palgrave macmillan law masters

sports law

palgrave macmillan law masters

Series editor: Marise Cremona

Business Law   Stephen Judge
Company Law   Janet Dine and Marios Koutsias
Constitutional and Administrative Law   John Alder
Contract Law   Ewan McKendrick
Criminal Law   Jonathan Herring
Employment Law   Deborah J. Lockton
Evidence   Raymond Emson
Family Law   Kate Standley and Paula Davies
Intellectual Property Law   Tina Hart, Simon Clark and Linda Fazzani
Land Law   Mark Davys
Landlord and Tenant Law   Margaret Wilkie, Peter Luxton and Desmond Kilcoyne
Legal Method   Ian McLeod
Legal Theory   Ian McLeod
Medical Law   Jo Samanta and Ash Samanta
Sports Law   Mark James
Torts   Alastair Mullis and Ken Oliphant
Trusts Law   Charlie Webb and Tim Akkouh

If you would like to comment on this book, or on the series generally, please write to
lawfeedback@palgrave.com.

palgrave macmillan law masters

sports law

mark james

Reader in Law, University of Salford
(as from September 2013)
Professor in Law, Northumbria University

Second edition

This edition first published 2013 by PALGRAVE MACMILLAN

Palgrave Macmillan in the UK is an imprint of Macmillan Publishers Limited, registered in England, company number 785998, of Houndmills, Basingstoke, Hampshire RG21 6XS.

Palgrave Macmillan in the US is a division of St Martin's Press LLC, 175 Fifth Avenue, New York, NY 10010.

Palgrave Macmillan is the global academic imprint of the above companies and has companies and representatives throughout the world.

Palgrave® and Macmillan® are registered trademarks in the United States, the United Kingdom, Europe and other countries

ISBN 978–1–137–02644–6 paperback

This book is printed on paper suitable for recycling and made from fully managed and sustained forest sources. Logging, pulping and manufacturing processes are expected to conform to the environmental regulations of the country of origin.

A catalogue record for this book is available from the British Library.

Contents

Part II   Sports participation and the law   67

Preface

Since completion of the first edition of this book in late 2009, sports law has continued to evolve at a rapid pace. The Court of Justice of the European Union (CJEU) handed down its opinion on the use of foreign decoder cards in 2011, match-fixing and racism have taken centre stage in debates on the use of the criminal law in sport, the publication of the Hillsborough Independent Panel Report finally resulted in many political and legal responses that will be felt for many years to come and the London 2012 Olympic and Paralympic Games were a resounding success. Meanwhile, the importance of the Court of Arbitration for Sport and its development of a *lex sportiva* has helped to clarify what we mean when we talk about sports law. The future looks like it will hold equally important sporting-legal developments: the World Anti-Doping Code is currently being revised for introduction in 2014; the International Cycling Union has appointed an independent panel to investigate the impact of the Lance Armstrong scandal; and the CJEU is scheduled to deliver its opinion on the legality of the UK's listed events regime during 2013, each of which provides further possibilities for how sport and the law interact with each other and to change how sport is played, administered and consumed.

The aim of this second edition remains to be to introduce readers to the challenges and controversies facing sport and the law when they interact with each other. It will explain how sport has evolved to take account of the requirements imposed on it by the law and how the law has provided sport with the legal tools necessary to govern itself more effectively and resolve the many and varied disputes to which it can give rise. By its very nature sports law requires an examination of the operation of the law in a specific context and as a result draws on issues and disputes from across a range of legal disciplines. These disparate strands are brought together here to provide a coherent insight into sports law and its location within the undergraduate curriculum. *Sports Law* is divided into four parts. Each of these parts contains groups of issues that can be studied together either because the applicable legal principles or the sporting subject matter are of a similar nature.

Part 1 provides an explanation of what sports law is and why it has become such an important and popular field of legal study in recent years. It traces the origins of sports law as a discrete subject and its legislative, judicial, political and sporting sources. It explains how and why the law becomes involved with sport and the ways by which the rules, decisions and procedures of the governing bodies of sport are most frequently challenged.

Chapter 1 analyses the juridification of sport and of the decision-making procedures followed by sports governing bodies. It highlights how a variety of sports law sources have evolved and how the *lex sportiva* of the Court of Arbitration for Sport is becoming as important as the jurisprudence of national and EU courts. Chapter 2 analyses the specific relationship between national law and the decision-making procedures followed by the governing bodies of sport. It explains how and why challenges are made to the rules and decisions of sports governing bodies and the impact that these decisions have had on the governance of sport. Chapter 3 examines how sporting disputes are referred to the Court of Arbitration for Sport and how its ever-evolving jurisprudence is having a corresponding impact on the operations of international sports federations, the International Olympic Committee and the World Anti-Doping Agency, enabling an understanding of how and why sport and the law interact in the ways that they do and of why a *lex sportiva* is developing to justify why sport requires differential treatment by the law.

Part 2 examines the application of the law to disputes involving on-field conduct and the legality of inherently dangerous sports. Cases involving sports injuries are some of the most commonly occurring applications of sports law as they can be based on incidents arising from any sport and at any level of participation, from the international elite to the recreational amateur player. The reporting of these cases has helped to bring sports law to the attention of the wider public, if only because of the media's frequent predictions (inaccurate so far) of the end of sport as we know it each time that a high profile player, coach, club or governing body is forced to change their behaviour when they have caused or contributed to the death or serious injury of an athlete.

Chapter 4 traces the development of the law of negligence and its application to sports injury cases. It focuses on actions between players and, where professionals are concerned, the vicarious liability of the defendant-player's club. Chapter 5 examines the extension of the law of negligence to a wider range of defendants including coaches and instructors, match officials, governing bodies, international federations and medical professionals. This recent growth in personal injury litigation is contrasted with the courts' reluctance to impose criminal liability for assaults that occur during the course of play, discussed in chapter 6. Here the long involvement of the criminal law with sports participation is examined in the context of the challenges posed by the prosecution of athletes for violent conduct, match-fixing and racism to a governing body's ability to self-regulate on matters of discipline. Chapter 7 concludes this part by examining the legal status of boxing and other combat sports from a variety of jurisprudential, social and moral perspectives. Despite their being acknowledged as lawful activities by the courts the legality of these sports continues to be debated each time that a participant is killed or seriously injured during the course of a bout.

In Part 3 the legal issues that arise from the organisation and hosting of a sports event are discussed. It explains how the owners and operators of sports venues can be held liable for the injuries caused to users of their facilities and the duty of care owed by sports participants to spectators. In particular the major sporting disasters of the twentieth century are examined to enable an analysis of the comparative importance of spectator safety and crowd disorder to be undertaken. By examining the stadium disasters that have occurred in football separately from issues of violence and disorder it is possible to see how the focus of both the government and the football authorities was turned away from spectator safety to crowd control during the 1970s and 1980s. The analysis of the historical and political contexts in which these responses took place demonstrates a disregard for sports' fans and their safety that has been brought back to the forefront of public discussion following the publication of the Hillsborough Independent Panel Report.

Chapter 8 focuses on the causes of action that can be used by a person who has been injured as a result of an incident that has occurred from the staging of a sports event. This includes actions brought against an event's organisers, the occupiers of the stadium where the event is taking place and the athletes competing in it by claimants including participants in the event, the spectators present at it and those living in the vicinity of the premises hosting the event. These claims include actions in negligence, private nuisance and under the Occupiers' Liability Acts 1957 and 1984. Chapters 9 and 10 unpick the problems associated with discussions surrounding spectator safety and crowd disorder. These two topics have often been examined together, leaving issues of spectator safety viewed through a 'hooligan lens' and being seen as secondary in importance to the apparently more pressing socio-political problem of how to control a disorderly crowd. Chapter 9 examines the political, legal and sporting build up to the Hillsborough disaster of 1989. It analyses the opportunities presented to, and wasted by, various governments to impose minimum standards of safety on sports grounds following official enquiries into the disasters at Burnden Park in 1946, Ibrox Park in 1971 and Valley Parade in 1985 and the ongoing social, sporting, political and criminal reactions to the Hillsborough Independent Panel Report. Chapter 10 examines governmental responses to sports-related disorder and in particular what is popularly referred to as football hooliganism. It analyses the piecemeal approach taken by Parliament in response to various high profile outbreaks of disorder that took place throughout the 1960–90s, the legality of Football Banning Orders and their relationship to changes in policing strategies and the collection of football-related intelligence.

Part 4 analyses the law's key role in the commercialisation of modern sport. It examines how the law has been used to challenge common practices that have become entrenched in sport and the role of the law in regulating the ways in which sport is administered, played and consumed. As governing bodies, clubs and event organisers have sought to exploit new income streams with ever increasing efficiency, they have resorted to the law to protect their commercial rights from unauthorised use by others. At the same time players have used the law to secure for themselves a greater share of this new income whilst fans have tried to find ways of limiting the near constant demands on their financial resources. These various strands of law and policy are brought together in an examination of the legal regulation of London 2012 and how the protections afforded to the Olympic Games are extended to other sporting mega-events.

Chapter 11 examines a variety of relationships and the ways that the law has been used to regulate some of the more unusual practices that have over time become commonplace in sport. It examines how challenges have been made to restrictive contractual terms, the potential impact on sport of the anti-discrimination protections enshrined in the Equality Act 2010 and the issues that are raised by the 'Football Creditors Rule'. Chapter 12 expands the analysis of these issues by examining how challenges to their legality can be made under the free movement and competition provisions of EU law. In this way the law is able to ensure a level of good governance is imposed on both governing bodies and clubs by subjecting them to a variety of checks on the quality of their administrative rules and procedures. In chapter 13 the ways in which the commercialisation and commodification of sport have had an impact on fan culture in its widest sense is examined. As fans are treated increasingly like loyal consumers by clubs and event organisers seeking ever more creative ways to grow their income streams, the law has been used to test the extent of the protections that can be afforded to the exploitation of these commercial rights. The regulation of secondary and grey markets in tickets, merchandise and broadcasting is examined through the application of criminal, EU and intellectual property law to issues affecting fans. In chapter 14 this analysis is developed further in respect of the specific ways in which the commercial rights in the Olympic Games are protected both in general and in respect of specific editions of the Games. In particular it examines the protections afforded to the Olympic symbols, the restrictions on advertising and attempts to prevent ambush marketing that are demanded by the International Olympic Committee and, increasingly, by the organisers of other sporting mega-events with a global appeal.

Throughout the book the appropriateness of the law as a mechanism for sports dispute resolution is examined. This provides a deeper understanding not only of what the law currently is but why it has evolved in the ways that it has and how sports law may develop further in the future. Each chapter contains a summary of the main points discussed in it, a detailed list of further reading and a more critical discussion of a key legal issue in the Hot Topics section. These should provide the reader with both an understanding of the subject under discussion in each chapter and with the tools to follow it up in greater detail should they need or want to.

To aid clarity 'claimant' is used to describe the person bringing the claim even where in the original judgment they would have been identified as the 'plaintiff'. For ease of cross-referencing where EU legislation is referred to, the Article numbers cited here are those currently used in the consolidated version of the Treaty on the Functioning of the European Union following the ratification of the Treaty of Lisbon, even if when the case was heard the corresponding provision had a different reference number at the time; likewise, the European Courts are referred to as the General Court of the European Union (formerly the Court of First Instance) and the Court of Justice of the European Union (formerly the European Court of Justice). A table of equivalence can be found at p.xiii.

The companion website for *Sports Law* can be found at: www.palgrave.com/law/james2e.

Here you will find links to relevant websites and additional documents on a chapter by chapter basis. Updates on the latest sports law developments will be posted here on a regular basis.

Many thanks to Rob Gibson at Palgrave Macmillan for his advice and support throughout the preparation of this second edition and for the helpful comments of the anonymous reviewers of the first edition. I would also like to thank in particular Guy Osborn, Richard Parrish, Geoff Pearson, Daniel Geey and David McArdle for their encouragement and advice throughout the thinking and writing up period, my wife Fiona for her endless supply of patience and support and Isla for her 'help' with annotations.

This book is based on material available to me on 1 December 2012.

Table of equivalences for the Treaty establishing the European Community and the Treaty on the functioning of the European Union

New numbering of the Treaty on the functioning of the European Union	Old numbering of the Treaty establishing the European Community	Original numbering of the Treaty establishing the European Economic Community
Article 18	Article 12	Article 6
Article 45	Article 39	Article 48
Article 49	Article 43	Article 52
Article 56	Article 49	Article 59
Article 101	Article 81	Article 85
Article 102	Article 82	Article 86
Article 106	Article 86	Article 90
Article 165	Article 149	Article 126
Article 263	Article 230	Article 173
Article 267	Article 234	Article 177

In this book, Treaty Articles will be referenced in the following way: Art.45 TFEU (ex Art.39 ECT) or Art.45 TFEU (ex Art.48 TEEC), providing both the new and original citations for the sake of clarity.

Table of cases

Table of legislation

Part I

Origins and sources of sports law

Why has the law become involved with sport? (1.1.1)

Sources of sports law (1.1.2)

The increasing importance of domestic and global sports law (1.1.3)

The governance of sport in the UK (1.1.4)

What is sports law and where do we find it? (1.1)

Domestic sports law (1.2)

Global sports law (1.3)

Decisions of the domestic courts (1.4.1)

Legislation from the national Parliament (1.4.2)

Investigations by the Office of Fair Trading (1.4.3)

National sports law (1.4)

What is sports law?

Decisions of the Court of Justice of the European Union (1.5.1)

Decisions of the European Commission on competition issues (1.5.2)

Sport and the European Treaties (1.5.3)

The development of European sports law (1.5.4)

European sports law (1.5)

European Convention on Spectator Violence and Misbehaviour at Sports Events and in Particular at Football Matches 1985 (1.6.1)

The Anti-Doping Convention 1989 (1.6.2)

International sports law (1.6)

Conclusion (1.7)

Chapter 1

What is sports law?

Key terms

▶ **Juridification** – the process by which a privately regulated sphere of activity becomes colonised by law and lawyers.

▶ **Domestic sports law** – the body of internally applicable legal norms created and adhered to by national governing bodies of sport.

▶ **Global sports law** – the autonomous transnational legal order through which the body of law and jurisprudence applied by international sports federations is created; in particular, it includes the jurisprudence of the Court of Arbitration for Sport and its creation and harmonisation of sporting-legal norms.

▶ **National sports law** – the law created by national parliaments, courts and enforcement agencies that directly affects the regulation or governance of sport or which has been developed to resolve sports disputes.

▶ **European sports law** – the law created by the institutions of the European Union, in particular the Court of Justice of the European Union, that affects the regulation or governance of sport or which has been developed to resolve sports disputes.

▶ **International sports law** – the general or universal principles of law which are part of international customary law, or the *jus commune*, that are applied to sports disputes.

▶ **National governing body** – the body responsible for the governance and administration of a sport, or a group of related sports, at national or state level.

▶ **International sports federation** – the body responsible for the governance and administration of a sport, or a group of related sports, at the continental or world level.

1.1 What is sports law and where do we find it?

UK law has no formal definition of sport and consequently no formal definition of sports law. Although we know what sport is when we see it and when we play it, we struggle to define it in a way that is neither so wide as to include all forms of physical exercise nor so narrow as to exclude specific activities that are normally considered to be sports. The same can be said of sports law; we know what it is, but we struggle to define it when called upon to do so.

The quest for a definition of sports law is complicated further by ongoing debates about the most appropriate name for the subject and the proliferation of sub-names and sub-branches that have been claimed for it. Some argue this is nothing more than the observable phenomenon of ordinary legal principles being applied to sports disputes and that we are therefore discussing sport and the law; the law as it applies to sport. On the other hand, it is claimed there is, or there is at least evolving, a common underpinning or unifying approach to sports disputes that overtly takes into consideration the sporting context to justify how and why the law applies differently to sport; this is sports law.

Further terminological confusions arise through the use of a number of Latin epithets that have appeared to provide a veneer of gravitas to what is still an emerging field of study and legal practice. Each of these terms is contested though a degree of consensus is beginning to emerge over their specific definitions: *lex sportiva* is being defined more narrowly as the binding precedents produced by the Court of Arbitration for Sport (CAS) that are applicable across both sporting and national boundaries; *lex ludica* refers to the rules of play and associated codes of conduct of specific sports; and *lex Olympica* to the law generated by and applicable to the Olympic Movement and more specifically the Olympic Games. What this confusion highlights is that, regardless of what this subject is called, the law is being applied to sports disputes and is providing or influencing the frameworks of sports dispute resolution and in return sports cases are bringing often complex legal issues directly into the public consciousness.

1.1.1 Why has the law become involved with sport?

The law's intervention in matters relating to sport prior to the 1980s was erratic and piecemeal. Until this time, there had been a disproportionately large number of prosecutions where the legality of boxing and prize fighting was explored and a few notable examinations of contractual and financial issues. This latter group of cases, including the clarification of the tax status of benefit events that were held for professional cricketers (*Seymour v Reed* [1927] AC 554) and a challenge to the transfer system in football (*Eastham v Newcastle United Football Club* [1964] Ch 413, see further chapter 11.4.2.4)) paved the way for the recent explosion in sports-related litigation. As a result, almost every field of law has infiltrated almost every aspect of sport, from the obvious freedom movement claim in *Union Royal Belge des Societe de Football Association ASBL v Bosman* (C-145/93) [1995] ECR I-4921 (see further, chapter 12.2) to the obscure regulations concerning advertising in the London Olympic and Paralympic Games Act 2006 (see further, chapter 14.3), and from the politically-motivated restrictions imposed on the movement of football fans in the Football Spectators Act 1989 (see further, chapter 10) to the faintly ridiculous trial to determine whether a father and his five-year-old son kicking a ball to each other in a park constituted a game of football (*Lawton v Fleming-Brown* [2006] EWHC 3146 (Admin)). There is now no doubt that sport is subject to the law and that this subjection has not resulted in the end of sport as we know it; a claim that is made by administrators and commentators almost every time that a high-profile sporting case reaches the courts.

The evolution of sports law is the product of a series of unrelated developments that were occurring in both sport and society from the late 1970s onwards and which combined to create the perfect conditions from which sports law could emerge. The commercialisation and commodification of sport during this period attracted law and lawyers like no previous period in sports history. As sport became more commercial, more money was invested into it and increased profits were created, which in turn led to disputes that required law and lawyers to resolve them (*Greig v Insole* [1978] 1 WLR 302, see further, chapter 11.3.2)). Alongside this commercialisation the marketing, branding and repackaging of sport became more sophisticated; games and events became products or commodities that could be sold to the highest bidder, with the best example in British sport being the creation of the Premier League in 1992. One by-product of these commercial developments was the great strain that they caused to the antiquated governance structures of many NGBs. Systems that had been designed to organise amateur sport in the latter part of the nineteenth century could no longer cope with the demands imposed on them by the newly professional players who challenged their procedures in court and forced them to modernise (*Jones v Welsh Rugby Union* (unreported) EWCA Civ 19 December 1997, see further, chapter 2).

Developments in the political sphere occurred at both the national and European levels. The stadium disasters of the 1980s finally forced the government to take legislative action and create regulatory frameworks that ensured that football stadiums became safer places for spectators to watch matches and football hooligans could be monitored and punished more effectively. At the same time, the European Commission had been warning UEFA that the transfer system did not comply with EU law; UEFA's failure to act on these warnings eventually resulted in the *Bosman* decision and the many cases that have followed it.

The only aspects of sport that are effectively immune from legal intervention are the rules and codes of ethics that regulate the actual playing of games. National and European courts as well as the Court of Arbitration for Sport have regularly stated that they will not review the decisions of match officials that are taken during the course of a game (*Mendy v Association Internationale de Boxing Amateur* CAS OG 1996/06, see further chapter 3.2). The aim of such an exemption is to uphold as far as is possible the authority of the match officials and to preserve the finality of the end of game result. The only time that the courts may consider such a claim to be justiciable is where their application of the rules of the game promotes illegality in some way.

Thus, the law has engaged with sport for a variety of reasons. A combination of changing circumstances in sport and society, together with the pursuit of specific political aims at national and EU levels, has been responsible for the emergence of sports law as such an important field of legal study and practice. This knowledge of the impact of the law on sport has fuelled further litigation as lawyers apply the lessons that they have learned in one area of sports law to others that have not previously been attempted. In response, NGBs and ISFs have amended their rules and procedures as a result of risk assessment strategies and in order to comply with the rules of natural justice in an attempt to avoid further litigation. This enables the discussion to move on from why do we have sports law to where we can find it.

1.1.2 Sources of sports law

Which still leaves the all important question: What is sports law? The most effective way to answer this question is to begin by identifying the various sources of sports law and the jurisprudence that each is developing. Building on the nomenclature developed by Foster in 'Is there a Global Sports Law?' (2003) 2(1) *Entertainment and Sports Law Journal*, online, two main groups of sports law sources can be identified. The first group reflects the application of legal principles by the tribunals granted jurisdiction to hear disputes by the national governing bodies of sport and by international sports federations; these are referred to here as domestic sports law and global sports law. These two sources highlight the desire of these bodies to self-regulate disputes that affect their sports and their claims that they are developing through CAS a completely new branch of law that is often referred to as *lex sportiva*.

The second group consists of the sources of sports law that evidence the application of national, European and international law, together with generally or universally applicable legal principles, before specific courts; these sources are referred to here as national sports law, European sports law and international sports law. This group of sources explains how the law of a nation state, or a group of nation states, applies to a sports dispute. The key distinction between the two groups of sources is that the former is underpinned by a series of contractual agreements entered into by, for example, the athlete, his or her club, their club's national governing body and the appropriate international sports federation; it is a private contractual order that claims to be making and applying its own set of rules. The latter is the law imposed by a nation state on its citizens or which is constituted by the treaties entered into by communities of nation states, for example, the members of the EU being bound by the law enshrined in the Treaty on the Functioning of the European Union.

1.1.3 The increasing importance of domestic and global sports law

One of the most important recent developments in sports law has been the growing sophistication and technicality of the jurisprudence of specialist sports tribunals and appeals panels. Where once these bodies acted almost exclusively as disciplinary tribunals, they now often hear cases that require a detailed knowledge of the law and a determination of how specific legal issues should apply in the context of a sports dispute.

The impact of this development can be seen in three specific ways. First it has required the further juridification and formalisation of how sports tribunals operate: their procedures have become more court-like in appearance as they are required to adhere to the rules of natural justice; legal representation is now commonplace where professional sport is concerned; lay panel members have been replaced by lawyers and judges; the applicable rules are more tightly drafted in order to minimise the scope for challenge; the decisions and reasons for reaching them are handed down in the same style as court judgments and the punishments imposed are justified in a similarly judicial style (see further, chapter 2.4). The juridification of these tribunals has ensured a greater degree of acceptance of their decisions by the parties appearing before them which, in turn, has led to fewer challenges to their authority coming before the courts.

Secondly, these specialist tribunals are able to utilise more easily a sports-sympathetic approach to the disputes coming before them. They are more readily prepared to accept the importance of protecting the 'specificity of sport' from the application of the law (see further, chapter 12.1.2) and are more likely to accept without question that certain aspects of sports governance are acceptable, unless they are the specific focus of the challenge before them. For example, the regulations concerning the transfer of players in professional team sports could eventually be the subject of a legal challenge under EU law. However they are currently accepted as lawful and valid by all sports tribunals up to and including CAS (*FC Shaktar Donetsk v Matuzalem Francelino da Silva, Real Zaragoza SAD and FIFA* CAS 2008/A/1519 and 1520) (see further, chapters 3.3.2, Hot Topic 3 and 12.2.2.2). The benefits of using alternative dispute resolution mechanisms such as these are well known: the panel has sport specific and/or sports law knowledge; the rules are less formal and less restrictive of the evidence that they can hear, and the disputes are usually settled much more quickly than they would be before the courts leading to significant savings on costs. One further advantage is that by keeping a dispute within the sporting community, the authority and stability of the international sports federation in question is maintained. The main disadvantage is that it can allow restrictive and potentially unlawful rules and practices to become entrenched in sporting culture.

Thirdly the increased use of specialist tribunals is preventing many sports disputes from coming before national and European courts. This can create a problem with legal certainty; the paucity of cases reaching the courts means that the judiciary is deprived of the opportunity to develop national and EU law in a way that is appropriate to both its general application and the development of any derogations or exemptions that may be necessary for the proper administration of sport. This, in turn, gives rise to the possibility that different interpretations of the law and applicable legal norms will be developed by the courts and the specialist sports panels leading to the potential for much more serious disputes in the future. Thus, the evolution of the relationship between the various sources of sports law will have a significant impact on its future development.

1.1.4   The governance of sport in the UK

In the UK, the state has a non-interventionist approach to sports governance when compared to many other countries. Sport in the UK is administered almost exclusively by private entities, the national governing bodies, whose rules bind other private entities, whether these are individual clubs or individual athletes. As a result, there has not been a need for the state to define sport as it has often been regarded as being one of Parliament's less important spheres of competence; the Minister for Sport is a junior minister in the Department for Culture, Media and Sport (DCMS) rather than a Secretary of State with cabinet level responsibilities. Even the Minister for the Olympics, who was based in the Cabinet Office, was only a junior minister detailed to provide specific advice to the Prime Minister and the Cabinet on matters relating to the London 2012 Olympic Games.

The role of DCMS is to provide access to, and encourage participation in, all levels of sport. In doing this, its twin aims are to promote health and a more active lifestyle amongst UK citizens whilst producing world class performers. To achieve these aims, DCMS distributes funding, particularly that raised by the National Lottery, to UK Sport and to the home country sports councils: Sport England, sportscotland, the Sports Council for Wales and the Sports Council for Northern Ireland. This funding is used, amongst other things, for building or improving sports facilities, widening participation schemes and supporting elite performers.

Of particular note has been DCMS' role in the development of policies and procedures that have increased safety and improved specific spheres of sports governance. For example DCMS, together with the National Society for the Prevention of Cruelty to Children, helped to establish the Child Protection in Sport Unit in 2001 (see further, chapter 6.5). It also oversees the work of the Sports Grounds Safety Authority (see further, chapter 9.6.2.4) and assists governing bodies in bidding to host sporting mega-events, as identified by the Golden Events Series proposals.

The implementation of DCMS' policies is carried out on a day-to-day basis by UK Sport and the four home country sports councils. The four sports councils' complementary aim is to encourage participation in sport through partnerships with clubs, local authorities and national and regional governing bodies. As of 14 December 2009, UK Sport's anti-doping functions were taken over by a newly-created specialist agency, UK Anti-Doping (UKAD). UKAD will fulfil the role of national anti-doping organisation, as required by Art.20.5 World Anti-Doping Agency Code, and will administer drug testing programmes throughout the UK. It will also work more closely with law enforcement agencies than has previously been the case in an attempt to control more effectively the importation and supply of banned performance-enhancing substances.

Thus, sport in the UK is not seen as being a public service that is the responsibility of the state. Instead, the day-to-day running of sport is left almost entirely to the private sector: athletes are members of clubs who provide them with training and the opportunity to participate; the clubs are members of local and/or national governing bodies who administer fixture lists, training for coaches and match officials, disciplinary tribunals and representative teams; the national governing bodies of sports are members of continental and/or world bodies that ensure harmonisation of their rules and procedures and which organise international club and representative tournaments. Although a simplistic outline of the governance structures of most sports, what should be clear from this brief description is that the role of the state in the everyday administration and governance of sport in the UK is minimal. Consequently, there is little legislation in place to govern sport directly unless it is introduced to regulate a specific issue, such as football disorder (see further, chapter 10) or is in response to a specific incident, for example the restrictions that were imposed on gun ownership in the Firearms (Amendment) Act 1997 following the shootings in Dunblane. Therefore, sports law in the UK has generally evolved in accordance with common law principles as applied by sports tribunals and national courts.

1.2 Domestic sports law

Domestic sports law is the creation of an autonomous legal order by a sport's national governing body (NGB) to regulate the conduct of its members and those playing its sport; it is the body of internally applicable law and procedure that has been developed by each sport's NGB. Every NGB has its own constitution that has been created by its members, or their representatives, which defines the extent of its powers and its jurisdiction over disputes affecting everyone connected to the sport. This constitution is administered, along with the body's other main organisational powers, by an executive or management committee. The power to administer the NGB's disciplinary powers in respect of the breach of its playing, financial or administrative rules is delegated to a specialist committee or tribunal. Thus, NGBs have in place an entire system to create and administer their own rules that replicates the machinery of justice of a nation state corresponding to its legislature, executive and courts.

Following challenges to the legitimacy of their rules, their decision-making procedures and ultimately the decisions handed down by them, the system of governance operated by many NGBs has become more formalised, often taking on a form that is quasi-judicial in both appearance and operation (see further, chapter 2). Some NGBs require their tribunal chairs to be legally qualified whilst at the elite levels of many sports, players and clubs will be legally represented as a matter of course. This process of juridification has also seen disciplinary tribunals publishing the charges laid against those who have transgressed the NGB's rules and the publication of both the determination of the hearing and a detailed explanation of how and why that decision was reached; in other words the tribunal is operating as a 'court' which is applying the 'laws' of its 'Parliament' and which is publishing its 'judgments' which can then be used as precedents in future cases.

The jurisprudence of sports disciplinary tribunals and associated arbitrations is becoming increasingly important as these panels become more court-like in their procedures and as they deal with ever more complex legal issues. For example, when Kevin Keegan claimed that he had been constructively dismissed by Newcastle United FC, the complex legal issues were heard before the Premier League Manager's Arbitration Tribunal, not the Employment Tribunal as might have been expected

(*Keegan v Newcastle United FC Ltd* Premier League Manager's Arbitration Tribunal 2 October 2009 and further, chapter 11.3.5). The Tribunal's analysis was considered to be sufficiently authoritative that when a similar case was heard before the Employment Appeal Tribunal, the Keegan decision was used as precedent (*McBride v Falkirk Football and Athletic Club* [2011] UKEAT 0058_10_1706). Further, in *The Football Association v Suarez* FA Regulatory Commission 20 December 2011 (see further, chapter 6.3.3), the judgment on what in the past might have been considered to be a straightforward misconduct hearing lasted several days with all parties legally represented and ending in a 107 page reasoned explanation of the panel's decision.

In addition to these internal hearings, the decisions of Sports Resolutions UK, particularly when it sits as the National Anti-Doping Panel, are becoming of increasing importance as more NGBs now make references to it. In the majority of cases coming before these tribunals, national legal norms are being applied to sports disputes rather than them creating entirely new law or legal principles; they are explaining how the law applies in the specific context of sport or using standard techniques of statutory and contractual interpretation and the rules of natural justice to determine the meaning and scope of an NGB's rules. Thus although domestic sports law is not a new legal specialism, because these tribunals are making and enforcing decisions on legal matters they are becoming an increasingly important source of sports law as the cases coming before them would otherwise end up being heard before the national courts.

1.3 Global sports law

In the same way that the basic structure of an NGB is mirrored on the world stage by that of an international sports federation (ISF), so is the development of domestic sports law mirrored in the transnational arena by the emergence of a global sports law. Global sports law aspires to be an autonomous transnational legal order created by the private bodies that govern sport at the world level. Each ISF regulates the conduct of its members, usually continental and national governing bodies, and through them the participants who play its sport. As with domestic sports law, global sports law is the body of internally applicable law and procedure that has been developed by each ISF through the operation of the tribunals to which they allow disputes affecting their sports to be submitted.

Most major ISFs now allow appeals from their own disciplinary tribunals or dispute resolution chambers to CAS, enabling a degree of standardization of sporting-legal issues to evolve into a global sports law that could be said to reach its apotheosis in what is frequently referred to as the *lex sportiva* created by CAS (see further, chapter 3). This distinctive body operates in parallel to existing national and transnational court structures to provide interpretations on the legality and applicability of the rules and decision-making procedures of many ISFs. Its aim is to create new legal and interpretative norms within sport that enable disputes to avoid having to be brought before national and European courts. Applications for arbitration and adjudication before CAS reinforce the desire for the self-regulation of all sports disputes by ISFs. This private system of justice, resort to which is enforced by contracts between the various parties, forces the World Anti-Doping Agency, ISFs, NGBs, clubs and individual participants to submit to the jurisdiction of CAS rather than to the courts, and is epitomized by the International Olympic Committee and its relationship with the Olympic Charter and CAS (see further, chapter 14).

As with domestic tribunals, CAS regularly hears applications that contain complex legal issues concerning for example the interpretation of the terms of a professional footballer's employment contract and whether they enabled him to move to another employer, the amount of compensation payable for breach of contract and the playing ban imposed for non-payment as in *FC Shaktar Donetsk v Matuzalem Francelino da Silva, Real Zaragoza SAD and FIFA* CAS 2008/A/1519 and 1520 (see further, chapters 3.3.2 and 12.2.2.2), and the legality of potentially discriminatory bans on the use of performance-enhancing equipment by a disabled athlete (*Pistorius v IAAF* CAS 2008/A/1480) (see further, chapters 3.3.1 and 11.5.4). As many of these applications would be heard by national courts if they were not brought before CAS, when the parties agree that the decision and its reasoning can be published, it can provide an important source of sports law that can be applied in other similar cases. However, as a private arbitral body, where the parties do not agree to have the decision published, or the rules of the relevant ISF do not allow for publication, it can occasionally be limited in its ability to provide guidance.

It can be argued that the decisions of an ISF's disciplinary tribunal or dispute resolution chamber, and of independent appeals and arbitration tribunals like CAS, are not creating a unique category of law or new legal norms, a true *lex sportiva*, but are instead simply applying national or EU law, or the general principles of international law, to transnational sports disputes. Global sports law sees the adjudicative or arbitral body approach sports disputes through a well-developed sports-specific lens. However its importance as a source of sports law is from its application of more traditional legal norms and principles that have the potential to form the basis of a distinct or unique jurisprudence.

1.4   National sports law

In contrast to domestic sports law, national sports law is the development of a body of law and legal principles that is applied directly to sport by Parliament and the judiciary. In other words national sports law is the Acts of Parliament and the decisions of the courts that affect the governance, administration, consumption and participation in sport in the UK; it is the application of 'real law' to sport.

There are no specific Acts of Parliament whose aim is to define 'sport' and the ways that sport should be governed in UK law. This is in stark contrast to France, for example, where the Loi du Sport (Loi No. 84-610 du 16–07–1984) provides a framework within which many aspects of sport are regulated. Without such a rigid public law framework being in place, the decisions of the UK courts are much more numerous than are the piecemeal and often reactive responses of the legislature. A further source of national sports law can be found in the decisions of the Office of Fair Trading (OFT), which investigates potential abuses of competition law and can demand changes in the activities of sports bodies that are found to have been acting anti-competitively.

1.4.1   Decisions of the domestic courts

Whatever the reasons behind the increased use of the law as a means of resolving sports disputes, as those involved with sport have become more litigious an ever-wider variety of legal problems have been brought before the UK courts. As a result, decisions of the national courts have had a profound impact on the way that sport is administered, played and consumed in the UK.

For example, cases have challenged the rules and accepted practices that govern the way that sports are administered. Eighty-four years before possibly the most well-known sports law case, *Union Royal Belge des Societe de Football Association ASBL v Jean-Marc Bosman* (C-415/93) [1995] ECR I-4921 (see further, chapter 12.2.1), the legality of the transfer system in English football was challenged in *Kingaby v Aston Villa Football Club* [1912] *The Times*, 28 March. Although this action failed, it should have alerted football's governing bodies to there being something strange, legally, about being able to 'buy' and 'sell' an employee.

Further cases challenged the procedures used by NGBs when applying these rules to specific cases brought before them. The finding of the High Court in *Jones v Welsh Rugby Union* [1998] *The Times*, 6 January (see further, chapter 2.4.4), which highlighted that many NGBs were failing to operate the rules of natural justice in their disciplinary tribunals and were therefore not acting fairly when conducting their hearings, led to many sports completely rewriting their decision-making procedures. This, in turn, can be said to have increased the process of juridification of the decision-making process of NGBs by making them more legalistic in their operations. This ability to challenge a governing body's internal rules and procedures in English law led to the International Amateur Athletics Federation moving its headquarters from London to Monaco in an attempt to protect itself from further legal actions (*Gasser v Stinson* (unreported) High Court (QBD), 15 June 1998) (see further, chapter 11.4.2.3).

In other cases, participants have sued each other for injuries that, until then, had been accepted as an unfortunate, but almost inevitable, risk of participation in contact sports (*Condon v Basi* [1985] 1 WLR 866 and further, chapter 4.4.1.1), the match officials for failing to apply the safety rules applicable to a specific aspect of a game (*Smoldon v Whitworth and Nolan* [1997] ELR 249 and further, chapter 5.3) and the NGB for failing to require appropriate medical provision (*Watson v British Boxing Board of Control* [2001] QB 1134 and further, chapter 5.4). This has, in turn, led to changes in the way that sports' rules are defined, the quality of training provided for coaches and match officials and the development and design of medical trauma care protocols.

The decisions of the UK courts are currently the most important source of national sports law because of the wide variety of legal principles that have been debated before them. What is somewhat strange, given the massive growth in sports-related litigation since the beginning of the 1980s, is how few sports cases have reached either the House of Lords or now the Supreme Court. In recent years, only *Rugby Football Union v Viagogo Ltd* [2012] UKSC 30 (see further, chapter 13.4.4) has been heard before the Supreme Court, and this was because of a highly controversial issue relating to the forced disclosure of suspected ticket touts' personal information by an internet ticket sales company, rather than the underlying sports law issue of restricting the operation of the secondary ticket market. This leaves sports lawyers with the problems of trying to determine when and why the law will engage with a sports dispute, trying to establish whether there is a pattern to the law's engagement with sport and trying to establish whether or not there is any underlying theory that unites the cases into a coherent body of sports law jurisprudence.

1.4.2 Legislation from the national Parliament

Direct state intervention by Parliament on issues relating to sport has generally been poor, rushed and reactive and as a result could often be described as panic law. Without a coherent policy for sport and its administration and with no clearly defined role for the state in this field of activity, this is unlikely to change significantly in the immediate future.

There is little doubt that some Parliamentary intervention has been both necessary for and beneficial to encouraging participation in sport. For example the Public Health Act 1875 allowed urban authorities to purchase land to be able to provide places for public recreation. The Act's aim was to ensure that the people living in the new urban centres had open spaces where they could exercise and hopefully maintain a basic level of fitness. Further, the establishment of the Football Licensing Authority (now the Sports Grounds Safety Authority) by the Football Spectators Act 1989 (see further, chapter 9.6.2.4) and the licensing regime imposed on adventure centres by the Activity Centres (Young Persons' Safety) Act 1995 (see further, chapter 8.5) have undoubtedly made watching football and engaging in outdoor pursuits safer activities than was previously the case.

However, this can be contrasted with the legislation passed to control the behaviour of disorderly football spectators and that which enables the London Olympic and Paralympic Games to take place in 2012, some of which appears to be ill thought through and overly restrictive. The many and varied Acts that have been passed in an attempt to control crowd disorder at football matches have led to the development of invasive surveillance techniques by the police and the imposition of quasi-criminal restraining orders, Football Banning Orders, by the courts (see further, chapter 10.6). These legal responses have been justified by the courts as being for the protection of the general public from football-related disorder, even where those subjected to them have never been proved to have acted criminally at or in connection with a football match (*Gough v Chief Constable of Derbyshire* [2002] EWCA Civ 351) and despite their appearing to be contrary to the provisions of the Human Rights Act 1998 (see further, chapter 10.6.2).

Although not suffering from the same claims of illegality, some sections of the London Olympic and Paralympic Games Act 2006 were inserted at the behest of a purely private body, the International Olympic Committee, rather than on the basis of a rational legal justification. Why the Olympic and Paralympic Games are so special that the use of their symbols and sales of tickets to their events required specific legislative protection, protections that have not been extended to other national or international sporting or cultural events held in the UK before or since, was never fully debated either in Parliament or before the courts (see further, chapter 14).

Thus, although Acts of Parliament can and do have a dramatic impact on sport, and are an important source of national sports law, there is little coherence to the justifications behind these interventions. Reasons as varied as the promotion of public health, the prevention of public disorder and the protection of commercial rights are behind some of the more recent legislative interventions; what is unclear, because of the lack of a clearly defined role for the state in respect of sport, is when and why the government will choose to intervene from one Parliamentary term to the next. The reality appears to be that the national sports law created by Parliament is driven more by political pragmatism than for the intrinsic benefit of sport.

1.4.3   Investigations by the Office of Fair Trading

The role and powers of the Office of Fair Trading (OFT) were consolidated in the Enterprise Act 2002 enabling it to act with the aim of promoting and protecting consumer interests and preventing anti-competitive behaviour. It has the power to enforce a wide range of consumer protection legislation, investigate and punish businesses for infringements of the Competition Act 1998 and refer conduct that distorts a particular market to the Competition Commission. Although relatively narrow in its overall remit, the investigations that have been undertaken by the OFT into sport have had a significant impact on the way that sport is administered and consumed.

In *Re Televising Premier League Football Matches* [2000] EMLR 78, the OFT referred the agreement between the FA Premier League and the broadcaster BSkyB to the Restrictive Practices Court to determine whether the collective selling of its media rights was anti-competitive. The Court's decision that it was in the public interest for a sports league to sell the rights to the entire competition, rather than allowing the individual clubs the right to sell their own home games, was based in part on the benefits to the consumer of only having to purchase one 'product' and the redistribution of income that was included in the collective agreement in an attempt to maintain a competitive balance between the teams in the league (see further, chapter 13.3.1). Further investigations have led to reductions in the price of replica kits after it was found that various retailers were guilty of fixing the prices at an artificially high level (*JJB Sports plc v OFT; Allsports Ltd v OFT* [2004] CAT 17) (see further, chapter 13.2.2).

Following complaints from fans of Tottenham Hotspur FC and Manchester United FC, the OFT investigated whether a number of terms in the season tickets of these two clubs and the information supplied by them concerning refunds and the purchasing of additional tickets were in breach of consumer protection legislation. As a result of the investigations, both clubs agreed to amend their terms and to provide clearer information to purchasers in order to avoid potential litigation. Thus, the OFT plays an important role in ensuring that businesses connected with sport are complying with competition law and consumer protection legislation. In its clarification of the applicable law in these fields, it is an important source of national sports law.

1.5 European sports law

The link between domestic and national sports law is replicated at the transnational level by the relationships between global sports law and European and international sports law. European sports law is the law generated by the institutions of the European Union (EU) and the explanations of how and why that law has been applied to sport in the decisions of the Court of Justice of the European Union (CJEU).

Following the ratification and entry into force of the Treaty on the Functioning of the European Union (TFEU), Arts.6 and 165 provide the EU with the competence to act in support of, to coordinate and to supplement the actions of member states in the field of sport. This specific reference to sport in the TFEU should enable a more coordinated approach to the development of European sports law to evolve in the future. The failure to mention sport in previous treaties has meant that the application of EU law and policy fell under the jurisdiction of several of the European Commission's Directorates General, including in particular the Directorate General for Education and Culture and the Directorate General for Competition. The Sport Unit, which is located within the Directorate General for Education and Culture, acts as an umbrella for the disparate sources of EU sports law and policy and is likely to play an increasingly important role in the future development of European sports law as a result of the implementation of Art.165 (below, 1.5.3).

The EU's involvement with sport to date has mainly occurred where specific sports practices have engaged EU law, in particular the provisions that protect the operation of the internal market and competition law. The EU's sports policy that has emerged from these interactions is derived from consultation with stakeholders in sport, particularly ISFs, social dialogue and through cooperation with the member states. The result has often been a piecemeal approach similar to that seen in the UK but with one significant difference: the UK Parliament chooses its non-interventionist approach to sport whereas the EU did not have a mandate to intervene directly on matters relating to sport prior to the ratification of the TFEU. This lack of coherence in the EU's approach to sport has been only partially remedied by the various decisions of the CJEU and the non-binding pronouncements of the European Commission and the Council of Ministers. Thus, to date, the most authoritative source of European sports law has been the rulings of the CJEU; what Art.165 TFEU has provided is the opportunity for the EU to take a more proactive and distinctive role in its future development, though its scope and remit remain unclear for the time being.

1.5.1 Decisions of the Court of Justice of the European Union

As sport has become more commercialised and more internationalised, it has developed a cross-border aspect that has engaged EU law. The European Commission Directorate-General Education and Culture's recently commissioned report, 'Study on the contribution of sport to economic growth and employment in the EU' published in November 2012 found that the total sport-related EU gross added value impact was almost €300bn or almost 3 per cent of EU gross added value. Further, over seven million people are engaged in sport-related employment, or over 3.5 per cent of the total EU workforce. Although the decisions of the CJEU have had the greatest impact on professional sports participants, there is no prohibition on the application of EU law to a purely amateur sportsperson. In the *Staff Working Document* (SEC (2007) 935) that accompanied the publication of the *White Paper on Sport* (COM (2007) 39 Final), it was stated that amateur sport was not outside the scope of the fundamental principles of free movement because access to sport is a social advantage that can affect a worker's ability to take up employment in another member state. Thus, all sporting relationships have the potential to be regulated by EU law.

In the early 1970s, the CJEU declared in *Walrave and Koch v Association Union Cycliste Internationale* (36/74) [1974] ECR 1405 that sporting relationships, particularly those involving professional sportspersons, were subject to EU law where the conduct in question constituted an economic activity (see further, chapter 12.1.2). From this point onwards, it became clear that sport did not have the immunity from EU law that it appeared to have assumed was the case. Since *Walrave*, the test for when sport will be subject to EU law has developed considerably with a detailed jurisprudence emerging that explains how and why it will become engaged with a sports dispute. These developments have occurred particularly in respect of the provisions relating to the free movement of workers and are doing so to an increasing extent in the field of competition law (see further, chapter 12).

The next major landmark was *Union Royal Belge des Societe de Football Association ASBLv Jean-Marc Bosman* (C-415/93) [1995] ECR I-4921 (see further, chapters 12.2.1), which involved an application of Art.45 TFEU (ex Art.48 TEEC) and determined the legality of the transfer system as it operated in Belgian football in particular and

European football in general. Where many media commentators, and many football fans, still consider 'doing a *Bosman'* to be something not quite right in sporting terms, in EU law terms it simply enabled an employee whose fixed-term employment contract had come to a natural end to seek work with another employer elsewhere in the EU without any restriction; something that all non-athletes would consider to be a normal part of their working life. *Bosman* and its progeny still have a significant impact on how sport is organised in the EU and beyond; to the Union of European Football Associations (UEFA) and the Federation of International Football Associations (FIFA) in particular, the decision has become something of a *bête-noire* as they seek ever-more elaborate rules that are capable of avoiding its application (see further, Hot Topic 12).

As applicants have become more creative in presenting their cases before national courts, so has the complexity of the references made to the CJEU on questions of EU law increased. When the compatibility of the IOC's anti-doping regime with EU law was challenged in *Meca-Medina and Majcen v Commision of the European Communities* (C-519/04 P) [2006] ECR I-6991 (see further, chapter 12.1.2), the eventual appeal to the CJEU was made in terms of breaching both competition law, contrary to Arts.101 and 102 TFEU (ex Arts.81 and 82 ECT), and the provisions on the freedom to provide services under Art.56 (ex Art.49 ECT). For procedural reasons the decision was handed down in terms of the anti-doping penalties being compatible with Arts.101 and 102 with no further comment being made on the applicability of Art.56 in these circumstances. The CJEU held that the rules had as their legitimate objective the proper conduct of competitive sport by ensuring healthy rivalry between the competitors. Later, in *Murphy v Media Protection Services Ltd* C-429/08 [2012] 1 CMLR 29, Art.56 was examined in detail and found to have been breached by the complex framework of contracts that resulted in a British citizen being prevented from receiving subscription television services from an undertaking based in Greece (see further, chapter 13.3.2). Following *Motosykletistiki Omospondia Ellados NPID (MOTOE) v Greece* (C-49/07) [2008] ECR I-4863, the possibility of claims that NGBs and ISFs are abusing their position through the application of rules that protect their own commercial interests, rather than acting for the benefit of their sport as a whole, is one that is likely to result in further litigation in the future (see further, chapter 12.5.1).

Until these and other cases were heard by the CJEU, transfer systems, anti-doping regulations and other monopolistic and restrictive practices had long been considered to be integral parts of the way that many sports operated. However, their impact on the relatively short careers of professional sports participants had not previously been interrogated from a legal perspective. The impact of the CJEU's decisions in these and other cases has had a dramatic impact on the way that sport is administered and consumed, ensuring that any new rules, such as those proposed by FIFA and UEFA concerning the constitution of professional football teams, must be designed and applied so that they conform with EU law.

Despite the best efforts of some ISFs, and some intensive lobbying by FIFA and UEFA in particular, sport is subject to EU law. Their attempts to argue for a specific exemption for sport from the operation of EU law have so far failed. The CJEU will now examine any sporting dispute that comes before it to determine whether, because of the 'specificity of sport', EU law should apply differently in a particular sporting context or whether the disputed conduct should be specifically exempted (see further, chapter 12). This development, whilst still in its infancy, may go some way to appeasing some ISFs. However, others continue to miss the point being made implicitly by the

CJEU; where rich and successful ISFs appear to be acting for their own commercial benefit and to protect the earnings of their star performers, the CJEU is attempting to act for the benefit of all levels of all sports. Until the ISFs can construct an argument that justifies the exemption of their rules from EU law, their views will continue to conflict with those of the CJEU and the decisions of the highest court in the EU will continue to provide an important source of European sports law.

1.5.2 Decisions of the European Commission on competition issues

Where an undertaking is suspected of engaging in anti-competitive conduct capable of interfering with the operation of the single market (see further, chapter 12.5), the European Commission has been granted special powers of investigation and sanction under Council Regulation (EC) 1/2003. The outcomes of the Commission's investigations are published as 'Decisions' and provide important guidance on how Arts.101 and 102 TFEU should be interpreted. The legality of these Decisions can be challenged before the European Courts following the Art.263 TFEU procedure (ex Art.230 ECT). The Commission can launch an investigation either on its own initiative, where it has reason to suspect an undertaking of anti-competitive behaviour, or following a complaint from a natural or legal person with a legitimate interest in curtailing the anti-competitive conduct, or at the instigation of a member state under Art.7 Regulation 1/2003.

Art.20 Regulation 1/2003 grants to the Commission the power to inspect the books, records and premises of an undertaking in order to determine whether a breach of the competition provisions has occurred. Under Art.23(1) Regulation 1/2003, failure to cooperate with the investigation process can result in an undertaking being fined up to one per cent of its turnover from the previous business year. Where an infringement of Arts.101 or 102 TFEU is established, a Decision taken in accordance with Art.7 Regulation 1/2003 can force changes to an undertaking's behaviour, or in extreme cases to its structure, in order to curtail the anti-competitive conduct. Alternatively where the undertaking's anti-competitive conduct is considered to be sufficiently serious, a fine of up to ten per cent of its turnover in the preceding business year can be imposed under Art.23(2) Regulation 1/2003.

The Commission has investigated the conduct of ISFs and major event organisers on a number of occasions. For example in *Royal Excelsior Mouscron* IP/99/965 9 December 1999 (see further, chapter 12.5.3.3), the Commission held that the 'home-and-away' rule operated by UEFA in its football competitions affected only the proper organisation of sport and therefore was not subject to Arts.101 and 102 TFEU, thus preventing the need for further litigation on the issue. Further, in *FIFA 2006 World Cup Ticketing Arrangements* IP/05/519 2 May 2005, an increased range of payment options was offered to purchasers of tickets to the World Cup Finals Tournament following a complaint made to the Commission by the consumer organisation *Which?*. Although not having the status of judgments of the European Courts, Decisions of the Commission on competition law issues have a great deal of authority because of the expertise of the body involved and its interest in creating consistency of interpretation across all member states of the EU. It is also able to provide a pre-emptive and quicker resolution to a potential dispute instead of requiring the parties to commence proceedings before a national court and hoping that the necessary reference under Art.267 TFEU will be made by one of the trial or appellate judges.

1.5.3   Sport and the European Treaties

The need to protect the special status of sport was recognised during the negotiations that led to the Treaty of Amsterdam in 1997. Although the Declaration that was appended to the Treaty was not legally binding, it enabled the EU to take into account the importance of sport to the citizens of the EU and to the EU's cultural makeup when developing its own law and policies. The most visible development that came out of the Declaration was the creation of the Directorate General for Education and Culture's Sport Unit.

> ▶ *Treaty of Amsterdam 1997 Declaration 29*
>
> The Conference emphasises the social significance of sport, in particular its role in forging identity and bringing people together. The Conference therefore calls on the bodies of the European Union to listen to sports associations when important questions affecting sport are at issue. In this connection, special consideration should be given to the particular characteristics of amateur sport.

At the end of the French Presidency of the EU in 2000, the Nice Declaration was annexed to the Presidency Conclusions. Like the Amsterdam Declaration it was not legally binding, however once again it reiterated the importance of sport by requiring the EU to take into consideration its social, educational and cultural functions when creating new laws and policies. The task of organising sport was left to the various NGBs and ISFs, although it was noted in the Declaration that these bodies must operate within national and EU law if they are to avoid censure.

Since these two Declarations were made, a group of the leading ISFs, spearheaded by FIFA and UEFA, has campaigned vigorously for sport to be specifically exempted from the operation of EU. This has not found favour with the European Council, Commission or Parliament and instead the EU has reserved for itself the competence to act on matters relating to sport within the limits provided by Arts.6 and 165 TFEU. This, in turn, could lead to a more proactive and coherent development of European sports law in the future, though it is unlikely that this will result in the exemption sought by the ISFs materialising.

> ▶ *Treaty on the Functioning of the European Union Art.165*
>
> 1. [The] Union shall contribute to the promotion of European sporting issues, while taking account of the specific nature of sport, its structures based on voluntary activity and its social and educational function.
> 2. Union action shall be aimed at:
>   [– developing] the European dimension in sport, by promoting fairness and openness in sporting competitions and cooperation between bodies responsible for sports, and by protecting the physical and moral integrity of sportsmen and sportswomen, especially the youngest sportsmen and sportswomen.
> 3. The Union and the member states shall foster cooperation with third countries and the competent international organisations in the field of education and sport, in particular the Council of Europe.

This amendment to the sphere of competence of the EU will enable it to support, coordinate and most importantly supplement the actions of the member states in respect of sport. The EU will be able to promote European sporting issues, ensure that the specific nature of sport is protected and develop its social and educational functions. In particular, it aims at promoting transparency in sporting competitions, cooperation between sporting bodies and protecting the physical and moral integrity of sports participants. However, despite the potential for an increased role for the EU in the regulation of sport provided for in Art.165, its potential impact remains vague, and its powers have remained relatively unused.

Importantly, it is implicit in the wording of Art.165 that the 'specificity of sport' will continue to be a decisive factor in determining whether or not EU law applies to a particular situation and that current administrative structures are to be protected. Thus, both the conditional autonomy currently enjoyed by governing bodies and the pyramidal structure according to which most European sport is organised are likely to be unaffected by the implementation of Art.165. The more likely areas of development will be in the creation of a more coherent sports policy aimed at protecting grassroots and youth sport rather than the creation of legal measures specifically aimed at the greater regulation of the commercial aspects of professional sport.

1.5.4   The development of European sports law

The further expansion of European sports law is dependent on the evolution of the relationship between the CJEU and CAS and on the interpretation of the scope of Art.165. The resolution of the tension that exists between the jurisprudence of CAS and the degree of influence that the EU is able to exert over sports disputes will be key to the harmonious development of both global and European sports law. As the scope of CAS's influence continues to grow, and as it hands down an increasing number of decisions requiring it to interpret and apply EU law, the opportunity for differences of opinion between the decisions of CAS and the CJEU becomes more likely. Even though CAS is bound by the interpretations of EU law delivered by the European Courts, the much more rapid development of its jurisprudence creates at least the possibility of divergence between the legal interpretations used by the two tribunals. With the language of CAS often replicating that of the CJEU, particularly where discussions of the 'specificity of sport' are concerned, a greater degree of consultation, or perhaps even collaboration, between these two bodies may eventually become necessary to ensure that the law develops in a way that is beneficial to sport.

Following the ratification of the TFEU, perhaps the clearest indication of how EU sports law and policy will develop can be found in the European Commission's *White Paper on Sport* (COM (2007) 39 Final). The *White Paper* provides a strategic orientation of the current societal role, economic dimension and organisational framework of sport and identifies how the Commission may see its own role in respect of these issues evolving in the future. The potential for the development of European sports law can be seen most explicitly in the chapters covering the societal role of sport and its organisation and governance. Regarding the former, the Commission appears to see a role for itself in developing policies and potentially law, covering, amongst other things, anti-racism, crowd disorder and doping control. However, it is in respect of the organisation of sport that the Commission could develop a more interventionist role in the creation of European sports law. It identifies freedom of movement, the transfer of players between clubs, the regulation of sports agents and the protection of minors as potential areas for regulatory development, albeit set against the emerging requirement that the specificity of sport to be taken into consideration if the Commission does eventually decide to act. Thus, the Commission has made it clear how and why it sees a more active role for the EU developing in respect of sport and, therefore potentially, sports law.

1.6 International sports law

International sports law is the general or universal principles of law, particularly of international law, that are applicable to sport. In some discussions, there is confusion between this definition of international sports law and global sports law, however, a clear distinction is drawn here between the two specific and different sources of sports law. According to Foster, these general principles are those which are a part of international customary law, or the *jus commune*, and include but are not limited to: the principle that agreements are binding; the prohibition on unjust enrichment; the guarantee of procedural fairness and that a body is bound to follow its own rules and procedures, the doctrines of proportionality and personal liability and the principle against double jeopardy, where a person cannot be punished twice for the same conduct. As these general principles of law are universally applicable, they cannot be avoided or reinterpreted by ISFs as they see fit. Moreover, as legal principles, they can be enforced before an appropriate national or transnational court; in other words, their existence limits an ISF's opportunity for complete self-regulation by imposing upon it basic standards of good governance. From a practical perspective, most of these universally applicable principles have been incorporated into sports law through national courts, as occurred in *Jones v Welsh Rugby Union* [1998] *The Times*, 6 January (see further, chapter 2.4.4) and more recently by CAS in *United States Olympic Committee v International Olympic Committee* CAS 2011/O/2422 (see further, Hot Topic 1 and chapter 3.3.5).

This kind of universally pervasive international law is further reflected in the mission of the Council of Europe, which seeks as one of its core aims to create a common legal area that ensures respect for human rights and the rule of law and is epitomised by its Conventions that seek to promote the harmonisation of legal principles and procedures rather than creating specific laws, as occurs in EU law. The Council of Europe is a supra-national organisation based in Strasbourg, France. It is separate from, and much larger than, the EU, counting 47 states amongst its members, including all current member states of the EU. Apart from the European sports law developed by the EU institutions and the principles of law that constitute the *jus commune*, the only significant current source of international sports law is that which can be found in the Conventions of the Council of Europe.

As the Conventions and Resolutions passed by the Council are not automatically binding on the UK Parliament, its role is much more relevant to the development of international sports policy and cooperation rather than sports law. This is evidenced most recently by the Council of Ministers of the Council of Europe adopting Resolution CM/Res (2007)/8, which created the Enlarged Partial Agreement on Sport. This sub-Convention level cooperation agreement focuses the work of the Council on sports ethics and the protection of the autonomy of sport from political interference rather than creating specific legal frameworks within which sport can function more effectively.

The Council has created two specific Conventions that apply to sport. The first, following the tragedy at the Heysel Stadium, Brussels in 1985, focuses on developing closer cooperation between members on issues relating to crowd disorder at football matches (see further, chapter 10.3.6). The second responds to the need for a more coordinated approach to the control of doping in sport (see further, chapter 3.3.3). Despite both Conventions being signed by the UK, they do not have legal effect in UK law, though both have played a significant part in developing UK policy in both of these areas. Thus, these Conventions are only weak sources of international sports law.

1.6.1 European Convention on Spectator Violence and Misbehaviour at Sports Events and in Particular at Football Matches 1985

The aim of the Convention on Spectator Violence is to create common and cooperative action amongst the signatories in their attempts to prevent and control spectator disorder. At the national level, it encourages greater cooperation among government, NGBs and the police to provide adequate resources to control public disorder and the development of an effective regime to punish those involved with acts of hooliganism, including banning them from attending matches. All of the recommendations made by the Convention reflect the findings of the various reports commissioned by the UK government into crowd control and spectator safety throughout the twentieth century (see further, chapter 9).

The Convention also recommends greater cooperation at the transnational level among signatories. In particular, it envisages the sharing of information on risk spectators between law enforcement and border control agencies and the prevention of known troublemakers from travelling abroad to watch football matches and potentially take part in disorder.

Although the Convention has no legal force in the UK, most of the policy initiatives raised within it have, in the aftermath of the disasters at Heysel Stadium, Brussels in 1985 and Hillsborough Stadium, Sheffield in 1989, been enacted. In particular, the exchange of information between police forces both within the UK and with their counterparts abroad and the imposition of Football Banning Orders on those convicted or suspected of being involved with football-related disorder have been cornerstones of the fight against football hooliganism (see further, chapter 10). Therefore, the regulatory framework provided by the Convention has been created, but the real source of the relevant law is national sports law rather than international sports law.

1.6.2 The Anti-Doping Convention 1989

The Council of Europe's Anti-Doping Convention was the culmination of over 20 years of discussions on the importance of producing a coordinated international response to doping in sport. Its importance can be seen from the fact that non-European nations including Australia, Canada and Tunisia have also considered it worthwhile to become signatories of the Convention and to ratify it. The Convention begins with the premise that doping is cheating and that it is important to reduce and ultimately eliminate it from all sporting competitions.

The Convention requires signatories to begin by coordinating the agencies responsible for their domestic response to anti-doping and to restrict the availability of banned substances and methods by legislation where appropriate. Alongside these measures, the Convention also encourages signatories to establish high-quality testing facilities and schemes to educate athletes about the moral and physical dangers associated with taking performance-enhancing drugs. Finally, as with the Convention on Spectator Violence, it encourages cooperation among signatories in eradicating doping in sport by, amongst other things, the exchange of information on testing procedures and on athletes who have tested positive for banned substances.

To a great extent, the purpose behind the Anti-Doping Convention has now been superseded by the activities of the World Anti-Doping Agency (WADA), its Code and the hearing of most major doping disputes before the Court of Arbitration for Sport. This global level of coordination and cooperation is the driving force behind WADA and its harmonisation of anti-doping procedures across sports and nations. However, recognition of the pioneering work of the Council of Europe can be seen in its position as a Foundation Board Member of WADA's Board and Executive Committee. Thus, although a weak source of international sports law, the Convention has been a key driver in the development of global anti-doping policies and has established the platform upon which CAS's anti-doping jurisprudence has been built.

1.7 Conclusion

When answering the question, 'What is sports law?' the answer is that it is a combination of the law and legal theory found in all of these different sources. It is the interaction of sport and the law, it is the law, legal principles and legal procedures that resolve sports disputes and it can be seen in action by the impact that it has had on how sport is currently administered, participated in and consumed. Whether it is referred to as 'sport and the law' or 'sports law', there is no doubt about its growing importance as a field of legal practice and academic enquiry. Sports law cases such as *Bosman* have changed the core features of sport as it had developed since the late 1800s and become part of the sporting-legal vernacular. Others have had a direct impact on the way that we watch sport and have led to changes in UK national law and the value of sports broadcasting rights, *Murphy v Media Protections Services Ltd*.

'Sport and the law' is more properly the simple application of national and EU law to a sports dispute. It does not specifically consider in any detail the special nature of sport, just whether or not the law is an appropriate forum for resolving the particular dispute that has arisen.

'Sports law' attempts to provide an underlying explanation of why sports as a group of related activities are, and should continue to be, treated differently by the law; it is the development of an underlying theory that draws together cases using disparate legal principles into a single coherent subject. It is not the piecemeal application of disparate fields of law to specific sporting disputes but a general approach to understanding the particular needs of sport and everyone who is involved with its playing, consumption and administration. This is at its clearest in the CJEU's development of what constitutes the 'specificity of sport' and that Court's provision of a more detailed explanation of the reasons why sport should be treated differently in certain circumstances. It is the 'specificity of sport' that allows monopolistic private bodies to control the conduct of huge sections of society without significant interference from the law; that enables participants to inflict injuries on each other with a degree of immunity from the law; that justifies the criminalisation of breach of contract when a tout resells a ticket to a football match or an Olympic event; that enables a governing body to prevent a player from earning a living from their chosen profession because they have boosted their performance by using particular substances or equipment; that prevents men and women from working together and competing against one another; that enables discriminatory nationality quotas to be imposed on employers and that forces employers to release their employees to another profit-making organisation without recompense. Sports law is the jurisprudence that has evolved to justify that sport is different and which enables a justification of how and why the law applies in the way that it does to be provided.

Hot topic ... ## The Court of Arbitration for Sport and fundamental principles of law

The Court of Arbitration for Sport (CAS) has been in existence since 30 June 1984 and in its current form since 22 November 1994. Its position as the world's leading sports law forum has been reinforced by it being the only tribunal that can hear disputes over the interpretation of the Olympic Charter, the sole tribunal of appeal from decisions of the World Anti-Doping Agency and the final tribunal of appeal for the majority of major international sports federations. This position at the apex of the sporting-legal world and the general acceptance of its decisions as being authoritative precedents on the interpretation of sports disputes has required CAS to ensure that its reasoning is robust and grounded in appropriate legal norms. In looking not only to the form and substance of the sporting rules before it but by drawing on what are generally considered to be universally accepted legal principles when forming its opinions and advices, it is creating what is coming to be known as *lex sportiva*; a transnational, universally applicable sports law.

CAS has often resorted to such principles, with the first review of its own jurisprudence on this issue coming in *AEK Athens and SK Slavia Prague v UEFA* CAS 1998/A/200 (see further, chapter 12.5.3.2). This case concerned whether it was fair for UEFA to ban from its competitions one or more teams that were owned by the same legal person, here an investment company called ENIC. In the course of its opinion, CAS stated that due to the transnational nature of the rules and decisions of ISFs being felt throughout the world, their conduct should not only be governed by their own rules and the law of the country in which they were established, but should be subject to, and bound by, general principles of law. These included, in particular, the prohibition on arbitrary and unreasonable rules, on sanctions that were excessive, unfair or disproportionate and the requirement of procedural fairness.

In *United States Olympic Committee v International Olympic Committee* CAS 2011/O/2422, this issue was returned to as one of two grounds for declaring what was at that time Rule 45 Olympic Charter unlawful. Rule 45 had been introduced to impose a greater sanction on athletes who had been found guilty of a doping offence and suspended from competition for six months or longer; in such a case, the athlete would be banned additionally from competing in the summer and winter Games immediately following the completion of their suspension. CAS held Rule 45 to be unlawful primarily on the grounds that by introducing an additional punishment unilaterally that was not sanctioned by the WADA Code, the IOC had not followed its own rules and procedures. In other words, it had acted *ultra vires*, or without procedural fairness or due process.

In response to a further claim put forward by the USOC, however, CAS also said that it could have found the additional punishment unlawful on the grounds that it offended against fundamental principles of law. In this instance, it was contrary to the principle of double jeopardy; no person can be punished twice for the same offence. As the athlete in question had already been punished for the doping offence by his ISF, the International Association of Athletics Federations, he could not then be punished again for the same offence by the IOC.

The introduction of fundamental, generally applicable or universally accepted principles of law into the jurisprudence of CAS is an important step in the creation of a *lex sportiva*. In particular, it provides CAS's decisions with an underpinning legalism that is grounded in the normative values that mature legal systems would consider to be integral to their operation. It also provides CAS with the opportunity to set minimum standards of procedural fairness and governance that are applicable across all sports and to challenge practices that have become entrenched or normalised through having been developed in isolation of legal review.

The *USOC v IOC* decision also demonstrates how CAS is prepared to develop its jurisprudence incrementally and use its previous decisions as precedent in what appears to be a distinctly common law approach. These signs that the jurisprudence of CAS is maturing and developing are as important to the development of sports law as is the creation of the principle of the specificity of sport in EU law. With CAS taking legal norms into consideration and national and European courts reciprocating by taking the needs of sport into consideration, there is scope for greater cooperation between the leading tribunals to ensure that sports law, or *lex sportiva* develops as a coherent single subject rather than being having different approaches adopted depending on in which tribunal a case is commenced.

Summary

1.1 There is no formal definition of sport in UK law. This can be explained, in part, by the non-interventionist approach of the UK Parliament to matters connected with sport. This, in turn, leaves the day-to-day governance of British sport to the NGBs; these bodies are in general answerable to the appropriate ISF rather than directly to Parliament or a government department. Thus, there is no single identifiable authoritative source of sports law. Instead the ability to identify the law, legal norms and legal procedures that constitute sports law requires an understanding of its various national and international sources.

1.2 As sports disputes have become increasingly juridified, so have the internal tribunals operated by NGBs taken on a more obviously quasi-judicial role in their resolution. Following a series of challenges to their authority and decision-making processes, these tribunals and independent bodies such as Sports Disputes UK are now capable of hearing and resolving sports disputes involving complex legal issues. They have become an important source of domestic sports law because although they rarely create new law and legal norms, they are hearing cases that would otherwise be heard before the national courts.

1.3 Global sports law is evolving from the autonomous legal order created by ISFs for resolving transnational sporting disputes. In particular, the jurisprudence of CAS provides leadership and guidance to affected parties by harmonising approaches across sports to the interpretation and application of legal norms to sporting disputes. The decisions of CAS and of the dispute resolution chambers of many ISFs provide an important source of global sports law by hearing complex legal issues that would otherwise be heard before national and European courts.

1.4 National sports law is that which is created by Parliament or found in the judgments and decisions of national courts and enforcement agencies. The non-interventionist approach to the governance of sport by the state in the UK means that there are few Acts of Parliament that apply specifically to sporting activities. Instead, the decisions of the courts and of bodies like the Office of Fair Trading have had the greatest impact on the administration of, participation in and consumption of sport.

1.5 In the absence of any specific mention of sport in the earlier treaties, the application of EU law to sport has largely been seen in the decisions of the CJEU when it has been called upon to interpret whether various provisions apply to the conduct of ISFs and NGBs. However, the EU has been active in the development of its own sports policy, and the 2007 *White Paper on Sport* gives a clear indication of how European sports law could develop following the ratification of the Treaty on the Functioning of the European Union and the powers granted to the EU in respect of sport in Arts.6 and 165.

1.6 The universally applicable principles of international customary law ensure that the parties to legal disputes are treated fairly and proportionately. They have been incorporated into

Summary cont'd

international sports law by actions before national courts and CAS that have forced NGBs and ISFs to adopt quasi-judicial procedures and norms when acting quasi-judicially. It is perhaps the most difficult source of sports law to identify because of sport being administered by a series of private relationships rather than through a network of international treaties ratified by nation states. Where such transnational agreements are in place, for example, the sports-specific Conventions of the Council of Europe, they are more likely to be indicators of how national sports law will develop rather than being specific sources of international sports law.

1.7 There continues to be discussion about whether 'sport and the law' or 'sports law' is the correct title of this field of legal enquiry. 'Sport and the law' accurately reflects how sports disputes are litigated before the courts; it is the application of discrete fields of law to a dispute that happens to be between parties connected with the administration of, participation in or consumption of sport. However, 'sports law' suggests that there is an underpinning theory that justifies how and why sports disputes are treated differently by the courts and why CAS considers that it is creating a new series of legal norms that it refers to as *lex sportiva*. This unifying theory has been identified by the CJEU as the 'specificity of sport' and goes a long way to explaining when it is appropriate for sport to be subjected to the law and when it should be left to regulate itself.

Further reading

Beloff et al, *Sports Law* (2nd edn, 2012, Hart) ch 1

Lewis and Taylor (eds), *Sport: Law and Practice* (2nd edn, 2008, Tottel) ch A1

Parrish and Miettinen, *The sporting exception in European Union Law* (2008, TMC Asser Press)

Beloff, 'Is there a *lex sportiva*?' [2008] 3 *International Sports Law Review* 49

Foster, 'Is there a Global Sports Law?' (2003) 2(1) *Entertainment and Sports Law Journal*, online

Humphrey, 'The politics of sport: the why, when and how of sports law development and implementation' [2008] 2/3 *International Sports Law Review* 30

Nafziger, 'Defining the scope and structure of international sports law: four conceptual issues' [2011] 3/4 *International Sports Law Journal* 14–15 and 18–21

Siekmann, 'What is sports law? Lex sportiva and lex ludica: a reassessment of content and terminology' [2011] 3/4 *International Sports Law Journal* 3–13

Taylor and O'Sullivan, 'How should national governing bodies of sport be governed in the UK? An exploratory study of board structure' (2009) 17(6) *Corporate Governance* 681

Links to relevant websites can be found at www.palgrave.com/law/james2e

Chapter 2 follows overleaf.

Challenging governing bodies in English Law

Key terms

> ▶ **Judicial review** – the power granted to the courts to review the decision-making procedures of public bodies.
> ▶ **Declaration** – a court order that states whether the procedure operated by an NGB is lawful or not.
> ▶ **Injunction** – a court order that requires its subject either to take specific action (mandatory injunction) or to stop doing something that is unlawful (prohibitory injunction).

2.1 The relationship between the two systems of sports law

In recent years, there has been a subtle though important shift in the relationship between national and European courts on the one hand and sporting tribunals on the other. During the latter part of the twentieth century, the archaic and unfair procedures of many sporting authorities and their tribunals were challenged before the courts and in the vast majority of cases, the system of sporting justice was required to update its processes to ensure that it met modern standards of procedural fairness, natural justice and due process.

The juridification of their procedures has led to a growing sophistication in the operation of these tribunals and an increasing confidence in their ability to hear complex legal cases. This has occurred to such an extent that both systems can now lay claim to having jurisdiction over many cases that would previously have been brought exclusively before one or other of them. The sporting legal system is now unrecognisable from the one that was in place when Lord Denning stated in *Enderby Town FC v The Football Association* [1971] Ch 591 at 605, that:

> 'In many cases it may be a good thing for the proceedings of a domestic tribunal to be conducted informally without legal representation. Justice can often be done in them better by a good layman than by a bad lawyer. This is especially so in activities like football and other sports, where no points of law are likely to arise, and it is all part of the proper regulation of the game.'

Points of law of the highest complexity are now most definitely heard before these sporting tribunals. Further, there is an expectation, particularly at the elite levels of sport, that not only will the parties be legally represented, but that they will be represented by sports law specialists arguing their case before a panel of sports law experts.

The opportunity for two systems that are both complementary and in competition to emerge can be traced to their almost identical frameworks of governance. Most national governing bodies of sport (NGBs) operate their own internal quasi-legal system. The NGB itself is the rule-making body (Parliament or legislature) whose rules (laws) are interpreted and enforced by a disciplinary tribunal, panel or committee (court).

In the same way that NGBs operate their own internal quasi-legal system, so too do international sports federations (ISFs). The role of the ISFs in this framework usually takes one or more of four forms. Firstly, the ISF will be responsible for defining the rules of the sport that it governs and for ensuring harmonisation in the implementation of those rules throughout the world. Secondly, it can ratify the decisions of NGBs and ensure that they are enforced worldwide. This ensures that, for example, a person banned from playing or coaching a sport in the UK does not simply move to France to ply their trade. Thirdly, the ISF may provide an appellate body to which appeals against the decisions of an NGB can be made. Fourthly, the ISF itself may provide the necessary disciplinary structures to be used at international representative fixtures, at other events that it organises or where a dispute contains a cross-border element. Where a dispute remains after the exhaustion of any available internal remedies, most major ISFs now allow an appeal to be made to the Court of Arbitration for Sport (CAS) for final determination of the matter (see further, chapter 3).

As is the case with the relationship between domestic and national sports law, the interactions between and overlap of global, international and European sports law only came to light with the increased internationalisation and commercialisation of sport. When the rules, decisions and common practices of ISFs began to affect sports participants' earnings, or spectators' safety when travelling abroad, or the ability of clubs to maximise their earnings, sports law began to develop a transnational perspective.

When originally created, these internal justice systems operated in an informal manner with no true separation of powers and very few procedural safeguards. Their main purpose was to enforce playing bans for on-field foul play and off-field financial misconduct. This ideal of self-regulation went unchallenged for most of the twentieth century as NGBs dealt with all aspects of sporting misconduct, or matters that brought their game into disrepute, in-house. When the occasional case did appear before the judiciary, the judges showed little enthusiasm to interfere in matters that they considered could be dealt with more efficiently and more effectively elsewhere.

This hands-off approach to the conduct of disciplinary hearings changed dramatically as sport in the UK became more openly professional and the participants became much more substantially rewarded. As bans began to affect not only an athlete's ability to take part in a sport but also their income, sports participants began to expect a more formal approach from their sporting justice systems and the ability to refer to the national courts to rectify any perceived inadequacies (*Jones v Welsh Rugby Union* [1998] The Times, 6 January) (below, 2.4.4). Further, with the financial rewards now available through increased commercial streams, particularly television money, clubs also began to expect not only a fair hearing but also a robust and legally defensible explanation of how and why the tribunal has reached its decision (*Sheffield United Football Club Ltd v Football Association Premier League Ltd* [2007] 3 ISLR SLR 77) (below, 2.4.3).

Much of the time, these panels are applying national and/or EU law or the underlying generic legal principles that are common to all modern legal systems, the *jus commune*, rather than creating completely new legal norms. However it is their development of the meaning of the 'specificity of sport', based on the reasoning in *Meca-Medina and Majcen v Commission* (C-519/04 P) [2006] ECR I-6991 (see further, chapter 12.1.2), and their ability to hear cases that might otherwise cause significant problems to both sport and the law if heard by national courts, as was the case in *FC Shaktar Donetsk v Matazulem and Real Zaragoza SAD and FIFA* CAS 2008/A/1519 and 1520 (below, 3.3.2 and chapter 12.2.2.2), that demonstrate the real importance of global sports law. As ISFs' final appeals tribunals in general and CAS in particular appear to be more prepared than the courts to examine the sporting context from which these disputes arise rather than mechanically applying the letter of the law, global sports law has developed a more sports-sympathetic approach to their resolution.

The relationship between the two sports law systems is an uneasy one, with both able to claim jurisdiction over the same disputes. Further, there is no doubt that their decisions can influence each other. However, although the sporting tribunals must apply national and EU law where necessary and appropriate to a dispute before it and the implementation of its decisions will be subject to the law of the state in which they are established and EU law, the national and European courts are not similarly bound to take account of the decisions of sporting tribunals. Therefore, it is imperative that any athlete challenging the conduct of an NGB or ISF begins their action in the correct forum as there is at least a possibility of the two systems reaching different answers to the case before them.

As all cases examine the conduct complained of in the context of the needs of the sport, and as the principles underpinning the *lex sportiva* being developed by CAS are common to EU law and the laws of all EU member states, they will usually arrive at the same result. This is of particular importance because of the number of applications heard by CAS and the final appeals tribunals of many ISFs that contain a significant EU law element. It would defeat the purpose of these panels if they were to get the law wrong, and the affected party were able to assert their rights before the national and European courts at a later date, as occurred in *Union Royale Belge des Societes de Football Association ASBL v Bosman* (Case C-415/93) [1995] ECR I-4921 (see further, chapter 12.2.1).

The tension that has arisen between the two systems is grounded in the sporting authorities' desire for self-regulation of all disputes that affect the governance and administration of their sports, coupled with the expectations of players and clubs that they will receive a standard of justice equivalent to that which is available in actions before the national courts; this tension has been key to the development of the procedural norms now applied in sports disciplinary tribunals. Instead of simply tracing the various challenges that have been made to the authority of, and procedures followed by, NGBs, this chapter explains how the decisions of the courts, the national sports law, have affected the operations of sports disciplinary tribunals and, consequently, domestic sports law. It begins by explaining the legal status of an NGB in English law before analysing how challenges to an NGB's rules, procedures and decisions can be brought before the national courts and the impact that these have had on the way that sports disciplinary tribunals now operate.

2.2   The role of governing bodies and their legal status in English law

Sport in the UK is organised on a private basis, meaning that there is very little direct state intervention in the day-to-day administration of sporting activities (see further, chapter 1.1.4). A governing body comprises its members, who will usually be the individual players as is the case with male professional tennis players being members of the ATP Tour, or a group of clubs as is the case for the vast majority of team sports in the UK. In either case, the clubs or the athletes will have agreed together, for the time being, to be bound by the rules and procedures of the NGB that they have created or of which they are constituent members.

2.2.1 The jurisdiction of governing bodies over their members

NGBs have no specific or inalienable legal right to govern the sport over which they have jurisdiction; their power derives only from the agreement of their current members to be bound by the NGB's rules. Thus, there must be in place a contract, or a relationship equivalent to that created by a contract, capable of binding all relevant parties to the rules and regulations of the NGB for it to be able to operate effectively. Such an agreement can be expressly entered into by the relevant parties or implied from their conduct, as can be seen in the litigation arising out of the suspension of professional tennis player Petr Korda for a doping offence.

▶ *The Petr Korda litigation*

On 7 May 1998, Petr Korda completed and signed the application form to compete in the All England Lawn Tennis and Croquet Club's Championships at Wimbledon. The application form stated that the event was to be played under the Rules of Tennis as approved by the International Tennis Federation (ITF), including its anti-doping and drug testing programme. Following his defeat in the Round of 16, Korda provided a urine sample for testing, which was later found to contain two metabolites of the banned substance nandrolone.

At a hearing before the Independent Anti-Doping Review Board (IADRB), it was concluded that Korda was guilty of a first violation of the ITF's Anti-Doping Programme and that he should be subject to the mandatory penalty of suspension from all ITF sanctioned events for one year and the forfeiture of all ranking points and prize money awarded at Wimbledon. Korda appealed to the ITF's Appeals Committee (AC) against the imposition of the suspension on the grounds that there were 'exceptional circumstances' for the presence of nandrolone in his urine sample. The AC accepted Korda's claim that he had not knowingly taken, or had administered to him, a prohibited substance and overturned the playing ban that had been imposed upon him.

The ITF lodged an appeal with CAS against this decision on the basis that the AC had incorrectly found there to be 'exceptional circumstances' that warranted a reduction in the penalty imposed. Korda applied to the High Court for an injunction preventing the ITF from pursuing its appeal to CAS on the basis he was not contractually bound by the ITF's rules and that even if he was, the rules did not provide for such an appeal in these circumstances.

▶ *Korda v ITF Ltd* **(unreported) High Court (Ch), 29 January 1999**

Contrary to Korda's claims, the High Court found there to be a contractual relationship in place between the player and the ITF. Although there had been neither a written nor an oral agreement between the two parties, the existence of a contract could be inferred from their conduct. Of particular importance was Korda's submission to the drug testing programme by his providing a urine sample, the exercise of his right to appeal from the original decision of the IADRB to the AC and his assertion that if the appeal to the AC were to go against him, then he would exercise his right to appeal to CAS. The Court held that Korda's submission to the jurisdiction of the AC was evidence of his acceptance of a contractual relationship between himself and the ITF whose terms required that the procedures provided for in the ITF's Anti-Doping Programme be followed.

▶ *Korda v ITF Ltd* **(unreported) Court of Appeal (Civ), 25 March 1999**

Having established the existence of a contractual relationship between the parties in the High Court, the dispute then focused on the circumstances in which the contract allowed an appeal to be made from a decision of the AC to CAS. The Court of Appeal interpreted s.(V)3 ITF Anti-Doping Programme to mean that either party could appeal to CAS for a full re-hearing of the case where there was any dispute arising from any decision made by the AC. As there was a clear dispute concerning whether the AC had correctly interpreted the meaning of 'exceptional circumstances' and whether it had imposed an appropriate punishment on Korda, s.(V)3 entitled the ITF to appeal to CAS for final resolution of the matter.

▶ *ITF Ltd v K* **CAS 99/A/223**

CAS began by agreeing with both of the findings of the English courts: first that a contractual relationship existed between Korda and the ITF and second, that s.(V)3 ITF Anti-Doping Programme allowed either party the right of appeal to CAS in the case of any dispute arising from any decision of the AC. Having established its jurisdiction to hear the appeal, the panel then went on to determine whether Korda was able to prove on the balance of probabilities that there were 'exceptional circumstances' present that could justify the imposition of a penalty lower than that required in the ordinary course of events by the Anti-Doping Programme. Their finding was that a claim by the athlete that he had no idea how a prohibited substance had come to be present in his urine sample, in the absence of any evidence that he was not at fault for the positive test, was not sufficient to establish the presence of 'exceptional circumstances' that could justify the imposition of a reduced penalty. Thus CAS reinstated the original penalties imposed by the IADRB of a one-year suspension from competition and the forfeiture of the ranking points and prize money earned at Wimbledon.

This series of hearings demonstrates how the governance of sport in English law is based firmly in contract. Without the existence of either an express or implied contract between the governing body and the clubs and/or athletes playing its sport, there is no legal basis for it being able to exercise regulatory powers over them. If a contract can be identified, then its terms need to be scrutinised to determine whether or not the governing body has the power to act in the way that it has. Further, as the relationship is based in contract, it should be possible to determine the circumstances in which the members of an NGB can decide not to submit to its jurisdiction any longer.

Shortly after the completion of the *Korda* litigation, a series of tribunal and court hearings based on an allegation of doping against Diane Modahl concluded. The key development in the Court of Appeal was how to determine the legal basis for whether or not an NGB's rules applied to the athlete and how and why the athlete should be bound by them.

▶ *Modahl v British Athletic Federation Ltd* **[2001] EWCA Civ 1447**

The claimant was a professional athlete of international standing. Following her participation in an event in Portugal, she submitted herself to the anti-doping programme that was being administered according to the rules of the International Amateur Athletics Federation, where her urine sample tested positive for the banned steroid testosterone. She was subsequently found to have committed a doping offence by BAF's Disciplinary Committee and banned from competition for four years. On appeal to the Independent Appeal Panel, Modahl was acquitted on the basis that there was scientific evidence that demonstrated a possibility that the samples provided by her had been degraded by bacterial contamination which could have affected the reliability of the results.

The claimant sought compensation from the defendant as she had not been able to earn money from competing for the period of time between the initial finding of guilt and her ultimate acquittal. She claimed that BAF had breached its contract with her by failing to act fairly during the disciplinary process as members of the panel at the first instance hearing were biased against her.

As no written or oral contract had been entered into between the claimant and the defendant, the Court of Appeal had to determine whether there were any grounds for implying the necessary contractual relationship. The Court found that there were three ways that the existence of contract could be justified: the 'club basis' (below), the 'participation basis' and the 'submission basis'. The 'participation basis' provides evidence of the existence of a contractual relationship because of the athlete's repeated participation in events organised or sanctioned by the NGB. As the claimant was an elite-level athlete taking part in such events, and in some representative events participating at the invitation of the defendant, both parties were aware of the existence of the applicable anti-doping and disciplinary regimes and knew that these must be operated fairly. The 'submission basis' is where athletes submit themselves to the anti-doping testing procedures and make use of the appeals procedures provided by the NGB. Latham LJ stated that a contract arose on the participation basis, whilst Mance LJ thought that a combination of the three bases would provide sufficient evidence of the existence of a contractual relationship. Thus, a contract was implied to be in place that contained a term that BAF must operate a fair disciplinary process.

Thus, there are three bases on which a contractual link between a governing body and an athlete can be established. The first is the 'club basis', where the existence of a contract between an athlete and the relevant decision-making body is established through a chain of mutually interdependent contracts. The first of these is the contract of membership or employment entered into between the athlete and their club, which will usually contain a term that requires the athlete to submit to the rules and disciplinary procedures of the relevant NGB and/or ISF. The second is the contract of membership between the club and the NGB, which will require the club and all those associated with it to abide by the NGB's rules and disciplinary procedures and those of the relevant ISF. The final contract, again one of membership, is between the NGB and ISF, which will also contain a term requiring the NGB to enforce the rules and disciplinary procedures operated by the ISF. This basis was used to establish the contractual link between *Modahl* and the BAF. Variations in this chain can occur, as was seen in *Jones v WRU* (below, 2.4.4) where the player's registration documents created a direct link with the NGB. However, the contractual link between athlete, club, NGB and ISF can be established on the production of comparatively basic documentation.

Secondly, the 'participation basis' is where the contractual relationship is established through the athlete having participated in a competition organised or authorised by an NGB or ISF and as a consequence has agreed to be bound by the sporting authority's rules and regulations. Both *Korda* and *Modahl* were also covered by this interpretation of the law. Finally, the 'submission basis' is where once an athlete has actively engaged with the relevant disciplinary procedure, they are bound by its findings even if they disagree with them; they cannot later dispute jurisdiction. This could also have been used as a basis for establishing the necessary contractual nexus between *Modahl* and the BAF and can also be used to justify the application of an NGB or ISF's rules to non-members, as occurred in *Bradley* (below, 2.3.3.2).

2.2.2 Establishing a rival organisation

Provided that the members follow the procedures by which they are currently bound, there is nothing to stop them from resigning their membership and establishing their own rival organisation when they no longer want to be bound by the rules or administrative structures of the existing NGB. For example, in 1992, a group of the leading professional darts players broke away from the British Darts Organisation (BDO) to establish the World Darts Council, now known as the Professional Darts Corporation (PDC). The PDC sees itself as being more professionally and commercially minded than the BDO and has established a series of lucrative professional competitions for its members. Meanwhile, the BDO has continued to organise darts at all levels of play, including professional competitions and to develop the game amongst young players and women. As a result, in 2005, it obtained the recognition of the four home country sports councils as the official NGB for darts in the UK. The two bodies provide administrative and organisational frameworks for the same sport, played according to the same rules, though with different missions and differing memberships.

In the most extreme case, this can result in a completely new sport being created as the breakaway organisation seeks to establish its own separate identity and ethos, as occurred in rugby. In 1895, a group of clubs from the north of England resigned their membership of the Rugby Football Union in order to establish the Northern Rugby Football Union following a dispute over paying players who had taken time off work to play for their club. Although Northern Union was originally played by the same rules that had been established by the Rugby Football Union, these quickly changed with the abolition of line-outs in 1897 and a reduction to 13 players per side in 1907. From a dispute over whether a club should be able to reimburse its players for the pay they lost whilst playing, the new sport of rugby league evolved. Thus, provided that those breaking away do so in accordance with the rules of membership of their original NGB or with the permission of the sport's regulator, as when members of the Football League resigned to set up the Premier League in conjunction with the Football Association (see *R v Football Association Ltd ex p Football League Ltd* [1993] 2 All ER 833), there is little that can be done to prevent them from leaving and establishing a new governing body and potentially a new sport.

2.2.3 The legal status of governing bodies

When originally created, the NGBs of English sport had a wide variety of legal forms. Some, like the Marylebone Cricket Club (MCC), are private members clubs that, over the years, have divested themselves of their powers of governance to more recently established limited companies, in this case, the England and Wales Cricket Board. Others were even more informal groupings of clubs that constituted unincorporated associations. These are bodies with no separate or distinct legal personality from that of its members; thus, if sued, each individual member is liable for a share of the damages payable to the successful claimant (*Brown v Lewis* (1896) 12 TLR 455).

To avoid the members being placed in the position of being individually liable for any claim made against the governing body, most NGBs have incorporated to become companies limited by guarantee. Where this has occurred, the NGB now has a separate legal personality that insulates its members from liability, leaving the NGB to be sued in its own right. Not only are the members protected by their NGB incorporating, but so is the sport. Following the debts accrued by the British Athletics Federation during its protracted litigation with Diane Modahl (above, 2.2.1), the Federation was forced into bankruptcy, and British athletics was left without a fully functioning NGB for a short period of time. However, because the Federation was incorporated and had few assets, the sport itself was relatively unaffected. After a review of the needs of the sport was conducted by an independent steering group in 1997 and 1998, a new NGB, UK Athletics Ltd, was formed in 1999, again as a company limited by guarantee.

The one high-profile exception to these more standard legal forms was the Jockey Club. Originally a private members club, the Jockey Club had, over time, taken on responsibility for the regulation of horseracing in the UK, in much the same way as the MCC originally had for cricket. In 1970, its powers over British horseracing were consolidated when it was re-established by Royal Charter. As its powers were now an exercise of the Royal Prerogative, the Jockey Club had the appearance of being an organ of the state, clearly differentiating its legal status from all other British NGBs. Despite this unusual position, in *R v Disciplinary Committee of the Jockey Club ex parte Aga Khan* [1993] 1 WLR 909, it was eventually established that even the Jockey Club was a private body whose framework of consensual relationships was not governed by public law (below, 2.3.1). What the various challenges to its authority did highlight, however, was that there was a potential conflict of interest between the Jockey Club's regulatory and commercial roles, an issue recently revisited by the CJEU in *Motosykletistiki Omospondia Ellados NPID (MOTOE) v Greece* (C-49/07) [2008] ECR I-4863 (see further, 12.5.1). In 2007, the British Horseracing Authority was established as the NGB for horseracing in the UK, taking over the regulatory work of the Jockey Club and leaving it free to pursue its commercial and charitable enterprises. The new Authority, like the vast majority of NGBs based in the UK, is a company limited by guarantee.

2.3 Challenging governing bodies' decisions in the English courts

Almost anyone connected with a sport, whether a player, coach, agent, club or owner, may have reason to challenge the decisions of an NGB. Most challenges are made because the individual or club involved has been punished in some way by the NGB, for example, by being banned from playing or working in a particular sport, having points docked, or being prevented from using a particular type of equipment. Most of the developments that have resulted in the juridification of sporting authorities' decision-making processes have been imposed on NGBs following a successful challenge to a rule, decision or procedure that was brought before the national courts because of its negative financial impact on the applicant. Although many NGBs, and the ISFs of which they are members, discourage recourse to national courts for the purposes of dispute resolution, dissatisfied parties can, and do, still bring legal actions in an attempt to reach a more favourable outcome for themselves.

For example, the terms of a membership contract can require the parties to submit to arbitration to the exclusion of pursuing legal actions before the courts, even under the court's supervisory jurisdiction (below, 2.3.2). Such agreements demonstrate clearly the growing importance of domestic sports law tribunals at the expense of national sports law heard before the courts. For example, in *Fulham Football Club (1987) Ltd v Sir David Richards and The Football Association Premier League Ltd* [2010] EWHC 3111 (Ch), under section S Premier League Rules, all disputes arising out of these Rules or otherwise must be submitted to final and binding arbitration. A similar rule is operated by the Football

Association under section K of its Rules. In each case, the arbitrator has the power to order a party to the arbitration to do or refrain from doing anything.

Following an allegation by Fulham that the first respondent, who at the time was the chairman of the Premier League, had acted inappropriately by assisting a rival club to sign a player who's services it hoped to secure for itself, the League had conducted an investigation that cleared Richards of any misconduct. Fulham claimed that such a decision was unfair prejudice against them and petitioned the court to prevent Richards from acting in future transfer negotiations and to have him removed from his post as chairman. The respondents sought a stay of these proceedings on the basis that the only means of resolving such a dispute under the League's Rules was by arbitration.

The court held that Fulham had no inalienable right to petition the court in the way that it had as the parties had agreed, by means of the contract of membership of the Premier League, that all such disputes would be submitted exclusively to arbitration. Provided that the dispute was one that was covered by the Rules in question, that third parties would not be bound by the resolutions of the arbitrator and that the remedy sought from him was one that he was legally entitled to impose (for example, not a term of imprisonment), then the agreement was valid, and the dispute could only be resolved by submission by the parties to the agreed arbitral process.

Where a dispute calls into question an interpretation of EU law, then a reference under Art.267 TFEU (ex Art.234 ECT) can be made to the CJEU to seek a definitive clarification of the law (see further, chapter 12.1.1). The decision on when to make such a reference lies with the court, not the parties to the dispute.

2.3.1 The unavailability of judicial review in England and Wales

Before discussing the causes of action by which a claimant can challenge the actions of an NGB, it is important to mention briefly one that cannot. Because the internal disciplinary framework of an NGB bears more than a passing resemblance to a fully operational justice system, it has long been argued by claimants that these decision-making procedures should be amenable to judicial review. Under Part 54 Civil Procedure Rules, judicial review enables a person who has been adversely affected by an enactment or a decision of a public body such as a local authority to challenge its lawfulness before the High Court. The purpose of the review is to establish whether the decision-making process followed by the relevant public body was lawful; the Court does not interfere with the substance of the decision. Thus, if the Court finds that the decision was taken in excess of the powers granted to the body and was therefore *ultra vires*, or that no reasonable body acting in that capacity would have come to the same decision according to the test established in *Associated Provincial Picture Houses Ltd v Wednesbury Corporation* [1948] 1 KB 223, or that it had failed to follow its own procedures in coming to its decision, or that the rules of natural justice were not complied with, or the rule against bias was breached, then the decision can be set aside. In such circumstances, the decision-making body must either retake the decision whilst following its own procedures correctly or, if the procedures themselves are defective, amend them before rehearing the complaint as though for the first time.

Judicial review is a quick and efficient means of remedying defective public law procedures and on the face of it would appear to be ideally suited to ensuring that any party coming before a sports disciplinary tribunal received a fair hearing. As each of the developments mentioned in chapter 2.4 are, in reality, public law concepts that have been incorporated into private relationships, judicial review would appear to be the most appropriate means of ensuring that the disciplinary mechanisms used by NGBs are in fact fair. However, despite the number of occasions that such an argument has been raised before the English courts, the judiciary has taken a narrow view of the 'public' nature of NGBs and repeatedly declared that as they are private bodies that are not exercising any recognisable public function, their actions cannot be subjected to judicial review.

▶ *R v Disciplinary Committee of the Jockey Club (ex parte Aga Khan)* **[1993] 1 WLR 909**

The Aga Khan was the owner of a racehorse, Aliysa, which had won the 1989 Oaks at Epsom. Following a routine examination after the race, a metabolite of camphor, a prohibited substance, was found in Aliysa's urine sample and the horse was disqualified by the Disciplinary Committee of the Jockey Club. The Aga Khan sought judicial review of the Committee's decision on the grounds of unfairness.

It was argued on behalf of the applicant that judicial review was the appropriate means of challenging the Committee's decision as the Jockey Club was acting as a public body in respect of its role as the regulator of horseracing in the UK. This was evidenced by the Jockey Club being the sole controller of a significant national activity, by its powers being of a nature and scope that affected a significant section of the public, by its establishment by means of a Royal Charter and because if the Jockey Club had not been granted these powers to act in this way, then the government would have been obliged to establish a body capable of carrying out its functions. It was further argued that the relationship between the Jockey Club and those who were involved with racing was not strictly consensual as they had no option but to submit to its jurisdiction if they wished to work in the racing industry in the UK. Therefore, it was argued that although the Jockey Club was not exercising governmental or statutory powers, by virtue of its monopolistic control of an activity of national significance that could have an impact on people's rights and ability to earn a living, it was, in reality, acting as a public body that should be susceptible to judicial review.

The Court rejected these arguments and held that despite the grant of a Royal Charter to the Jockey Club, it remained a private body because its powers were in no sense governmental, and it could not in any way be described as being an emanation of the state. The power accorded to the Jockey Club over all persons associated with racing derived from the agreement of those persons to be bound by the Rules of Racing as administered by the Club. This was a private relationship, the lawfulness of which could be reviewed in the law of contract, or where no contract existed through the supervisory jurisdiction of the courts; it was not a public law relationship that was susceptible to judicial review.

The best chance of the actions of any NGB being found capable of being subjected to judicial review was if the Jockey Club had been declared to be exercising a public function. Since even a body that had been established by Royal Prerogative was found to be acting only as a private entity then, despite their monopolistic attributes and their decisions having an impact on wide sections of society, no NGB can have its decisions judicially reviewed in England and Wales. Despite the ongoing debate that NGBs should be subject to the judicial review procedure, all potential lines of argument now appear to have been closed. This outcome does not leave aggrieved parties without the ability to challenge the decision-making procedures of an NGB before the courts; this can be achieved by invoking the supervisory jurisdiction of the court (*Nagle v Feilden* [1966] 2 QB 633) (below, 2.3.2) by claiming that the decision was in breach of contract (*Aberavon and Port Talbot Rugby Football Club v Welsh Rugby Union Ltd* [2003] EWCA Civ 584) (below, 2.3.3.1) or that the NGB has acted in restraint of trade (*Eastham v Newcastle United FC and the Football Association* [1964] Ch 413) (see further, chapter 11.4.2.4).

In reality, the protections sought by applicants through judicial review have been imposed on NGBs through these alternative causes of action. Although it has been argued in some quarters that the procedural protections contained in the Human Rights Act 1998 should be imposed on NGBs post-*Bradley* (below, 2.3.2), it is unlikely that such a claim will be sustained as they are not public authorities; where necessary and appropriate, such protections would be likely to be imposed through the supervisory jurisdiction of the courts as being in the public interest.

2.3.2   Supervisory jurisdiction of the courts

It has long been accepted by the courts that although the decision-making procedures of NGBs and their tribunals cannot be subjected to judicial review under Part 54 Civil Procedure Rules, they can be reviewed under the courts' inherent supervisory jurisdiction at common law (*Nagle v Feilden* [1966] 2 QB 633). There is no need to establish the existence of a contractual relationship to engage this jurisdiction, although where such a contract is in place, an additional cause of action may be raised by a claimant (below, 2.3.3). To enable a decision to be reviewed by the courts, the claimant must establish that the NGB exercised a significant degree of control over a significant part of a sport and that its decision had a significant impact on the claimant, particularly where it affects the claimant's ability to earn a living from the sport, by the exercise of its regulatory functions. The NGB is under an obligation to act fairly and within its own rules and the law; it is not obliged to get the decision correct. Complaints about the correctness of a decision should be cured by an appeal to the appropriate appeals or arbitration tribunal, not the courts, which exercise only a supervisory, not an appellate, function.

▶ *Bradley v Jockey Club* **[2005] EWCA Civ 1056**

The applicant, a former jockey and now bloodstock agent, had been a witness in the trial of another jockey on charges of drug smuggling. In the course of cross-examination at the trial, the applicant admitted that he had received gifts from a third party in exchange for information relating to races. He was charged by the Jockey Club with breaching the prohibitions on providing information to prospective gamblers contained in the Rules of Racing. The Disciplinary Committee of the Jockey Club disqualified the applicant for eight years, which was later reduced by an independent Appeals Board to five years. The applicant challenged the length of the disqualification on the basis that it was disproportionate and would have the effect of preventing him from conducting his business as a bloodstock agent.

As there was no contract in place between the applicant and the Appeals Board, it was accepted that the Jockey Club should stand as defendant to the application as it would be the body that implemented the Appeals Board's decision. The Court was unequivocal in its finding that, even in the absence of a contract, the court had jurisdiction to grant declarations and injunctions in respect of the decisions of private tribunals that affect a person's right to work. However, such jurisdiction was supervisory only, not appellate in function; the function of the court was not to take the primary decision on the merits of the case but to ensure that the primary decision-maker had operated within lawful limits.

In exercising this supervisory jurisdiction, the court will follow a very similar procedure to that used during a judicial review under Part 54 Civil Procedure Rules, even though it was determining questions of private law. Thus, the court will determine whether the decision-making procedure followed was fair, whether there had been any errors of law in making the decision and whether any exercise of discretion or judgment, including the penalty imposed, fell within the range of available options open to the tribunal.

Provided that the decision of the NGB, or its designated tribunal, has sufficient impact on the person or organisation that is its subject, the process followed by the sports body is capable of being reviewed by the courts under its common law supervisory jurisdiction. Further, as *Bradley* had engaged voluntarily engaged with the Appeals Board, the court's supervisory jurisdiction could also have been justified on the 'submission basis' (above, 2.2.1) The grounds for review will be the same as those used by the Administrative Court when challenges are made to the decision-making procedures of a public body and include claims that the NGB, or its disciplinary bodies, have acted: outside the scope of their powers as defined in their own rules or regulations; contrary to national law; contrary to the rules of natural justice; contrary to the rule against bias; unreasonably, irrationally, arbitrarily, capriciously or disproportionately or on the basis of irrelevant considerations or where it has failed to take account of relevant considerations.

A similar approach to the review of a decision-making process was taken in a Football Association Premier League Rule S Arbitration, *Sheffield United Football Club Ltd v Football Association Premier League Ltd* [2007] 3 ISLR SLR 77. The Panel held that the League was the appropriate respondent even though the decision being challenged had been made by an independent tribunal to which disciplinary powers had been delegated. Further, the same grounds of review as had been identified in *Bradley* were accepted as being appropriate in cases falling under the Panel's jurisdiction. Thus, the same approach to review has emerged in both domestic and national sports law.

Whereas previous cases invoking the supervisory jurisdiction of the courts sought to challenge the legality of the NGB's rules or the proportionality of the punishment imposed, in *McKeown v British Horseracing Authority* [2010] EWHC 508 (Admin), the claimant attempted to challenge the factual conclusions of the defendant's Disciplinary Panel and Appeal Board. Stadlen J held that there are four factors that must be taken into consideration by a court when deciding whether or not it should interfere with the findings of fact of a sport's disciplinary tribunal: (1) The function of the court is not to make findings of fact but to decide whether it is satisfied that no reasonable tribunal could have made a finding of fact made by the sporting tribunal on the evidence before it; (2) In considering whether it is so satisfied, the court should allow for the special expertise of the tribunal and the fact that it saw and heard the witnesses and/or video evidence; (3) The fact that the tribunal had a special expertise does not, however, prevent the court from carefully examining the evidence brought before the tribunal and concluding in an appropriate case that no reasonable tribunal could have made the findings of fact which were, in fact, made; (4) The importance of the court not showing unthinkingly servile obeisance to the decision of an expert sporting tribunal is particularly important where the decision being challenged affects a person's livelihood. Thus, the court will not replace the sporting tribunal as the primary finder of fact but can assess whether the conclusions reached by it were arbitrary, or perverse, or were of a kind that no reasonable decision-making body could have made.

2.3.3 Actions of the NGB amounting to a breach of contract

In many cases, the relationship between the person or body affected by a decision and the NGB making it will have been created by a contract, making it much easier for the aggrieved party to seek clarification of the legality of the NGB's conduct before the courts. Where a contractual nexus between the parties can be established (above, 2.2.1), the party disputing the lawfulness of the decision or the decision-making process of the NGB can therefore bring an action for breach of either the express or implied terms of any contract existing between them. The contractual nexus can be either direct or indirect; it is direct if a contract has been specifically entered into by the parties and indirect where a chain of relationships needs to be established to create the necessary link. Once the existence of a contract can be proved, the claimant can bring an action for either a declaration or injunction that will force the NGB to amend its procedures, or for compensation for any losses caused.

2.3.3.1 Direct contractual relationship

Where a claim is made by a member of a sport's governing body against the NGB itself, proving the existence of a contract between them will be a relatively straightforward exercise.

▶ *Aberavon and Port Talbot Rugby Football Club v Welsh Rugby Union Ltd* **[2003] EWCA Civ 584**

The claimant was a club member of the defendant NGB, the Welsh Rugby Union (WRU). At the end of the 2000–01 season, the claimant finished first in the First Division of the WRU National League and sought to be promoted to the Premier League. As a result of changes to the structure of the leagues in Wales before the start of the 2000–01 season, the Premier League was to be reduced in size, the consequence of which was that Aberavon, although the winners of their league, were not promoted.

Aberavon claimed that it was contractually entitled to be promoted on the basis of a promise made by the defendants at a Special General Meeting in 1997 that it would give at least 12 months' notice before implementing any changes to the league structure, particularly if such changes affected promotion and relegation. It was further claimed that the club had expended large amounts of money on securing promotion, which it otherwise would not have done, on the basis that no changes could take place before the start of the 2001–02 season.

The Court found that there was in existence an 'umbrella contract' between the club and the NGB that consisted of the Constitution and bye-laws of the WRU, resolutions passed by it and the membership agreement entered into by the parties. However, a fetter on the ability of the WRU to make changes to the way that it ran its business in the way claimed could only have been made by means of change to its Constitution. Such a change would have required a formal resolution to have been passed by two-thirds of the voting members present at the SGM in 1997, and as there was no evidence that this had occurred, the claimant failed to establish that the contract in place between the parties had been amended in the way claimed.

Where athletes are concerned, a completed registration form which contains an undertaking that they will observe the bye-laws, resolutions and regulations of the NGB provides evidence of a binding contractual relationship between them. On the one hand, the athlete agrees to be bound by the relevant rules of the NGB, whilst on the other, the NGB agrees to operate its decision-making processes fairly (*Jones v Welsh Rugby Union* (unreported) Court of Appeal (Civ), 19 December 1997) (below, 2.4.4).

2.3.3.2 Indirect contractual relationship

In some cases, although there is a clear relationship between the person affected by the decision and the NGB making it, it is difficult to identify immediately the existence of a contract. This will usually be because there is at least one other body standing between, for example, the athlete and the NGB. Traditionally, the courts had shown a high degree of reluctance to invent what they saw as fictitious contracts simply for the purposes of legal expediency (*Enderby Town FC v The Football Association* [1971] Ch 591). In these circumstances, the affected party would not be left without any possibility of resorting to the law as they would still be able to engage the supervisory jurisdiction of the courts.

However, where a claimant is seeking compensation for harm caused by the unlawful conduct of their NGB, the action must be brought in contract as only a declaration or injunction can be applied for under the court's supervisory jurisdiction. This has led claimants to seek to establish a sufficiently strong contractual nexus between themselves and the NGB so that a contract can be implied to be in place to govern their relationship. This can be proved where a series of contracts link an athlete to their club and then to its governing body and ultimately to the relevant NGB or ISF, such as that linking *Modahl* to the BAF (above, 2.2.1). More recently in *Bradley* (above, 2.3.2), a link between a bloodstock agent and the Jockey Club was implied on the basis of the claimant's choice to submit to the jurisdiction of the Club as though he had been licensed by it.

2.3.3.3 Breach of the contract

Once a contractual relationship has been established, the claimant must then prove that there has been a breach of that contract by the conduct of the NGB. The breach could be of a specific term of the contract, for example, where the NGB has not followed its own rules or procedures, or more likely where the NGB has breached an implied term of the contract that the court has found it necessary to include for the proper functioning of the relationship. In all cases, it has been found that the contract either expressly or impliedly contains terms that mirror the grounds for review found under the court's supervisory jurisdiction (above, 2.3.2). In other words, the court will review whether the NGB's procedures were fair, whether there had been any errors of law in making the decision and whether any exercise of discretion or judgment fell within the range of available options open to the tribunal (below, 2.4). Thus, even though the decision-making procedures of an NGB cannot be challenged in public law by judicial review, the same outcome can be arrived at by a claimant engaging the supervisory jurisdiction of the court or by bringing an action for breach of contract.

Alternatively, the rules and decisions of an NGB, as well as the contracts that it enters into with its members and competitors, are all capable of being in restraint of trade by either restricting a person from earning a living from their chosen profession or preventing an undertaking from maximising its profits (see further, chapter 11.4). However, the mere fact that a restriction exists does not mean that the NGB is acting in restraint of trade. Where the rules are necessary and proportionate for the proper administration of a sport, and they are in the public interest, as has been held to be the case in respect of properly administered anti-doping regimes, then the restraint can be justified.

The extension of the supervisory jurisdiction of the courts and developments in UK and EU competition law (see further, chapter 12.5) mean that this cause of action is only infrequently relied upon when challenging the decisions of an NGB. However, significant challenges have been made to the restrictive practices of many NGBs using the doctrine of restraint of trade over the years, and it remains a powerful means of reviewing the lawfulness of such restraints.

2.4 The impact of national sports law on disciplinary and appeals tribunals

The structure of most NGBs' disciplinary mechanisms used to follow the same basic pattern. The executive committee, comprising representatives of the NGB's members, would appoint the members of the disciplinary tribunal and, where necessary, the members of any second-tier appeals tribunal. Often, though not always, the disciplinary tribunal members would be a sub-committee of the national executive committee. In some cases, the members of the appeals tribunal would be drawn from the same sub-committee as the members of the first-instance disciplinary tribunal. It was possible, therefore, for a member of the rule-making body to sit on the panel which had the task of interpreting and enforcing those rules and for that same person to sit on the appeals tribunal when they had already been a member of the panel that heard the initial complaint.

In public law terms, there was no effective separation of powers among the various roles being carried out by the legislative, executive and judicial branches of the governing body, and no ability for one part of the system to provide the necessary checks and balances on the decision-making processes of the other parts, because they were all too closely interlinked. Further, questions began to be raised about whether the defendant in a disciplinary system that operated in this way was receiving a fair hearing. Despite Lord Denning MR's faith in NGBs being capable of regulating themselves more effectively without the intervention of lawyers (above, 2.1), as sports participants began to have more at stake on the outcome of a disciplinary hearing, it became apparent that changes to NGBs' procedures were required to ensure that a fair hearing was given to all who appeared before them. Thus, as a body of national sports law began to develop following the legal challenges made to NGBs' decision-making procedures, the norms adhered to by these tribunals and committees began to be juridified, taking on a more obviously legalistic approach to sporting justice. The following examples, which have resulted from a variety of challenges brought under the supervisory jurisdiction of the courts, or for breaches of contract, or because of restraints of trade, demonstrate how this process of juridification has occurred over time and how procedural fairness is now embedded in the sporting justice system.

2.4.1 The NGB must act within its own rules and in accordance with the law

In *Aberavon v WRU* (above, 2.3.3.1) the claimant argued that the WRU was contractually obliged to follow a rule that, it was claimed, had been amended at a Special General

Meeting of the Union. The amended rule would have required the WRU to give 12 months' notice to its members, including Aberavon, before implementing changes to the league structures in Wales. If the amended rule had been followed, Aberavon would have been promoted to the Premier League. The Court held that the WRU could only amend its own rules by following the procedures laid down in them. The change claimed by Aberavon would have required two-thirds of the members present at the SGM to vote in favour of the rule change. As there was no evidence that this procedure had been followed, the rule stood in its original form, enabling the WRU to alter the league structures and to deny promotion to Aberavon.

As well as following their own rules and the decision-making procedures laid down in them, NGBs must also act within the general law. Each of the following sections provides specific instances of where breaches or misinterpretations of the law, or of general principles of the law, have been raised by claimants who have been affected by the conduct of NGBs.

2.4.2 The NGB must not base its decision on errors of fact

When hearing the appeal against the decision of the Disciplinary Committee in *Modahl v BAF* (above, 2.2.1), the Appeal Panel held that the original finding of guilt had been based on an error of fact. New scientific evidence that had not been available at the first-instance hearing provided evidence of a possibility that the samples provided by Modahl had been degraded by bacterial contamination; this, in turn, could have affected the reliability of the results. Thus, as the factual basis on which the Disciplinary Committee based its decision was wrong, the Appeal Panel overturned its decision and acquitted Modahl of any wrongdoing.

2.4.3 The NGB must not take into account irrelevant considerations

This ground of challenge to an NGB's conduct has two bases; firstly that the NGB must take into consideration all relevant factors, and secondly that it must not take into account any irrelevant considerations. Challenges to a decision on these grounds often form an integral aspect of a claim that the NGB has acted unreasonably in coming to its decision (below, 2.4.6).

▶ *Sheffield United Football Club Ltd v Football Association Premier League Ltd* [2007] 3 ISLR SLR 77

As a result of the Premier League's Disciplinary Commission failing to deduct points from West Ham United FC for fielding an ineligible player, Sheffield United FC challenged the Commission's decision before an arbitration panel constituted under s.S Football Association Premier League Rules. The basis of Sheffield United's claim was that in coming to its decision on the penalty to be imposed on West Ham, the Disciplinary Commission had taken into account irrelevant considerations whilst failing to take proper account of other relevant considerations. Firstly, Sheffield United challenged the Disciplinary Commission's decision to give weight to West Ham being under new ownership at the time that the penalty was imposed as this did not prevent the breach of the rules from having taken place nor its impact on the Premier League in general and Sheffield United in particular. Secondly, by taking into account that a deduction in points after the completion of the season would guarantee West Ham's relegation, the Disciplinary Commission failed to consider that by imposing only a fine, Sheffield United was condemned to be relegated when it should not have been. Finally, when taking account of the adverse impact that relegation would have on the players and fans of West Ham, no account had been taken of the impact that relegation would have on Sheffield United, its players and fans. Furthermore, Sheffield United claimed that the Commission had failed to take into account the need to restore competitive balance to the league and that it had given insufficient weight to the deliberateness of the deceit practised by West Ham in concealing the true nature of Tevez's contractual position.

The panel held that although on the basis of these claims it would have made a points deduction, the Disciplinary Commission's decision to impose only a fine on West Ham was within the reasonable range of conclusions that it could have reached. Thus, despite the admitted and deliberate breach of the Rules practised by West Ham and the negative impact that the decision had on the finances of Sheffield United and the morale of its players and fans, the original penalty was upheld.

2.4.4   The NGB must act in accordance with the rules of natural justice

The rules of natural justice guarantee that certain minimum standards of procedural fairness are conformed to by NGBs and their disciplinary panels. There is no definitive list of rules with which an NGB's procedures must always comply; instead, it is under an obligation to act fairly in its dealings with those who are affected by its decisions and those of its associated tribunals. The fluid definition given by the courts to 'fairness' means that different safeguards can be required depending on whether the affected person is applying to join a body, or where they have an expectation that they will be treated in a particular way, or where they have been brought before a disciplinary tribunal that has the power to suspend them from participation in the sport (*McInnes v Onslow-Fane* [1978] 1 WLR 1520). Moreover, the need for procedural safeguards can change over time, for example, where the informal procedures established to hear cases involving amateur players no longer meet the requirements of hearings involving highly-paid professionals (*Jones v WRU*) (below).

From the cases where challenges have been made to the procedures followed by NGBs, or the panels to which they have delegated jurisdiction to hear specific cases, a series of procedural requirements can be identified. Firstly, the NGB is under a general duty to act fairly when coming to its decisions, though consideration is always given to NGBs being private domestic bodies and not courts or tribunals that are accountable in public law (*Enderby Town FC v The Football Association* [1971] Ch 591).

Secondly, the NGB must allow the person subject to its jurisdiction a proper opportunity to be heard. This requires that the NGB provide the person who will be affected by its decision with details of the case against them, with the opportunity to respond to and cross-examine the case against them and the ability to adduce evidence in support of their own case.

▶ *Jones v Welsh Rugby Union* **(unreported) High Court (QBD), 27 February 1997**

Jones was a professional rugby union player who had been sent off for fighting during a league game. At his disciplinary hearing before the WRU's Disciplinary Committee, Jones was not permitted to question the evidence put forward by the referee nor to put forward his own version of events, nor was he allowed to be formally represented, although a club representative was allowed to speak on his behalf as he suffered from a stammer. Furthermore, the Disciplinary Committee retired to consider video evidence of the incident in private and did not allow Jones to provide his own interpretation or explanation of the events as they unfolded. As a result, the Disciplinary Committee found Jones guilty of punching an opponent and banned him from playing for four weeks.

Jones applied to the High Court for a declaration that the WRU had acted in breach of contract by failing to provide him with a fair hearing. The Court held that the Disciplinary Committee's failure to examine the video in public, which was an important part of the evidence against Jones, its failure to allow him to challenge the evidence laid against him and the failure to allow him to adduce evidence in his own defence constituted procedural defects that resulted in a failure to provide him with a fair hearing.

The original decision of the Disciplinary Committee was set aside, and the WRU were required to amend their disciplinary procedures before rehearing the case. Despite the new procedural safeguards being in place, Jones failed to attend the new hearing and was again banned for four weeks (*Jones v WRU* (unreported) Court of Appeal (Civ), 19 December 1997).

The conclusion of the Court was less clear in respect of the right of the player to be represented. An outright ban on representation will be held to be unfair, though an NGB can retain the discretion to allow a legal or other representative to be present at a hearing. In reality, most NGBs do now allow those appearing before them to be represented, and it is good practice to do so.

Thirdly, the NGB must require an appropriate burden of proof in order for a case to be both proved and defended. Where the NGB is seeking to suspend a player or club, it must be prepared to prove its case to a high standard, generally so that the tribunal is satisfied that the ban should be imposed. Where the burden falls on the player or club, it will be to prove their version of events or to disprove the case against them on the balance of probabilities. In doping cases, the NGB is permitted to presume the liability of a participant whose A and B samples have tested positive for a prohibited substance. However, the participant must be given the opportunity to rebut any such presumption on the balance of probabilities (*Wilander v Tobin (No.1)* (unreported) Court of Appeal (Civ), 26 March 1996).

Fourthly, when determining whether or not the procedures followed by an NGB are defective, it is important that the court examine the entire decision-making process, not just individual aspects of it. Thus, where there are defects at the stage of the initial hearing, there is no unfairness to the respondent where they have been able to make recourse to an appropriate appeals tribunal that rectifies the problem encountered at first instance (*Modahl v British Athletic Federation (No.2)* [2001] EWCA Civ 1447) (above, 2.2.1).

An example of how disciplinary tribunals have changed their formalities since *Jones v WRU* can be seen in the transcript of the disciplinary appeal hearings, *RFU v Jennings*, 10 May 2010 and 14 July 2010. Not only are the findings laid out like court transcripts, but it is clear from the outset that the hearing was quasi-judicial in its form and procedure. The parties' legal representatives were present at the hearings, and witnesses were called by both sides.

In Part One of the hearing, the Panel made clear their findings of fact. This included, in particular, that Jennings had performed a hand-off to the eye of an opponent with the heel of his hand, causing it to implode and blind his victim, instead of with the flat part of his palm, and that it required expert evidence on the application of the Laws of the Game to the findings of fact made it had made.

In Part Two, the Panel analyses the expert opinion and provides a full and robust explanation of why a five-year ban should be imposed on Jennings. In particular, it defined the use of the heel of the hand to be a striking of the opponent and not a hand-off. As a result, the Panel found that this 'striking' was intentional and that Jennings had been reckless as to the degree of harm that would be caused by such an act. As he had shown no remorse, had not apologised and had sought to deny foul play, these aggravating factors were used to increase the initial ban of 78 weeks to one of five years. It is only because of the changes that have occurred since *Jones v WRU* that such a severe punishment can be imposed without fear of it being reopened before the national courts.

It is worth noting that the rules of natural justice are supplemented by the protections contained in the European Convention on Human Rights and Fundamental Freedoms as enacted by the Human Rights Act 1998, where the hearing is before a tribunal that is subject to public law. Although the decisions of the national courts will be informed by these rights when hearing sports law cases, it must be remembered that NGBs are not public bodies and so, at present, are not directly affected by the Convention (*Bradley v Jockey Club* [2005] EWCA Civ 1056) (above, 2.3.2).

2.4.5 The NGB must not reach its decision under the influence of bias

The person or body responsible for making a decision must neither show bias towards one outcome or another, nor must there be a perception of bias in the decision-making process; justice must not only be done, it must be seen to be done. Actual bias is where the decision-maker demonstrates a predisposition against a party's case for reasons unconnected with its merits. The test for establishing a perception of bias is objective and requires that a fair-minded person would conclude on the facts that there was a real possibility that the decision-maker was biased. Furthermore, the decision-maker must not have any financial interest in the outcome of the decision.

One of the claims put forward in the *Modahl* litigation was that certain members of the Disciplinary Committee were biased against the athlete and had prejudged the case against her. The Court of Appeal found that there was no evidence of actual bias and could find no perception that the decision-making body had been tainted by bias. The Court also held that even if members of the Disciplinary Committee had reached a biased conclusion, this would have been rendered irrelevant as the unbiased decision of the Appeal Panel would have cured any defects in the first-instance hearing.

In *Flaherty v National Greyhound Racing Club* [2005] EWCA Civ 1117, actual bias and a perception of bias was alleged against a witness, and procedural impropriety was alleged on the basis that the chief executive of the defendants retired with the panel members whilst they discussed the merits of the case in private. The Court of Appeal rejected any allegations of bias concerning the witness before turning to the issue concerning the presence of the chief executive at the deliberations. Although this was an irregularity that had the potential to undermine the separation of powers between the executive and judicial branches of the defendant, the chief executive's explanation that he was acting as a clerk who was advising the panel only on how previous cases had been determined and on interpretations of the rules of the Club was accepted by the court. As this was a minor defect in the procedure, it did not taint the proceedings to an extent that rendered them either biased or unfair.

2.4.6 The NGB must not act unreasonably, arbitrarily or capriciously

A claim of unreasonable, arbitrary or capricious conduct by the NGB in arriving at its decision can only be established where the person challenging its findings can prove that no similarly constituted body that had properly instructed itself according to the rules by which it was governed could have reached the same conclusion. In *Nagle v Feilden* [1966] 2 QB 633, the Jockey Club had repeatedly refused to grant the applicant a trainer's licence on the sole ground that she was a woman. The Court or Appeal held that in doing so, the Club was acting arbitrarily and capriciously and that it should consider her application on its merits not on her gender.

The boundaries of unreasonableness have been extended to include the ability of the court to analyse the proportionality of the punishments handed down by an NGB or its disciplinary panel. In *Bradley* (above, 2.3.2), the claimant argued that a suspension from all activities associated with racing for five years would effectively prevent him from being able to act as a bloodstock agent. The Court of Appeal found that the decision of the Appeals Board was within range of acceptable responses available to it because of the threat to the integrity of the sport caused by *Bradley's* actions and therefore that a reasonable and proportionate punishment had been imposed.

2.4.7 The development of the current structural framework

As a result of these developments, all NGBs now ensure that the rules of natural justice are adhered to in their tribunals. This has, in turn, led to an increased juridification of the procedures that are followed in many sports hearings and the ways in which the panels' decisions are formulated. Further, many now also ensure that there is complete separation of powers between the rule-making body and the members of the disciplinary panels, particularly at the appeals level. Where, usually for reasons of cost, it is not reasonably practicable for an NGB to operate such a system, it will often allow an appeal to a specialist independent tribunal, such as Sports Disputes UK, which operates in much the same way as CAS does but at a national level, ensuring that the standard of justice now available from NGBs is approaching that which is available before the courts.

Hot topic ... Dwain Chambers and the legality of the Olympic ban for doping

On 12 July 2008, Dwain Chambers won the 100m at the Olympic Trials. Under normal circumstances, he would have been invited by the British Olympic Association (BOA) to represent Team GB in this event at the Olympic Games in Beijing. However, as a person who had previously been found guilty of a serious doping offence, Chambers was not considered to be eligible for selection under the BOA's Bye-law 25. The following week, Chambers applied to the High Court for an interlocutory injunction that would prevent the BOA from enforcing Bye-law 25 and, in effect, force them to select him for the 100m at the Olympics.

The grounds of his claim were that the Bye-law operated as a restraint of trade at common law, that it was in conflict with Arts.101 and 102 Treaty on the Functioning of the European Union (TFEU) and that it was irrational and should be set aside under the court's supervisory jurisdiction; although the EU law challenges were not pursued at the hearing, following the decisions in *Meca-Medina and Majcen v Commission of the European Communities* (C-519/04 P) [2006]

ECR I-6991 and *Motosykletistiki Omospondia Ellados NPID (MOTOE) v Greece* (C-49/07) [2008] ECR I-4863 (see further, chapters 12.1.2 and 12.5), there was at least an arguable case that Bye-law 25 was anti-competitive.

As this was an application for an injunction and not a full trial of the legality of Bye-law 25, the judge would normally only have to be satisfied that the applicant had proved that he had a serious issue to be tried. However, in this case, if the injunction had been granted, the final trial would never have taken place as Chambers would have already competed in Beijing and would have seen no point in arguing further about the Bye-law's lawfulness. In such circumstances, the judge is permitted to take into account the underlying merits of the case and will only grant an injunction where satisfied with a high degree of assurance that the applicant will succeed at trial.

To establish that the Bye-law was a restraint of trade, Chambers had to prove that it prevented him from earning his living as a professional athlete. The Court held that it would be difficult for Chambers to establish that his ability to earn money as an athlete had been restrained because he was only prevented from competing in one championship, the Olympics, where, in any event, no prize money is awarded. Further, it was held unlikely that he would have been placed highly enough in his event to earn significant sums through sponsorships and endorsements as a result of his participation in the Games. This reasoning contrasts starkly with the decision of the CJEU in *Deliège v ASBL Ligue Francophone de Judo and others* (Cases C-51/96 and C-191/97) [2000] ECR I-2549 (see further, chapter 12.3.1), where it was held that restricting an athlete's ability to earn money indirectly from competition through sponsorship agreements or state contributions towards training costs was capable of constituting an infringement of Art.56 TFEU.

The judge also stated that even if this reasoning was wrong, he considered the Bye-law to be necessary and proportionate for pursuing a legitimate aim of the BOA, namely to protect the Olympic ideal of fair play. Therefore, the judge was not sufficiently satisfied that there was an actionable restraint of trade to grant the injunction. This line of reasoning is also questionable. Although the protection of the ethos and ideals of the Olympics is undoubtedly a legitimate goal of the BOA, its automatic refusal to consider in any capacity a person who had been found guilty of a serious doping offence for life did not take into account that all ISFs anticipate the possibility of an athlete's rehabilitation after serving a period of suspension. The assumption of Bye-law 25 was that dopers can never be rehabilitated and can never act as a good example to young athletes. Further, as the BOA was the only NOC to impose a lifetime ban, it was difficult for it to claim that it was single-handedly upholding the Fundamental Principles of Olympism when even the IOC did not take such an extreme stance towards doping.

The judge also refused to exercise the court's supervisory discretion on the grounds of delay, as occurred in the *Stevenage Borough FC* case. Chambers was well aware of Bye-law 25 at the time that he resumed his athletic career in 2008 and that the BOA would be unlikely to select him because of his previous doping infringement. He could, therefore, have made his challenge at any time from when he restarted his training programme with the intention of competing in Beijing and, in particular, following his second placing at the World Indoor Athletic Championships in March 2008, four months before he eventually commenced his legal proceedings. Instead, he left making his application so late to that the hearing took place less than 72 hours before the BOA had to send its final team selection to the International Olympic Committee (IOC), and no full trial of the issues was possible. As a result, the judge refused to grant an injunction, and Chambers did not go to Beijing.

In pleading such wide-ranging and complex legal arguments, perhaps the most straightforward claim was overlooked; that Bye-law 25 was *ultra vires*, or that the BOA had acted in excess of its powers, by introducing a rule that constituted an additional punishment not sanctioned by Art.23 WADA Code. Following the annulment of the IOC's similar, but less restrictive, rule in *United States Olympic Committee v International Olympic Committee* CAS 2011/O/2422 (see further, Hot Topic 1 and chapter 3.3.5), WADA declared the BOA non-compliant with the WADA Code. The BOA challenged this decision before CAS, which handed down its opinion in almost identical terms to the *USOC* decision; Bye-law 25 was an additional punishment not sanctioned by the WADA Code and was therefore unlawful. *British Olympic Association v World Anti-Doping Agency* CAS 2011/A/2658.

This decision enabled Chambers and others such as cyclist David Millar to compete at London 2012 just as they are free to compete in all other events. Despite these two CAS decisions, the issue of an additional or increased period of suspension that would include the next Olympic Games is still very much under consideration. The next version of the WADA Code is due to be published in late 2013, and during discussions on its revision, increasing the minimum period of suspension for a first offence from two years to four is being considered to ensure that athletes will inevitably be banned from at least one Olympic Games when a serious doping violation has been committed.

Summary

2.1 A symbiotic relationship has developed between domestic and national sports law in respect of challenges to the decision-making procedures operated by NGBs. Where those affected by the decisions of NGBs have successfully challenged their unlawful practices before the courts, NGBs have changed their procedures and developed new procedural norms. As NGBs' procedures have become increasingly juridified, the decisions of sporting and legal tribunals are able to inform each other on the most effective means of resolving sports disputes.

2.2 NGBs have no special legal status in English law. Their existence is based on consensus with their power deriving from the agreement of their members to be subject to their rules. As a result, many sporting relationships are based on either express or implied contracts. Most NGBs are now companies limited by guarantee so that the body itself has a separate legal identity that can be sued, rather than its members being exposed to the prospect of individual liability if it remains as an unincorporated association.

2.3 There are three main causes of action by which the decision of an NGB can be challenged. Firstly, where there is no contract in place between the parties, the challenger can invoke the supervisory jurisdiction of the court to review the lawfulness of the decision-making process. Secondly, where a contract is in place between the parties, the challenger can allege that the NGB is in breach of contract by acting unlawfully. Where there is no contract expressly entered into by the parties, a contractual relationship can be implied on one of three bases: the club basis, the participation basis and the submission basis. Thirdly, the challenger can claim that the decision on the NGB operates in restraint of trade. A challenger will be successful against an NGB where it has acted unfairly, outside of the jurisdiction granted to it by its own rules or unlawfully. NGBs cannot be subjected to the judicial review process under Part 54 Civil Procedure Rules as they are not public bodies.

2.4 As a result of the challenges made to the conduct of NGBs and their disciplinary tribunals, the procedures followed by them have become increasingly juridified. NGBs must act within their own rules and within the law, they must only take into account relevant considerations and not irrelevant factors, and they must act in accordance with the rules of natural justice and procedural fairness by allowing persons appearing before them a proper opportunity to be heard, to defend themselves and to be adequately represented. Further, NGBs must make their decisions fairly and without bias and impose reasonable and proportionate sanctions on those who are found to be in breach of their rules.

Further reading

Beloff et al, *Sports Law* (2nd edn, 2012, Hart) chs 3 and 7

Lewis and Taylor (eds), *Sport: Law and Practice* (2nd edn, 2008, Tottel) ch A4

Bradley and Ewing, *Constitutional and Administrative Law* (15th edn, 2010, Pearson) chs 5, 30 and 31

Anderson, 'An accident of history: why the decisions of sports governing bodies are not amenable to judicial review' (2006) 35(3) *Common Law World Review* 173

Beloff, 'Judicial review in England and Wales: the state of the art revisited' (2009) 13(2) *Jersey and Guernsey Law Review* 143

Beloff, 'Watching out for the googly: judicial review in the world of sport' (2009) 14(2) *Judicial Review* 136

Further reading cont'd

Ellson and Lohn, 'Whose rules are we playing by?' (2005) 3(2) *Entertainment and Sports Law Journal*, online

Taylor and O'Sullivan, 'How should national governing bodies of sport be governed in the UK? An exploratory study of board structure' (2009) 17(6) *Corporate Governance* 681

Links to relevant websites can be found at www.palgrave.com/law/james2e

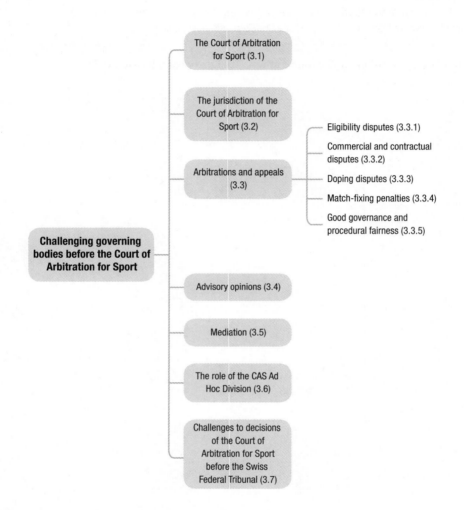

Chapter 3

Challenging governing bodies
before the Court of Arbitration
for Sport

Key terms

▶ **Lex sportiva** – the body of sports-specific jurisprudence and redefined legal norms created mainly by the Court of Arbitration for Sport for application in sports law cases.

▶ **Member state** – one of the 27 nation states that are full members of the European Union.

▶ **Undertaking** – an entity that is, for the purposes of European Union law, engaged in economic activity, irrespective of its legal form or the way that it is financed.

3.1 The Court of Arbitration for Sport

The operation of the Court of Arbitration for sport (CAS) and its impact on sporting justice worldwide is of increasing importance as an ever greater number of ISFs engage its services as a final court of appeal. Its position at the apex of the sporting justice system enables it to set the standards for procedural fairness and good governance throughout the sporting world and provide precedents to which all bodies should adhere. CAS does not operate in isolation of national and EU law, however, as its decisions can themselves be reviewed by the Swiss Federal Tribunal, a phenomenon that highlights clearly the increasingly symbiotic relationship that exists between sports law in the national and European courts and sports law before sporting tribunals.

CAS was established in 1984 under the auspices of the International Olympic Committee (IOC). There was some initial concern that CAS was merely an emanation of the IOC and that there was no real separation of powers between the two organisations leading to claims that its decisions could not therefore be truly impartial and independent. This came to a head following CAS's decision in *Gundel v FEI* CAS 1992/A/63, where the applicant who had been banned for one month following a partially successful appeal to CAS challenged the legality of its finding before the Swiss courts. The Swiss Federal Tribunal declared CAS to be a true court under Swiss law and that it was sufficiently independent of the FEI that its decision was legally valid (*Gundel v FEI and CAS* Recueil Officiel des Arêtes du Tribunal Fédéral 119 II 271, 15 March 1993). However, it also stated that because of the links that existed at the time between CAS and the IOC, CAS could not be considered to be truly independent where the IOC was a party to any proceedings before it and that any decision that it made in these circumstances would be invalid.

In order to address the issues raised by the Swiss Federal Court and to secure for itself the position as the world's most important sports tribunal, CAS was re-established as a completely independent body in 1994 to ensure that there could be no undue influence exerted on it by either the IOC or any ISF. CAS is based in Lausanne, Switzerland and is regulated by Swiss law; it has two further permanent offices in Sydney, Australia and New York. It also sits at many finals tournaments and major championships, including the UEFA European Football Championships, the Commonwealth Games and the Olympics, as the CAS Ad Hoc Division. When sitting in its *ad hoc* capacity, CAS provides rapid responses to disputes that arise during the course of these intensive short-term championships (below, 3.5 and chapter 13.4).

Although most major ISFs operate their own independent dispute resolution chambers and arbitral panels to hear disputes arising out of their own sports, almost all now allow an appeal to CAS for a final and binding decision. These decisions are binding arbitration agreements that are legally enforceable by each of the parties to the dispute. As well as acting as a tribunal of final appeal, CAS provides a number of services that are aimed at keeping sports disputes out of the courts, including arbitration and mediation facilities. It also had the power to provide advisory opinions to sporting authorities seeking clarification on a point of law or on the interpretation of a particular rule. This more proactive role could ensure that a sport is able to revise its rules or procedures before the dispute escalates into litigation (below, 3.3).

The decisions and opinions of CAS are becoming increasingly important as a source of sports law, or *lex sportiva* as CAS refers to it, because of the number of applications that it hears that would otherwise have the potential to be heard before national and/or European courts. In particular, its decisions on the interpretation and application of FIFA's Regulations for the Status and Transfer of Players have undoubtedly prevented highly complex litigation from reaching the CJEU. More important, however, is its ability to impose a degree of harmonisation on the decision-making procedures of ISFs; regardless of the sport from which the dispute arose, CAS will impose the same standards of procedural fairness and due process on all governing bodies and adhere to the same interpretative norms when establishing the true meaning of their rules.

Hearings are generally before a panel of three arbitrators. Each party selects an arbitrator from CAS's list, and an independent chair is then chosen by either the parties' arbitrators or by the President of the Ordinary Arbitration Division or the Appeals Arbitration Division, depending on the nature of the procedure being followed. The outcomes of ordinary arbitrations and mediations are private and usually confidential, however, the decisions of the Appeals Arbitration Division and Advisory Opinions are generally published in full on the CAS website and in abridged form in the regular bulletins that are published on its website.

CAS has been a key driver in the modernisation and standardisation of the rules and procedures of many sporting authorities. Its sports-sympathetic approach has ensured its acceptance amongst the sporting community and its development of the meaning of the 'specificity of sport' has helped it to justify how and why it interprets legal norms in the way that it does. Whether it is truly developing a completely new *lex sportiva* is, however, an evolving debate.

3.2   The jurisdiction of the Court of Arbitration for Sport

CAS has the general jurisdiction to hear any dispute that is either directly or indirectly linked to sport. More specifically, it will hear applications where the rules of an ISF allow the parties to make a reference to it or where they have agreed to submit to CAS's jurisdiction. For the most part, it hears commercial, doping and disciplinary disputes, although its jurisdiction is not specifically limited to these issues. As with the other sources of sports law, the cases coming before it can usually be sub-divided further according to two underlying themes: good governance and procedural fairness (see further, chapter 1.6). In many ways, it could be said to operate a supervisory jurisdiction over sports disputes similar to that of the High Court (see further, chapter 2.3.2), however, one that allows it to review the substance of a sporting authority's decisions and impose its own final ruling when acting in its appellate capacity. Thus, CAS will examine whether the rules of an ISF are reasonable and being applied and interpreted lawfully and that any penalties imposed are necessary, reasonable and proportionate.

CAS has made it clear on a number of occasions, however, that it will not review the in-game decisions of the match officials unless bad faith or illegality can be proved against them. In refusing jurisdiction over such disputes, its aim is to preserve the autonomy of the match officials in coming to their decisions in the heat of competition and to uphold the finality of the outcome of the sporting event in question. It is also an acknowledgment that whereas the match officials are trained to take decisions in relation to their sport, the CAS panel is not.

> ▶ *Mendy v Association Internationale de Boxing Amateur* **(AIBA) CAS 1996/H/OG Atlanta 1996/006**
>
> The claimant had been disqualified from the boxing tournament at the Atlanta Olympics for landing a punch below the belt of his opponent. He applied to have the disqualification overturned on the grounds that the point of impact was clearly above the belt and therefore lawful. CAS refused to review the decision of the AIBA on the basis that the application of the purely technical rules of the sport was the responsibility of the ISF concerned. The justification for this stance was because the CAS panel was less well-placed to decide an in-game issue after the event than was a qualified referee who was in the ring, or the team of judges who were based ringside.

This refusal of jurisdiction was taken to its extreme in *Yang Tae Young and Korean Olympic Committee v International Gymnastics Federation (FIG)* CAS 2004/A/704, where the panel refused to intervene in a dispute where the judging panel in the men's all-around final failed to follow the correct procedures in scoring Young's performance. Although a simple recalculation of the marks awarded could have been applied, and which would have resulted in Young finishing in the gold medal position, CAS refused to intervene on the basis that he should have followed the correct procedures as laid down by FIG and appealed within one round of the mistake occurring. Thus, even though it was acknowledged that the officials had made a mistake that could be rectified with comparative ease, the panel remained resolute in its position that the in-game decisions of match officials are non-justiciable before CAS just as they are before the national courts; the officials' decisions are final (see further, chapter 14.4).

3.3 Arbitrations and appeals

CAS has jurisdiction to hear two specific kinds of arbitration: ordinary arbitrations and appeals arbitrations. Ordinary arbitrations can only take place where both parties agree to submit to a private dispute resolution procedure. Their consent to submit to arbitration can be by formal agreement to have an individual dispute resolved by an arbitrator or panel of arbitrators, or can be in accordance with the rules of the governing body concerned. The decision of the arbitrators is binding on both parties and avoids the need for the dispute to be heard in court. Ordinary arbitrations usually involve preliminary clarifications of the meaning of a rule before a more formal appeal is made against the final decision on an ISF (*Boxing Australia v Association Internationale de Boxing Amateur* CAS 2008/O/1455).

Appeals arbitrations are appeals from the decisions of ISFs to CAS, which then acts as a tribunal of last instance following a rehearing of the dispute. The level of legal complexity and the breadth of law involved in the appeals applications that are made to CAS are evidence of its growing importance as a source of sports law.

3.3.1   Eligibility disputes

Eligibility to compete in a sporting event or championships is usually determined by reference to the rules of the particular competition or its organiser. Although challenges to these rules are relatively rare, when disputes about the right to compete do arise, they can engage complex and unusual areas of the law. In *Pistorius v International Association of Athletics Federations (IAAF)* CAS 2008/A/1480 (see further, chapter 11.5.4), CAS was asked to determine whether the IAAF's refusal to allow 400m runner Oscar Pistorius to use the 'Cheetah Flex-Foot' prosthetic legs was unlawful on the grounds of disability discrimination. On finding for Pistorius, CAS held that the IAAF's decision to classify the prosthetics as capable of unfairly enhancing an athlete's performance was not a conclusion that could reasonably be drawn from the scientific evidence. The ban on him using them in IAAF-sanctioned events was therefore discriminatory as it was not objectively justifiable in the light of current scientific knowledge. As a result, Pistorius was free to compete against able-bodied athletes whilst using this particular piece of equipment, enabling him to compete at both the London Olympics and Paralympic Games in 2012.

A more politically sensitive issue has been raised in respect of whether Gibraltar is eligible to compete in international tournaments in its own right, as opposed to its athletes being a constituent part of any British team taking part. In *Gibraltar Badminton Association (GBA) v International Badminton Federation (IBF)* CAS 2001/A/309, the GBA asked CAS to set aside the conditions imposed on it by the IBF (now the Badminton World Federation) that would enable Gibraltar to compete in the 2001 World Team Championships in Seville, Spain. The IBF had stated that players from Gibraltar could only take part in the opening ceremony as members of an IBF team competing under the IBF flag, with no mention of their representing Gibraltar and that the players would not be able to wear tracksuits or competition shirts that had the name Gibraltar printed on the back. The GBA claimed that as a full member of the IBF, it should be able to compete under the same conditions as any other member association and that the IBF was acting in a discriminatory manner by imposing these additional conditions on its players.

CAS dismissed the application on two grounds. Firstly, that the IBF had not acted discriminatorily against Gibraltar as discrimination was defined in its Rules and by the Olympic Charter as being where there was differential treatment against a country or an individual on the grounds of a person's race, religion, politics or sex. As Gibraltar was, according to international law, an overseas territory of the UK and not an independent nation state, it was not a 'country' and therefore could not be the subject of discrimination. Furthermore, CAS noted that any conditions imposed on the GBA were for the benefit of the sport as a whole as they were necessary and proportionate in order for the competition to take place in Spain and for the Gibraltar team to participate in it; therefore, the conditions imposed on the GBA were lawful. Gibraltar has faced similar recognition difficulties in other sports; for example, it has been campaigning for 10 years for membership of UEFA. In October 2012, the Gibraltar FA was granted provisional membership of UEFA.

One issue of growing concern for many governing bodies is the increasing number of athletes seeking to represent at international level a country other than the one for which they are most obviously eligible on the basis of their birth or citizenship (also below, 3.3). ISFs generally have strict criteria for determining the international team for which an athlete is eligible to compete; those of FIFA came under scrutiny in the politically sensitive hearing of *Irish Football Association v Football Association of Ireland, Daniel Kearns and FIFA* CAS 2010/A/2071. The IFA was established in 1880 and has been affiliated to FIFA since 1911. The FAI was founded in 1921 following the creation of the Irish Free State and has been a member of FIFA since 1923. At first, both bodies claimed the right to select players born anywhere on the island of Ireland to play for their representative teams. Following an exchange of letters in the years up to and including 1950, the two associations agreed to only select players born in or with a connection to their own territory; the IFA would only select players from Northern Ireland and the FAI those from the Republic of Ireland.

Kearns was born in Antrim, Northern Ireland to parents who had also been born in Northern Ireland but who had dual British-Irish nationality. Kearns had represented the IFA's Northern Ireland teams at under-15, 16, 17 and 19 levels but had not yet been selected to represent its 'A' team. At the age of 18, he filed a request with FIFA for a change of association in order to play for the Republic of Ireland teams selected by the FAI on the basis of his Irish nationality. The IFA claimed that this was a breach of FIFA's eligibility rules as according to Art.16 Application Regulations of the FIFA Statutes 2009 (Application Regulations 2009), a player must fulfil at least one of the following conditions: that he had been born on the territory of the relevant Association; that at least one of his biological parents or grandparents had been born on the territory of the relevant Association; or that he has lived continuously on the territory of the relevant Association for at least two years. As Kearns did not fulfil any of these criteria, the IFA claimed that he was only eligible to represent Northern Ireland. In response, the FAI claimed that in accordance with Arts.15 and 18, as Kearns was a national of the Republic of Ireland, he was free to choose to represent the FAI's teams on the basis of his nationality and because he had not yet played for the Northern Ireland senior team.

In upholding the decision of the FIFA Players' Status Committee, CAS held that despite any historical construction that could have been placed on previous eligibility criteria, the Application Regulations 2009 were clear in their meaning and how they should apply in this case; Art.15 conferred eligibility to play for an Association on those with permanent nationality of the territory in which it is based, Art.16 on those with a significant connection with an Association's territory, Art.17 defined the conditions under which a player may change nationality and Art.18 the circumstances in which a player can opt to change Associations. Therefore, as Kearns was qualified to represent the IFA on the basis of his nationality, the nationality of his parents, his place of birth and his residence and the FAI on the basis of his nationality, he was free to choose which of the two associations he wished to represent at senior level, and his application to transfer his eligibility to the FAI was upheld.

3.3.2 Commercial and contractual disputes

Many of the commercial disputes that have been brought before CAS have arisen out of the complexity of the FIFA Regulations for the Status and Transfer of Players and appeals brought by either players or clubs against the decisions of FIFA's Dispute Resolution Chamber (DRC). These Regulations, which have been developed post-*Bosman* in an attempt to maintain and regulate a transfer system of some kind in professional football, have given rise to a number of disputes that almost undoubtedly would have ended up being heard before both national and European courts, were it not for the existence of CAS.

▶ *FC Shaktar Donetsk v Matuzalem Francelino da Silva, Real Zaragoza SAD and FIFA* **CAS 2008/A/1519 and 1520**

Three years into a five-year playing contract, Matuzalem, a Brazilian national, unilaterally and without any due cause terminated his contractual relationship with the Ukrainian football club FC Shaktar Donetsk, claiming to have done so in accordance with Art.17 FIFA Regulations. Two days later, he signed a three-year contract with the Spanish club Real Zaragoza. Shaktar initiated proceedings against both the player and Zaragoza before FIFA's DRC claiming €25m, the minimum fee payable under the contract's release clause. Shaktar was awarded €6.8m in compensation and appealed to CAS in the hope of securing a much higher sum for the loss of its top scorer and captain.

CAS began by stating that Art.17 did not give players the right to unilaterally breach their playing contracts and move to a new club. As its purpose was to reinforce contractual stability, not create greater uncertainty, it should instead be read as defining the consequences of either a player or club choosing to breach their agreement. Thus, as Matuzalem had breached his contract by failing to report for training at Shaktar and signing for Zaragoza, compensation was due to Shaktar.

Having established the breach of contract, it was held the amount of compensation payable should be calculated in accordance with Art.17 FIFA Regulations, not the release clause, as the circumstances in which Matuzalem had left Shaktar were not those anticipated by the contract. The release clause could only be activated where a club seeking to secure Matuzalem's services directly approached Shaktar with an offer of €25m or greater; it did not cover the situation where Matuzalem unilaterally breached his contract. CAS held that the value of the player's services to Shaktar, his status and standing at the club, his behaviour and the timing of his departure should all be taken into account when calculating the amount of compensation payable. This amount should then be reduced by the sum of money that Shaktar would not have to pay Matuzalem in terms of his salary. Thus the total amount payable was €11.9m.

The comparative simplicity of this decision, that one party to a contract does not have the unfettered right to refuse to perform their obligations with impunity, hides the extraordinarily wide range of legal issues that are raised by this case (see further Hot Topic 2 and chapters 11.3.1 and 12.2.2.2). The first question was to determine the law applicable to the dispute. Although a contract to work in the Ukraine was at issue, CAS held that as it contained no choice-of-law clause, the applicable law was, according to the FIFA Regulations, Swiss law, not Ukrainian law.

Secondly, it had to determine whether the release clause was a properly constructed liquidated damages clause or a genuine buy-out clause. The former would explain how the amount of compensation payable on breach should be calculated, whilst the latter would identify the amount payable by a club seeking to secure the transfer of Matuzalem. CAS held that the release clause was a buy-out clause that would be triggered automatically where another club paid Shaktar at least €25m; in such circumstances, Shaktar would have to release Matuzalem, whether it wanted to or not. A liquidated damages clause would have to set out clearly the factors to be taken into account when calculating the amount of compensation payable, not simply state a fixed sum to be paid on breach.

Thirdly CAS identified how the sum to be paid should be calculated following a breach of contract of this kind. This needed to take into account not only the specific requirements of Art.17 but also the domestic law of the country where the employment relationship took place. Although no submissions were made on this point in *Matuzalem*, local law could be a significant complicating factor in the light of the various ways in which compensation for breach of contract is calculated in different jurisdictions and their differing views on the legality of release and liquidated damages clauses.

Matuzalem is a clear example of a dispute that would normally be expected to be heard before the national courts of the country where the work is taking place and potentially even the CJEU where an EU national is involved (see further, chapter 12.2.2.2). Instead, it was resolved (in legal terms) quickly by two expert sports tribunals with all the attendant costs savings to both parties. By keeping disputes such as this away from the national courts (in the first instance at least), there is the added advantage to FIFA that there was no detailed investigation of the legality of its Regulations and the transfer system as it currently operates. Before CAS, it was assumed without question that the Regulations were lawful, and the case turned instead on the interpretation of the disputed contractual term and Art.17. This leaves open the possibility of further disputes in future cases challenging not only the interpretation of the Regulations but also their legality under national and EU law (below, Hot Topic 2 for further discussion of the *Matuzalem* litigation).

3.3.3 Doping disputes

One of the most common reasons for appealing to CAS is to challenge the legality of bans imposed for anti-doping infringements. Since 2003, Art.13 World Anti-Doping Code (WADA Code) has included a provision nominating CAS as the final tribunal of appeal for all doping disputes arising from participation in an International Event or which involve an International-Level Athlete. An International Event is defined as one that is organised by the IOC, an ISF, the International Paralympic Committee or a major event organiser such as the Commonwealth Games Committee. An International-Level Athlete is one who is on the registered testing list for at least one ISF. All national-level disputes would be heard by the National Anti-Doping Panel, a role fulfilled by Sports Resolutions UK in the UK (see further, chapter 1.2).

The WADA Code continues to evolve significantly in response to sporting, pharmaceutical and legal developments and is due to be revised significantly in 2013. Of particular importance from a legal perspective, and as a means of avoiding the litigation and uncertainty previously experienced in countries like the UK, is that the preamble of the Code states unequivocally that it applies to all athletes and their support personnel on the basis of their participation in the sport. This is reinforced by a requirement that ISFs bring to the attention of all participants the relevant anti-doping rules and procedures, effectively ensuring that athletes are also subject to the Code on the submission basis (see further, chapter 2.2). Art.3 of the WADA Code imposes the burden of proof on the body seeking to prove the anti-doping violation and requires it to establish its case to the comfortable satisfaction of the panel; this standard lies somewhere between the balance of probabilities required to prove a civil action in the UK and the proof beyond reasonable doubt that is needed for a criminal conviction. Further, the Code defines and enshrines the right to a fair hearing in Art.8.

The result of these developments is that most doping appeals now focus on challenges to the length of the ban imposed on an athlete or procedural impropriety, on the basis that the correct rules and procedures have not been followed, or problems with the chain of custody of the sample so that it might have been tampered with or degraded in transit, rather than challenging the existence of the anti-doping regime itself. After the decision of the CJEU in *Meca-Medina and Majcen v Commission of the European Communities* (C-519/04P) [2006] ECR I-6991 (see further, chapter 12.1.2), it is unlikely that the anti-doping regime as a whole could now be challenged as being unlawful. As all ISFs that are members of the IOC, as well as National Olympic Committees, national governments and transnational bodies such as the Council of Europe have ratified the WADA Code, the position of CAS as the tribunal responsible for its interpretation has enabled its panels to play a significant role in clarifying and harmonising anti-doping procedures and establishing appropriate legal norms in doping disputes.

The anti-doping regime in operation in almost all major sports around the world is now governed by the provisions of the WADA Code, as administered by the World Anti-Doping Agency (WADA). Doping is defined in Art.1 WADA Code as being one or more of the rule violations defined in Arts.2.1–2.8. In order these are: presence of a prohibited substance in the athlete's sample; use or attempted use by an athlete of a prohibited substance or method; refusing or failing to provide a sample or otherwise evading the provision of a sample; being unavailable or failing to provide information on whereabouts on three occasions in an 18-month period; tampering or attempting to tamper with doping control procedures; possession of prohibited substances or methods; trafficking or attempted trafficking in any prohibited substance or methods; the administration or attempted administration of a prohibited substance or method to another athlete; and the assisting, encouraging, aiding, abetting, covering up or any other complicity in an anti-doping violation.

The most basic and most commonly committed forms of doping are the presence of a prohibited substance in an athlete's sample and the use of a prohibited method, such as blood doping. Once an athlete has submitted to doping control, they must provide either a blood or urine sample to be tested. The sample is then divided into two parts. If the 'A' sample is negative, the athlete is clean and free to continue competing; if it is positive, they have the option of either admitting to doping or having the 'B' sample tested. If this second sample also returns a positive result for a prohibited substance, then a doping offence is committed.

Under Art.2.1.1 WADA Code, a duty is imposed on the athlete to ensure that no prohibited substances enter their body. In *Baxter v International Olympic Committee* CAS 2002/A/376, a British slalom skier was disqualified from competing at the Salt Lake City Winter Olympics in 2002 and stripped of his bronze medal after testing positive for a metabolite of amphetamine. Baxter was known to suffer from nasal congestion and usually used an over-the-counter Vicks inhaler, the British version of which contained no prohibited substances. Whilst in the USA, he purchased the American version of the same Vicks inhaler without consulting with the team doctor or checking the US Anti-Doping

Agency's website, on the assumption that it would have the same ingredients as its British equivalent. This assumption was incorrect, and it was clearly stated on the USADA website that this product contained a prohibited substance. As a result, he was guilty of doping by having a prohibited substance present in his sample and was disqualified and subsequently banned for three months by his governing body, the International Skiing Federation.

The relevant anti-doping agency does not need to prove fault on the part of the athlete who has returned a positive test or adverse analytical finding; there is no need to prove that the athlete intentionally or negligently or knowingly ingested a prohibited substance, or that they intended to enhance their performance by ingesting the prohibited substance. The mere presence of a prohibited substance in the athlete's body, particularly those that are banned because of their inherently performance-enhancing qualities, is considered to undermine the integrity of the result of the event in which they are competing. For example, in *Raducan v International Olympic Committee* CAS OG 00/011, a young gymnast was given a Nurofen Cold and Flu tablet by her team doctor to help reduce the symptoms of a heavy cold. This led to her sample showing small traces of the prohibited substance pseudoephedrine, and as a result, she was disqualified from Women's All-Around event and stripped of her gold medal. Despite there being no intention to dope, and no fault on the part of the gymnast, the disqualification was upheld in accordance with what is now Art.9 WADA Code. An athlete can only overturn a disqualification where they can prove, on the balance of probabilities, (Art.3.1) not only that were they not at fault for ingesting the prohibited-substance but also that the prohibited substance was not performance enhancing in their case (Art.10.1.1), a test that will be almost impossible to discharge where a substance has been banned because of its performance-enhancing qualities, as was the case with both Baxter and Raducan.

Where it was accepted that there was no fault on the part of Ruducan but that the prohibited substance still had the potential to enhance her performance, Baxter had acted at least negligently by failing to seek clarification of the contents of the medication that he was taking. These cases highlight the extreme difficulties faced by an athlete seeking to prove that they acted without fault or negligence and the need for compelling evidence to support their contention, as was highlighted by the combined cases of *International Tennis Federation v Gasquet* CAS 2009/A/1926 and *World Anti-Doping Agency v Gasquet* CAS 2009/A/1930. Gasquet returned an adverse analytical finding for minute traces of cocaine in a sample provided after a night out with a group of friends and acquaintances. He claimed that the only way that he could have ingested cocaine was by kissing a woman that he had met that evening and that therefore he had acted with no fault or negligence in returning the positive test. The original Independent Anti-Doping Tribunal of the ITF had dismissed his claim of no fault on the basis that he should not kiss strangers in nightclubs as there is a risk that they might have been taking recreational drugs; however, they allowed a claim of no significant fault as Gasquet did not know that the person he kissed was using cocaine and could not have known of the risk of ingesting cocaine through kissing. As a result, he was banned for a comparatively short period 2.5 months.

Both the ITF and WADA appealed this decision, requesting that CAS significantly increase the punishment imposed on Gasquet. CAS found that, on the balance of probabilities, Gasquet had established that he had ingested the prohibited substance by kissing a person who had been using cocaine. However, even if he had exercised the utmost caution, it was impossible for him to know that kissing someone whom he had met in a totally unsuspicious environment could result in his being contaminated with cocaine to such an extent that he would return an adverse analytical finding the following day. Therefore, he had not acted with any fault or negligence, and the appeals of the ITF and WADA were dismissed. Inexplicably, Gasquet had not appealed against the Anti-Doping Tribunal's decision, and as a result, CAS was unable to substitute its finding of no fault for the original finding of no significant fault. Thus, the original decision stood, and Gasquet was banned for 2.5 months despite CAS finding him to have acted with no fault.

3.3.4 Match-fixing penalties

In contrast to the clear regulatory framework that is in place to counter doping, no such global approach has yet to be coordinated to combat match-fixing and corruption. Each sport approaches the matter differently, even if only slightly in many cases, and attaches different degrees of seriousness to the different categories of match-fixing and other gambling-related misconduct and corruption in which persons connected with sport may be engaged.

Many of these issues were raised in *Savic v Professional Tennis Integrity Officers* CAS 2011/A/2621. Savic was found guilty of a corruption offence by an Anti-Corruption Hearing Officer (AHO), on the basis of evidence that he had approached a fellow professional tennis player in order to fix who would win which sets in a match and ultimately predetermine its outcome. He was fined $100,000 and banned for life by being declared permanently ineligible to compete in professional tennis activities. Savic appealed to CAS on the grounds that as he had been accused of conduct amounting to criminality, a higher standard of proof than that of 'a preponderance of the evidence' should have been used. Further, he claimed that there was no factual proof of his having approached any other player about match-fixing and that even if he was still found guilty, the penalties imposed were disproportionate.

CAS held that the standard of proof to be used before the AHO was determined by the law applicable to the dispute, in this case the law of the state of Florida in the USA. This jurisdiction allowed a case to be proved on the preponderance of the evidence and did not require a higher standard to be imposed that was based on the seriousness of the alleged misconduct; therefore, the correct standard had been used by the AHO. Further, CAS considered that not only was there sufficient evidence to prove the case against Savic on the preponderance of the evidence, but that the panel considered that the case had been proved to the higher standard of its comfortable satisfaction. Therefore, the charge of corruption against Savic was proved.

Finally, CAS addressed the issue of the appropriate level of punishment. In doing so, it stated that the following factors should be taken into consideration: the sanctions imposed by the AHO must not be disproportionate; that a lifetime ban for match-fixing could be a proportionate penalty in some circumstances because of the damage that such conduct could cause to the integrity and image of a sport; that match-fixing had been identified by the tennis authorities as the most serious corruption offence that could be committed in that sport as it could be committed by an individual acting alone; that Savic had attempted to corrupt another player into fixing the outcome of a match; and that a long period of suspension was required to act as a deterrent to others. On the basis of these considerations, a lifetime ban was found to be a proportionate punishment to impose for match-fixing in this particular instance.

Finally, CAS overturned the $100,000 as being unnecessary and disproportionate in the circumstances. First, it was considered that the period of suspension was sufficient to punish the player and act as a deterrent to others who might contemplate engaging in match-fixing and other corrupt activities. Secondly, as the ban would remove Savic's main source of income, he would find it significantly more difficult, if not impossible, to pay the fine now he could no longer earn money as a professional tennis player.

This approach demonstrates clearly how serious sporting authorities and the sporting justice system currently consider match-fixing and corruption to be. As proceedings such as this are likely to overlap with prosecutions for criminal offences (see further, chapter 6.4 and Hot Topic 6), the sporting justice system will need to cooperate fully with national criminal justice systems to ensure that the cases heard before both are not compromised in any way by the actions of each other.

3.3.5 Good governance and procedural fairness

In much the same way as the High Court has used its supervisory jurisdiction to improve the procedural fairness of the disciplinary and decision-making processes of the UK's NGBs (see further, chapter 2.4), so has CAS acted in a similar manner in respect of ISFs and the IOC. CAS will always ensure that the rules and procedures of the decision-making body have been constituted in an appropriate and lawful manner and in particular that they are neither arbitrary nor unfair (*USA Shooting and Quigley v Union Internationale de Tir* CAS 94/129). It has also ensured that when appearing in an ISFs proceedings that there is a general right to be heard and be able to respond to the charges being laid against an athlete (*A v Fédération Internationale de Luttes Associées* AS 2001/A/317) and that any punishments imposed are reasonable and proportionate and supported by a reasoned judgment (*AEK Athens and SK Slavia Prague v UEFA* CAS 98/200).

The opinion of CAS in *United States Olympic Committee v International Olympic Committee* CAS 2011/O/2422 (see further Hot Topic 1) is the latest in the long line of cases that have ensured that the rules of natural justice or due process are adhered to by ISFs. In this case, CAS held that the IOC had not followed its own rules as defined in the Olympic Charter by imposing an additional punishment on athletes who had been found guilty of serious doping violations that was not sanctioned by the WADA Code; in public law terms, the IOC had acted *ultra vires* or unlawfully by acting outside of its own rule-making competence. CAS also extended the general principles of law to which it will make reference to include the prohibition against double jeopardy, to ensure that an athlete cannot be punished twice for the same doping violation. By requiring ISFs to take into consideration universally applicable principles of law that transcend state law, CAS is ensuring that both procedural justice and internal decision-making are improved and that a more legalistic standard of sporting justice is adopted.

3.4 Advisory opinions

Much less used, but no less important, was the ability of CAS to provide Advisory Opinions to the IOC, ISFs, WADA, National Olympic Committees and the organising committees of each edition of the Olympic Games. This pre-emptive procedure enabled each of these bodies to request CAS to provide advice on the legality of an existing or proposed rule or procedure. CAS would then provide an opinion only where to do so did not involve an investigation of the underlying merits of a potential case or where the request for an opinion did not subvert the normal appeals procedure through which the case should be heard. For example, in *Australian Olympic Committee (AOC)* CAS 2000/C/267, CAS was asked by the AOC to investigate the legality of the then recently introduced 'sharkskin' half-body swimming suits. It declined to do so on the basis that as FINA had followed the correct procedures when coming to its decision, it was not within the jurisdiction of CAS to comment on the technical merits of whether or not these swimming suits were buoyancy aids. As of 1 January 2012, CAS withdrew its competence to provide advisory opinions due to a lack of recourse by sports bodies to this procedure.

CAS provided opinions where there was a genuine concern about the legality of a rule or the way that it was being interpreted, or a clear loophole that had not been considered by the rule's drafters was identified by affected parties. In *International Baseball Association* CAS 1998/C/215, CAS was asked whether it was possible for a player with dual nationality to change their sporting nationality. By drawing an analogy with a person who changed their sporting and/or legal nationality from one country to another, it advised that there was no reason why a player with dual nationality could not change their sporting nationality between the countries of which they were legal nationals. In such a situation, the player would have to wait three years from either their last appearance for one country before being eligible to play for another, or from the time of informing the relevant ISF that they wished to change their sporting nationality.

3.5 Mediation

Mediation is similar to arbitration except that the outcome is non-binding. It requires that both parties agree to submit to the mediation process during which a neutral third-party mediator attempts to achieve a settlement of the dispute that is acceptable to both parties. If successful, it obviates the need for further litigation as the aim of mediation is to achieve agreement between the parties. Mediation is a private mechanism, and as with ordinary arbitrations, the outcome of the parties' discussions cannot be published without the agreement of everyone who is engaged in the process.

3.6 The role of the CAS Ad Hoc Division

The CAS Ad Hoc Division provides an instant hearing and appeals framework at many major international events, including the Olympics and the Commonwealth Games. Its aim is to provide rapid and authoritative responses to emerging disputes, thereby enabling decisions to be made that minimise delays to the competitions in progress; its aim is to provide a definitive determination on all cases coming before it within 24 hours and it often sits overnight in order to ensure as little disruption to a tournament as possible.

The Ad Hoc Division follows the same basic rules and procedures that CAS would follow normally but within a significantly shorter timeframe. Although the majority of its work is the same as that usually undertaken by CAS, in the heat of competition some more unusual disputes have come before the Ad Hoc Division (see further, chapter 14.4). For example, in *A, W and L v NOC Cape Verde* CAS 1996/H/OG Atlanta 96/002 and 005, a dispute had arisen over who should carry the Cape Verde national flag at the opening ceremony of the Atlanta Olympics in 1996. The sole athlete representing Cape Verde had snatched the flag from the Chef de Mission and carried it into the stadium himself and as a result had had his accreditation revoked by his National Olympic Committee. Without expressing a view on the underlying merits of the case, the Ad Hoc Division required that due process was followed in punishing the athlete in this manner, which it had not in this case as the incorrect procedure had been followed, and reminded all involved about the need to uphold the Olympic spirit in situations such as these.

3.7 Challenges to decisions of the Court of Arbitration for Sport before the Swiss Federal Tribunal

It has become increasingly common for those who have not achieved the desired result before CAS to challenge its decisions before the Swiss Federal Tribunal (SFT), the Supreme Court in Switzerland. The SFT has the ability to review the decisions of CAS and ensure that it is acting lawfully and in adherence to the rules of natural justice and in accordance with public policy considerations. Despite the increase in challenges, the decisions and opinions of CAS have proven to be robust and have been overturned on only a very few occasions.

The SFT does not act as an appellate panel but provides an opportunity to review the decision-making process used by CAS. There are four overarching grounds of review provided for in s.190(2)(a-d) Swiss Private International Law Act: the arbitrator or arbitral panel was not properly appointed, including that they have a lack of independence from one of the parties; the arbitral tribunal incorrectly accepted, or declined, jurisdiction to hear a case; the arbitral tribunal either went beyond the claims submitted to it or failed to address a specific element of the case before it; and that there has been a violation of due process or in some way a failure to guarantee procedural fairness. The first time that the SFT seriously considered overturning CAS was in a challenge to its decision in *Gundel v FEI* CAS 1992/A/63 (*Gundel v FEI and CAS* Decision 4P.217/1992 of 15 March 1993). Although the CAS decision was allowed to stand, the SFT made it clear that if the defendant had been the IOC, rather than the FEI, then it would have found that CAS was insufficiently independent of the IOC to hear cases in which it was a party. As a result, CAS was reconstituted in 1994 to ensure that there was in future an appropriate separation of powers between itself and the organisations that would be appearing before it, particularly the IOC.

The first CAS decision to be overturned was *WADA v International Ice Hockey Federation and Busch* CAS 2008/A/1564 (*A v WADA* Decision 4A.358/2009 of 6 November 2009). The player, Busch, had refused to submit to doping control and was subsequently banned for two years by CAS, following an appeal against the leniency of the national anti-doping panel by WADA. CAS determined that it had jurisdiction to hear the appeal on the basis of a player entry form completed and signed by Busch in respect of a previous tournament. The SFT annulled the CAS finding that it had jurisdiction to hear the case as the player entry form was time limited. Thus, the player could only have his case heard before CAS on the basis of events that occurred during the period of the specific tournament; it did not provide an indefinite jurisdiction over the player from that point in time onwards.

In the most recent instalment of the *Matuzalem* litigation, the CAS decision to uphold the playing ban imposed by FIFA's Dispute Resolution Chamber was overturned by the SFT (below, Hot Topic). In *FC Shaktar Donetsk v Matuzalem Francelino da Silva, Real*

Zaragoza and FIFA 2008/A/1519 and 1520, Matuzalem and Real Zaragoza were held to be jointly and severally liable for damages for breach of contract amounting to almost €11.9m. Having failed to pay this sum, FIFA's Dispute Resolution Chamber declared on 31 August 2010 that unless the full amount were paid within 90 days, Matuzalem would be banned indefinitely from all professional football activities worldwide; this decision was upheld by CAS in an unreported decision of 29 June 2011.

Matuzalem challenged the decisions of FIFA and CAS in *Matuzalem v FIFA* Decision 4A.558/2011 of 27 March 2012, claiming that they breached fundamental legal principles and generally recognised values by preventing him from earning a living from professional football and earning sufficient money to be in a position to pay some, even if not all, of the compensation due to FC Shaktar Donetsk. The SFT held that to prevent someone from working indefinitely, and in effect permanently, from their chosen profession was a grave encroachment of his privacy rights and contrary to public policy. Further, as Matuzalem would never be likely to be in a position to pay the compensation in full, the purpose of the ban was questionable and disproportionate, especially as the award could be equally, if not more effectively, enforced under the New York Convention on the Recognition and Enforcement of Arbitral Awards 1958. Thus, the decisions of the FIFA Dispute Resolution Chamber and CAS, in as far as they amounted to an indefinite playing ban, were annulled.

Hot topic … The relationship and interplay between *lex sportiva* and national law

The *Matuzalem* litigation highlights not only the complexity of modern sports law but also the uneasy relationship between the sporting and national justice systems (see further, chapters 1.1.3, 1.4, 3.3.2 and 12.2.2.2). Where sport still aims for the ideal of self-regulation, the sporting justice system including CAS ultimately remains subject to the law and its decisions can be reviewed before an appropriate national court. In much the same way that ISFs have only conditional autonomy and are subject to EU law (see further, chapter 12.1.2), CAS only has conditional autonomy and its decisions and opinions are ultimately subject to review before the Swiss Federal Tribunal (SFT), the Supreme Court of Switzerland.

The initial dispute (Matuzalem 1) focused on whether there had been a breach of the employment contract between Matuzalem and FC Shaktar Donetsk. CAS began by declaring that the dispute would be governed by Swiss law as there was no choice-of-law clause in the contract, despite this clearly being an employment relationship with links to no other jurisdiction than the Ukraine. CAS then decided that the disputed clause of the contract was a buyout clause, not a liquidated damages clause; it would have required Shaktar to release Matuzalem from his obligations if another club paid it €25m, but this was not an indication of how the compensation payable should be calculated on breach. Further, CAS also held that FIFA's Transfer Regulations did not allow players to unilaterally terminate their contracts without sporting just cause. Finally, CAS calculated the compensation payable to Shaktar as being €11.9m

In Matuzalem 2, the player appealed to the SFT to review the legality of the CAS award on the basis of it being unfair and dispro-

portionate. The SFT held that CAS has acted lawfully despite the size of the award made against the player. The Tribunal further stated that as the player was fully aware of the potential consequences of his unilaterally breaching his contract in this manner, he could not then complain later that this was unfair when those consequences eventuated.

Neither Matuzalem nor Real Zaragoza, which was jointly and severally liable for the €11.9m damages, were in a position to pay the compensation that was due to Shaktar. As a result of this non-payment, Shaktar requested FIFA's Dispute Resolution Chamber (DRC) to enforce the award against both club and player. The DRC acceded to Shaktar's request and gave Matuzalem and Real Zaragoza 90 days to pay the award, plus an additional CHF 30,000 fine or be banned until the award was paid. The DRC's decision was upheld by

CAS in Matuzalem 3, meaning that Matuzalem was banned from all professional football activities until the original CAS award in Matuzalem 1 was paid in full.

In the final instalment, Matuzalem 4, the player returned to the SFT to challenge the ban imposed on him for non-payment of the original award. He claimed that the indefinite worldwide ban imposed on him by the DRC and upheld by CAS breached fundamental legal principles and generally recognised values and was contrary to public policy. This time, the SFT overturned the CAS award as being contrary to public policy, disproportionate and unnecessary. Firstly, the ban would prevent Matuzalem from earning a living, which was unlawful, and which in turn would ensure that he would not be in a position to make any contributions to the sum owed to Shaktar. Thus, the ban was not only unlawful but also counterintuitive. Secondly, as Matuzalem was unlikely ever to be in a position where he could pay Shaktar's damages, the purpose of the ban was questionable as it would not have the effect of forcing him to pay the award. Finally, it was disproportionate as the award could be enforced more effectively under the New York Convention on the Recognition and Enforcement of Arbitral Awards 1958. The end result is that Matuzalem still owes Shaktar the compensation for breach of contract but cannot be banned from playing indefinitely until the award is met.

The national and European courts before which sports law cases are heard are generally accepting of the sporting justice system's jurisdiction over sports disputes. However, where procedural fairness is compromised, or illegality is established, or fundamental principles of law are infringed, the courts will not hesitate to review the rules and decisions of NGBs, ISFs and CAS. Despite CAS's role in improving and standardising the procedures of other tribunals, its decisions are still susceptible to review. This conditional autonomy ensures that in the vast majority of cases, sport is able to regulate itself, but where the fundamental rights of the parties are compromised, the courts will readily review sporting justice system to ensure that it operates fairly.

Matuzalem 1: *FC Shaktar Donetsk v Matuzalem Francelino da Silva, Real Zaragoza and FIFA* 2008/A/1519 and 1520

Matuzalem 2: *Matuzalem v FIFA and CAS* Decision 4A.320/2009 of 2 June 2010

Matuzalem 3: *Matuzalem v FIFA* CAS (unreported) 29 June 2011

Matuzalem 4: *Matuzalem v FIFA* Decision 4A.558/2011 of 27 March 2012

Summary

3.1 The jurisprudence of CAS is becoming an increasingly important source of sports law in the light of the number and complexity of the cases that it hears. As one of its aims is to standardise the legal norms applied by all sports bodies, its proactive approach to the development of legally robust rules and procedures has played a significant role in the development of sporting justice. Its sports-sympathetic approach attempts to improve standards of good governance and fairness whilst minimising the negative impact of its decisions on ISFs. However, the development by CAS of a *lex sportiva* may, at some point in the future, come into conflict with the jurisprudence of the CJEU in disputes requiring an interpretation of EU law.

3.2 CAS can hear any sporting dispute where either the parties have agreed to submit to its jurisdiction or where the rules of the sporting body allow for an appeal to it. Thus, its jurisdiction is based on a series of contractual relationships. CAS has repeatedly held that it will not review the in-game decisions of the match officials.

3.3 Despite the breadth of its potential jurisdiction, the disputes before it generally fall into five main categories: eligibility to compete in a specific event; commercial and contractual disputes; doping appeals; issues related to match-fixing; and the improvement of procedural justice and good governance. Its position at the apex of the sporting justice system has enabled it to impose improvements across all sports and provide precedents for how decision-making procedures should develop in the future.

3.4 Advisory Opinions provided an opportunity for parties to determine the legality of a rule pre-emptively. However, it was so little used that CAS terminated this service on 1 January 2012.

Summary cont'd

3.5 As an alternative to a full hearing before CAS, mediation services are also provided to parties. As the results of mediation are private and not published, they cannot be used as a precedent for the development of good governance and procedural justice.

3.6 The Ad Hoc Division of CAS has sat at all Olympic Games since 1996 and a variety of other tournaments and championships since then. It provides an expedited procedure to ensure that its decisions are handed down within 24 hours of the dispute arising so that as little interruption as possible is caused to the on-going event.

3.7 The decisions and awards of CAS are themselves subject to review by the Swiss Federal Tribunal. Although its awards are generally legally robust, and the vast majority of its opinions have been upheld, where CAS has infringed public policy or fundamental legal principles, the Swiss Federal Tribunal has not hesitated to annul the disputed decision.

Further reading

Beloff et al, *Sports Law* (2nd edn, 2012, Hart) ch 7

Lewis and Taylor (eds), *Sport: Law and Practice* (2nd edn, 2008, Tottel) chs B2 and 3

Beloff, 'The Court of Arbitration for Sport at the Beijing Olympics' [2009] 1 *International Sports Law Review* 3

Foster, 'Lex sportiva and lex ludica: the Court of Arbitration for Sport's jurisprudence' (2004) 3(2) *Entertainment and Sports Law Journal*, online

Haas, 'Role and application of Article 6 of the European Convention on Human Rights in CAS procedures' [2012] 3 *International Sports Law Review* 43

Mavromati, 'Jurisprudence of the Swiss Federal Tribunal appeals against CAS awards' [2011] 2 *International Sports Law Review* 37

Rigozzi, 'Challenging awards of the Court of Arbitration for Sport' (2010) 1(1) *Journal of International Dispute Settlement* 217

Links to relevant websites can be found at www.palgrave.com/law/james2e

Sports participation and the law

The growth of sports torts (4.1)

Choice of tort – negligence or trespass to the person? (4.1.1)

Trespass to the person (4.2)

Battery (4.2.1)

Direct contact (4.2.1.1)

Intentional contact (4.2.1.2)

Contact without the claimant's consent (4.2.1.3)

Negligence (4.3)

Negligence in sports cases (4.4)

Duty of care (4.4.1)

The emergence of a sport-specific duty of care (4.4.1.1)

Defining sports negligence (4.4.1.2)

The playing culture of a sport (4.4.1.3)

Codes of conduct (4.4.1.4)

Breach of duty and the expected standard of behaviour (4.4.2)

The reasonable and competent player (4.4.2.1)

A variable standard of care? (4.4.2.2)

Negligence v. reckless disregard (4.4.2.3)

Judicial use of reckless disregard (4.4.2.3.1)

Wooldridge v Sumner [1963] 2 QB 43 (4.4.2.3.2)

Civil procedure (4.4.2.3.3)

The causal link between the breach of duty and the harm caused (4.4.3)

Causation in fact – the 'but for' test (4.4.3.1)

Causation in law – the foreseeability of the injuries caused (4.4.3.2)

Liability for injuries caused by other participants

Vicarious liability (4.5)

Bringing a claim based on vicarious liability (4.5.1)

Vicarious liability for negligent acts (4.5.2)

Vicarious liability for deliberate acts (4.5.3)

Dual employment (4.5.4)

Defences (4.6)

Defences to trespass to the person (4.6.1)

Consent (4.6.1.1)

Self-defence (4.6.1.2)

Defences to negligence (4.6.2)

Volenti non fit injria or the voluntary assumption of risk (4.6.2.1)

Contributory negligence (4.6.2.2)

Compensation (4.7)

Calculating compensation (4.7.1)

Chapter 4

Liability for injuries caused by other participants

Key terms

▶ **Damages** – the compensation awarded to a claimant following a successful claim.
▶ **Man of straw** – a defendant, or potential defendant, who has insufficient funds to meet any award of damages made against him.
▶ **Negligence** – the defendant owes a duty of care not to cause harm to the claimant and has breached that duty by falling below the standard of conduct expected in the circumstances and has caused reasonably foreseeable harm.
▶ **Tort** – unlawful conduct actionable in the civil courts, usually to recover damages.
▶ **Trespass to the person (battery)** – the direct and intentional application of force to the person of the claimant by the defendant where the touching was made without the claimant's consent.
▶ **Vicarious liability** – the employer is responsible for the tortious acts of its employee where the tort committed has sufficient connection to the employee's employment.

4.1 The growth of sports torts

The use of the law of tort to secure compensation for injury is the most commonly occurring example of sports law in action. Although only attracting mainstream media attention where there has been a catastrophic injury or where the injured person is a high profile athlete, many thousands of claims are made each year at all levels of participation and across many different sporting disciplines. The growth in litigation in this area has been rapid: the first reported case involving one sportsperson suing another came before the Court of Appeal as recently as 1985 in *Condon v Basi* [1985] 1 WLR 866 (below, 4.4.1.1). Perhaps the only surprising point to be made about this rapid expansion of the law is the lack of a definitive ruling from the House of Lords or Supreme Court on the application of the law of tort to cases involving sports injuries.

This area of sports law, as with all tortious claims for personal injury, is dominated by issues of public policy and insurance. Whether or not the defendant is adequately insured will often determine whether or not a claim should be brought against them; if the defendant is an uninsured 'man of straw', then any judgment entered against them will be, at best, a hollow victory for the claimant. The ability or otherwise of the defendant to meet any damages award may trigger a search for other potential defendants against whom a claim is not only likely to be successful but who can also afford to pay the compensation awarded (see further, chapter 5).

There is no specific identifiable reason for the growth in the use of the law to resolve sports disputes of this kind. The existence of a so-called compensation culture may help to explain why people have a greater knowledge of their legal rights when they are injured, or it may be that potential claimants are less likely to accept that accidents happen rather than there being someone to blame for their misfortune. Section 1 Compensation Act 2006 was introduced to limit specifically the deterrent effect that excessive litigation might have on participation in, and the organisation of, risky activities such as sports; the paucity of cases making reference to it, however, means that its impact on the ongoing juridification of this area is as yet uncertain.

4.1.1 Choice of tort – negligence or trespass to the person?

The first important decision that an injured sportsperson will have to make is whether to pursue their claim in trespass to the person or negligence. Until *Gravil v Carroll and Redruth Rugby Football Club* [2008] EWCA Civ 689 (below, 4.5.3), where the claimant received compensation for injuries caused by a punch thrown by an opponent, it was assumed that only very rarely would a claimant rely on trespass to the person as the appropriate cause of action because most insurance policies exclude liability for deliberately caused injury. In *Elliott v Saunders and Liverpool FC* (unreported) High Court (QBD) 10 June 1994, the initial claim for trespass, arising from a challenge in a professional football match, was dropped, and only the claim in negligence pursued after it was brought to the attention of the claimant that Liverpool FC's employer's liability insurance would not meet a claim for deliberately inflicted injury. Thus, in the vast majority of cases, the claimant will bring their claim in negligence.

4.2 Trespass to the person

Trespass to the person comprises three distinct torts: assault, battery and false imprisonment. In the sports context, only battery will be considered as the other two torts are unlikely ever to be actionable. This is because they rarely result in physical injury to the claimant and are generally used to protect rights rather than secure compensation for harm caused. The tort of assault is committed where the defendant threatens the claimant with immediate unlawful force. The tort of false imprisonment is where the defendant imposes a total restraint on the claimant's freedom of movement from a particular place. Where athletes are involved, battery, which requires that the defendant applies physical force to the claimant, will be the most appropriate cause of action.

4.2.1 Battery

In order to establish a successful claim in battery, the claimant must prove that there has been a direct and intentional application of force to their person by the defendant and that the touching was made without their consent. There is no need to establish that any injury has been caused; the tort is completed by the defendant interfering with the claimant's right not to have their bodily integrity interfered with as every person's body is considered inviolate (*Collins v Wilcock* [1984] 1 WLR 1172). The degree of injury caused will only affect the quantum of damages awarded as compensation, not whether the tort has been committed in the first place.

4.2.1.1 Direct contact

The contact made with the claimant must be direct. In essence, this means that there must be actual physical contact between the defendant and the claimant. Direct contacts include those where the defendant causes an object, such as a hockey stick, or a projectile, such as a ball, to come into contact with the claimant (*Scott v Shepherd* (1773) 96 ER 525). The unlawful contact can also include what is referred to as a 'continuing battery'. This is where a contact which was originally lawful (for example, because it was consented to) becomes unlawful because it continues to be performed by the defendant for a length of time or with a degree of force to which the claimant does not consent (*Fagan v Metropolitan Police Commissioner* [1969] 1 QB 439). For example, if a defendant wrestler is awarded a bout on the basis of a submission but refuses to let go of the claimant after the referee has counted his opponent out, the continuing nature of the contact will mean that what was originally a legitimate touching becomes an unlawful and actionable battery.

4.2.1.2 Intentional contact

The contact with the claimant must be made intentionally by the defendant. Where the contact is made carelessly, any legal action should be brought in negligence (*Letang v Cooper* [1965] QB 232). There is no specific definition of 'intention' in the case law, however, it can be described as a requirement that the defendant acts deliberately and that contact with the claimant is the desired outcome of the deliberately performed act. There is no need for the defendant to intend any harm to be caused to the claimant. The difficulties associated with proving not only that the defendant intended to act in the way that he did, but also that he intended to make contact with the claimant, mean that battery will only rarely be pleaded.

4.2.1.3 Contact without the claimant's consent

Finally, the contact must be made without, or in excess of, the consent of the claimant (below, 4.6.1.1). Consent can either be express or implied. Express consent is where the claimant agrees in advance that certain contacts may be made with him or her in certain circumstances. Implied consent is where the claimant's agreement to the contact can be inferred from the situation in which they have placed themselves. For example, a rugby player may not specifically explain to each of his opponents before kick-off that they can tackle him when he has the ball, however it can be inferred by his taking to the field to participate in the game that he has agreed to be tackled in ways allowed by the rules. Thus, a tackle around the legs when the player is carrying the ball will be consented to, but a punch thrown at him at any time will not.

4.3 Negligence

An action in negligence is the most common means of securing compensation for injuries caused during sporting competition. The tort of negligence has developed over the years to provide compensation to those who have been caused harm by the careless actions of others. It judges a defendant objectively against the standard of behaviour expected of the reasonable person performing the injury-causing activity with a reasonable degree of care and skill. If the defendant has acted in accordance with those standards, then the duty is discharged and no liability will be imposed, however if the appropriate standard of behaviour has not been reached then liability is likely to follow.

To establish negligence against a defendant, the claimant must prove that a duty of care was owed to them in the circumstances in which the activity was taking place (*Caparo Industries plc v Dickman* [1990] 2 AC 605). If a duty was owed, then it must be established that when injuring the claimant, the defendant had breached the duty by dropping below the expected standard of behaviour in the circumstances (*Nettleship v Weston* [1971] 2 QB 691). If breach of duty can also be established, then the claimant must next prove that there was a causal link between the breach and any harm caused by asking whether, but for the actions of the defendant, the claimant would still have suffered the same harm (*Barnett v Chelsea and Kensington Hospital Management Committee* [1969] 1 QB 428). Finally, the claimant must establish that the injuries suffered were a reasonably foreseeable consequence of the defendant's actions (*The Wagon Mound (No1)* [1961] AC 388). Where each of these elements of the tort are established on the balance of probabilities by the claimant, and the defendant is unable to raise any appropriate defence (below, 4.6), then the action in negligence will be successful.

4.4 Negligence in sports cases

To date, there has not been a negligence claim involving sports injuries that has reached the House of Lords or Supreme Court. Despite this, the law has become relatively settled over the years. As will be seen, there are still some areas where vagueness and inconsistency would benefit from clarification from the Supreme Court, however, the cases that have been reported provide sufficient guidance to cover the vast majority of incidents that occur.

4.4.1 Duty of care

4.4.1.1 The emergence of a sport-specific duty of care

The first step towards establishing a claim of negligence is to define the duty of care owed by the defendant to the claimant.

▶ *Condon v Basi* **[1985] 1 WLR 866**

The defendant challenged the claimant in an attempt to tackle him whilst playing in an amateur football match. The tackle was performed by means of a slide from about three metres away, and contact was made with the back of the claimant's leg about 30 cm off the ground with the studs pointing forwards. The tackle, for which the defendant was sent off, was described as reckless and dangerous and broke the claimant's right leg. The Court of Appeal held that despite the lack of previous authority on the point, a duty of care was owed by those taking part in competitive sport to their co-participants and which was objectively defined according to all the relevant circumstances. If a player fell below the standard of care reasonably to be expected of those taking part in the game, then he would be liable to anyone injured as a consequence of his actions.

At trial, Judge Wootton saw no need to define the duty of care as there was, in his opinion, such a clear breach of the expected standards of play by the defendant because he had injured the claimant by an act of serious and dangerous foul play. In the Court of Appeal, Donaldson MR accepted the conclusions of the trial judge and put forward two alternative definitions of the duty of care as had been formulated in the Australian case of *Rootes v Shelton* [1968] ALR 33. On the one hand, the duty was to take reasonable care not to cause harm to those reasonably foreseeably at risk from the conduct, but injuries caused by inherent risks of participation in the activity would be considered to have been consented to and therefore not actionable. On the other hand, the duty was to take all reasonable care not to cause harm to those reasonably foreseeably at risk from the conduct, but the circumstances in which the activity was taking place must always be taken into account. According to either formulation, the defendant's conduct was so far below that which would have been expected in the circumstances that negligence was established.

Donaldson MR preferred the latter construction of the duty, which is also more in line with the way that the generalised duty of care was originally defined by Lord Aitken in *Donoghue v Stevenson* [1932] AC 502. By leaving it open for subsequent courts to choose which version of the duty to impose, however, the Court of Appeal introduced an unnecessary degree of uncertainty and confusion.

Since the judgment of the Court of Appeal in *Condon*, it has been accepted that a duty of care is owed by a sports participant to each and every other participant in the contest. What remained at issue was the precise definition of this duty. The cases which were reported over the following 16 years added to this confusion by mixing issues of consent into the definition of duty as required by the first alternative definition above, and by introducing elements of the standard of care into the definition of the duty owed. This leaves many of the cases decided between 1985 and 2001 as being of factual interest but little legal value.

4.4.1.2 Defining sports negligence

In 2001, the Court of Appeal handed down one of its most important sports judgments in *Caldwell v Maguire and Fitzgerald* [2001] EWCA Civ 1054. In approving Holland J's propositions concerning the definition of the duty of care owed by sports participants, the Court of Appeal also clarified how the duty could be breached.

▶ *Caldwell v Maguire and Fitzgerald* [2001] EWCA Civ 1054

The parties were professional jockeys competing in a race. As they entered the final straight, the defendants, who were placed first and second, moved towards the inside barrier, causing the third-placed horse to move in front of and trip up the fourth-placed horse, ridden by the claimant. The claimant was seriously injured as a result of being unseated from his horse. The defendants were found guilty of careless riding by the stewards and banned for three days. The Court of Appeal held:

1 Each Contestant in a lawful sporting contest … owes a duty of care to each and all other contestants.
2 That duty is to exercise in the course of the contest all care that is objectively reasonable in the prevailing circumstances for the avoidance of infliction of injury to such fellow contestants.
3 The prevailing circumstances are all such properly attendant upon the contest and include its object, the demands inevitably made upon its contestants, its inherent dangers (if any), its rules, conventions and customs, and the standards, skills and judgment reasonably to be expected of a contestant. (For a discussion of the appropriate standard of care see below, 4.4.2.)

The claim failed on the basis that the interference that had occurred was a commonly occurring inherent risk of professional horse racing that did not fall below the standard of riding expected of a professional jockey.

The first of these propositions merely confirms the basic finding of the Court in *Condon*: that a duty of care is owed. The second proposition is a modern restatement of the law as originally defined in *Donoghue v Stevenson*, with its focus on the need to take account of the prevailing circumstances in which the incident took place. It is the third proposition that provides the detail necessary to enable a court to determine the scope of the specific duty owed by a sports participant in any given situation. By highlighting the various circumstances that may be relevant to a case of sports negligence, the Court enables the same basic test to be used regardless of the sport actually being played at the time that the injury occurred.

In *Caldwell* the Court stated that in the particular case of a horse race, the prevailing circumstances include the jockey's obligation to ride their horse over a given course whilst competing with the remaining contestants for the best possible placing, if not for a win. The circumstances must also include the rules or laws of the sport in question, in this case the Rules of Racing, and the standards, skills and judgement of a professional jockey, all as expected by their co-participants. Thus, a very specific duty of care can be defined in respect of professional jockeys when competing in a race that takes into consideration their knowledge and training. Further, by making reference to the inherent dangers associated with participating in sport, the test also takes into account that injuries can and do happen to sports participants without being caused by the negligence of the other competitors.

4.4.1.3 The playing culture of a sport

The only part of the judgment that is neither fully explained nor immediately obvious is the reference to the 'conventions and customs' of the game. Assuming that both the trial court and the Court of Appeal did not simply add in this phrase gratuitously, some meaning must be attached to it. It appears to be something beyond the rules of the game as these are specifically mentioned immediately before this phrase, but it has not been explained further by later courts.

Perhaps the most appropriate interpretation of the 'conventions and customs' of a game is if this phrase extends acceptable play to include the unofficial rules or interpretations of how a game is actually played, in contrast to how the letter of the rules of the sport states that it ought to be played. By extending the circumstances which must be taken into account by a court to include the playing culture of a sport, a duty of care that is most appropriate to the actual level of the particular sport can be imposed. This will ensure that commonly occurring acts that are technically foul play, or foul play that is generally not injury-causing, will be considered acceptable either because it is a prevailing circumstance associated with playing the particular game or because it is an inherent risk associated with it.

For example, pushing an opponent is against the rules of both football and basketball. It is entirely possible that someone may fall and be injured by such a push, however, this kind of foul play occurs with such regularity in these sports that it would be considered to be an acceptable means of playing the game because it is within the playing culture of the sport, even though a foul would be awarded against the pusher. Where such low-level foul play is known to occur, players can guard against it or take evasive action. Only those fouls more likely to result in serious injury would then be legally actionable as those playing the game would be taken to appreciate that such conduct is unacceptable and unconnected with the proper playing of the game. Although such a view is contrary to the opinions of writers such as Grayson, who considered that all foul play that resulted in injury should be actionable, the introduction of the playing culture of a sport as a relevant circumstance reflects more accurately the way that sport is, in fact, played.

▶ *Leatherland v Edwards*, (unreported) High Court (QBD), 28 October 1998

The claimant and defendant were engaged in a game of uni-hockey, a fast-moving, non-contact, short-form version of hockey. It was understood by all participants that the ball was not supposed to rise above the surface of the pitch and that the plastic sticks should not be raised above waist height. The defendant took a shot at goal and continued his follow-through into the face of the claimant, causing his eye to implode. It was held that by raising his stick above shoulder height, the defendant had breached a core safety rule of the game that was central to its purpose and spirit. Such dangerous conduct, when players were moving at speed and in close proximity to each other, was a clear breach of the duty of care owed by one participant to another, and the defendant was found liable for the injuries caused to the claimant.

In contrast, the defendant in *Pitcher v Huddersfield Town Football Club* [2001] All ER (D) 223 was found not liable for a mistimed challenge which broke the claimant's leg. Although both injuries resulted from the foul play of the defendant, only the challenge in *Leatherland* was considered negligent as it was a breach of a safety rule of the game and was therefore totally prohibited; the challenge in *Pitcher* was considered to be an error of judgement that any reasonable First Division footballer could have made.

4.4.1.4 Codes of conduct

In some cases, the parties have relied on a code of conduct drawn up by a sport's governing body or international federation that explains specifically the kind of behaviour expected of those participating in that sport. Many sporting codes of conduct are of little use in this context as their phrasing is too vague or because they are nothing more than entreaties to play fair and play by the rules. Others are of such detail that they can almost be elevated to the status of rules of the game.

▶ *Lyon v Maidment* [2002] EWHC 1227

The parties were involved in a collision whilst on a skiing holiday together. The defendant had set off down the hill first, followed shortly afterwards by the claimant. When defining the scope of the duty of care owed by one skier to another, both the claimant's expert witness and the trial judge made specific reference to the International Ski Federation's '10 FIS Rules for Conduct.' These Rules are applicable to all skiers and snowboarders skiing anywhere in the world and, according to FIS, must be considered an ideal pattern of conduct for a responsible and careful skier or snowboarder, and their purpose is to avoid accidents on the piste. The preamble to the Rules also gives a clear warning that a failure to adhere to them could expose a skier or snowboarder to civil and/or criminal liability in the event of a collision.

This document and the accompanying explanatory notes make it clear that a duty is imposed on a skier higher up the mountain to look out for, take care to avoid and leave sufficient room when overtaking a skier who is lower down the mountain. Dismissing the claim, the court held that as the claimant had come from higher up the mountain, he, not the defendant, should have taken care to ensure that the collision did not take place.

Although an unusual example of an ISF taking such a proactive stance on safety issues, to the extent of informing those who read the Rules of their potential legal liability if they breach them, this is the kind of document that is likely to become more common in the future. Not only does it make the sport safer by explaining how a participant should act in certain circumstances and why, it also helps to insulate FIS from any potential legal action (see further, chapter 5.4).

4.4.2 Breach of duty and the expected standard of behaviour

As with the definition of the duty of care owed, a detailed explanation of how the duty can be breached by a sports participant is, to some extent, still lacking. The basic tortious test for breach of duty is to determine objectively whether or not the conduct of the defendant dropped below the standard of a reasonable and competent person acting in those circumstances. On the face of it, that appears to mean that the test to be applied should be, for example, that of the reasonable and competent rugby player, swimmer, basketball player or jockey. Such a broadly defined test gives rise to a number of what appear to be sport-specific problems: who is the relevant comparator, or the reasonable and competent player? Is there a variable standard of care within and among sports, and if so, how and why does it vary? Does the defendant merely have to drop below the expected standard of care, or does he or she have to act with a reckless disregard for the health and safety of the claimant?

4.4.2.1 The reasonable and competent player

Identifying against whom the defendant's conduct ought to be judged has been a constant source of debate and confusion since *Condon*. To speak of the 'reasonable footballer' is a gross over-simplification of the court's task. Firstly, this does not take into account that the duty element of the tort requires an examination of all the relevant circumstances, which will include the level at which the game was being played. Secondly, it does not take into account the hierarchical structure within which most sport in this country is organised, where participants, including teams, of similar ability play against each other for a season. Promotion and relegation, whether moving between leagues or up and down ranking tables, is the norm with the aim being to keep mismatches to a minimum.

Unlike driving on the road, for example, sport is not a closed system but a series of closed systems. When using the highway, everyone needs to be judged by the same basic standard of care to ensure that a minimum degree of skill is attained and maintained by all road users. This is a closed system where one standard is both necessary and appropriate for all actors (*Nettleship*). Where sport is concerned, each league, or perhaps each competition is itself a closed system; as the circumstances change, such as the league or ranking status of the participants, the standard of care changes.

This issue has caused much controversy over the years. The confusion began in *Condon* when Donaldson MR stated that there would be a higher degree of care required of a player in a First Division football match than of a player in a local league football match. Drake J distanced himself from this comment in *Elliott* and returned to the one-size-fits-all test, which has attracted much approval. The difficulty with both of these formulations is that they approach the issue from the wrong perspective. Both confuse the duty owed with the standard of care against which the defendant should be judged, and both assume that the key to liability lies in the degree of care owed by the defendant to the claimant.

In reality, these never change; the defendant owes a duty to act with reasonable care to avoid causing reasonably foreseeable injury to other participants in the contest, taking into account all relevant circumstances, one of which is the level of competition at which the incident occurs. The standard of care owed is that of the reasonable player in the circumstances in which the incident took place; this requires the defendant to be judged against the standard of the reasonable player who is playing the same sport at the same level of the sporting pyramid as they are.

4.4.2.2 A variable standard of care?

There is nothing in the law of tort that would consider such an approach to be inappropriate. This is not introducing a variable standard of care that allows a less skilled player to cause more injury than could a more skilled player. It is instead analogous to the tests which are applicable in professional negligence cases. Following *Bolam v Friern Hospital Management Committee* [1957] 1 WLR 582, the court can enquire what the reasonable person of the same level of skill or training or qualification would have done in those circumstances. It also allows the court to ask the defendant to justify the option that they took that led to the injury being caused, as per *Bolitho v City and Hackney Health Authority* [1998] AC 232.

This means that, far from allowing less skilled players to cause more injury or to take less care than those who are more skilled, the test asks whether or not the defendant was competent to perform the particular move that led to the claimant's injury. In determining the defendant's level of competence, the court will look at their level of training, the degree of skill expected at that level of the sporting pyramid and the expectations of others playing at the same level. Thus, more skilled players may be able to take greater risks as they are more highly trained in performing the particular action safely, and their opponents will be more highly skilled in taking the necessary evasive action.

More recent cases have started to define the standard of care in this more specific manner almost as a matter of course. In *Caldwell*, the High Court and Court of Appeal referred to the standard of the professional jockey. In *Pitcher,* the High Court referred to the standard of the reasonable First Division footballer, and in *Richardson v Davies* [2006] 1 CL 405, the County Court applied the standard of care and skill to be expected of a player in an amateur Sunday league football match.

The civil courts have long been able to apply different standards of care based on a defendant's training, qualifications and expected skill levels. The sports negligence cases are finally coming round to defining the test for breach of duty in line with the way that the law is applied in analogous situations. This is not so much introducing a variable standard of care but ensuring that all the relevant circumstances of the case are properly taken into account when determining the liability of the defendant.

4.4.2.3 Negligence v. reckless disregard

The standard of conduct sufficient to breach the duty of care owed by a sports participant has generated a disproportionate amount of comment and confusion. There are three distinct strands to this confusion. Firstly, most of the early reported cases described the defendants' behaviour as being in reckless disregard of the claimants' health and safety. Secondly, there has been a misguided reliance on the *dicta* of Diplock LJ in *Wooldridge v Sumner* [1963] 2 QB 43 (see chapter 8.4.3), where he refers to a sports participant being liable in negligence to a spectator at the event only where he has acted with a reckless disregard for the spectator's safety. Thirdly, the adversarial nature of English civil litigation means that each side will try to define the parties' conduct in the most extreme terms.

Before addressing each of these issues in turn, it is important to state from the outset that the correct standard to be applied is negligence in all the circumstances. This test is fluid enough to take account of the fact that sports can range from the non-contact, such as tennis, to the full-contact, such as ice hockey. This test is applied throughout the law of negligence, and to date there is no authority that requires the application of the less stringent reckless disregard test. The key to the determination of any case is, therefore, the identification by the court of the relevant circumstances with sufficient precision.

4.4.2.3.1 *Judicial use of reckless disregard*

From *Condon* onwards, many of the reported cases have recorded that the defendant acted with a reckless disregard for the claimant's safety. More confusingly, as in *Elliott*, the duty is defined in terms of negligence in all the circumstances, yet the defendant was found not liable on the basis that he was not guilty of dangerous or reckless play. Again, it was the Court of Appeal in *Caldwell* that clarified the situation in its final two propositions.

▶ *Caldwell v Maguire and Fitzgerald* **[2001] EWCA Civ 1054**

'4 Given the nature of such prevailing circumstances [above, 4.4.1.2] the threshold for liability is in practice inevitably high; the proof of a breach of duty will not flow from proof of no more than an error of judgement or from mere proof of a momentary lapse in skill (and thus care) respectively when subject to the stresses of [competition]. Such are no more than incidents inherent in the nature of the sport.

5 In practice it may therefore be difficult to prove any such breach of duty absent proof of conduct that in point of fact amounts to reckless disregard for the fellow contestant's safety. I emphasise the distinction between the expression of legal principle and the practicalities of the evidential burden.'

Proposition 4 reinforces that an examination of the circumstances in which the incident took place is of paramount importance. Further, it specifically takes into account that the playing of sport is rarely an exercise in perfection; mistakes are made, errors of judgement occur, and injuries happen. Thus, before imposing liability for an act of sporting negligence, the court needs to convince itself that the injury-causing act is something more than poor play and is something that no reasonable participant would have done; a clear application of negligence in the circumstances.

Proposition 5 attempts to explain the very fine distinction between the correct legal test and the evidence required to prove breach of duty. The legal test remains that of negligence in all the circumstances, but, depending on the act committed or the sport being played, more cogent evidence may be required in order to prove the breach. This simply ensures that the court carries out a full analysis of the acceptability or otherwise of the particular conduct of the defendant. Where dangerous contacts are an inherent part of a sport, then more evidence will be required to prove that the injury-causing act was more than an error of judgement or a mistake. Alternatively, where interpersonal contact is not usually part of the normal playing of the sport, it may be much easier to prove that the injuries caused by such a contact were negligently inflicted. As the level of interference committed by the defendants was of a kind to be expected in a fast-moving sport, such as national hunt racing, the claimant was unable to establish that the duty of care owed to him had been breached.

Following this clear statement of the law and how it should apply to sport, judgments couched in terms of reckless disregard should be considered to be the court making a finding of fact that the challenge was carried out with a reckless disregard for the safety of the claimant. Alternatively, it may be the court attempting to discourage an appeal against its judgment by stating that the act was not just negligent but fell well below the standard of play expected of the defendant. If this is the case, then the application of the law is correct even though the use of the specific phrase may cause confusion; the standard of care, however, remains whether the defendant has dropped below the standard of the reasonable and competent athlete in that game.

4.4.2.3.2 Wooldridge v Sumner [1963] 2 QB 43

A further justification put forward for using the reckless disregard standard comes from a purported reliance on the dictum of Diplock LJ in *Wooldridge* (see further, chapter 8.4.3). Although not referred to by either court in *Condon*, *Wooldridge* is first cited, though not relied on, in *Elliott*. The confusing reference to the defendant in *Elliott* not having acted dangerously or recklessly may have inadvertently left open the door to later parties to rebut a claim of negligence on the basis that reckless disregard should instead be relied on. Thus, by sheer force of repetition, the reckless disregard standard has been elevated beyond its original status and meaning.

The first criticism that can be made of any specific reliance on *Wooldridge* is that it involves an incident that takes place between a participant in an event and a spectator at it, not two sports participants. It is, therefore, neither a direct nor a particularly good authority on which to rely. If the correct test of negligence in all the circumstances is applied, then the main distinguishing circumstance here is the status of the claimants. The dynamic interaction between two participants with each other and a participant with a spectator are so different as to negate any possible claim that the cases are analogous.

The second criticism is that the passages from *Wooldridge* relied on by those who wish to develop the reckless disregard standard have been taken out of their proper context. There is no doubt that Sellers LJ stated that if the conduct is reckless and in disregard of all safety of others, then liability might attach and that later in the judgment Diplock LJ felt that a person attending a sporting event voluntarily runs the risk of injury unless the participant's conduct is such as to evince a reckless disregard of the spectator's safety. However a closer reading of the surrounding passages makes clear that these statements are a description of the evidence potentially needed to prove a claim in negligence, as per Holland J and Tuckey LJ in *Caldwell*, not an attempt to create a completely new tort of reckless disregard; it is sufficient, though not necessary, to prove that a person acted with reckless disregard in order to establish a claim of negligence against them.

4.4.2.3.3 Civil procedure

That this discussion persists is most likely explained by the adversarial nature of English civil litigation. All claimants will plead their case in terms of the defendant having dropped below the standard of the reasonable and competent participant at that level of that sport. All defendants will argue that they should only be found liable in negligence if it can be proved that they acted with a reckless disregard for the health and safety of the claimant, a much more difficult standard for the claimant to prove.

Although a defendant's attempted reliance on the reckless disregard standard is wrong in law, by defending their case in this way, counsel will be hoping to sow seeds of doubt in the mind of the court. By claiming that he or she should only be liable on a finding of reckless disregard, the defendant will be attempting to demonstrate that the incident was less serious, or more acceptable, than it might otherwise have seemed. This tactical use of reckless disregard is entirely understandable from the defendant's perspective. As long as the judge applies the correct test, no harm is done to the law.

4.4.3 The causal link between the breach of duty and the harm caused

Causation in negligence is examined from two perspectives: causation in fact and causation in law. The former identifies which parties have the relevant proximity to the incident to be potential defendants. The latter limits the ramifications of the negligent act to only those consequences that are reasonably foreseeable.

4.4.3.1 Causation in fact – the 'but for' test

Establishing causation in fact is often referred to as a need to satisfy the 'but for' test (*Barnett*). This simply requires the court to ask itself, 'But for the actions of the defendant, would the claimant have been caused this harm?' If the answer is no, then the defendant's actions are a factually relevant cause of the claimant's injuries. Where one participant is accused of injuring another during a sporting contest, establishing this element of the causal link between the breach of the duty and the harm caused should not pose any difficulties as there will usually have been direct contact between the parties.

4.4.3.2 Causation in law – the foreseeability of the injuries caused

The general rule for establishing causation in law is that the defendant is liable for all reasonably foreseeable harm flowing from their negligent injury-causing act (*The Wagon Mound No 1*). Thus, if the type of harm (for example, personal injury by interpersonal contact) is reasonably foreseeable from the point of view of the reasonable person in the position of the defendant at the time that the duty of care is breached, then liability in negligence will be established. In the vast majority of sports negligence cases, this element of the tort will not be problematic; even where the reasonable person would only anticipate a minor injury, such as a bruise, but a more serious injury, such as a fracture, was caused, the broad type of harm is reasonably foreseeable and liability will be imposed.

Following *Watson and Bradford City AFC (1983) Ltd v Gray and Huddersfield Town AFC Ltd* (1998) The Times 26 November, several cases have applied a variation of this test for which there is neither explanation nor authority. In *Watson v Gray*, Hooper J held that, 'such a forceful, high challenge ... was one that a reasonable professional player would have known carried with it a significant risk of serious injury.' More recently, in *Richardson*, it was held that, 'a reasonable amateur player in the defendant's position would have known that there was a significant risk that his actions would result in serious injury to [the claimant].'

These variations contain an important error: it is the type of harm caused, such as personal injury, not the degree of harm caused, for example serious injury, that must be foreseen by the reasonable person (*Smith v Leech Brain and Co Ltd* [1962] 2 QB 405). Although the courts may be attempting to filter out claims for minor injuries and ensure that the floodgates are not opened to such actions, this should be done by categorising the injury as an inherent risk of the sport, not by redefining the test for foreseeability of harm.

4.5 Vicarious liability

Vicarious liability is when an employer is held responsible for the tortious acts of one of its employees. It is imposed on an employer where the tort committed has a sufficiently close connection to the employee's employment or job (*Lister v Hesley Hall Ltd* [2001] UKHL 22). The employer does not have to be found liable in negligence for anything that it has done; it is simply liable for the negligent conduct of its employee.

The purpose of vicarious liability is to give the claimant a better opportunity to receive their damages in full as the employer is likely to be better able to meet the award either because it has more available money or better insurance cover than the employee. The justification for imposing liability on the employer despite it not having done anything wrong is twofold. Firstly, because the employer reaps the benefit of the acts of the employee, it should pay for the consequences of any wrongdoing by that employee. Secondly, the threat of vicarious liability being imposed on the employer should ensure that it requires certain levels of conduct from, and provides sufficient training to, its employees. Taken together, the employer is provided with an incentive to deter its employees from behaving unlawfully whilst acting in the course of their employment.

4.5.1 Bringing a claim based on vicarious liability

To bring a claim based on vicarious liability, the claimant must first establish that there is a contract of employment in place between the defendant and the club. This includes part-time or semi-professional players, not just full-time professionals, but is not available where the defendant is an amateur or unpaid player as the relationship is not sufficiently formal to be regarded as contractual in nature (*Gravil*).

Once the existence of an employment contract has been proved, the employer must be added as a defendant to the claim. For example, in *McCord v Cornforth and Swansea City AFC* (1997) The Times 11 February, the defendant player, Cornforth, was a professional footballer employed full-time by Swansea City FC. Here, Cornforth was accused of having acted negligently by causing injury through foul play, whilst Swansea City FC were claimed to be vicariously liable for his negligent conduct. In some more recent cases, for example, *Pitcher v Huddersfield Town FC* and *Gaynor v Blackpool FC* [2002] CLY 3280, the player who caused the claimant's injuries is not listed as a defendant because it was accepted from the outset that if a tort can be established against the player, then the club will be liable to pay the damages awarded on the basis of vicarious liability. The club is not seeking to deny that what occurred did so in the course of the player's employment, only that the injury-causing act was not tortious.

4.5.2 Vicarious liability for negligent acts

Vicarious liability can only be imposed on an employer if it can be established that the employee has committed a tort, in this case negligence, and that the tort has a sufficiently close connection with the purpose of the employment. The existence of a close connection between the negligent act of the employee and the terms of their employment with their employer is usually established by proving that the act was a wrongful and unauthorised mode of carrying out an act otherwise authorised by the employer.

This approach is wide enough to include most negligent acts, including acts of foul play, which occur in the course of playing sport. For example, tackling an opponent is authorised by employers of football and rugby players. However, as occurred in *McCord*, where the tackle is high and late and causes injury, the poor quality of the challenge will be held to be an unauthorised mode of carrying out an authorised act for which the employer will be vicariously liable.

▶ *Thomas v Thornton and Bramley Rugby League Club (unreported) County Court (Leeds), 15 January 1999*

During the course of a professional rugby league match, the defendant, who was in possession of the ball, ran at the claimant, who was about to attempt to tackle him. As the players drew close together, the defendant raised his arm to hand off the claimant in an attempt to avoid being tackled. Instead of using his hand, however, the defendant used his forearm and struck the claimant in the face, fracturing his jaw. In holding the defendant liable, the court held that despite players clattering into each other with great force, and that it is not always possible for them to time or execute their manoeuvres as they may wish, this was such dangerous play that a reasonable professional player would have known that it carried with it a significant risk of serious injury to the claimant; this was an unauthorised manner of carrying out an otherwise acceptable move. Having established the negligence of the participant-employee and that they were acting in the course of their employment, liability was imposed on the employing club without the need for proof of any wrongdoing on its part.

4.5.3 Vicarious liability for deliberate acts

Although the following extension of the meaning of 'in the course of the employee's employment' was developed in respect of claims based in negligence (*Mattis v Pollock* [2003] EWCA Civ 887), in reality it is used to cover situations where the defendant employee has acted deliberately when causing harm to the claimant. Thus, where the unauthorised act was so closely connected with the employee's employment that it would be fair and just to hold the employer vicariously liable, or where the risk of wrongdoing can fairly be said to be reasonably incidental to the employer's business, the act will be held to have been committed in the course of the employee's employment, even where the employee caused harm to the claimant deliberately (*Lister*).

▶ *Gravil v Carroll and Redruth Rugby Football Club* [2008] EWCA Civ 689

Following a scrum in a semi-professional rugby union game, and after the referee had blown his whistle to stop play, a fight broke out during which the first defendant hit the claimant, causing him serious facial injuries. Having established that the first defendant had committed an actionable battery against the claimant, the question on appeal was whether the second defendant should be vicariously liable for the actions of its employee.

In the Court of Appeal, Clarke MR held that melees of the kind that preceded the punch were frequent occurrences in rugby union matches and that punching was not uncommon. He further described the incident as being an 'ordinary though undesirable' part of modern rugby. Thus the deliberate infliction of injury in circumstances amounting to an actionable battery could be considered to be in the course of the first defendant's employment as a rugby union player because the risk of such wrongdoing can fairly be said to be reasonably incidental to the employer's business of running a rugby club. In other words, a sufficiently close connection between the employee's terms of employment and the injury-causing incident could be established. Further, despite a contractual term specifically prohibiting fighting, it was fair and just to impose vicarious liability on the defendant club because it was better placed to influence and punish the conduct of its players and to purchase adequate insurance to cover their transgressions. Thus, the club was found vicariously liable for the acts of its player.

Gravil, though perhaps surprising to non-lawyers, is a simple extension of the law of vicarious liability that was developed in *Lister* and *Mattis* to a sporting context. A specific prohibition on fighting is not of itself sufficient to exonerate the employer from liability (*Rose v Plenty* [1976] 1 WLR 141). Only where the employing club has a strict and well-used internal disciplinary procedure might it be possible for it to avoid liability in a situation like this. Otherwise, for injury-causing acts that occur on the field of play, whether they are deliberate or negligent, the club should expect to be found vicariously liable for the acts of its employee players.

4.5.4   Dual employment

Where a sportsperson has two or more employments, the sports employer can be vicariously liable for the acts that occur during the course of the sporting employment. In many professional team sports, the opportunity for dual employment of this kind is usually limited to playing representative fixtures on top of the contractual obligation to play for the main employing club. Being picked to play in a representative match might take two legal forms; a lending of the player by the club to the international team, as in football, or a separate contract of employment, often referred to as a 'central contract', between the governing body and the player, as occurs in English cricket.

In both cases, the international team, not the club, will be vicariously liable for the tortious actions of the player. Where the player is lent to the representative team, the governing body will be entitled to exercise control over their actions as the player will be integrated into their business for the period of the lending (*Mersey Docks and Harbour Board v Coggins and Griffith (Liverpool) Ltd* [1947] AC 1). In cases where players are released by their main employer to fulfil international representative fixtures, the governing body will be liable for any tortious acts committed during that period.

Where the player is concurrently employed by both a club and the governing body under a central contract, the situation is even more straightforward. In the same way that Redruth RFC was only responsible for the tortious acts of its employees when they were playing rugby for the club (*Gravil*), vicarious liability will only be imposed on the employer for whom the player was playing at the time that they committed the tort. Thus, if the tort takes place during an international representative fixture, the governing body will be liable, but if it occurs whilst the player is playing a club fixture, then the employing club will be vicariously liable.

4.6   Defences

Defendants have two options when defending a claim. Firstly, they can deny or adduce evidence to prove that they did not commit the tort of which they are accused. Secondly, where the claimant has succeeded in proving, on the balance of probabilities, that a tort has been committed by the defendant, the latter may be able to raise a defence to the claim made. Different defences can be raised, depending on which cause of action is pursued by the claimant.

4.6.1 Defences to trespass to the person

There are two defences open to a defendant to plead when accused of having committed a battery: consent and self-defence. Consent will generally apply to specific contacts that have been inflicted as a necessary or inherent part of the game, such as rugby tackles, but not to acts unconnected with ongoing play, such as punching an opponent (*Gravil*). Self-defence can generally only be raised where the defendant was being, or was about to be, attacked by another person. Both defences, if successful, are complete defences to a claim.

4.6.1.1 Consent

Where the claimant has given full, free and informed consent to the actions of the defendant, the latter will have a complete defence to any claim made against him (*Re F* [1990] 2 AC 1). The consent given can be either express or implied. Express consent is where the claimant grants permission in advance of participation to the defendant to perform certain specific acts on them in the course of the game. Implied consent is where the claimant is deemed to have consented to all reasonable contacts being made with them, on the basis that they are participating in the particular sporting contest. As the vast majority of sports participants do not discuss with their opponents in advance what is and is not an acceptable level of interpersonal contact, a claimant's consent will usually be implied from their participation in the game.

Full, free and informed consent means that, either expressly or impliedly, the claimant was aware of, and agreed to, the risks of participating in the sport under consideration. In sporting contests, consent will be an objectively defined standard applicable to all participants in the contest; a game would become impossible to manage if each individual player could define which contacts could or could not be applied to them during the game. For example, rugby players expect and consent to being tackled even if they would rather not be, whereas tennis players would neither expect nor consent to any interpersonal contact with an opponent during the playing of the game.

The scope of the consent given by a sports participant is defined by reference to the relevant circumstances and playing culture of the game (above, 4.4.1.3–4). Sports participants consent to all interpersonal contact that is an integral part of the game, such as a challenge for the ball, to all contacts accepted as occurring as a normal part of playing the game, such as collisions, and commonly occurring acts of foul play, such as pushing. All contacts unconnected with playing the game, such as those occurring when the action has moved to a different part of the arena or after play has stopped, or fighting of any kind, are not consented to (*Gravil*).

4.6.1.2 Self-defence

This defence will only rarely be raised in sports cases as it is only available where the defendant is actually being attacked by another person or on the basis of an honest belief that an attack by another person is about to occur. The defendant must honestly believe that there is a need for the use of some force to defend themselves, and this belief must be based on reasonable grounds, for example where the defendant is already being hit or is being threatened. The force actually used in defence must be reasonable and proportionate in the circumstances in which it was used (*Ashley v Chief Constable of Sussex* [2008] 1 AC 962). For example, a defendant could punch a person whom he honestly believed was punching him, but he could not chase after and punch someone who was running away from him as there is no longer an imminent threat of being attacked; the defendant is not given a licence to use an unlimited degree of force. The burden of proof is on the defendant to establish on the balance of probabilities that all elements of the defence were present at the time he hit the claimant.

4.6.2   Defences to negligence

There are two defences available to a defendant accused of negligently causing injury. *Volenti non fit injuria*, or voluntary assumption of risk, acts as a complete defence to negligence claims where the defendant can prove that the claimant agreed in advance to the defendant acting negligently. Contributory negligence is a partial defence that enables the defendant to reduce the amount of damages payable on the basis that the claimant has, in some way, contributed to their own harm.

4.6.2.1 *Volenti non fit injuria or the voluntary assumption of risk*

Volenti is a defence that is often pleaded but whose application is rarely fully understood. For *volenti* to apply, the claimant must have agreed to the defendant acting negligently, not just to the risk of injury inherent in the sporting activity (*Smoldon v Whitworth and Nolan* [1997] ELR 249) (see further, chapter 5.3). It will be an unusual case indeed where the claimant agrees, whether expressly or impliedly, to allow the defendant to act with anything other than reasonable care.

The practical effect of the sports negligence cases decided in recent years is to render this defence functionally obsolete. By requiring an explicit and detailed analysis of the relevant circumstances in which an incident took place, and the playing culture of the particular sport, *volenti* is left with little, and perhaps no, role to play. If the injury-causing conduct of the defendant is an acceptable means of playing the sport in question or is within its playing culture, then there is no breach of duty and therefore no liability (*Elliott*). If liability cannot be established, then an analysis of *volenti* is unnecessary.

Alternatively, if the injury-causing conduct of the defendant is an unacceptable means of playing the sport in question because it is too dangerous, unconnected with the playing of the game or outside of its playing culture, then negligence is established. No question of *volenti* arises as participants do not agree to allow players to act in a manner that is incompatible with the playing culture of the sport. Sports participants agree to the inherent risks associated with playing the game, such as mistakes and errors of judgement, but they do not permit the defendant to act negligently.

▶ *Rollason v Matthews, (unreported) County Court (Bristol), 31 January 2006*

The defendant, in attempting to regain possession of a football of which he had lost control, slid towards the ball and tried to knock it out of the way of the claimant. The claimant got to the ball first, and in following through with his challenge, the defendant made contact with and broke the claimant's left leg just below the knee. The court held that in carrying out this initially legitimate attempt to recover possession of the ball, the defendant had fallen below the standard of care expected of him by performing the challenge with both feet raised and with his studs pointing at, and making contact with, the claimant's leg.

Thus, it will now be extremely difficult to raise the defence of *volenti* because of the requirement for a very detailed examination of the applicable duty and its breach. Although defence counsel will often plead *volenti* alongside any appropriate denial of liability, to all intents and purposes the denial is likely to be the more effective approach.

4.6.2.2 Contributory negligence

Contributory negligence is a statutory defence that reduces the amount of compensation payable by a defendant to a claimant.

> ▶ *Law Reform (Contributory Negligence) Act 1945 s.1(1) – apportionment of liability in case of contributory negligence*
>
> Where any person suffers damage as the result partly of his own fault and partly of the fault of any other person or persons, a claim in respect of that damage shall not be defeated by reason of the fault of the person suffering the damage, but the damages recoverable in respect thereof shall be reduced to such extent as the court thinks just and equitable having regard to the claimant's share in the responsibility for the damage.

Where the defendant can prove, on the balance of probabilities, that the claimant has failed to take reasonable care for their own safety and has contributed to the extent of the harm caused, the damages payable will be reduced accordingly (though never to zero). For example, a claim of contributory negligence may succeed where the claimant has knowingly put themselves at risk of injury by the defendant by, for example, playing whilst injured, attempting a challenge in the knowledge that contact would be made with the defendant or playing in a game or in a position for which they had not received adequate pre-participation training (see further, chapter 5.2.2). In one of the few cases to address this issue, Lord Brailsford held in *Phee v Gordon* [2011] CSOH 181 that in the time available to the claimant to react to a shout of 'fore' on a golf course, he had not failed to take reasonable care for his own safety by crouching down and then looking up to try see the direction in which the ball was heading. It was the defendant's lack of skill, not the claimant looking up, which led to the ball hitting the claimant in the eye, causing it to implode. Contributory negligence is not assessed with hindsight but in the context of the circumstances prevailing at the time of the injury.

4.7 Compensation

The compensation awarded to a claimant is calculated, so far as is financially possible, to put them in the same position as they were before the tort was committed. The award is usually split into 'special' and 'general' damages. Special damages are pre-trial losses that are precisely quantifiable and include loss of earnings, medical expenses and damage caused to property, such as clothing and sports equipment, during the accident. General damages are more speculative in nature as they are estimates of future losses. Compensation for the pain and suffering caused by the injury, any loss of amenity, or inability to perform acts that the claimant could before the injury occurred and loss of future earnings, including loss of earnings capacity, fall under this part of the claim.

In very limited cases, the amount of compensation payable to a claimant can be increased by an award of aggravated damages. Where the court considers that the manner in which the defendant committed the tort also caused injury to the claimant's proper feelings of dignity or pride, then an enhanced award can be made (*Rookes v Barnard (No.1)* [1964] AC 1129). Although there have been no UK cases on this point, and it would undoubtedly be a very complex point to argue, the Australian case of *Rogers v Bugden and Canterbury-Bankstown* (1993) ATR 81-246 held that aggravated damages should be awarded to the claimant, a professional rugby league player, for the emotional impact of knowing that he had been the victim of a deliberate assault carried out by an opposing player live on national television.

4.7.1   Calculating compensation

The amount of compensation payable for pain, suffering and loss of amenity is calculated by reference to a tariff system, set out in the Judicial College's 'Guidelines for the assessment of general damages in personal injury cases.' Each injury attracts a specific amount of compensation, which can be increased to take account of further complications, such as a permanent limp.

The more difficult assessment is usually the calculation of lost earnings, particularly the speculation on lost future earnings. In *Collett v Smith and Middlesbrough Football and Athletics Company (1986) Ltd* [2008] EWHC 1962 and [2009] EWCA Civ 583 the High Court was asked to assess the quantum of damages payable to an aspiring professional football whose career had been ended by a negligent tackle before he had played a first team match for his club, Manchester United. The calculation, upheld by the Court of Appeal, highlighted three issues that need to be addressed in the calculation: the level at which the player would have played had he not been injured; the amount that he would have been paid; and the length of his career.

The Court was referred to a wide range of expert opinion on the claimant's potential as a professional footballer, players whose careers could be used an appropriate comparator and statistical evidence about average pay and career length in making its assessment. The Court concluded that the claimant would have had a post-trial career of 11 years, of which one-third would have been with clubs playing in the Premier League, and two-thirds with Championship clubs. His lost pay was based on the average earnings of a well-paying Championship club with Premier League ambitions and an average Premier League club. In each case, his pay was uplifted to reflect his good chances of being a successful player, bonuses and signing-on fees. A discount of 15 per cent was applied to reflect the risk of injury and other contingencies that could lead to a reduced income. Taking into account these variables, the eventual sum payable was almost £4.5m.

Hot topic ... | # The evolution of vicarious liability and its impact on sport

The law of vicarious liability has been developing rapidly over the last 15 years in a way that has made it easier to claim that an employer is legally responsible for the harms caused by its employees. These developments either have had, or have the potential to have, an impact on sport in three specific ways. Firstly, it has extended the scope of the conduct for which an employer-club is liable. Secondly, it could increase the range of relationships for which a club may be vicariously liable. Thirdly, it will make employer-clubs more risk averse when deciding whether or not to select a player with a 'hard' or violent reputation.

In *Gravil v Carroll and Redruth RFC*, it was held that an employer-club is not just responsible for the actions of an employee-player performing authorised acts negligently but also for acts that are so closely connected with the discharge of the employee's contractual duties that it is fair, just and reasonable for an employer-club to be vicariously liable for any harm caused. This decision sees the range of conduct for which the club is liable extend from negligently performed tackles in *McCord v Cornforth and Swansea City AFC* to deliberately thrown punches in *Gravil*. Perhaps more importantly, *Redruth* was held vicariously liable despite its extreme stance against the use of violence by its players.

Following *JGE v Trustees of Portsmouth Roman Catholic Diocesan Trust*, the Court of Appeal discussed not just employment relationships, which would include professional and semi-professional sports participants, but relationships that are 'akin to being an employee'. These would usually arise where some payment changed hands between the parties, there was at least some degree of control over the conduct of the athlete, the athlete was per-forming on behalf of or in some way furthering the aims or inter-ests of the club and it was fair, just and reasonable to impose liability on the club. As a result, there is an outside chance that in certain circumstances, for example, where the club is a commercial entity and the player is paid expenses to play for the club, a relationship akin to employment could be established. However, where both club and player are genuinely amateur, vicarious liability remains unlikely.

The 'hard man' of a team has been elevated to an almost mythi-cal status amongst British sports fans. Despite the fact that such players will often have hassled and hustled, kicked and punched their way through a significant portion of their careers, they are remembered fondly by fans and commentators alike as players who gave their all for club and country and who never failed to put their bodies on the line for the sake of the team. They were picked both to protect their own team's star players and to in-timidate those of the opposition in the hope that they would be put off their game. Although most of these players were in their prime before the law's more regular in-volvement in sport since *Condon*, their like still exists even if there is now less scope for overt foul play when every move of the profes-sional player can be replayed and analysed in television studios and in online discussions.

The leading cases on vicarious liability have held that where an employer knows of the violent tendencies of an employee, or seeks to exploit them for their own benefit, then the employer will be liable for any harm caused by the employee exhibiting those tendencies. Furthermore where the employer is aware of such a tendency but ignores it, or other-wise fails to control, discipline or retrain the employee, then again the employer will be vicariously liable for any harm caused by the employee that is connected to his employment.

This has the potential to cause significant problems for clubs that employ a player with a known reputation for foul play, or one who over a period of time develops such a reputation whilst playing for a club. Whereas in the past it could have been argued that deliberately violent conduct was outside of the course of their employment as a sportsperson, or that this was a revenge attack in some way unconnected with the playing of the game, *Gravil* demonstrates that this is no longer the case. A club can now be vicariously liable for one of their players who causes deliberate injury to an opponent. Taken as a whole, these develop-ments are likely to result in clubs being more circumspect when assessing the risks associated with selecting a player with a reputation for physical or violent play and the end of the hard men of sport.

Summary

4.1 There has been a rapid development in the law as it applies to sports injuries since *Condon v Basi* in 1985. As a result, the most important issues for anyone suffering an injury whilst playing sport are to identify the potential defendants to a claim and to determine whether the appropriate cause of action lies in trespass to the person or negligence.

4.2 A battery is the direct and intentional application of force by the defendant to the claimant without their consent. Claimants rarely pursue an action in battery as most insurance policies exclude claims for deliberately inflicted injury. However, after *Gravil v Carroll and Redruth RFC*, an employing club may now be vicariously liable for any conduct of its employee-players that is sufficiently connected to its business, including batteries.

4.3 The generally applicable definition of negligence requires claimants to establish that they were owed a duty of care by the defendant, that the defendant has breached this duty by dropping below the standard of conduct generally expected of a person in their position and that this

Summary cont'd

breach has caused reasonably foreseeable harm to the claimant. This definition has been refined by *Caldwell v Maguire and Fitzgerald* in particular in respect of its application to sports cases.

4.4 *Caldwell v Maguire and Fitzgerald* also provided clarification of the standard of care required of athletes to discharge the duty of care owed by them and of the standard of proof required to prove a negligence claim. The examination of the reasonableness of an athlete's conduct will take into account the specific sporting circumstances in which the injury occurred. Further, because of the dangers inherent in many sports, it was also acknowledged that something more than an error of judgement would be required to establish the defendant's negligence.

4.5 An employer-club is responsible for the negligent actions of its employee-players who cause injury to another person whilst they are acting in the course of their employment. Following *Gravil v Carroll and Redruth RFC*, this vicarious liability of the employer-club has been extended to include batteries that are so closely connected to the playing of the game that they can be considered to have occurred in the course of the player's employment. This would appear to include fighting that occurs during the game but, without further legal examination, will not extend beyond to fights after the game has ended.

4.6 Where the claimant has consented to the injury-causing conduct happening to them, the defendant has a complete defence to a claim of battery. Where the claimant consciously ran the risk of the defendant acting negligently, the defendant will be able to raise the defence of *volenti non fit injuria*. After *Caldwell v Maguire and Fitzgerald* both of these defences will be examined alongside the issue of whether or not the defendant has breached their duty of care towards the claimant. The possibility that the defendant could raise the defence of contributory negligence has not yet been fully explored before the courts, however, it was accepted as a possibility in *Phee v Gordon*.

4.7 The compensation payable to a claimant is split into special and general damages. Pain, suffering and loss of amenity are calculated by reference to the Judicial College's 'Guidelines'. In *Collett v Smith and Middlesbrough*, the criteria for calculating lost earnings were found to be determining the level of play at which the claimant would have played, the appropriate rate of pay, the length of his lost career and identifying an appropriate comparator player who can act as a benchmark.

Further reading

Beloff et al, *Sports Law* (2nd edn, 2012, Hart) ch 5

Grayson, *Sport and the Law* (3rd edn, 2000, Butterworths) chs 1 and 15

Griggs, 'Dangerous recreational activities – stay at home and be safe!' [2010] 1 *International Sports Law Review* 9

Lewis and Taylor (eds), *Sport: Law and Practice* (2nd edn, 2008, Tottel) ch D5

Steele, *Tort Law: text, cases and materials* (2nd edn, 2010, Oxford University Press) chs 3 and 5

Anderson, 'Personal injury liability in sport: emerging trends' (2008) 16 *Tort Law Review* 95

Cox, 'Civil liability for foul play in sport' (2003) 54 *Northern Ireland Law Quarterly* 351

Goodhart, 'The sportsman's charter' (1962) 78 *Law Quarterly Review* 490

Grayson, 'Drake's drumbeat for sporting remedies/injuries' (1994) 144 *New Law Journal* 1094

Harris, 'Personal injury: a sporting chance' (2012) 162 *New Law Journal* 1248

James and McArdle, 'Player violence or violent players? Vicarious liability for sports participants' (2004) 12 *Tort Law Review* 131

McArdle, 'The enduring legacy of reckless disregard' (2005) 34 (4) *Common Law World Review* 316

McArdle and James, 'Are you experienced? Playing cultures, sporting rules and personal injury litigation after Caldwell v Maguire' (2005) 13 (3) *Tort Law Review* 193

Yeo, 'Determining consent in body contact sports' (1998) 6 *Tort Law Review* 199

Links to relevant websites can be found at www.palgrave.com/law/james2e

Liability for injuries caused by non-participants

Extending sports negligence to new defendants (5.1)
- Possible explanations for the expansion of negligence liability (5.1.1)
- Recent restrictions on liability (5.1.2)

Coaches, instructors and supervisors (5.2)
- Establishing a claim (5.2.1)
  - Duty of care (5.2.1.1)
  - Breach of duty and the appropriate standard of care (5.2.1.2)
- Defences (5.2.2)

Referees and match officials (5.3)
- Establishing a claim (5.3.1)
  - Duty of care (5.3.1.1)
  - Breach of duty and the appropriate standard of care (5.3.1.2)
  - Foreseeability of harm (5.3.1.3)
- Defences (5.3.2)

Governing bodies and international federations (5.4)
- Establishing a claim (5.4.1)
  - Duty of care (5.4.1.1)
    - Pre-event administration and licensing (5.4.1.1.1)
    - Safety provision and risk management (5.4.1.1.2)
    - The rules of the game (5.4.1.1.3)
  - Breach of duty and the appropriate standard of care (5.4.1.2)
- Defences (5.4.2)

Medical professionals (5.5)
- First aid and the initial injury (5.5.1)
- The design and implementation of return to fitness programmes (5.5.2)
- Referrals for specialist medical treatment (5.5.3)
- Confidentiality and the disclosure of medical records (5.5.4)

Liability for injuries caused by non-participants

Key terms

- **Man of straw** – a defendant, or potential defendant, who has insufficient funds to meet any award of damages made against him.
- **Vicarious liability** – the employer is responsible for the tortious acts of an employee where the tort committed has sufficient connection to the employee's employment.

5.1 Extending sports negligence to new defendants

Since *Condon v Basi* [1985] 1 WLR 866 (see further, chapter 4.4.1.1), the range of potential defendants has increased dramatically. What limited authority that previously existed has since been clarified and often extended. Successful personal injury claims have been brought against coaches, instructors and supervisors, match officials, governing bodies and medical staff, all of which are discussed in this chapter. The liability of facility owners and event organisers is explored in Chapter 8 as it brings in the additional causes of action found in the Occupiers' Liability Acts 1957 and 1984 and the law of nuisance. Despite this seemingly massive extension in the number of people who can be sued, the law has not yet fully tested the scope of what these defendants might be liable for.

5.1.1 Possible explanations for the expansion of negligence liability

There is no definitive explanation for why there has been this explosion in sports negligence cases, though several theories may help to explain the increase in litigation. Firstly, where the injuries were caused by an opponent, the person who actually caused the harm may be unable to meet any claim brought against him. This then leads to a search for others who may have been at fault for facilitating, encouraging or in some other way contributing to the harm caused to the claimant, but who also have deeper pockets or better insurance than the defendant athlete.

Secondly, claimants may now be more aware of their legal rights than in earlier times. Whether this is because of claims handlers specifically aiming adverts at injured sports participants or because people are now less likely to accept that blameless injury can occur during play, sports negligence litigation continues to grow, whether or not there is any proof of a 'compensation culture.'

Thirdly, since the introduction of conditional fee arrangements in s.58 Courts and Legal Services Act 1990, some of the financial risk of commencing litigation has been removed from claimants. Where such an arrangement is in place, claimants no longer have to pay for their legal advice up front or on an ongoing basis during the course of negotiations. Instead, their lawyers only receive their fees if they win, when they are paid directly by the defendants. Thus, where previously the threat of having to meet your own costs up front and, in the case of losing, the total costs of both sides was enough to discourage many good claims from being initiated, that gamble can now be avoided by using a conditional fee arrangement.

Regardless of how or why these claims are being made, this area of the law is one that has developed rapidly in recent years. Not only that, it continues to do so and continues to extend legal liability to new contexts and new defendants who sometimes had not previously been thought to be at risk from litigation.

5.1.2 Recent restrictions on liability

This growth in litigation has not gone completely unchecked; many cases fail because the injury has been caused by the obvious or inherent risks associated with the activity. Furthermore, Parliament has specifically legislated to protect risky but socially beneficial activities.

▶ *Compensation Act 2006 s.1 – deterrent effect of potential liability*

A court considering a claim in negligence or breach of statutory duty may, in determining whether the defendant should have taken particular steps to meet a standard of care (whether by taking precautions against a risk or otherwise), have regard to whether a requirement to take those steps might –

(a) prevent a desirable activity from being undertaken at all, to a particular extent or in a particular way, or
(b) discourage persons from undertaking functions in connection with a desirable activity.

Although judges rarely refer to this section as a reason for their decisions, there has been a clear indication that by the use of phrases like 'responsibility for their own personal autonomy' and 'personal responsibility for the risks that they have run', the judiciary does not want to see sport litigated out of existence. Instead, there has been a growth in successful contributory negligence claims and this tension between a claimant being responsible for running acceptable risks and a defendant's unacceptable negligence is a constant theme of this chapter.

5.2 Coaches, instructors and supervisors

Liability for injuries caused by a failure to train or supervise a sports participant has grown out of a series of cases from the early twentieth century where successful negligence claims were brought against PE teachers and instructors. Although the duty of care owed to children is always higher than that owed to adults (*Jolley v Sutton LBC* [2000] 1 WLR 1082) the teacher cases are illustrative of how and why the law has developed to encompass sports coaches and instructors. For example, in *Gibbs v Barking Corporation* [1936] 1 All ER 115, a PE teacher was held to be liable in negligence for the injuries caused to one of his pupils when he failed to assist the boy to land safely on the mats following his vaulting over a horse during a gym session. As the pupils were not yet proficient in completing a vault unaided, the duty imposed on the teacher was to ensure that a procedure was in place to enable them to land safely. The system in place did not provide a sufficient level of assistance to the vaulters and therefore the Corporation was vicariously liable for the negligence of the teacher.

In most of the cases involving a coach's potential liability, the argument focuses on whether or not the defendant has followed appropriate procedures, used appropriate techniques, supervised the performances of those under their tuition and generally acted within their sphere of competence. Where coaches have kept their training and qualifications up to date and are working with groups of athletes that they have been trained to coach, it is almost impossible for a claimant to establish liability.

5.2.1   Establishing a claim

The first step in any claim is to ascertain the most appropriate cause of action. In *Moore v Hotelplan Ltd (t/a Inghams Travel)* [2010] EWHC 276, the claimant suffered catastrophic injuries after she lost control of a snowmobile. She had been unable to bring her vehicle to a stop before crashing into a parked car as she had not been shown how to use the emergency engine cut-off button. If this had been engaged, it would have brought the vehicle to a stop before the impact occurred. This failure in instruction constituted negligence on the part of the expedition organiser; however, the court had to determine whether this claim should be brought in contract against the defendant or in tort against the organiser of the excursion. It was held that the arrangements made between the claimant's party and the defendant's representative at the resort constituted a contract for the supply of a snowmobile excursion. The defendant was, therefore, liable for the injuries caused by the negligence of the organiser of the snowmobile expedition under the terms of the excursion contract.

The interplay of the very different duties imposed by the Health and Safety at Work Act 1974 and the law of tort were discussed in *R v Upper Bay Limited* [2010] EWCA Crim 495. The child victim almost drowned in a swimming pool operated by the defendant and as a result suffered severe brain damage. It was found that the defendant had failed to provide sufficient numbers of lifeguards around the pool and therefore had not done all that was reasonably practicable to ensure that persons not employed by it were not exposed to risks to their health and safety contrary to ss.3(1) and 33(1)(a) of the Act. Criminal liability was therefore established against the defendant. However, it was clear that the victim's father had also failed to keep a proper lookout for his child's safety and was, therefore, in breach of his own duty to supervise the victim. The court held that the duty of a parent to supervise their children is concurrent with the duties imposed on the defendant under the Health and Safety at Work Act 1974. Thus, the behaviour of the parent did not affect the finding of guilt under the 1974 Act but would reduce, and perhaps even extinguish, any finding of fault against the defendant if a civil action, in either negligence or under the Occupiers Liability Act 1957, were commenced.

5.2.1.1 Duty of care

The duty imposed on a coach is to take reasonable care to ensure that they are training the players under their control in a manner that does not cause them reasonably foreseeable harm. This duty, subject to additional detail relevant to the particular activity, will always be imposed on every coach and instructor. It must be noted from the outset that this duty is not absolute; it does not require perfection on the part of the coach. It requires only that the coach take reasonable care to ensure that those under their tuition are taught how to perform moves relevant to the sport in question and appropriate to their own level of skill and experience. It does not require that the activity take place in a completely risk-free environment, only that the risks are appropriately managed. As was seen in *Gibbs*, participants are allowed to be taught new skills that carry with them a risk of injury, provided that the coach has in place and operates a system that ensures that they are reasonably safe when performing the task.

5.2.1.2 Breach of duty and the appropriate standard of care

The more difficult question for the court will usually be determining whether or not the duty has been breached by the coach's conduct. The general test for determining a breach of duty is to measure the conduct of the defendant against the standard of the reasonable and competent person performing that task. As with the liability of sports participants, this is not an abstract concept or a one-size-fits-all test: all of the relevant circumstances in which the incident took place will need to be taken into account, including the particular sport, the level of experience and perhaps the age of the participants, their skill levels and the inherent risks of performing the particular move that leads to the injury, as well as the level of qualification, training and experience of the coach (see further, chapter 4.4.2).

The specialist nature of sports coaching means that the professional negligence tests developed from *Bolam v Friern Hospital Management Committee* [1957] 1 WLR 582 and *Bolitho v City and Hackney Health Authority* [1998] AC 232 will be used when a defendant coach's competence is called into question. Following *Bolam*, the court can enquire what the reasonable person of the same level of skill or training or qualification would have done in those circumstances. If a body of similarly qualified coaches would have acted in the same way, then it is likely that the defendant will be able to establish that they have not breached the duty of care owed to the claimant.

To ensure that negligent practices do not become entrenched through repetition, however, *Bolitho* allows the court to ask the defendant to justify the option that they took that led to the injury being caused. Thus, a defendant must prove not only that other coaches would have acted in the same way, but also that there was good reason for their having acted in that way. Where a claimant cannot prove, on the balance of probabilities, that the coaching team did anything other than act in accordance with standard safe practice, the injuries caused will be considered to be nothing more than an unfortunate accident.

▶ *Hopkins v Pullen and Taylor (trading as Ippon Judo Club)* **(unreported) Crown Court (Preston), 8 December 2005**

During his first judo training session, the claimant was injured whilst performing the Kesa Gatame move. Instruction in how to perform the move was given by an experienced judo coach who was being further supervised by the second defendant. The claimant alleged that he had not been taught how to fall or roll away from his training partner. Further, he alleged that his partner was significantly larger than he was and that as a result, when his partner fell on top of him whilst performing the move, he fractured his right clavicle. The court held that although the club owed a duty to ensure that adequate training and supervision were given to the novices by reasonable and competent coaches, this duty had not been breached in these circumstances. All reasonable steps had been taken to ensure the safety of the claimant: he was adequately supervised at all times and the move being performed by him was one that was appropriate to his status as a complete beginner.

In contrast, *Gannon v Rotherham Metropolitan Borough Council* (unreported) Crown Court (Nottingham) 6 February 1991 held that no reasonable or competent swimming coach would allow anyone, and particularly not those lacking sufficient skill and experience, to dive off racing blocks into the shallow end of the pool. Having shown the swimmers the basic technique, the coach allowed the claimant and others to continue to practise diving from the blocks at the shallow end of the pool. The claimant hit his head on the bottom of the pool and broke his neck. Negligence was established against the coach and the Council was held vicariously liable.

As a further example, a rugby player cannot complain of being injured by a legitimate tackle performed either during training or as a part of the game. However, where the tackle is performed on a schoolboy by an older and much larger player, and the disparity in size leads to the claimant being injured, then negligence will be established against those picking and coaching the larger player's team.

▶ *Mountford v Newlands School* **[2007] EWCA Civ 21**

The claimant was playing in an under-15 age group rugby union match for his school against the defendant school. The defendant's rugby coach had picked an overage player in its team who was considerably taller and heavier than the claimant who, when lawfully tackled by this larger player, suffered a broken elbow. According to the Junior Rugby Guidelines of the England Rugby Football Schools' Union, players should not normally play in age groupings other than their own as this could compromise the safety of younger and smaller players. The court held that having regard to the older player's size and age, the defendant's rugby coach should not have picked him to play in this fixture. As the rule had been devised to prevent this specific type of harm from eventuating, the defendant was vicariously liable for the negligent selection of the older boy by the coach.

Being tackled in such a way by someone substantially larger is not a risk inherent in age-restricted games. Further, where the injury is caused by a tackle performed by an adult coach on a child participant, this will also be considered to be beyond the normal, inherent risks of the sport and liability will be established against the defendant (*Affuto-Nartoy v Clarke and Inner London Education Authority* (1984) *The Times*, 9 February).

When determining whether or not there has been a breach of duty, the Court of Appeal in *Gouldbourn v Balkan Holidays Ltd and Another* [2010] EWCA Civ 372 held that local practice and standards must be the benchmark against which the conduct is judged unless there is evidence of the acceptance of higher international standards of care being adhered to in the jurisdiction where the accident occurred. Here, local Bulgarian standards of ski instruction, where the culture was that the learner had to opt out of activities that were beyond their competence, were the standards against which the defendant ski instructor's conduct had to be judged, not those of the Fédération Internationale de Ski, which stated that instructors should never allow pupils to take risks beyond their capabilities (see further, *Anderson v Lyotier, Lyotier and Portejoie* (5.2.2) and *Lyon v Maidment* (4.4.1.4)).

5.2.2   Defences

A coach accused of negligence can raise either of the two general defences to negligence: *volenti non fit injuria*, or voluntary assumption of risk, and contributory negligence (see further, chapter 4.6.2). For a successful claim of *volenti*, the claimant must have agreed to the defendant acting negligently, not just to the risk of injury inherent in the sporting activity. Unless the player has specifically agreed in advance to run the risk of injury from, for example, the use of a novel training technique not sanctioned or taught as a part of a normal coaching course, then this defence is unlikely to succeed.

Practically, it is more likely and more advisable that a defendant raise the partial defence of contributory negligence (s.1(1) Law Reform (Contributory Negligence) Act 1945) (see further, chapter 4.6.2.2). Contributory negligence can be established where it can be proved on the balance of probabilities that the claimant has failed to take reasonable care for their own safety and has contributed to the extent of the harm caused. The damages payable will be reduced proportionately to the degree of fault exhibited by the claimant, where it is just and equitable to do so. With all sports defendants, there is an inherent tension in many of the cases, recognised in s.1 Compensation Act 2006, between the need for care to be taken by the defendant and the risks inherent in many sporting activities. On the one hand, the courts do not want to be seen to be allowing or encouraging negligent conduct in the name of sport. On the other hand, they do not want sports participants to be absolved of all responsibility for their own safety nor to litigate risky activities out of existence.

> ▶ *Anderson v Lyotier, Lyotier and Portejoie* [2008] EWHC 2790
>
> The claimant had been a member of a mixed-ability skiing group that had been under the instruction of the third defendant. They had descended a number of slopes of varying difficulty and had skied off-piste on two occasions during the week's holiday. On the second occasion, the claimant had found the trail particularly challenging and had fallen a number of times. On the final day, the third defendant took the group down a particularly steep off-piste trail that descended through some trees. The claimant lost control and skied into a tree, suffering catastrophic injuries as a result. The High Court was asked directly to determine whether this was a case of negligent training, instruction and supervision or a situation where the claimant should have taken personal responsibility for their voluntary participation in a high-risk activity.
>
> It was held that the instructor had acted negligently by failing to assess the competence of each member of the group individually before making the off-piste descent and that he had failed to appreciate the claimant's lack of ability and confidence when skiing off the main trails. By failing to take account of the individual circumstances of each member of the group and failing to determine prospectively and objectively whether the terrain was reasonably safe for each of them, the instructor had breached his duty. However, as the claimant had been contributorily negligent by failing to draw the instructor's attention to his own lack of competence to descend this particular trail, his damages were reduced by one-third.

Balancing these contrasting approaches is a difficult task. It is obvious to all skiers, whether they are novices or highly experienced, that there is a risk of falling and being injured at almost any time. It is also obvious that there are additional dangers when skiing off-piste, particularly if the trail runs through trees. This risk of injury through falling and/or crashing is increased where the skier lacks the necessary skill and experience to ski off-piste. By failing to voice his fears and voluntarily descending this particular off-piste section in the knowledge that he lacked the necessary skill and confidence, the claimant appears implicitly to be running not only the inherent risks of skiing but also the risks associated with the defendant's misplaced belief that he could ski this specific trail.

After instructing him every day for the past six days however, it should have been obvious to the defendant that the claimant lacked these skills and either should not have been allowed to ski this section or should have been more closely supervised during the descent. Thus, this is also a case where the instructor had failed to teach the necessary skills and provide an appropriate safe system of learning (*Gibbs*) or had failed to provide a reasonably safe system of supervision (*Gannon*). A further reading of this scenario could be that this was a case of the instructor incrementally building up a novice's skills by testing them towards the upper limits of their ability. Liability would be established where instructors had pushed their trainee beyond the limits of their competence but not if they were teaching skills and techniques that were appropriate to their skill level. In contrast to *Anderson*, the court in *MacIntyre v Ministry of Defence* [2011] EWHC 1690, absolved an appropriately qualified climbing instructor who had conducted the necessary risk assessments and taken into consideration the claimant's prior experience before starting the climb. It held that although the route taken up the mountain was ambitious and challenging, it was not beyond the competence of the claimant.

The court in *Anderson* eventually held that the instructor's suggestion was not a reasonable one of undertaking something incrementally more challenging but an unreasonable one that required the claimant to engage in an activity that was dangerous and beyond the his capabilities and therefore negligent. However, the decision whether or not to make the descent was collaborative, and the claimant could not abdicate all responsibility for his own safety to the instructor; the claimant was, therefore, contributorily negligent and had his damages reduced significantly. Although the balance was struck in favour of the claimant, the implications of this decision are potentially wide-ranging for both sides (see also *Moore v Hotelplan* (5.2.1) where damages were also reduced by 30 per cent on the basis of contributory negligence).

5.3 Referees and match officials

In 1996, it was widely reported that the UK was about to witness the end of sport as we then knew it. The cause of this hysteria was the decision in *Smoldon v Whitworth and Nolan* [1997] ELR 249, the first reported case of an injured athlete successfully suing a match official in negligence. As has so often been the case where sport and the law collide, sport has been able to adapt to the new challenges laid down by the law and continues in much the same way as it always has. What *Smoldon* did highlight specifically was that injury, in this case catastrophic injury, can be caused by those who have no direct involvement in the contest itself but who are present to ensure the smooth running of the game.

▶ *Smoldon v Whitworth and Nolan* [1997] ELR 249

The claimant was playing in the front row of a rugby union scrum when it collapsed, causing him serious spinal injuries that paralysed him from the neck down. He alleged that the cause of the collapse was the second defendant referee's mismanagement of the engagement of the scrum and his failure to adhere to specific safety rules that were in place for the protection of front row forwards. The court held that referees and other match officials owe a duty to ensure that those playing the game under their control are reasonably safe and that by failing to impose a variety of safety rules specifically designed to prevent scrums from collapsing, the referee was in breach of that duty of care. Further, the claimant could not be considered to have voluntarily run the risk of injury from the second defendant's failure to uphold the safety rules; although he did agree to run the inherent risks involved with playing in the front row, he did not agree to the referee failing to ensure that the game was being played safely.

Liability will only rarely be imposed on match officials. Evidence to support a claim of negligence will usually have to focus on their failure to impose or uphold the safety rules of a sport or on their having acted outside of their sphere of competence, for example, by refereeing a level or type of match for which they were not qualified, as was part of the problem in *Smoldon*. In reality, although most actions will be brought against the referee, the aim will be to secure a payout from the referee's own insurers or, if vicarious liability can be proved, against the insurers of the sport's governing body.

5.3.1   Establishing a claim

5.3.1.1 *Duty of care*

The extension of liability in negligence to match officials was a natural incremental step for the law to take. There are no logical, legal or policy reasons why match officials should be immune from the operation of the law if they behave with such a degree of incompetence that they cause injury to those who are playing sport under their control. After reviewing the previous authorities on sports negligence, both the trial judge and the Court of Appeal in *Smoldon* came to the conclusion that a match official did owe a duty of care to the players and that full account must be taken of the factual context in which the incident occurred. This involved a simple application of negligence in all the circumstances applied to a novel situation: referees officiating a fast-moving contact sport.

In defining the applicable duty, the Court took into consideration that referees provide a 'protective mantle' for the players under their control and that they must ensure that the game is played with the players' safety in mind. Thus, the match officials owe all of the players in the game a duty to take reasonable care to enforce the rules of the particular sport, to apply them fairly, to control the match in a manner that does not expose the players to an unnecessary risk of injury and, in this particular case, to have especial regard to the age of the players as this was an under-19s match.

Referees will not be liable for injuries caused by the inherent risks of participation in an activity. They will, however, be liable for their failure to ensure that the players are able to play the game in a reasonably safe environment. *Smoldon* ensures that this includes upholding the safety rules of the sport in question, but there is no reason why this could not be extended to the various pre-match inspections that the officials must carry out, including, for example, whether the playing surface is safe and free from dangerous articles, whether playing equipment (like studs) meets relevant guidelines and whether goalposts are erected properly and padded where necessary (see further, chapter 8.2.5).

Again, this is a duty to act reasonably, not to ensure absolutely that no injury can take place. As Bingham LCJ held in *Smoldon* at p.139,

> [The referee] could not be properly held liable for errors of judgement, oversights or lapses of which any referee might be guilty in the context of a fast-moving and vigorous contest. The threshold of liability is a high one. It will not be easily crossed.

This last comment explains why so few cases involving the negligence of match officials have been reported. Liability will only be imposed where the number or seriousness of the breaches committed cannot be considered to be an inherent risk of participation in the sport.

5.3.1.2 Breach of duty and the appropriate standard of care

The standard of care against which a match official will be judged is that of the reasonable and competent person officiating at that level of the sport being played. They will be expected to know and to apply the relevant playing and safety rules and to control the players in a way that avoids them being caused or causing each other injury. The reported cases involving referees raise very different issues regarding breach of duty. In the first three cases, the claimant suffered a broken neck following the collapse of a scrum; in the fourth, the claimant was seriously injured by a crash in a motocross event

In *Smoldon*, the sheer number of instances of mismanagement of the game ultimately led to the referee being found liable. This was not a case of a referee making the occasional mistake in the heat of the moment but a prolonged period of incompetent refereeing. It was found that the referee:

▶ Failed to ensure that each scrum consisted of eight players from each side; each team had had a forward sent off, one after 25 minutes play, the other 20 minutes into the second half. Thus, for 35 minutes, the scrums were unstable and wheeling, placing additional strain and pressure on the necks and backs of the front row forwards.
▶ Failed to use the 'crouch-touch-pause-engage' procedure to ensure that the scrums were set correctly without the two packs of forwards charging into each other with undue force.
▶ Ignored the warnings and advice of the two touch judges, who were also the coaches of the two contesting teams.
▶ Failed to establish why the scrums were continually collapsing, thereby allowing between three and four times the normal number of collapses for a game at this level.

Any of these mistakes, particularly his allowing at least 25 scrums to collapse, provides potent evidence of negligence. Taken as a whole, this course of conduct was sufficient evidence to prove that the referee had dropped below the standard of conduct expected of him.

In *Vowles v Evans and The Welsh Rugby Union Ltd* [2003] EWCA Civ 318, the seriousness of an incorrect decision formed the basis of the referee's liability. The claimant was the hooker for Llanharan RFC. When one of the prop forwards with whom he was playing had to leave the field with an injury, Llanharan had no trained front-row replacement to act as his substitute. The team captain, who had some experience of playing prop, offered to fulfil the role and informed the referee that he was capable of playing in this specialist position.

When a scrum collapsed later in the game, the referee was held liable for the claimant's resulting injuries on the basis that he should not have allowed the Llanharan captain the choice to try himself out in the prop forward position. Either they had a specialist front-row replacement who could be used, in which case the game could continue without any necessary changes to the playing rules, or they did not, in which case depowered scrums, where no pushing is allowed, should have been imposed. By allowing the Llanharan captain the option to determine that he was a specialist, instead of insisting on them using either a specialist front-row replacement or moving to depowered scrums, the referee had breached his duty to apply the safety rules of the sport, resulting in the very injury that the rule was designed to prevent.

A further issue, similar to that in *Smoldon*, also arises in the case, although it was not fully explored in the judgments because the referee's failure to impose depowered scrums was considered to be so serious as to dispose of the issue of negligence. The scrum that caused the claimant's injuries occurred over 50 minutes after the replacement of the original prop forward by the Llanharan captain. At almost every scrum from that point onwards, there was at least one collapse. The referee should have carried out a constant review of the replacement front row's competence and, when it became apparent that he was not able to scrummage safely, the referee should have moved to depowered scrums. In this way, the replacement could have been given the opportunity to prove that he had the necessary skills to play in the position, yet the referee would have retained the ability to declare that the player was, in fact, incompetent to play at prop forward. Using either approach, the seriousness of his oversights was sufficient to justify the imposition of liability.

In *Allport v Wilbraham* [2004] EWCA Civ 1668, the lack of evidence and unreliability of the claimant and his witnesses led to a finding of no negligence on the part of the referee. Further, the incident occurred at only the fourth scrummage of the match and after only 20 minutes of play. In contrast to *Smoldon* and *Vowles*, there was no evidence of a sustained course of mismanagement of the safety aspects of the game, making it significantly more difficult for the claimant to establish the match officials' negligence.

Most recently, in *Stanley v Bryn Close t/a Armthorpe Moto Parc* [2009] EWHC 2849, the defendant track owner and organiser of motocross events was held liable for the injuries caused by the negligence of one of his marshals. The accident happened following the restart of a practice session after an accident had required the riders to come to a stop. Once the original accident had been cleared, one of the track marshals lowered his yellow flag, indicating proceed from restart with caution, before noticing that the claimant had stalled and had not exited his area of control. Before the marshal could raise his red 'stop-danger' flag to prevent riders from entering the jump zone under his control, two riders accelerated up the slope and jumped onto the flat surface at its top; one of them hit the claimant in the head with his bike. The defendant was found vicariously liable in negligence for the track marshal's failure to operate his section of the course reasonably safely, and directly liable for failing to provide adequate training to the marshals in his employ.

5.3.1.3 Foreseeability of harm

It was argued in *Smoldon* that to be actionable, a serious spinal injury should be a highly probable outcome of a collapsed scrum and that as it was not, then such a serious injury could not be considered to be reasonably foreseeable. As was held by the court, this would set the test for causation at too high a level. The outcome of the negligent conduct does not need to be a probable outcome, just one that is not fanciful or far-fetched. In other words, because it is reasonably foreseeable as a possibility that a collapsed scrum may cause a serious spinal injury to a front-row forward, causation in law is established.

5.3.2   Defences

The two usual defences of *volenti* and contributory negligence may be available to a match official accused of negligence. Both will, however, be difficult to raise successfully unless the claimant player has in some way actively contributed to the harm that he has suffered. In *Smoldon*, the defendant referee argued that because the claimant was aware of the rules of the game and the dangers associated with collapsed scrums, he had impliedly consented to the risk of injury being caused by the non-application of the various safety rules. In respect of *volenti*, Bingham LCJ stated in *Smoldon* at p.146:

> The [claimant] had of course consented to the ordinary incidents of a game of rugby football of the kind in which he was taking part. Given, however, that the rules were framed for the protection of him and other players in the same position, he cannot possibly be said to have consented to a breach of duty on the part of the official whose duty it was to apply the rules and ensure so far as possible that they were observed. If the [claimant] were identified as a prime culprit in causing the collapse of the scrums, then [*volenti* and contributory negligence] might call for consideration.

Thus, if a scrum collapses in the ordinary course of the playing of the game, it will be considered to be a non-actionable inherent risk of the sport, as occurred in *Allport*. Where the match officials have failed to implement the safety rules of the sport and injury is caused as a result of this mismanagement of the game, then negligence will be established and no defence can be raised by the match officials against the claim. Such a conclusion is reinforced by the fact that in most sports in general, and rugby union in particular, there is little or no scope to debate these issues with the match officials without the risk of disciplinary sanctions being imposed. The failure to complain about the risks created by the match officials will not lead to a finding that the claimant has agreed to run them, though following *Anderson v Lyotier* (above, 5.2.2) this may lead to a reduction in damages in certain limited circumstances on the basis of contributory negligence. *Volenti* will fail, however, because the players do not agree to run the risk of injury from the match officials' failure to enforce the safety rules of the game.

As noted by Bingham LCJ, the possibility of a successful claim of contributory negligence is increased where the claimant has, to some degree, contributed to the occurrence of the injury-causing incident. His Lordship identified specifically that where the claimant is the main cause of the collapse, a finding of contributory negligence will be appropriate. Other situations where the defence may succeed could include where the claimant is aware that he or she lacks the appropriate skills to perform a specific task or play in a specific position. For example, if the Llanharan captain had been injured whilst playing at prop forward, then as he was aware that he lacked the necessary experience and training to play there, a finding of contributory negligence would have been appropriate. Unless there has been a specific agreement to run a risk or the claimant has voluntarily and knowingly continued to participate in the specific risky environment, then *volenti* and contributory negligence will be extremely difficult for a match official to establish where they are overseeing a game that is being played without adherence to the necessary safety rules and procedures.

5.4   Governing bodies and international federations

This is the least-explored area of liability for sports injuries. Although most challenges to the actions of an NGB or ISF occur in respect of their general administrative decisions (see further Chapters 2 and 3), the UK courts have accepted that it is fair, just and reasonable to impose a duty of care on them in respect of the safety of sports participants in certain circumstances. The definition and scope of this duty has not yet been fully established or explored before the courts.

Actions based on vicarious liability can be brought against NGBs and ISFs in their roles as employers, just as they can against other organisations. *Vowles* established that an NGB can be vicariously liable for the negligent conduct of its referees. Further, where an NGB employs players, coaches and other support staff for its international teams or uses a system of central contracts for elite performers these will be treated as being analogous to the position of professional clubs (see further, chapter 4.5 and above 5.2.1). This section will focus on the direct liability of NGBs and ISFs for harm caused to athletes.

5.4.1 Establishing a claim

5.4.1.1 Duty of care

The duty of care owed by an NGB derives from the need for the safety of the competitors to be its paramount concern. This can be defined as being the duty to take reasonable care to ensure the safety of the participants taking part in the sporting activity (*Watson v British Boxing Board of Control* [2001] QB 1134). It can be activated in three main spheres of activity: pre-event administrative checks and the granting of licences to organisers; during event safety provision and associated risk-management research; and the playing and safety rules of the game itself.

5.4.1.1.1 Pre-event administration and licensing

Many of the claims brought against NGBs are cases where the organisers of an event have also been sued. The claimant's line of argument is usually that the organiser has dropped below the standard of care expected of them but that this was either because they had been following guidelines prepared negligently by the NGB or that an appropriate permission or licence had been granted negligently to the organiser by the NGB. In either case, the accident would not have occurred if the NGB had taken greater care in discharging its own duty to take reasonable care of the safety of the participants.

The first reported instance of an NGB being sued in negligence for harm caused to a competitor was *Stratton v Hughes and Cumberland Sporting Car Club Ltd and Royal Automobile Club Motor Sports Association Ltd (RAC)* (unreported) Court of Appeal, 17 March 1998. The claimant, the co-driver and navigator of a rally car, sued the driver, event organiser and NGB of the sport. The precise nature of the duty owed is not discussed in great length in the court, however, it is assumed that not only is a duty owed but that it is defined in the same terms as that imposed on the organiser; that there is a duty to take reasonable care for the safety of the competitors and that in the context of a specialist activity such as this, conduct should be assessed by reference to the standards of the reasonable and competent organisers of motor rallies.

The role of the RAC as a defendant is because it has responsibility for the production of the competition regulations and the granting of racing permits. One of the conditions of granting such a permit or licence is that the track is appropriate for the particular event being held and that it is reasonably safe for those using it. Although there had been some minor breaches of its regulations, these had not been causative of the accident that occurred. Thus, as the regulations themselves were not challenged and the court held that in testing the driving skill of the competitors the layout of this particular track was safe, the granting of the permission to race was not negligent. The liability of NGBs and ISFs has, however, been revisited and extended.

▶ *Wattleworth v Goodwood Road Racing Company Ltd and Royal Automobile Club Motor Sports Association Ltd and Federation Internationale de l'Automobile* **[2004] EWHC 140**

Whilst taking part in an informal, non-competitive 'track day' at a motor racing circuit owned and operated by the first defendant, the claimant lost control of his car and crashed into a tyre wall with fatal consequences. The action, brought on behalf of his estate, claimed that the first defendant had acted negligently in its design of the racing track by relying on the advice given to it by the second defendant. Furthermore, it was alleged that the RAC, as NGB and the body responsible for inspecting and licensing motorsports circuits in the UK, and Federation Internationale de l'Automobile (FIA) as ISF and originator of the relevant safety guidelines, owed a duty to take reasonable care to ensure that competent and accurate advice on track design and safety was given to the track owners. It was claimed that this duty should be owed to the deceased as he would have expected that the track would be designed and constructed in a manner that ensured that it was safe enough to be used by drivers such as him.

After a comprehensive review of the relevant sporting and non-sporting authorities, the court came to the conclusion that the RAC owed a duty of care to both the race track owner and those driving on it but that it had not been breached in this case because the appropriate advice had been given by reasonable and competent experts in race track safety. The design of the track and attendant safety features such as the tyre wall were sufficient to ensure that it was reasonably safe for the kind of racing with which the claimant was involved and that the inspections carried out by the second defendant prior to granting the relevant licence had been carried out with appropriate care and skill. No duty was owed to the claimant by the FIA as it had legitimately delegated track safety inspections to the appropriate NGB, the RAC.

The duty to the race track owner is easily justified here. The RAC was the sole body able to inspect and license both racing tracks and motorsport events in the UK. Its inspectors worked closely with the track owners and provided expert technical advice over a prolonged period of time, enabling the owners to construct a track that was in accordance with the then-current safety guidelines issued by the FIA.

The duty owed to the users of the track was justified on the basis that where advice is given by one person to another that has a direct and foreseeable effect on the safety of a third, then the advisor owes a duty to both the advised party and the third party. Although the RAC was only giving advice to enable the track owners to run competitive events, not informal track days, the nature of safety advice given was said to be the 'highest common denominator.' In other words, if the advice was appropriate to enable a competitive event to be run safely, then it would also enable a track day to be run safely.

The FIA owed no duty to either the track owners or the drivers because of the structure of governance in place between it, as the ISF, and the RAC as the NGB. Regarding track safety and inspections, the FIA delegated all responsibility for domestic arrangements to the RAC. It was, therefore, sufficiently removed from the advising and inspection process to be absolved of responsibility for the safety advice given, though the court did note that the FIA maintained responsibility for safety arrangements at all international level meetings. Although no further comment was made on this, presumably if a similar incident was to occur at an international competitive fixture, for example the Formula One British Grand Prix, then a duty commensurate to that owed by the RAC in *Wattleworth* would be imposed.

Thus, an NGB owes a duty to take reasonable care to ensure that the advice it provides to event organisers, whether through inspections or guidelines, is sufficient to enable the organisers to provide facilities that are reasonably safe for the participants in the sport. This duty is also owed to the participants; the advice given must be sufficient to enable them to compete reasonably safely in their chosen sport.

Further, whether or not a duty is owed by an ISF will depend on the relationship between the parties to the action. In *Wattleworth*, the FIA had delegated responsibility for safety to the RAC. In cases where such delegation does not take place, then there is no reason why the ISF should not owe exactly the same duty to both organisers and participants that is owed by the NGB: a duty to take reasonable care to ensure that the advice it provides to event organisers, whether through inspections or guidelines, is sufficient to enable the organisers to provide facilities that are reasonably safe for the participants in the sport and that this advice must be sufficient to enable participants to compete reasonably safely in the circumstances of the sport.

5.4.1.1.2 Safety provision and risk management

Pre-dating *Wattleworth* by several years, *Watson v British Boxing Board of Control* [2001] QB 1134 concerns such an unusual aspect of a governing body's liability in negligence that it requires separate attention. The claimant suffered a catastrophic brain injury from a punch, or series of punches, inflicted on him during the course of a world championship professional boxing bout. His claim was not that boxing was dangerous but that the governing body of professional boxing in the UK, the BBBC, had failed to provide adequate guidelines to those organising boxing contests regarding the quality of ringside medical provision.

> ▶ *Watson v British Boxing Board of Control* [2001] QB 1134
>
> The claimant had been knocked out towards the end of a professional boxing bout, causing him to suffer intra-cranial bleeding. Current best practice guidelines provided that treatment of the bleeding and subsequent clotting should take place as soon as possible and preferably within one hour of the injury occurring. The emergency medical provision required of the event organisers by the defendant did not enable pre-operative procedures and emergency first aid to be carried out within this time frame. Furthermore, the nearest hospital to where the event took place did not have the necessary neurosurgical arrangements in place. The claimant was eventually operated on over 90 minutes after he had lost consciousness in the ring, and this delay in treatment was causative of his lasting brain injury. The court held that the defendant had, through its position as the sole governing body for the sport in the UK, assumed responsibility for determining the nature of the medical facilities and personnel that should be present at a bout and that it should keep itself informed of current best practice relating to all reasonably foreseeable injuries likely to occur during a fight. It was also reasonable for a boxer to rely on the defendant to take reasonable care for his safety during and after a bout. Therefore, the defendant had breached the duty it owed the claimant to take reasonable care of his safety.

Almost the entire discussion in the case focuses on whether or not a duty should be imposed on the BBBC in respect of the medical guidelines that it produced for, and required to be implemented by, the organisers of boxing bouts. The Court of Appeal, in upholding the decision of the trial court, came to a series of important conclusions. Firstly, that because of the degree of control that the BBBC had over every aspect of boxing, it was in the best position to determine what safety protocols ought to be in place. Everyone involved in boxing can only fulfil their role if they have been licensed by the BBBC, leaving it as the sole authority on issues related to participation and safety.

Secondly, that as it considered the safety of boxers to be of paramount importance, the BBBC was under a duty to minimise the risks inherent in this dangerous sport. This included providing guidelines on adequate ringside medical treatment. Thirdly, that this was a body that had, or more rightly ought to have had, special knowledge about the risks involved in the sport that it was overseeing and how those risks could and should be addressed by the drafting of adequate safety protocols. Fourthly, that those advising it on medical and safety issues should have been cognisant of current best practice in the treatment of injuries that were reasonably likely to occur during the course of a bout; this included the initial emergency treatment of serious traumatic brain injuries such as those sustained by the claimant.

In coming to the conclusion that a duty of care was owed to the boxers by the Board, the Court held that the duty was not to take reasonable care to avoid causing personal injury but to take reasonable care to ensure that reasonably foreseeable personal injuries sustained were treated properly. It was fair, just and reasonable to impose a duty on the BBBC because of the degree of control it possessed over the sport as a whole and because it was best placed to keep itself informed on developments in relevant fields of medicine. Finally, as in *Wattleworth*, the governing body owed to the participant a duty to ensure that the advice that it gave to event organisers was sufficiently well prepared to enable the organisers to run a contest safely.

This duty could only be discharged if the BBBC had formulated sufficiently detailed and accurate regulations imposing duties on others to act reasonably and competently. By failing to require suitably qualified medical staff to be present ringside during the bout, with suitable equipment and medical supplies available to them, the BBBC had failed to act as a reasonable and competent governing body and was therefore in breach of its duty towards the boxers fighting under its rules.

Although not explored in other cases, the liability imposed on the BBBC could be imposed on other governing bodies should they fail to take adequate steps to ensure the safety of participants in their sports. Governing bodies need to ensure not only that their game is safe to play but also that there are protocols in place to ensure that an injured player's position is, as a minimum requirement, not made any worse by the actions of those who treat him.

5.4.1.1.3 The rules of the game

To date, there have been no reported cases in the UK of a sports participant suing a rule-making body for the rules of a sport being unsafe. On the face of it, there would appear to be no reason why the law could not be developed incrementally to impose a duty of care on such a body in these circumstances. Indeed, the imposition of a duty, although likely to be fiercely resisted by those who run sport, would not be that much of a step for the law to take in the light of both *Watson* and *Wattleworth*. The difficulty would be in proving that there had been a breach of the duty. This would undoubtedly lead to a rehearsal of the many theoretical and public policy arguments on the meaning and function of sport in our society and to debates on whether it can ever be justifiable to encourage the causing of serious injury in the name of sport and games.

The International Rugby Board was one of the defendants in the Australian case of *Agar v Hyde* [2000] HCA 41, where it was claimed that the known risk of serious neck or spinal injuries being caused by a collapsed scrum was such that it was negligent to allow scrums to continue to be a part of the game. Although the action failed on procedural grounds, there is still a possibility that a similar claim may succeed in the future where the risk of serious injury from the inherent dangers of a sport is high.

This does not mean that ISFs will automatically be found liable for the injuries caused by the dangerous elements of a sport, such as rugby scrums or bouncers in cricket. However, it does mean that they may be required to prove that these elements of their sports are integral to their proper functioning and are as safe as is reasonably practicable. This will mean that risk-management strategies and patterns of injury will need to be reviewed in order to determine whether a sport needs to be made safer and, if so, how. It is unlikely that the potential liability of sports' rule makers will continue to be ignored in the way that it has to date.

Any development in this area of the law will have to be made alongside the further clarification of the role and scope of voluntary assumption of risk and contributory negligence. The vast majority of sports participants are well aware of the degree of risk that they are running when they take part in dangerous sporting activities. As was held in *Anderson v Lyotier, Lyotier and Portejoie* [2008] EWHC 2790 (above, 5.2.2), the decision to run a risk is a collaborative one that is taken by the athlete and, depending on the specific circumstances of the accident, their coach, the match official, and the rule-making body. Thus, the potential liability of NGBs and ISFs for maintaining the riskier aspects of their sports will be ameliorated by the need to impose a degree of responsibility on the participants for their own actions. This could ensure that the unique characteristics of a sport do not need to be changed significantly whilst requiring sports bodies to make their sports as safe as is reasonably practicable.

5.4.1.2 Breach of duty and the appropriate standard of care

The standard of care imposed on an NGB or ISF will follow the same structure as is used in cases involving coaches and match officials; the NGB or ISF will be judged by the standard of the reasonable and competent body in the context in which it is acting, whether as an advisor, licensor or rule maker. It will be expected to make decisions and draft guidance and rules in a competent manner and to ensure that what it produces is defensible; something achieved by the RAC in *Wattleworth* but not by the BBBC in *Watson*.

The main difficulty for a claimant bringing an action against either an NGB or ISF will be providing the necessary evidence to prove that the standard of care has been breached. In each of these cases, many technical experts have given evidence, both from within and outside of sport, in an attempt to establish whether or not the NGB and ISF have acted in a reasonable and competent manner. The difficulty in proving that such a body has acted in breach of this standard of care means that it is likely that negligence will only be established in cases where the governing bodies of sport have failed to keep their technical and safety knowledge up to date, along with training on these matters for their relevant members.

5.4.2 Defences

In *Wattleworth*, although not necessary for the disposal of the case and therefore technically *obiter dicta*, the judge addressed claims of both *volenti non fit injura* and contributory negligence. *Volenti* was considered to be an unsustainable defence for the same reasons that were given in *Smoldon* and *Vowles*; although the participant clearly ran the risks inherently involved with motor racing, such as losing control of his car and crashing, he did not voluntarily run the risk that the body with overall responsibility for the safety of the sport would fail to ensure that the track was safe to use.

More interestingly, Davis J held that had there been a breach of the relevant duties by the defendants, then the claimant would have been held 20 per cent contributorily negligent. This finding was on the basis that the claimant had taken the wrong racing line when entering a corner and allowed his wheels to go on to the grass verge on the outside of the bend and losing control of his vehicle. This demonstrates quite clearly that although establishing a defence is difficult, it is not impossible, particularly where the claimant's lack of skill in performing a manoeuvre has contributed to the extent of the injuries that they have suffered.

5.5 Medical professionals

In recent years, one further group of potential defendants has been added to what is a rapidly-expanding list: medical professionals. To some extent, this is a fairly obvious fusion of the well-established field of medical law with the growing field of sports law. However, the duties imposed on medical practitioners do not always fit well with the way that sports clubs, particularly professional clubs, operate on a day-to-day basis.

The cases of *Bolam* and *Bolitho*, which have already referred to on several occasions, were both medical negligence cases. Both highlight that a duty of care is owed by a medical practitioner to their patients and require that the medic reaches the standard of the reasonable and competent person acting in their field of medicine. This is judged by whether the medical professional's conduct would be considered to have been appropriate according to a competent body of similarly qualified medical practitioners. Where more than one alternative course of conduct is open, then the choice must be capable of being justified logically. The cases discussed here do not doubt or alter this basic approach. Instead, certain specific problems that sports medicine professionals might come across during their practice are highlighted.

5.5.1 First aid and the initial injury

How any initial injury is treated will depend on the sport in question, the level at which it is being played and the medical protocols in place. Following *Watson*, the BBBC overhauled its medical protocols to ensure that emergency treatment and preparation for major surgery can be performed ringside by appropriately qualified experts at professional boxing bouts.

The initial treatment carried out at the scene of injury will attract, as a minimum, a duty not to make the injured person's situation any worse. Depending on who else is required to be present during the game, duties appropriate to the level of qualification of the medical personnel present and the equipment and medical supplies to which they have access will be imposed. Where the initial treatment is carried out by someone who holds a first aid certificate, they will be judged by the standard of the reasonable and competent first aider, *Catley v St John's Ambulance Brigade* (unreported) High Court, 25 November 1988. A growing number of sports now require anyone providing initial on-field first aid to hold a specialist certificate. For example, the FA Premier League requires the attending medical officer to hold the Advanced Resuscitation and Emergency Aid

Certificate, the Rugby Football League requires the Immediate Medical Management on the Field of Play certificate and the Rugby Football Union requires the Pitch-side Immediate Trauma Care certificate. In these cases, the defendant will be judged by the standard of the reasonable sports medic qualified in immediate trauma care. Where, as in boxing, more specialised personnel are required to be present, these will be judged by the standards of their specific specialism, such as the reasonable and competent anaesthetist.

5.5.2 The design and implementation of return to fitness programmes

Where a physiotherapist, for example, is part of the team designing a rehabilitation or return to fitness programme, they must also ensure that they discharge their duties in a manner that is both reasonable and competent. The programme must be appropriate for the player, the sport and the injury that they have suffered. The medical professional must also ensure that they have properly and accurately advised the player on when he or she is actually fit to return to play. Just because the player wishes to return to play before being fit enough to do so, or the club insists that they return before being physically and mentally ready, does not absolve the club of responsibility. Where the use of drugs is part of the rehabilitation programme, the athlete remains responsible for ensuring that they have not breached the relevant provisions of the WADA Code or have applied for an appropriate Therapeutic Use Exemption (Art.4.4 WADA Code), *Baxter v International Olympic Committee* CAS 2002/A/376 (see further, chapter 3.3.3).

Where a potential conflict of interest such as this arises, accurate and contemporaneous note-taking is essential. In *Brady v Sunderland AFC Ltd* (unreported) Court of Appeal, 17 November 1998, although the quality of the notes taken by a member of the medical team was poor, they were sufficient to demonstrate that appropriate action had been taken in trying to determine the nature of the condition suffered by the claimant.

5.5.3 Referrals for specialist medical treatment

Where an injury is particularly serious, it may require treatment from a specialist rather than a member of the club's in-house medical team.

> ▶ *West Bromwich Albion Football Club Ltd v El-Safty* [2006] EWCA Civ 1299
>
> The defendant consultant surgeon had operated on a member of the claimant's first team professional football squad. The defendant had admitted acting negligently in treating the injury with the result that the player had been forced to retire prematurely from professional football. The claimant brought an action arguing that the defendant owed it a duty to perform the diagnosis and operation competently and that as he had not done so, they should be able to claim from him the losses, running into millions of pounds, that they had incurred as a result of needing to recruit a replacement player of similar quality.
>
> The Court of Appeal held that where referrals such as this were concerned, the medical professional owed a duty of care to act reasonably and competently only to their actual patient, not to the patient's employer. This was despite the fact that the referral was made by one of the club's in-house medical team, that the bill was sent to the club and that it was ultimately to be paid for by the club's medical insurance. Even though a negligently performed operation would lead to reasonably foreseeable loss to the club, in that it would have to incur additional expenditure in recruiting a replacement for him, no duty to act with reasonable care and skill was owed to them.

5.5.4 Confidentiality and the disclosure of medical records

The last two points also raise issues relating to doctor-patient confidentiality and the disclosure of medical records. In general, a medical professional cannot disclose the medical records of their patient to anyone else without the patient's consent as they are confidential. In practice, medical records can be disclosed in certain situations.

Firstly, because of the size of many modern medical teams, a number of staff may require access to a patient's records. In this situation, the patient's consent to disclose their medical records to enable effective treatment by the team is given implicitly.

Secondly, where an examination is required by an employer to determine whether an employee is fit for work, the notes of the examination can be disclosed to the employer. The General Medical Council's guidance on this point recommends that the purpose of the examination and scope of its disclosure be explained to the patient and that a copy of the report be given to them as well as the employer. For good measure, the patient's consent to disclose the information should be sought at the outset of the examination. Thus, where a member of the in-house medical team examines a player to determine whether they are fit to play, the outcome of such an examination can be disclosed to the team manager or coach to enable a decision to be made regarding the player's fitness, although the player ought to be made aware of this in advance.

However, in the *El-Safty* situation above, the consultant owed the duty of confidentiality to the patient alone and was not in a position to disclose the results of his initial negligent examination to the football club. The only situation in which West Bromwich Albion could have legitimately come into possession of the medical records would have been if the player had consented to their disclosure.

In many professional sports, a clause will be inserted into the employment contract of the player granting explicit consent to the club to have access to all of their medical records and reports. If such a clause exists, even if the external medical professional were to refuse to disclose the medical report to anyone other than the patient, the player would then be contractually obliged to disclose the information to the club.

Hot topic ... **Developing defences to claims of sporting negligence**

After the rapid expansion of the law of negligence into so many sporting relationships in the 1990s and early 2000s, the courts have more recently begun to check this juridification of sporting disputes through the application of two key defences: *volenti non fit injuria*, or voluntary assumption of risk, and contributory negligence. This judicial brake on sports negligence claims mirrors the position of Parliament and its own attempts to control what is often referred to as the UK's 'compensation culture'.

By s.1 Compensation Act 2006, judges must specifically take into consideration when determining liability in negligence whether a finding against the defendant might discourage or prevent the provision of a desirable activity that brings benefit to the community, such as is the case with organised sports. This legislative direction has only rarely been relied on explicitly by the judiciary, with *Sutton v Syston Rugby Football Club Ltd* [2011] EWCA Civ 1182 (see further, 8.2.5.1) being

one of the very few sporting references to the provision; however, its underlying sentiment is clearly influencing judicial reasoning in cases involving sporting activities and attempts to limit the scope of defendants' liability.

The application of *volenti*, in conjunction with analyses of breach of duty, has been used to justify how and why injuries caused by the inherent dangers of a sport are not actionable. It has been accepted by the courts in both *Smoldon v Whitworth* and

Allport v Wilbraham (as well as in other rugby playing common law countries such as Australia in *Hyde v Agar* and Canada in *Hamstra v British Columbia Rugby Union* (1989) 1 CCLT (2d) 78), that injuries caused by collapsing scrums are an inherent risk of playing in one of the forward positions in rugby union. Similarly, being punched in the head is an inherent risk of competing as a boxer, *Watson v BBBC*. What is not an inherent risk of competing in these sports, however, is that the match officials and NGBs will fail to have sufficient regard for the safety of the athletes. *Volenti* will not apply in these situations but will help to explain why liability is not imposed for inherent risks. This defence has become particularly important in the occupiers' liability cases where the claimant has ignored safety warnings, *Tomlinson v Congleton Borough Council* [2003] UKHL 47,

or taken an obvious risk, *Grimes v Hawkins* [2011] EWHC 2004 (see further Chapter 8).

Even more important is the development of the law of contributory negligence as it allows for the apportionment of blame between the parties rather than absolving the defendant completely from responsibility for his negligent conduct. The detailed analysis of its application to sports negligence cases in *Anderson v Lyotier* is extremely important to the future development of the law in these cases. By acknowledging the symbiotic relationship between athlete and coach, as *Smoldon* had between players and match officials, the court accepted that the decision-making process is rarely the exclusive responsibility of one person. Instead, the claimant's knowledge of the risks inherent in a sport (*Allport*), his own levels of skill and competence (*Anderson*)

or the lower standards employed in less regulated environments (*Gouldbourn*) have ensured that it is essential to examine not only the defendant's conduct but also the claimant's.

The combination of these two defences with the generally more sophisticated analyses of breach of duty and applicable standard of care that are now undertaken by the courts means that claimants can no longer guarantee being able to recover the entirety of their damages. The law will continue to provide sporting activities with the protection required to ensure that they can continue without undue interference in line with the underlying rationale of s.1 Compensation Act 2006, but what this approach also requires is that claimants take greater personal responsibility for their own safety when engaging in inherently risky sporting activities.

Summary

5.1 After a comparatively late entry to the field of litigation, sports negligence cases have mushroomed in recent years. Successful claims have been made against defendants who have acted in almost every role connected to the playing, coaching and administering of sport and at all levels of participation.

5.2 Coaches and instructors must ensure that they conduct appropriate risk assessments on all participants and equipment to ensure their suitability for the particular session that they are running. However, participants cannot abdicate all responsibility for their personal safety to their coach. Following *Anderson v Lyotier, Lyotier and Portejoie*, they must bring to their coach's attention any concerns that they have over their own competence to participate in a particular activity.

5.3 Referees and match officials must ensure that they enforce the safety rules of the sport under their control, as the safety of the players is of paramount importance. Where they fail to do so, and an injury occurs that should have been prevented by the application of the rule the referee will be liable for breaching their duty to ensure that the game has been played in a reasonably safe manner.

5.4 Litigation involving NGBs and ISFs is currently an under-explored field. Although actions against the bodies running sport are likely to increase as claimants search for the defendant most capable of paying their compensation, the creation, implementation and regular revision of effective risk-management procedures should ensure that few cases against them can be sustained.

Summary cont'd

5.5 Although the reported cases to date have focussed on injuries caused to professional sports participants, sports-medical litigation is already having an impact on the practice of medicine in this area. The professionalisation of sports and exercise medicine, at the expense of the 'man with the cold sponge' is creating an environment where players' health is taken more seriously than in the past. The creation of the Faculty of Sports and Exercise Medicine is clarifying further the standard of conduct required of those working in this specialist field of medical practice.

Further reading

Beloff et al, *Sports Law* (2nd edn, 2012, Hart) ch 5

Jackson, *Medical Law: text, cases and materials* (2nd edn, 2010, Oxford University Press) ch 3

Lewis and Taylor (eds), *Sport: Law and Practice* (2nd edn, 2008, Tottel) ch D5

Steele, *Tort Law: text, cases and materials* (2nd edn, 2010, Oxford University Press) chs 3 and 5

Elvin, 'Liability for negligently refereeing of a rugby match' (2003) 119 *Law Quarterly Review* 560

Gardiner, Liability for sporting injuries' [2008] 1 *Journal of Personal Injury Law* 16

George, 'Negligent rule-making in the Court of Appeal' (2002) 65(1) *Modern Law Review* 106

Kevan, 'Sports personal injury' [2005] 3 *International Sports Law Review* 61

James and Gillett, 'Sports medicine and the law – defining the standard of care' [2009] Apr *Sports Law and Practice* 11

James and Gillett, 'Immediate treatment for on-field injuries' [2009] Jun *Sports Law Administration and Practice* 1

Morgan, 'Tort, insurance and incoherence' (2004) 67(3) *Modern Law Review* 384

Norris, 'The duty of care owed by instructors in a sporting context' [2010] 4 *Journal of Personal Injury Law* 183

Opie, 'Negligence liability of rule making bodies in sport' [2002] 2 *International Sports Law Review* 60

Links to relevant websites can be found at www.palgrave.com/law/james2e

Sports participation and the criminal law

Regulating athletes' conduct with the criminal law (6.1)
- The role of sports disciplinary tribunals (6.1.1)

Criminal violence in sports (6.2)
- Overview of the applicable offences (6.2.1)
  - Common assault (6.2.1.1)
  - Offences Against the Person Act 1861 s.47 – assault occasioning actual bodily harm (6.2.1.2)
  - Offences Against the Person Act 1861 s.20 – assault inflicting grievous bodily harm (6.2.1.3)
  - Offences Against the Person Act 1861 s.18 – causing grievous bodily harm or wounding with intent (6.2.1.4)
- R v Barnes – prosecuting sports violence (6.2.2)
- Application of the law and sentencing (6.2.3)
  - Common assault (6.2.3.1)
  - Offences Against the Person Act 1861 s.47 (6.2.3.2)
  - Offences Against the Person Act 1861 s.20 (6.2.3.3)
  - Offences Against the Person Act 1861 s.18 (6.2.3.4)
- Defences (6.2.4)
  - Consent (6.2.4.1)
  - Involuntary reflex (6.2.4.2)
- Homicide (6.2.5)
  - Unlawful act manslaughter (6.2.5.1)
  - Corporate manslaughter (6.2.5.2)

Public disorder and racism (6.3)
- Public Order Act 1986 ss. 4A and 5 – causing harassment, alarm and distress (6.3.1)
- Breach of the peace and inciting crowd disorder (6.3.2)
- Racial abuse (6.3.3)
- Assaulting the crowd (6.3.4)

Match fixing, spot-fixing and corruption (6.4)
- Criminal conspiracies (6.4.1)
- Fraud Act 2006 – fraud (6.4.2)
- Gambling Act 2005 s.42 – cheating at gambling (6.4.3)

Sexual offences and child abuse (6.5)

Sports participation and the criminal law

Key terms

- ▶ **Assault** – intentionally or recklessly, the defendant causes another person to apprehend the immediate infliction of unlawful personal force upon themselves.
- ▶ **Battery** – the intentional or reckless infliction of unlawful force on another person by the defendant.
- ▶ **Consent** – where, expressly or by implication from the surrounding circumstances, the victim allows the defendant to apply force to their person; in sport, the victim consents to all injury-causing contacts that are part of the acceptable way of playing the particular game.
- ▶ **Mens rea** – the state of mind required to commit a criminal offence, for example, intention or recklessness.
- ▶ **Match-fixing** – deliberately manipulating the outcome of a sporting event with a view to winning, or enabling others to win, at gambling.
- ▶ **Spot-fixing** – deliberately manipulating a specific element of a sporting contest with a view to winning, or enabling others to win, at gambling.

6.1 Regulating athletes' conduct with the criminal law

One of the oldest interactions between sport and the law is the prosecution of players for acts of violence towards each other. The first prosecution for violent conduct, *R v Bradshaw* (1878) 14 Cox CC 83 (below, 6.2 and 6.2.7.1), occurred over a hundred years before the corresponding first reported negligence claim in *Condon v Basi* [1985] 1 WLR 866 (see further, chapter 4.4.1.1); many of the cases relating to boxing are even older (see chapter 7).

Although rarely resorted to, the Public Order Act 1986 has also been used to punish incidences of anti-social behaviour amongst players where their actions have the potential to result in crowd disorder (R *v* Bowyer (unreported) Newcastle Magistrates' Court, 5 July 2005, see further, chapter 6.3.1). Throughout 2011 and 2012, racist abuse made the headlines both on the field of play and on Twitter, raising the possibility that racially-aggravated public order offences had been committed by the players concerned (see further, 6.3.3).

Finally, developments in gambling technology and organized crime have seen a growth in match-fixing and its more sophisticated offspring, spot-fixing. The regulation of corruption is a key focus of many governing bodies and a growing number have established their own anti-corruption units. Offences under the Fraud Act 2006, the common law offence of conspiracy to defraud and cheating at gambling under s.42 Gambling Act 2005 can all apply to anyone involved in sports betting scandals.

The ongoing battle between the proponents of internal self-regulation and external legal regulation has been at the heart of the discussions of the regulation of sport by the criminal law and is a major theme of this chapter. As the law becomes increasingly settled, a pattern of response is emerging where the more serious the misconduct, the more likely it is that criminal charges will be pursued, particularly where participants attack spectators, racially abuse opponents or fix matches, or coaches abuse young athletes under their supervision.

6.1.1 The role of sports disciplinary tribunals

Although more pronounced at the elite level of sport, fewer criminal cases are being reported from all levels of the sporting pyramid. The increased robustness of many tribunals' procedures has ensured that many clearly criminal acts are no longer considered appropriate for the criminal justice system (see further, chapter 2) and the legalisation of NGBs' procedural justice has restricted athletes' opportunities to complain that they have been treated unfairly. For example, the decisions of the FA Commission in the racial abuse case against Luis Suarez and violent conduct case against Joey Barton follow the same structure and level of detail and are perhaps even longer than a corresponding legal judgment would be (see further, 6.3.3 and 6.2.3). Further, the more stringent the penalty imposed, the less cause there is for the victim to complain that the incident had not been treated with an appropriate degree of seriousness, whilst in many anti-corruption cases, the entire investigation replicates that which would be seen operated by the criminal justice system. This raises an important point of discussion: whether self-regulation is more appropriate in these circumstances than legal regulation and whether it is ever appropriate for any form of violent conduct to be dealt with outside of the criminal justice system.

6.2 Criminal violence in sports

The courts and some commentators have long held that in-game violence should be treated in exactly the same way as of violence committed anywhere else; this has rarely occurred in practice. There is no clear reason why this should be the case, though there are a number of possible explanations. Firstly, that injury, even where deliberately inflicted, is often considered to be an inherent risk of playing sport that players should tolerate. Secondly, there appears to be a general feeling amongst athletes that these issues should be sorted out within the sport itself, either by retaliation during the game or by the relevant governing body's disciplinary tribunal after the event. Thirdly, that sports violence is not real violence and should not get in the way of the everyday workings of the courts.

Bradshaw set the scene for how the criminal law ought to develop in respect of sports assaults. In directing the jury on whether a fatal challenge of an opponent was criminal, or simply part of the lawful playing of the game, Bramwell LJ stated at p.85 that:

> 'No rules or practice of any game whatever can make that lawful which is unlawful by the law of the land … [If] a man is playing according to the rules and practice of the game and not going beyond it, it may be reasonable to infer … that he is not acting in a manner which he knows will be likely to be productive of death or injury. But … if the [defendant] intended to cause serious hurt to the deceased, or … was indifferent or reckless as to whether he would produce serious injury or not, then the act would be unlawful.'

Much like the corresponding tortious cases (see further, chapter 4.4.1.3), the court required an analysis of the player's conduct in the specific context of it having taken place whilst playing a lawful contact sport, rather than treating the challenge as a random act of violence. Bramwell LJ directed the jury to consider whether the act was in accordance not just with the rules of the game, but with its 'rules and practice'.

Unfortunately, 'practice' is not defined in the judgment but must mean something beyond a strict interpretation of the rules of the sport in question. This paves the way for a wider interpretation of acceptable conduct that has been referred to by Williams as a sport's 'working culture' and, more recently, as its 'playing culture' (see further, chapter 4.4.1.3 and below, 6.2.3), concepts wide enough to encompass not just acts that are within a sport's constituent rules but also acts of commonly-occurring foul play.

When these issues were revisited by the courts a century later, it was clear that the judiciary were unwilling to impose the full force of the law on those committing sports assaults. In *R v Billinghurst* [1978] Crim LR 553, the defendant argued that he had not committed the offence of inflicting grievous bodily harm contrary to s.20 Offences Against the Person Act 1861 (see further, 6.2.1.3) because fighting in rugby union was commonplace and therefore consented to. The judge rejected this line of argument and held that players consent in law only to applications of force that are of a kind that could reasonably be expected to occur during a game and that there was no unlimited licence to use force against an opponent. Despite breaking his victim's jaw in two places, the defendant's nine-month prison sentence was suspended for two years.

The continuing lack of reported cases on sports assaults, particularly at appellate level, made it difficult to identify a coherent set of principles that were underpinning judicial thinking in this area. This was reinforced in the Law Commission's two Consultation Papers on the law of consent. The first of these, *Consent and Offences against the Person* (LCCP No 134, 1994), focuses on determining the reasonableness of the defendant's conduct as the key to determining their criminal liability, though without explaining how this is to be determined across a range of sports. The second, *Consent in the Criminal Law* (LCCP No 139, 1995), proposes in the light of responses to LCCP No 134 that sports participants should be able to consent to all injury inflicted within the rules of the game but not to deliberately inflicted harm or recklessly inflicted 'seriously disabling injury'. The former proposal ignores the developments of the law concerning the playing culture of a sport, whilst the latter predicates criminality on the degree of injury caused rather than the legality of the contact made, meaning that a defendant would have to wait until the outcome of a challenge was known before being able to determine whether an assault had been committed. These proposals have not resulted in the promised third and final Paper, leaving the law in a state of flux until clarification was provided by *R v Barnes* [2004] EWCA Crim 3246 (see further, 6.2.3).

6.2.1 Overview of the applicable offences

The foundations of the law of offences against the person are found in the definition of common assault. This crime can be committed in two ways: by assaulting another person or by battering them. Although 'assault' and 'battery' have very specific meanings in the criminal law, the term 'assault' is generally used, whichever of the two meanings is at issue. The aggravated offences of assault in the Offences Against the Person Act 1861 (OAPA 1861) all require that the defendant has committed a common assault in the first instance; the actual offence charged is dependent on the severity of the harm caused to the victim and the defendant's *mens rea* when the assault was committed.

One of the key issues in these cases can be the choice of offence with which to charge the defendant. Unfortunately, the factors affecting this choice are not reported in the cases, creating confusion where the same injuries can result in successful charges under either ss.47 or 20 OAPA 1861. There are three main reasons why similar injuries might be prosecuted under either of these two sections. Firstly, as there are no formal definitions of the two main levels of harm that a victim might suffer, the determination of whether an injury constitutes actual or grievous bodily harm is not an exact science. Secondly, a player may be charged with the more serious offence under s.20 in the hope that they will then plead guilty to the lesser offence under s.47 and avoid the need for a trial. Thirdly, the defendant might not have the requisite *mens rea* for the s.20 offence (below, 6.2.1.2–3).

6.2.1.1 Common assault

An assault is where the defendant intentionally or recklessly causes the victim to apprehend the immediate infliction of unlawful personal force to their person; it is the threat that unlawful contact will be made with the victim. Battery is the intentional or reckless application of force to the victim, the carrying out of the threat (*Fagan v Metropolitan Police Commissioner* [1969] 1 QB 439). It is touching another person without their consent that is the crime, not causing them harm.

The aim of the offence is to prevent any unwanted interference with a person's bodily integrity by criminalising the merest touching of another person. However, where the victim has consented to the touching, the defendant will have a complete defence to the charge (below, 6.2.6.1). Common assaults, technically batteries, form the basis of all offences against the person committed by sports participants. If the initial common assault cannot be proved, then no offence has been committed.

The *mens rea* of battery is that the defendant acted intentionally or recklessly when making contact with the victim (*R v Savage; DPP v Parmenter* [1992] 1 AC 699). 'Intention' means that the defendant desired to make contact with or apply physical force to the victim, for example, by pushing or punching them. Alternatively, the offence can be committed subjectively recklessly, where the defendant foresaw the risk of making contact with the victim but carried on regardless. For example, a footballer can foresee that they not only might get the ball but also might come into contact with the opposing player when attempting a sliding tackle. By carrying on with the challenge regardless of the possibility of making contact with their opponent, the defendant acts subjectively recklessly. The *mens rea* for battery is the same for all of the assault offences discussed in this chapter, though some of the aggravated offences in the OAPA 1861 require additional elements of *mens rea* regarding the degree of harm caused to the victim.

6.2.1.2 Offences Against the Person Act 1861 s.47 – assault occasioning actual bodily harm

The most common charge in a case of sports assault is under s.47 OAPA 1861. This offence is committed where the defendant intentionally or recklessly assaults another person and, as a matter of fact, the assault causes the victim actual bodily harm (ABH). Put simply, it is a common assault that causes the victim ABH. The *mens rea* is the same as for common assault: the defendant must have intentionally or recklessly made contact with the victim. However, no further *mens rea* is required for the causing of ABH; if the assault causes ABH, then the s.47 offence is committed. ABH is not defined in the Act but over the years has come to mean any harm that interferes with the health and comfort of the victim. From a practical perspective, this will include serious bruising, concussion and most minor fractures.

6.2.1.3 Offences Against the Person Act 1861 s.20 – assault inflicting grievous bodily harm

The s.20 offence also requires that the defendant intentionally or recklessly assaults another person. However, both the degree and/or type of harm caused must be more serious and there are more stringent *mens rea* requirements than under s.47.

For a charge under s.20 OAPA 1861, the victim must suffer either grievous bodily harm (GBH) or a wound. GBH is not defined in the Act but has been described as being really serious harm, such as major fractures and internal injuries (*R v Miller* [1954] 2 QB 282). For historical reasons, wounds of whatever degree of severity are considered to be particularly serious types of injury and are therefore specifically included in this section. A wound is any injury that breaks the external skin of the victim (*Moriarty v Brookes* (1834) 6 C&P 684).

In addition to the initial *mens rea* that the contact must be made intentionally or recklessly, s.20 also requires that the defendant foresaw that the assault would cause some harm to the victim (*R v Savage; DPP v Parmenter* [1992] 1 AC 699). The defendant does not need to foresee that the assault will cause either GBH or a wound, just that some harm will result from the contact. Thus, a defendant can commit the s.20 OAPA 1861 offence without intending or even appreciating in advance the precise degree of harm ultimately caused to the victim.

6.2.1.4 Offences Against the Person Act 1861 s.18 – causing grievous bodily harm or wounding with intent

Section 18 OAPA 1861 is the most serious of the non-fatal offences against the person. It can be defined succinctly as being where the defendant committed an intentional assault with the intent to cause GBH or a wound to the victim. Where there was no intent to cause GBH or a wound, only to assault, then the defendant must be charged under s.20 OAPA 1861. The high degree of intention required by s.18 OAPA 1861 means that charges under this section are comparatively rare in sport.

6.2.2 *R v Barnes* – prosecuting sports violence

The application of the criminal law to sports violence has been clarified substantially by the case of *Barnes*. In a wide-ranging judgment, the Court of Appeal explained the public policy underpinning its approach to prosecuting sports assaults, the situations in which a prosecution is appropriate and the circumstances that must be taken into account when deciding whether an injury-causing act is an unlawful assault or lawfully consented to as an integral part of the game being played.

▶ *R v Barnes* [2004] EWCA Crim 3246

Towards the end of a football match, the victim, a forward, gained control of the ball and ran towards his opponent's goal, shot and scored. After the ball had been kicked by the victim, the defendant tackled him from behind by performing a sliding challenge that caused serious injury to the victim's right ankle and fibula. After making the challenge, the defendant was heard to say something to the effect of 'Have that' to the victim. The defendant was sent off for violent conduct; the referee considered the challenge to have been a late, high, two-footed lunge as opposed to the defendant's claim that he was attempting to perform a sliding tackle. The judge directed the jury that the defendant could only be guilty of an assault under s.20 OAPA 1861 if the prosecution could prove that the challenge had not been done by way of 'legitimate sport' or that it was 'over and above what is generally acceptable in a football game.' The conviction under s.20 OAPA 1861 was justified on the basis that the injury-causing challenge was intentional, in that the defendant intended to make contact with the victim. Furthermore, when making the challenge, he would have been able to foresee some harm, such as bruising being caused to the victim.

The Court of Appeal, however, allowed the appeal on the basis that the judge's failure to provide the jury with an adequate explanation of what constituted 'legitimate sport' was a misdirection on the law and that the conviction was therefore unsafe. It held that only rarely should cases involving sports participants be heard before the criminal courts rather than the relevant governing body's disciplinary tribunal. Where cases were appropriate for prosecution, the jury should consider the type of sport being played, the level at which it was being played, the nature of the act, the degree of force used, the extent of the risk of injury and the state of mind of the defendant when determining whether the defendant's conduct was objectively acceptable, or criminal, in the circumstances.

This conclusion is explicable only on the basis that the judge had not provided examples of what he meant by 'legitimate sport' in response to specific questions from the jury. Somewhat strangely, however, having provided the fuller explanation of 'rules and practices' or 'expected conduct' or 'legitimate sport' or 'playing culture' that the law required, the Court then failed to apply this new test to the facts that had been found by the jury to exist, allowing the defendant's appeal and quashing his conviction.

In allowing the appeal, the Court began by making a very clear policy statement: that because most sports have governing bodies which administer their own internal disciplinary regimes then in the vast majority of cases it will be undesirable to encourage recourse to the criminal law as well as, or instead of, making use of these tribunals. Only where the conduct was sufficiently grave should a prosecution be pursued. Ignoring the inherent circularity in this statement and the lack of any further justification of why this specific form of violence should be granted an exemption from prosecution, the Court made it abundantly clear that they did not consider it appropriate for sports assault cases to be heard before the criminal courts.

If the Court of Appeal's aim was not only to clarify the law but also to discourage during-the-game incidents from being prosecuted, then the dearth of reported cases since *Barnes* would indicate that it has been successful. In *R v Chapman* (unreported) Warwick Crown Court 3 March 2010, one of the few post-*Barnes* cases, a conviction under s.20 OAPA 1861 was secured on very similar facts and the defendant was sentenced to six months in jail, highlighting that *Barnes* is on the borderline of what is and what is not lawful play. In the future, it is unlikely that anything other than the most obviously deliberate foul will be considered by a court to be a criminal assault, for example, where the injuries were caused by a fight or were in some other way 'off-the-ball' or 'behind-the-play' as was the elbow to the face in *R v Cotterill* [2007] EWCA Crim 526. In all other cases, the sport's disciplinary tribunal will be the appropriate forum. For example, in the FA Regulatory Commission Decision, *The Football Association v Barton* 23 May 2012, Queens Park Rangers footballer Joey Barton was found guilty of kicking one opponent and attempting to head-butt another. He was banned for eight matches and fined £75,000 but not prosecuted despite two criminal assaults being committed.

6.2.3   Application of the law and sentencing

Following *Barnes*, the courts will focus not only on the severity of the injuries caused but also on the *mens rea* of the defendant and the response of the appropriate NGB. Further, athletes who are convicted of sports assaults can usually expect to receive a significantly lower sentence than for corresponding offences committed in other circumstances. Despite stating that 'sport is not a licence for thuggery', the court in *R v Lloyd* (1989) 11 Cr App Rep (S) 36 only imposed an 18-month prison sentence for a conviction under s.18 OAPA 1861 where the defendant rugby player had deliberately kicked his opponent, who was lying on the ground, so hard that it fractured his cheekbone. Moreover, where sports assaults are concerned the courts seem more willing to accept a much wider range of arguments in mitigation of sentence than would usually be the case, including provocation (*R v Lincoln* (1990) 12 Cr App Rep (S) 250) and the length of the playing ban imposed (*R v Goodwin* (1995) 16 Cr App Rep (S) 885).

6.2.3.1 Common assault

Common assault is rarely charged in respect of sports assaults, either because the contact was consented to or because the degree of harm caused was sufficiently severe to be prosecuted under s.47 OAPA 1861. However, in *R v Brownbill* (unreported) Crown Court (Preston), 4 February 2004, the defendant was convicted of common assault despite having repeatedly punched his opponent in an ice hockey game with such force that his two front teeth were knocked out; he was fined £250 and ordered to pay £250 costs. This case can be considered something of an anomaly as the degree of injury inflicted was at least sufficient to constitute an offence under s.47 OAPA 1861.

A more usual response was that in *R v Evans* (unreported) Crown Court (Newcastle), 14 June 2006, where the defendant was accused of having stamped on his victim's head in a rugby union game. The judge directed the jury to acquit on the basis that the 'slight bruise' on the victim's forehead was insufficient to constitute an actionable injury arising from the normal playing of rugby.

6.2.3.2 Offences Against the Person Act 1861 s.47

R v Birkin (1988) 10 Cr App R (S) 303 is a classic example of how and why the law applies to sports assaults. The defendant footballer was the subject of a late foul tackle by his victim that was part of the normal playing of the game. As the two players ran off to take up their positions for the resulting free kick, the defendant punched the victim on the side of his face and broke his jaw in two places. The assault was off-the-ball and clearly retaliatory. It was neither within the 'rules and practices' of football nor an act that could reasonably be expected to occur during a football match. The defendant was convicted and sentenced to six months imprisonment with the court taking into account that the degree of injury was neither expected nor intended.

6.2.3.3 Offences Against the Person Act 1861 s.20

Although there is a high degree of overlap between the use of ss.47 and 20 OAPA 1861, charges brought under s.20 generally reflect the greater degree of injury caused to the victim and/or that the defendant acted with particular violence towards the victim. In *Cotterill*, the defendant deliberately elbowed the opposing forward in the face, fracturing his jaw in two places. His comparatively low four-month jail sentence was based on his instant admission and guilty plea, his lengthy playing ban and the termination of his professional playing contract.

6.2.3.4 Offences Against the Person Act 1861 s.18

The high degree of intent required by s.18 OAPA 1861 means that charges under this section are comparatively rare in sport, but conviction will almost always result in imprisonment. Unless the defendant has kicked or stamped on another player's head (*R v Garfield* [2008] EWCA Crim 130), bitten them (*R v Johnson* (1986) 8 Cr App R (S) 343) or head-butted them (*R v Piff* (1994) 15 Cr App R (S) 737), then the appropriate charge will usually be s.20 OAPA 1861. In each of these cases, there was substantial mitigation, including guilty pleas and loss of employment; prison sentences were imposed for 15 months, six months and six months, respectively. Biting is a particularly unpleasant but clear-cut example of a s.18 assault. The initial assault, the bite, can really only be carried out intentionally and by biting through the skin, most commonly the ear lobe, there can be little doubt that the resulting wound and/or GBH was also inflicted intentionally.

6.2.4 Defences

As most contacts that occur whilst playing sport are, in legal terms, intentional or reckless, then for sport to be able to continue in the forms that we currently know it, some mechanism must operate to prevent these contacts from being criminal assaults. The most important defence in these circumstances is consent, which ensures that those contacts that are truly part of the playing of the game are lawful and cannot form the basis of a criminal charge.

In certain circumstances, self-defence may be raised by a defendant where they honestly believed in the need to use reasonable force to prevent an attack upon themselves (*R v Williams* [1987] 3 All ER 411). As this is really only relevant in the context of fights or where a fight is about to break out (*R v Hardy* (unreported) Central Criminal Court, 26 July 1994), this defence is not discussed further here. In the United States, 'involuntary reflex' has been successfully raised to explain why a defendant hit and injured his opponent; however, such an argument is unlikely to succeed in the UK (below, 6.2.4.2).

6.2.4.1 Consent

It has long been accepted that sport, particularly contact sports, must be treated differently to other situations in which injury is suffered (*Attorney-General's Reference (No 6 of 1980)* [1981] QB 715). The simple reason for this is that without some kind of exemption to the general prohibition on being able to consent to ABH or greater being inflicted upon oneself (*R v Brown* [1994] 1 AC 212), many popular sports would be unable to function in the way that they do currently.

Outside of sport, the general law on consent to injury is that nobody can consent to the infliction of ABH or greater upon their person (*Brown*). Without further elaboration, a person could consent to a common assault being perpetrated on them but not the aggravated assaults contained in the OAPA 1861. For example, if a rugby player tackles an opponent, there is intentional contact between them and therefore an assault. If the tackle breaks the leg of the opponent, injury constituting at least ABH will have been suffered, and therefore an assault under s.47 OAPA 1861 is committed. As *Barnes* held that it would not be in the public interest to criminalise conduct of this nature, the courts have acknowledged that some accommodation for sport needs to be reached.

In *Bradshaw* Bramwell LJ noted that contacts that were within the 'rules and practices' of the sport in question were lawful and could be consented to, regardless of the degree of harm caused to the victim. A hundred years later in *Billinghurst*, the court held that injurious conduct that was 'of a kind which could reasonably be expected to happen during a game' could be consented to. In *Barnes*, the Court reviewed the law as it had developed over the previous 130 years before Lord Woolf CJ at para.15 provides a comprehensive set of circumstances that should be taken into account when determining the lawfulness of a sports participant's conduct:

> '[The] fact that the play is within the rules and practice of the game and does not go beyond them, will be a firm indication that what has happened is not criminal. In making a judgment as to whether conduct is criminal or not, it has to be borne in mind that, in highly competitive sports, conduct outside the rules can be expected to occur in the heat of the moment, and even if the conduct justifies not only being penalised but also a warning or even a sending off, it still may not reach the threshold level required for it to be criminal. That level is an objective one and does not depend upon the views of individual players. *The type of the sport, the level at which it is played, the nature of the act, the degree of force used, the extent of the risk of injury, the state of mind of the defendant are all likely to be relevant in determining whether the defendant's actions go beyond the threshold.'* [Emphasis added.]

First of all, Lord Woolf CJ reiterates that injuries caused by contacts that are an accepted and expected part of the playing of the game, including many contacts that are technically foul play, are part of its playing culture and are therefore lawfully consented to. Instinctive reactions and errors of judgement made in the heat of competition are not considered appropriate cases for prosecution, though they could constitute negligence on the part of the opposition players (see further, chapter 4.4). In particular, where the governing body of a sport has taken prompt, decisive and meaningful action following an incident of violent conduct, the police and Crown Prosecution Service have been reluctant to take the matter further.

Secondly, where a player's conduct is considered to be something other than an error of judgement, then the Court provided a non-exhaustive list of the circumstances surrounding the incident that should be taken into account in order to determine its lawfulness. In doing this, the Court provided a more detailed explanation of the phrase 'legitimate sport' that had been used at trial. By examining these criteria in detail, it should be possible to determine whether a particular act was an acceptable way of playing the game or so inherently dangerous that it ought to be criminal. It also enables courts to maintain an overview of all sporting conduct, ensuring that the governing bodies of sport are not able to determine unilaterally the extent of a player's consent; vigorous and hard play can be justified, but dangerous and violent conduct cannot be.

Applying these criteria to the facts established by the jury in *Barnes*, it must be taken into account that this was a competitive football match and that therefore challenges for the ball were an integral part of the game. Secondly, this was a Sunday league game, where a sliding tackle such as occurred here would be a normal part of play at this level.

The third criterion is key to establishing whether the conduct was criminal: the nature of the act. In *Barnes*, the court had to determine whether this was a vigorous but fair challenge for the ball, as the defendant claimed, or a late, high, unnecessary foul tackle from behind, as argued by the prosecution. In reaching a conclusion on this point, the remaining circumstances will also have to be considered: the degree of force used; the extent of the risk of injury and the state of mind of the defendant. At trial, the jury appeared to consider that the degree of force used was excessive as the chances of the defendant playing the ball were remote, that the risk of injury was high as the defendant appeared to have stamped on the back of his victim's leg and that he had done so deliberately, or at least recklessly, as evidenced by his reaction. Although the Court of Appeal overturned the conviction, this was on the basis of a technical misdirection on the law. The later case of *Chapman* demonstrates that this kind of challenge will more usually be held to be unlawful.

6.2.4.2 Involuntary reflex

In *Barnes* the Court of Appeal referred to a player's 'instinctive reaction' as being an insufficient basis for establishing criminal liability. The strict legal explanation for this is because where a defendant has acted without thinking, instinctively, they will be trying to establish that they did not have the requisite *mens rea* at the time the assault was committed. If this is a denial of having acted unlawfully, then there is nothing inherently wrong with such a claim. If it is an attempt to establish the defence of automatism however, then it will fail (*Bratty v Attorney-General for Northern Ireland* [1963] AC 386). The cause of the involuntary conduct must be something external to the defendant, such as a blow to the head that leads to concussion. Where sports participants are concerned, they will rarely be able to claim that they had no control whatsoever over what they were doing; if their training caused them to react in a certain way, they will still have had sufficient control over what that they were doing to be acting with *mens rea*. In the American state of Minnesota, a claim of involuntary reflex helped to raise a sufficient doubt in the minds of the jury that a mistrial had been declared.

▶ *State v Forbes (unreported) Case 63280, Minn Dist Ct, 12 September 1975*

The defendant and his victim were opposing professional ice hockey players in an NHL game. Following an on-ice altercation between them, both were sent to the penalty box for seven minutes. Throughout the period of the penalty, the defendant threatened his opponent. As they returned to the ice, the victim skated up behind the defendant, causing the defendant to hit the victim in the face with the butt end of his stick. He then fell upon his prone victim and repeatedly punched him in the face, fracturing his eye socket and causing a wound that required 25 stitches. The defendant was banned from playing professional ice hockey for ten games and charged with aggravated assault by use of a dangerous weapon.

The defendant argued that his initial assault was an instinctive reaction to the training that he had received throughout his career and that where an opponent was approaching from behind, his actions were defensive to prevent an attack being carried out on him. This argument was sufficient to result in a hung jury with a mistrial declared, despite the defendant having caused serious facial injuries to his victim. A retrial was not sought by the prosecutors as it was considered that if conviction could not be secured on these facts, then it was unlikely that any court would ever convict for a sports assault, a prediction that has proven to be true by the dearth of prosecutions since.

Although this line of argument is unlikely to succeed in the UK, it is a clear indication of how the seeds of doubt can be sown in the minds of a jury in a criminal trial. In the Canadian case of *R v Green* (1970) 16 DLR 3d 137, the judge relied on a similar justification for finding that no assault had been committed when an ice hockey player hit an opponent on the upper arm with an ice hockey stick; it was simply an instinctive warning to his opponent to keep away, not a criminal assault.

6.2.5 Homicide

There are only two forms of homicide that are relevant where a person has been killed whilst participating in sport: unlawful act manslaughter and corporate manslaughter. To establish a murder charge, the court must be satisfied so that it is sure that the defendant intended to kill their victim or that the defendant intended to cause them GBH and that the victim died as a result of the intentional assault (*R v Cunningham* [1982] AC 566); if a defendant commits a s.18 OAPA 1861 assault against a victim who later dies from their injuries, then murder is established. The high standard of proof and the need to prove intention to kill or cause GBH mean that murder charges will be extremely rare in sports unless there is a fight that results in death.

6.2.5.1 Unlawful act manslaughter

Manslaughter occurs where the defendant commits an unlawful and dangerous act that causes the victim's death. In this context, 'dangerous' means that all sober and reasonable people would inevitably recognise the risk that some harm (not death) would be caused by the defendant's act (*R v Church* [1966] 1 QB 59). Usually, the unlawful act that forms the basis of the charge will be an assault under either s.47 or s.20 OAPA 1861. The test is objective so that it is unnecessary to prove that the defendant was aware that their actions were dangerous; if the reasonable person would have recognised that there was a risk of harm being caused to the victim, then the act is dangerous.

Two of the earliest sports assault cases provide a useful comparison of how a sports assault can result in a manslaughter charge. In *Bradshaw*, the defendant attempted to either challenge the deceased for possession or to intercept the ball. In making the challenge, the defendant charged the deceased by jumping at him with his knees raised and pointing towards the deceased's midriff, leading to the deceased dying the following day from a rupture to his intestines. The judge directed the jury that football was a rough but lawful game and that only where the defendant intended to cause, or was reckless as to causing, serious injury would a conviction be appropriate. In acquitting the defendant of manslaughter, it would appear that the jury considered that the defendant had committed a rough but ultimately fair challenge that was within the rules and practices of football as then understood, and therefore consented, to by the deceased.

In contrast, the defendant in *R v Moore* (1898) 15 TLR 229 was found guilty of manslaughter, having charged the deceased from behind, throwing him violently against the knee of the goalkeeper. Again, the deceased died from internal injuries a few days later. In this case, the jury considered the challenge to be both unlawful and dangerous and therefore incapable of being consented to, presumably because the defendant had no chance of getting to the ball and had deliberately and violently charged the deceased.

In both cases, it can be seen that there was at least a reckless, if not an intentional, assault committed on the deceased players and that it was objectively foreseeable to the reasonable person that some harm may have been caused to them as a result of the challenges. However, *Bradshaw*'s act was within the rules and practices of football because it was a rough challenge for the ball, whereas *Moore*'s was not as there was no attempt to play the ball, only the opposing player. A more modern example has come before the courts in Canada, where the law of manslaughter is similar to English law.

▶ *R v CC 2009 ONCJ 249*

The defendant performed an intentional 'spear tackle' on the victim by driving his shoulder into the victim's stomach, lifting him up and propelling him backwards and head-first into the ground. The victim died later as a result of catastrophic injuries to his spinal cord. The trial judge found that a tackle performed in this way was not within the rules of the game, was unconnected with the playing of this particular game as it occurred behind the play and was not a mistimed attempt to get the ball and that there was no unwritten code of conduct that could justify conduct of this nature as being within its playing culture. Thus, the tackle was not within the implied consent of those playing rugby union and the offence of manslaughter was made out.

The similarities between English and Canadian law on this point are very close as both can trace their roots to the Canadian case of *R v Cey* (1989) 48 CCC 3d 480 (Sask CA). If an analogous situation were to occur in England, a similar result could be expected to follow.

6.2.5.2 Corporate manslaughter

Prior to the enacting of the Corporate Manslaughter and Corporate Homicide Act 2007 (CMCHA 2007), there had always been significant difficulties in bringing manslaughter actions against corporate entities. The main problem was identifying the person who was the 'controlling mind and will' of the company who would be the person who formed the *mens rea* of the offence on its behalf.

Under the common law, a company would have to be charged with gross negligence manslaughter. With a similar structure to the tort of negligence, the offence is committed where the defendant owed the deceased a duty of care, the duty was breached by the defendant's conduct, the breach caused the deceased's death and the breach of duty was so gross as to justify conviction (*R v Adomako* [1995] 1 AC 171).

When trying to establish that a company had acted grossly negligently, the court could not aggregate the conduct of two or more employees; instead, a single controlling mind and will had to be identified and that person alone had to have acted with gross negligence (*Attorney-General's Reference (No2 of 1999)* [2000] QB 796). There were virtually no prosecutions for corporate manslaughter, because the larger and more complex the management structure of the company, the more difficult it was to identify its controlling mind and will (*R v P & O European Ferries (Dover) Ltd* (1991) 93 Cr App R 72). One of the very few successful prosecutions for corporate manslaughter under the old common law was against a company that organised outdoor adventure pursuits for children.

▶ *R v Kite and OLL Ltd* [1996] 2 Cr App R (S) 295

The defendant was the sole director of a company that provided outward bound and adventure activities to groups of children. Eight schoolchildren, a teacher and two of his instructors embarked on a sea canoeing expedition across Lyme Bay. Contrary to British Canoe Union guidelines, all members of the group were inexperienced novices and should not have been out on the open sea and the instructors were not sufficiently experienced to be guiding an expedition of this nature. The entire group got into difficulties and four of the children drowned before they could be rescued. The defendant was under a duty to provide a safe system of management that would ensure the safety of those taking part in the activities that he was providing. His failure to adhere to relevant BCU guidelines, failure to provide sufficiently qualified expedition leaders and failure to respond to the safety concerns brought to his attention by two former employees were evidence of his having fallen far below the expected standard of care owed to the children and were sufficient to amount to gross negligence.

The corporation, of which the defendant was the sole director and therefore the controlling mind and will, had breached its duty to take reasonable care of those who were taking part in its activities by failing to have in place an adequate system to ensure their safety. The breach was gross because of the high risk of danger to all involved in the trip and previous warnings that he had received concerning lapses in safety procedures. The company was convicted of gross negligence manslaughter and its managing director, Kite, was sentenced to two years imprisonment.

This case highlighted that it was much easier to bring cases against small companies because the controlling mind and will was clearly identifiable and was one of the reasons for the eventual enactment of both the Activity Centres (Young Persons' Safety) Act 1995 (see further, chapter 8.5.1) and the CMCHA 2007. The new Act should ensure that even a large corporation could now be found guilty as long as it can be proved that mismanagement by its senior managers contributed significantly to the deaths that its activities caused.

Section 20 CMCHA 2007 abolishes the common law offence of gross negligence as it applies to corporations and s.1 of the Act replaces it with a new offence known as corporate manslaughter in England, Wales and Northern Ireland and corporate homicide in Scotland. The new offence is very similar to the one that it replaces, except that it no longer requires the identification of a single directing mind and will of the corporation.

Corporate manslaughter is defined in s.1 CMCHA 2007 as being committed where the activities of a corporation cause a person's death by a gross breach of a duty owed to the deceased. The existence of a duty of care is indentified in much the same way as it is for the law of negligence (see further, chapter 4.4) and includes the duties owed under the Occupiers' Liability Acts, s.2 CMCHA 2007. Under s.4(b), a breach of the relevant duty is considered to be gross where the conduct of the corporation falls far below what could reasonably be expected of it in the circumstances in which it operates. Finally, the grossly negligent conduct is attributable to the corporation only if its senior management, defined in s.4(c) as being the persons who play significant roles in making decisions, managing and/or organising the whole or a substantial part of the corporation, played a substantial role in breaching the duty.

In theory, the new offence makes it easier to establish criminal liability against corporations that have caused deaths by their activities. To date, the few prosecutions under the Act make it unclear whether or not this will actually be the case. Until a clearer picture of how the CMCHA 2007 will be used to regulate corporate conduct, this field of litigation will continue to be as controversial as it always has been.

6.3 Public disorder and racism

Cases involving public disorder and racial abuse are more usually associated with the misbehaviour of spectators, not players (see further, chapter 10). Where the players' behaviour is particularly anti-social and/or is likely to incite disorder amongst the spectators, the Public Order Act 1986 and related offences can be used to punish their conduct.

6.3.1 Public Order Act 1986 ss.4A and 5 – causing harassment, alarm and distress

Section 5 of the Public Order Act 1986 contains the offence of using threatening, abusive or insulting words or behaviour within the hearing or sight of a person likely to be caused harassment, alarm or distress by the defendant's conduct. Section 4A creates an aggravated version of the offence where the defendant intends to, and does actually, cause harassment, alarm or distress to another person. As with breach of the peace (see further, 6.3.2), these offences would appear to be most appropriate to punish a participant's behaviour where it has caused, or was likely to cause, some kind of reaction in the crowd (see further, chapter 10.5.1.1).

In *R v Bowyer* (unreported) Magistrates' Court (Newcastle), 5 July 2005, the defendant pleaded guilty to a charge under s.5 Public Order Act 1986 following an on-field scuffle with teammate, Kieron Dyer. As Bowyer eventually pleaded guilty, there was no explanation why this charge was proffered, as opposed to a charge of common assault, and no explanation of who was likely to have been harassed, alarmed or distressed by his conduct. Dyer was not keen to pursue charges against Bowyer, and there were no official complaints from spectators, so presumably those who were harassed, alarmed or distressed by the altercation were police officers on duty at the ground. In contrast, in *R v Thomas* (unreported) Bexley Magistrates' Court, 13 February 2006, the defendant professional footballer was acquitted of a charge under s.5 on the basis that there was insufficient evidence to prove that any of the fans watching the game were harassed, alarmed or distressed by his gesturing at them with his middle finger.

6.3.2 Breach of the peace and inciting crowd disorder

The on-field conduct of sports participants is capable of being particularly provocative to those who are watching the game. Where the behaviour of the players causes a threat to another person or their property, in this case by causing crowd disorder, then a breach of the peace may have occurred under s.115 Magistrates' Court Act 1980 or the Justices of the Peace Act 1361. In *Butcher v Jessop* (1989) SLT 593, the former Glasgow Rangers and England football captain was bound over to keep the peace following an on-field altercation between him and the Glasgow Celtic centre forward Frank McAvennie, which resulted in Butcher pushing McAvennie over. Butcher was bound over to keep the peace and fined £250 on the basis that in the highly charged environment of a Glasgow derby, pushing a Celtic player directly in front of the Celtic fans had the potential to cause serious crowd disorder.

6.3.3   Racial abuse

Racism in British sport is now seen as much less of a problem than it has been in the past. That said, a number of very high-profile incidents in football during 2011 and 2012 highlighted that although advances have been made, it cannot be said that racism has been eradicated from sport in general and football in particular.

Racially aggravated versions of ss.4A and 5 Public Order Act 1986 are created by s.31 Crime and Disorder Act 1998. These offences are racially aggravated where the offender demonstrates hostility towards the victim based on the latter's membership of a racial group, or the offence is motivated in some way by hostility to members of a racial group, s.28(1) Crime and Disorder Act 1998. The necessary hostility can be demonstrated by the use of threatening, abusive or insulting words or behaviour, as would fulfil the requirements of ss.4A and 5 Public Order Act 1986. A racial group is defined in s.28(4) as being based on race, colour, nationality, citizenship, ethnic or national origins. Further, these offences can be religiously aggravated where reference is made to a person's religious belief, or lack thereof, under s 28(5) of the Act.

It was under s.5 Public Order Act 1986 and s.31 Crime and Disorder Act 1998, that John Terry, the former Chelsea and England football captain, was charged following an allegation that he racially abused Anton Ferdinand of Queens Park Rangers during a Premier League football match (*R v Terry* (unreported) Westminster Magistrates' Court, 13 July 2012). Terry admitted using a string of expletives towards Ferdinand, including the phrase 'fucking black cunt,' but claimed that this had been said in the context of repeating back to Ferdinand an accusation that he believed had been made; in effect, he was claiming that he asked Ferdinand, 'Did you just say that I called you a fucking black cunt?' The lack of evidence from anyone else on the pitch, coupled with the obvious inability of the expert lip readers to infer 'tone of voice', led to Terry's acquittal on the basis that he had introduced a significant element of doubt into the proceedings.

At the later internal hearing, Terry was found guilty of misconduct by using abusive and/or insulting words that included a reference to ethnic origin and/or colour and/or race contrary to Rules E.3(1) and (2) FA Rules and Regulations(FA Regulatory Commission Decision *The Football Association v Terry* 24–27 September 2012). The difference between the two outcomes can be explained by the Chief Magistrate finding Terry to be a credible witness who had introduced doubt into the prosecution's case, whereas the FA Regulatory Commission found Terry's explanation 'improbable, implausible and contrived' and that the charge was made out on the balance of probabilities, the lower standard of proof used in disciplinary tribunals. Terry was banned for four games and fined £220,000.

In the aftermath of the failed prosecution, Ferdinand's brother and Manchester United player Rio appeared to endorse the comment of a Twitter user that Ashley Cole was a 'choc ice' for having given evidence on behalf of Terry. This is considered to be an offensive and insulting means of questioning a person's identity by indicating that although black on the outside, they act as a white person on the inside. In his defence, Rio Ferdinand claimed that he meant only that Cole was a fake. Ferdinand was also found guilty by the FA Regulatory Commission of making abusive comments that made reference to Cole's colour, contrary to Rules E3(1) and (2), but had not acted in a racist manner; it was also taken into account that he had repeated the comments of another person rather than initiating them himself. He was fined £45,000 but was not the subject of a criminal investigation (FA Regulatory Commission Decision *The Football Association v Ferdinand* 13 August 2012).

The third of these incidents involved Liverpool player Luis Suarez repeatedly calling Manchester United's Patrice Evra the Spanish word 'negro'. The FA Regulatory Commission Decision *The Football Association v Suarez* 20 December 2011 held that charges under FA Rules E.3(1) and (2) were again made out on the basis that Suarez was using insulting and abusive words towards Evra that made reference to his colour. The Commission accepted that the word 'negro' translated as 'black', not 'nigger', and was therefore not a racist term in its own right but a reference to Evra's skin colour. Suarez was banned for eight games and fined £40,000, but the matter was not investigated by the police.

Following the lead of the violence cases, particularly *Barnes* (see further, 6.2.3), it would appear that the police and CPS are prepared for what are perceived as being less-serious cases of racial abuse to be dealt with by sports disciplinary panels, as with *Suarez* and *Ferdinand*, but where more serious allegations are made, a prosecution will follow. This is a very fine distinction to make and leaves both the courts and governing bodies open to criticisms of not taking racism seriously where charges are not made or punishments that are perceived to be lenient are imposed. Whilst s.5 Public Order Act 1986 requires only that insulting or abusive words are used, that these caused an onlooker to feel harassed, alarmed or distressed and that this can be racially aggravated by making reference to a person's colour, there is certainly scope for further prosecutions for racial abuse by players in the future, particularly after the controversy that was raised by these three cases.

6.3.4 Assaulting the crowd

Although extremely unusual, a few participants have been convicted of assaulting the spectators at events at which they were performing. As these actions are unconnected with the actual playing of sport, no special consideration is made for the players who react in this way.

The most infamous incident of a player assaulting a spectator is *R v Cantona* (1995) The Times, 25 March. Having been sent off for a foul challenge on an opponent, the defendant was verbally abused by an individual in the crowd. The defendant reacted by performing a flying kick that caught the spectator in the chest, causing him minor bruising. The defendant was convicted of common assault and sentenced to 120 hours of community service. As can be seen from this example, the courts will treat attacks on spectators as 'ordinary' acts of violence and deal with them as either common assaults or offences under the OAPA 1861.

6.4 Match fixing, spot-fixing and corruption

It is now widely acknowledged across many sports that gambling-related corruption is, or is likely to become, a serious problem. In recent years, horse racing, cricket, tennis and snooker have all come under scrutiny and in many sports, NGBs and ISFs have begun to introduce education campaigns through codes of conduct and their own investigatory bodies to ensure that those engaging in corrupt activities are found and punished.

There are two main methods by which sports contests can be manipulated to the benefit of gamblers. Match-fixing is where the result, or the final score, of a contest is determined in advance so that those gambling on it can back the correct outcome. Spot-fixing is where a particular event within a contest is manipulated so that gamblers can bet on it, such as a no ball being bowled on a specific ball in cricket, or a double fault on a particular point in tennis. In both cases, people actively engaged in the contest, including players and/or match officials, will need to be part of the process to ensure that the predetermined outcome of the fix eventuates. Alongside of the sport-specific disciplinary measures, a number of criminal offences may also be committed.

6.4.1 Criminal conspiracies

Much of what would previously have been caught by this offence will now be prosecuted under the provisions of the Fraud Act 2006. However, where the agreement to make a gain for oneself or another or a loss to another covers a wide variety of conduct and/or defendants, then such a conspiracy may be charged as either statutory conspiracy under s.1 Criminal Law Act 1977 (a conspiracy to commit a specific offence) or as the common law offence of conspiracy to defraud. The key aspect of a conspiracy is that it is complete on agreement. Money need not change hands, or if it has, the match to be fixed need not have yet taken place. The agreement itself is the crime, not the performance of the agreed acts, *R v Anderson* [1986] AC 27.

In *R v Fallon and others (unreported) Central Criminal Court, 7 December 2007,* the former champion jockey Kieren Fallon and five others were charged with agreeing not to use their best efforts to win, thereby affecting the result in specific races. The prosecution alleged that, in effect, the three jockeys deliberately lost certain races that they had been expected to win, which in turn enabled their co-conspirators to bet against the jockeys on the Betfair betting exchange. Those affected by the conspiracy were any users of Betfair who bet on the races with the defendants thinking that the jockeys would be riding to win. Despite a lengthy investigation and trial, the prosecution collapsed when the judge ordered the jury to acquit each of the defendants of all charges. Forbes J found that he could attach little weight to the evidence of the prosecution's main witness, the Australian racing steward Mr Murrihy, after he had admitted in cross-examination that he had little knowledge of the rules and culture of British racing. This led Forbes J to conclude that Mr Murrihy's evidence fell 'far, far short of establishing a prima facie breach of UK racing rules' and, therefore, that no conspiracy to defraud could be established. This is, perhaps, as much of a salutary lesson in the choice of expert witnesses as it is an example of the difficulties associated with establishing a case against those suspected of match-fixing.

Successful prosecutions have been brought against four Pakistani cricketers who were involved with 'spot-fixing' by agreeing to bowl no balls on specific balls in specific overs during a Test match against England. Mazhar Majeed, who represented a number of Pakistani players, acted as intermediary between what he thought was a gambling syndicate and the players involved in the game; in reality, it was an undercover *News of the World* reporter trying to expose corruption in cricket. Majeed approached the team captain, Salman Butt, who in turn approached two of his bowlers, Mohammad Asif and Mohammad Amir. The bowlers bowled no balls as agreed, and each of the four took a share of the money offered by the reporter.

All four were charged with conspiracy to do acts to enable others to cheat at gambling by their agreeing to bowl no balls on predetermined occasions (see further, 6.4.3). Majeed was also charged with conspiracy to corruptly give an inducement to Butt, Asif and Amir, with the three players being charged in turn with conspiracy to accept corrupt payments; the underlying charge for the conspiracy was under s.1(1) Prevention of Corruption Act 1906. Majeed and Amir pleaded guilty to both charges, and Butt and Asif were found guilty at trial. In sentencing the three players, their playing bans and the impact on their careers was taken into account as were the guilty pleas of Majeed and Amir, *R v Majeed, Butt, Asif and Amir* (unreported) Southwark Crown Court, 3 November 2011. Majeed was sentenced to 32 months in prison, Butt 30 months and a 10-year playing ban, Asif 12 months and a seven-year ban and Amir six months and a five-year ban.

In contrast to these cases, in what was one of the most complex instances of corruption in British sport, the matter was dealt with entirely by the governing body despite its findings that conspiracies to defraud and to cheat at gambling had taken place, *Re Quinn, Fitzsimmons, Doe, Fairley, Milczarek and others* Decision of the British Horse Racing Authority, 15 December 2011. In this case, owners and gamblers had paid jockeys not to win so that they could lay bets against them. In finding the allegations proved, the British Horseracing Authority banned five jockeys for between six months and 12 years and two owners for 14 years from any involvement in horseracing.

6.4.2 Fraud Act 2006 – fraud

The Fraud Act 2006 radically redefines the scope of what had been the deception offences found in the Theft Acts of 1968 and 1978. The general offence of fraud in s.1 Fraud Act 2006 highlights the three specific ways in which the offence can be committed, which are defined more fully in ss.2–4. In sport, it is likely that fraud by false representation under s.2 will be the most appropriate charge.

▶ *Fraud Act 2006 s.2*

(1) A person is in breach of this section if he—
   (a) dishonestly makes a false representation, and
   (b) intends, by making the false representation—
      (i) to make a gain for himself or another, or
      (ii) to cause loss to another or to expose another to a risk of loss.
(2) A representation is false if—
   (a) it is untrue or misleading, and
   (b) the person making it knows that it is, or might be, untrue or misleading.
(3) "Representation" means any representation as to fact or law, including a representation as to the state of mind of—
   (a) the person making the representation, or
   (b) any other person.
(4) A representation may be express or implied.
(5) For the purposes of this section a representation may be regarded as made if it (or anything implying it) is submitted in any form to any system of device designed to receive, convey or respond to communications (with or without human intervention).

The false representation could be that a jockey is trying to win the race when he is not, or that a footballer is trying to pass the ball to a team-mate when he is trying to increase the number of corners conceded, or a batsman trying to get out instead of scoring runs. The gain can be to the participant or another member of a betting syndicate. The loss could be to a bookmaker or to other users of a betting exchange. It is important to note that the offence is committed where there is the intent to make the gain/loss; it is irrelevant whether, in fact, a gain was made, or a loss inflicted.

6.4.3 Gambling Act 2005 s.42 – cheating at gambling

For offences occurring after 1 September 2007, a charge of cheating contrary to s.42 Gambling Act 2005 may be brought against a corrupt athlete.

▶ *Gambling Act 2005 s.42*

(1) A person commits an offence if he—
   (a) cheats at gambling, or
   (b) does anything for the purpose of enabling or assisting another person to cheat at gambling.
(2) For the purposes of subsection (1) it is immaterial whether a person who cheats—
   (a) improves his chances of winning anything, or
   (b) wins anything.
(3) Without prejudice to the generality of subsection (1) cheating at gambling may, in particular, consist of actual or attempted deception or interference in connection with—
   (a) the process by which gambling is conducted, or
   (b) a real or virtual game, race or other event or process to which gambling relates.

This provision is aimed at catching corrupt athletes who, regardless of whether or not they have accepted money, attempt to influence the outcome of a game or race, or some aspect of it, that might form the basis of a bet. It was the underlying offence for the conspiracy charges against Majeed, Butt, Asif and Amir and is likely to be the cornerstone of future prosecutions of corrupt athletes.

6.5 Sexual offences and child abuse

There is a growing body of research into the relationships that exist between coaches and sports participants, particularly where those participants are children. The main concern of this research is that sport can provide an opportunity for the exploitation of the relationship and that physical and sexual abuse of the young athlete can occur. This was particularly highlighted in the 1990s when there was a series of high-profile prosecutions for sexual offences committed by coaches on the athletes under their instruction.

Where an athlete has been sexually or physically abused, criminal charges under the Sexual Offences Act 2003 (SOA 2003) and the OAPA 1861 (above, 6.2) will be laid against the abuser. The SOA 2003 applies to sexual offences committed in sport, as it would in any other setting. For example, in *R v Hickson* [1997] Crim LR 494, a British Olympic swimming coach was convicted of two counts of rape, two counts of anal rape (both now under s.1 SOA 2003) and 11 counts of sexual assault (now s.3 SOA 2003) against female swimmers whom he had coached over the course of his career. The fact that these incidents took place in the context of sport was only relevant in that it provided the defendant with the opportunity to commit the offences. The applicable law is not varied in any way where abuse of this nature is concerned, because it is impossible to claim in any way that sexual abuse is an expected or accepted part of participation in, or training for, sport.

The SOA 2003 was a comprehensive overhaul of the law relating to sexual offences. Of particular note in the context of sport is the range of offences that can be committed against children (ss.9–21 SOA 2003), including abuse of a position of trust by engaging in sexual activity with a child (s.16). For these purposes, a child is a person under the age of 16 and the defendant must be over the age of 18. Inexplicably, s.16 SOA 2003 only applies to adults working in the public sector, such as teachers, and not those working in the private sector, such as many sports coaches.

Further safeguards are provided by extra-legal bodies and the extensive documentation that they have developed. In particular, the work of the Child Protection in Sport Unit (CPSU), a cooperative venture established in 2001 by the National Society for the Prevention of Cruelty to Children and the UK's four regional sports councils, has ensured that child protection has become an important focus of the work of many NGBs. The CPSU provides advice and guidance to governing bodies, coaches, athletes and parents on a wide range of child protection issues. It also produces the 'Standards for Safeguarding and Protecting Children in Sport' which provides guidelines to and sets benchmark standards of good practice for governing bodies including a child protection policy template. The aim of these benchmarks is to ensure that certain minimum standards have been reached in respect of their child protection procedures and that these are being implemented by NGBs.

Hot topic … | ## Controlling gambling and match-fixing in sport

Gambling has a long association with sport. Indeed, the early codification of some sports was to ensure that odds could be calculated accurately, and bets paid out on specific outcomes. Despite this link, attitudes towards sports betting change regularly and in large parts of the world gambling on sports is unlawful.

Gambling-related corruption is now seen by many ISFs and NGBs as a serious threat to the integrity of sport, perhaps even more so than doping, particularly as gambling technologies and organised criminal gambling syndicates have become increasingly sophisticated. Any sport that is gambled on is at risk of related corruption, though some are at more risk than others. For example, it is more difficult to fix the overall result of team sports without multiple parties being involved, including players, officials, club personnel and gamblers playing some sort of role, as was the case in the Italian football scandal. In contrast, where only one person can be corrupted to influence the result, as in horse racing, tennis or snooker, there is a much higher risk of individual participants being corrupted. Further, it is easier to manipulate or spot-fix specific set pieces in a sporting contest, such as deliberately bowling no balls or wides in cricket, or double faulting in tennis, rather than trying to force a footballer to score more goals, over which he may have very little control.

Advances in gambling and gambling-related technology have also facilitated corruption in a way that could not have happened in the past. First, it is now possible to bet on almost any aspect of a sporting contest, not just its result or outcome, inadvertently creating the opportunity for spot-fixing. Secondly, the advent of betting exchanges where individuals can act as bookmakers in their own right and set their own odds, including accepting bets that an athlete might lose instead of win, has created increased risks of players being offered financial incentives to manipulate the sporting contest. Although the major gambling companies and exchanges have protocols in place to reduce the risk of corrupt gambling practices, these have no application in countries where gambling is illegal and engaged in by privately organised criminal syndicates operating outside of the traditional betting forums.

In the light of recent scandals, sport authorities are themselves becoming more sophisticated in their anti-corruption regimes.

Many have introduced codes of conduct for everyone involved in the sport and particularly for players, coaches and match officials. These operate alongside education programmes, whistleblowing hotlines and anti-corruption investigative units. For example, the International Cricket Council has implemented the Anti-Corruption Code and established the Anti-Corruption and Security Unit to investigate corruption and misconduct by those involved with cricket. There have even been calls in some quarters for a WADA-style World Anti-Corruption Agency to be established to combat gambling-related crime.

Bans for engaging in corruption are substantial and usually significantly longer than those that are imposed for doping or acts of violence. Courts have refused to interfere with these lengthy bans even when they will, in practice, lead to the end of the player's career, as occurred when the High Court refused to exercise its supervisory jurisdiction to overturn the five-year ban imposed on Graham Bradley (*Bradley v Jockey Club* [2005] EWCA Civ 1056). A similar approach was followed by CAS when it upheld life bans on Serbian tennis player David Savic and Austrian Daniel Koellerer, after each was separately found guilty of match-fixing following investigations by the Tennis Integrity Unit

into contraventions of the Uniform Tennis Anti-Corruption Program (*Savic v Professional Tennis Integrity Officers* CAS 2011/A/2621 and *Koellerer v Association of Tennis Professionals, Women's Tennis Association, International Tennis Federation and Grand Slam Committee* CAS 2011/A/2490). The length of these bans is justified on the grounds that corrupt practices of this nature are the antithesis of sporting integrity and undermine the nature of sport so completely that a substantial and even a life ban can be seen as reasonable and proportionate, where a doper would usually be given at least a chance of redemption.

In the UK, the Sports Betting Intelligence Unit was created by the Gambling Commission in 2005. It focuses on collecting and analysing information and intelligence relating to potentially criminal activity in respect of sports betting, where the sporting event either takes place in the UK or involves one or more parties who are based in the UK, or involves a gambling company licensed by the Gambling Commission. The information gathered by the SBIU can be used to bring prosecutions or regulatory action under the Gambling Act 2005. By working with the police, NGBs and related international organisations, the SBIU hopes to maintain the integrity of both British sport and the British gambling industry.

Summary

6.1 Despite the longevity of the jurisprudence in this area, an uneasy relationship continues to exist between the criminal law and sports participation. The courts' aim is to punish all criminal acts, including those which occur in sports. However, the judiciary also appears to consider that NGBs should be playing a more proactive role in keeping their own houses in order. These mixed messages have led to much confusion about whether or not the criminal law ever has a role to play in the punishment and control of sports violence.

Summary cont'd

6.2 Common assault is the foundation stone of all offences against the person. Sections 47 and 20 OAPA are the most common charges brought against athletes accused of acting violently. Players are much less frequently charged with intentionally causing GBH under s.18 OAPA because of the much more stringent *mens rea* requirements. As a general rule, after *R v Barnes,* it is likely that the assault offences defined in the OAPA will only be used to prosecute acts of violence that are completely unconnected with the playing of the game in question. Homicide charges arising out of sport will be extremely rare. They will usually only be appropriate following a deliberate or reckless criminal assault that has resulted in the death of the victim as in *R v CC.*

6.3 Prosecutions for public order offences committed by athletes are likely to be extremely rare. It will only be where the behaviour of the player is likely or intended to incite disorder in the crowd that such offences will be committed. In most other cases, a prosecution for common assault will be more appropriate. Racially-aggravated public order offences can be appropriate where players have engaged in racial abuse directed at either their opponents or spectators.

6.4 Corruption in sport linked to gambling is a growing concern in many sports as it undermines the integrity of the sporting contest and the image of the sport. Although a range of criminal offences, including conspiracy and cheating at gambling, can be committed by players engaging in match- or spot-fixing, NGBs and ISFs are taking an increasingly proactive stance in the regulation and punishment of these corrupt practices.

6.5 Sexual assaults should have nothing to do with the actual playing of sport. What sport does provide is the setting in which sexual abuse and the abuse of relationships of trust can take place. Hopefully, the leadership and advice provided by the Child Protection in Sport Unit and the policies that it is helping to develop with many NGBs will continue to raise awareness of the threats posed to athletes, particularly those who are young and vulnerable.

Further reading

Grayson, *Sport and the Law* (3rd edn, 2000, Butterworths) appendix 6

Herring, *Criminal Law: text, cases and materials* (3rd edn, 2008, Oxford University Press) ch 6

Law Commission, *Consent and offences against the Person*, LCCP No 134 (1994, HMSO)

Law Commission, *Consent in the Criminal Law*, LCCP No 139 (1995, HMSO)

Lewis and Taylor (eds), *Sport: Law and Practice* (2nd edn, 2008, Tottel) ch D6

Alldridge, 'R v Majeed: corruption – conspiracy to give corrupt payments – accepting corrupt payments' [2012] *Criminal Law Review* 965

Anderson, 'Policing the sports field' [2005] 2 ISLR 25

Anderson, 'No licence for thuggery: violence, sport and the criminal law' [2008] *Criminal Law Review* 751

Carpenter, 'Match-fixing – the biggest threat to sport in the 21st century?' [2012] 2 *International Sports Law Review* 13

Gardiner, 'The law and hate speech: "Ooh aah Cantona" and the demonstration of the other' in Brown (ed), *Fanatics! Power, Identity and Fandom in Football* (1998, Routledge)

Gardiner, 'Not playing the game: Is it a crime?' [1993] *Solicitors Journal* 628

Grayson and Bond, 'Making foul play a crime' [1993] *Solicitors Journal* 693

James and Gardiner, 'Touchlines and guidelines: the Lord Advocate's response to sportsfield violence' [1997] *Criminal Law Review* 41

Further Reading cont'd

Naidoo, 'On the front foot against corruption' [2004] 1 *International Sports Law Review* 3
Naidoo and Gardiner, 'On the front foot against corruption' [2007] 1/2 *International Sports Law Journal* 21.
Williams, 'Consent and public policy' [1962] *Criminal Law Review* 74

Links to relevant websites can be found at www.palgrave.com/law/james2e

Chapter 7

The legality of fighting sports

- Context (7.1)

- The legal status of traditional fighting sports (7.2)
  - Distinguishing between sparring and prize-fighting (7.2.1)
    - Causing danger to the participants (7.2.1.1)
    - The tendency of prize-fighting to cause a breach of the peace (7.2.1.2)
    - An alternative approach – the reasonableness of the rules of the game (7.2.1.3)

- The legal status of modern fighting sports (7.3)
  - The anomalous position of fighting sports (7.3.1)
  - Properly conducted sports (7.3.2)

- Justifying the legal status of fighting sports (7.4)
  - The public policy arguments (7.4.1)
    - Boxing should be lawful because it is a sport (7.4.1.1)
    - Boxing should be lawful because it promotes fitness (7.4.1.2)
    - Boxing should be lawful because it instils discipline (7.4.1.3)
    - Boxing should be lawful because it offers financial security (7.4.1.4)
    - Boxing should be lawful because it is popular (7.4.1.5)
    - Boxing should be lawful because it is traditional (7.4.1.6)
    - Boxing should not be lawful because it is too dangerous (7.4.1.7)
    - Boxing should not be lawful because it encourages violence (7.4.1.8)
    - Boxing should not be lawful because it encourages gambling (7.4.1.9)
    - Boxing should not be lawful because it creates public disorder (7.4.1.10)
    - Summary of the public policy arguments (7.4.1.11)
  - The legal arguments and R v Brown (7.4.2)
    - The extent of the injuries caused is unknown in advance (7.4.2.1)
    - There is insufficient regulation of the causing of serious injury (7.4.2.2)
    - There is a potential for the cross-infection of blood-borne diseases (7.4.2.3)
    - The activity promotes a cult of violence in society (7.4.2.4)
    - Summary of the legal arguments (7.4.2.5)
  - The jurisprudential arguments (7.4.3)
    - Liberalism (7.4.3.1)
    - Paternalism (7.4.3.2)
    - Legal moralism (7.4.3.3)
    - Summary of the jurisprudential arguments (7.4.3.4)
  - Conclusion (7.4.4)

The legality of fighting sports

- ▶ **Aiding and abetting** – providing assistance or encouragement to those who are committing a criminal offence.
- ▶ **Prize-fight** – an unlawful boxing contest between participants who fight until one of them is physically unable to continue, usually for reward.
- ▶ **Seconds** – a boxer's assistants who are present at ringside and able to provide advice and basic first aid as required.
- ▶ **Sparring** – a lawful boxing contest that tests the participants' skill, strength and dexterity.
- ▶ **Mixed Martial Arts** – a fighting contest between exponents of different fighting disciplines where the rules of the bout are limited to enable a wider variety of moves to be performed; widely known by various commercial names such as *UFC* and *Cage Fighting*.

7.1 Context

Fighting sports are amongst the oldest, most established and most popular sporting disciplines in the world. Of the 28 sports currently included in the Olympic Summer Programme, five are modern forms of traditional fighting sports: boxing, fencing, judo, taekwondo and wrestling. Most of these sports and many others of a similar type can trace their origins to military training regimes. However, as warfare became increasingly mechanised and the need for these skills became less important for battle, a number of these activities evolved into the recognisable fighting sports of today.

This category of sport has always received a significant degree of protection from the normal operation of the law; without this protection, fighting sports would constitute a range of offences from criminal assault to homicide (see further, chapter 6.2) To accommodate them, the law of consent has developed an exemption for fighting sports with the classic explanation originating in Foster's *Crown Law*, where it is stated in relation to wrestling and cudgelling:

> 'Here is the appearance of combat, but it is in reality no more than a friendly exertion of strength and dexterity. They are manly diversions, they tend to give strength, skill and activity, and make fit people for defence ... I would not be understood to speak of prize-fighting and public boxing-matches, or any other exertions ... of the like kind ... which are exhibited for lucre, and can serve no valuable purpose; but on the contrary encourage a spirit of idleness and debauchery.'

Not only does Foster explain why these sports should be protected, he also identifies the key issue that has troubled the courts ever since: whether, apart from creating 'fit people for defence', there are any legal, moral or public policy reasons why fighting sports should be exempted from the normal operation of the criminal law. He clearly feels that anyone fighting for money should not benefit from the exemption granted to those who are simply testing their skill, strength and dexterity. This distinction and its specific manifestation in respect of prize-fighting and sparring came before the courts on a number of occasions throughout the eighteenth and nineteenth centuries and continues to influence legal discussions on consent to the present day.

As sport became more organised, and less tolerance was shown towards bloodshed for the sake of entertainment, the legality of fighting sports began to be questioned more frequently. Although there is no doubt that some of these sports are completely lawful, the legal status of others occupies a greyer area, where public policy, morality and legal theory collide with equal force.

7.2 The legal status of traditional fighting sports

Without some measure of exemption from the operation of the law of offences against the person and homicide, participation in any fighting sport would be at least a series of criminal assaults. From before Foster's time, it had been acknowledged that in limited circumstances, it was possible to provide a valid consent to blows that were struck in the name of sport or for the purposes of military training but that all prize-fights were illegal. The only real question was where precisely to draw the line between what Foster refers to as 'manly diversions' and criminal assaults.

7.2.1 Distinguishing between sparring and prize-fighting

Throughout the 1800s, a number of cases focused their discussions on where to draw this line by creating a distinction between sparring, which was lawful, and prize-fighting, which was not. Sparring is described variously as being an exercise of pugilistic skill, a demonstration of the ability to attack and defend oneself, that promotes strength and agility and where violence was not the aim of the participants who would fight wearing padded gloves for a pre-determined number of rounds. Prize-fighting, on the other hand, involved bouts that were accompanied by violence and personal danger to the participants and the threat of a breach of the peace amongst the spectators. The threat of violence posed to the fighters was created by the bouts often being bare-knuckle and their continuing until one or other of the participants was physically incapable of fighting any longer. The threat of a breach of the peace came from disorder in the crowds that was usually associated with the gambling that accompanied prize-fights.

Not only was prize-fighting itself illegal, so was the training of fighters to compete in prize-fights (*Hunt v Bell* (1822) 1 Bingham 1) and the organisation of prize-fighting contests (*R v Coney* (1881–82) 8 QBD 534) (below, 7.2.1.1). There are therefore two strands to the distinction between lawful and unlawful fighting sports: the dangerousness of the contest to the protagonists themselves when compared to the comparative safety of genuine tests of skill and the potential of some sports to cause a breach of the peace. Whether or not the fight was for money appears not to have been considered as important a concern as the risk of injury and disorder.

7.2.1.1 Causing danger to the participants

The potential dangers to which the participants in a prize-fight are exposed range from minor cuts and bruises to death. The seriousness of the harm that could be caused to a prize-fighter was exacerbated by bouts being fought bare-knuckle and over an unlimited number of rounds. Conversely, sparring was not considered to be dangerous.

▶ *R v Young and others* (1866) 10 Cox CC 371

The defendants were charged with manslaughter following the death of Young's opponent in an organised fight. The remaining defendants were the organisers of, and seconds at, the contest. In the final round, the deceased lost his balance and fell, hitting his head against a post that ran up through the centre of the ring. The court considered that it was important to take into account that the fight had taken place in a private room containing a boxing ring, that the fighters were both wearing padded gloves and that the only other people present were friends of the fighters and their seconds. In directing the jury, the judge noted that where a contest began as lawful exhibition of sparring, it was possible for it to become a criminal assault where the participants continued to fight until they were in such a state of exhaustion that it was *probable* that one would fall and might, as a result, be injured and die.

All of the defendants were acquitted on the basis that this was an accident caused during the course of a lawful sparring contest. The jury reached this conclusion by relying primarily on the expert evidence of the house-surgeon from Charing Cross Hospital, who stated that sparring with gloves in this manner would be very unlikely to cause injuries that would lead to death. Furthermore, the presence of the seconds to look after the participants reduced the inherent dangers of the fight to both of them.

The key distinction identified in *Young* that led to sparring being held to be a lawful activity is that there was some form of regulation in place. Where the activity is inherently dangerous, it is important that there are safety systems and rules in place to make it as safe as is reasonably possible. Unlawful prize-fighting, however, has few of these safeguards in place, creating a high risk of serious injury being caused to the participants. This reasoning was developed further to require the court to examine the true aim of the fight, not just its form.

▶ *R v Orton* (1878) 14 Cox CC 226

The defendants had paid to enter premises to watch a fight. The fighters each wore padded gloves, fought in a ring and were attended to by seconds. The Court held that where a fight was organised to be an exhibition of skill in sparring, then the contest was lawful. However, if the parties intended that the fight would continue until one or other of the participants could not continue, either because of the severity of the injuries that they had received or through exhaustion, then the contest was an unlawful prize-fight. The court held that it was not the existence of safety measures, such as the wearing of protective equipment and the attendance of seconds, that determined the lawfulness of the event; the focus should instead be on the intentions of the participants and of those who had organised the contest.

Where the aim was to fight until one of the participants was so exhausted or so injured that they could not continue, then the fight was a series of unlawful assaults. Furthermore, if the fight was for money, it was an unlawful prize-fight. If it was a test of attacking and defensive skill, and after 1865 preferably in accordance with the Marquis of Queensbury's Rules, then it would be a lawful bout of sparring regardless of whether or not the spectators had paid an entrance fee to watch the event.

7.2.1.2 The tendency of prize-fighting to cause a breach of the peace

In neither *Young* nor *Orton* was it necessary to discuss in any detail whether there had been a breach of the peace as the activities taking place were held to be lawful sporting contests. It would appear from the charges laid against the defendants that where the spectators are at a private venue and have not paid to view the bout, there is no breach of the peace as there is no threat to public order (*Young*). However, where the spectators have paid to gain entry to the event, then a breach of the peace is at least a possibility because of the public nature of the event (*Orton*) (see also *Butcher v Jessop*, chapter 6.3.2).

▶ *R v Coney and others* (1881–82) 8 QBD 534

The defendants were prosecuted for being involved in various roles connected with a prize-fight, including in particular the competitors, the organisers and some of the spectators. The fight itself had taken place on private ground in a ring where the participants were separated from the spectators by a rope. Although a crowd of over a hundred people was present, and betting was taking place, there was no evidence of crowd disorder. The defendants were found guilty of aiding and abetting an assault and appealed against their convictions.

The Court for Crown Cases Reserved, where an almost unprecedented 11 judgments were handed down, held that participation in a prize-fight is illegal because of the inherent risk of serious injury being caused to the participants and the additional risk of a breach of the peace occurring amongst the onlookers; the consent of the participants is irrelevant and cannot make lawful that which is unlawful. Further, the Court held that all those who were aiding and abetting the prize-fight, in particular those who had organised it and those who were acting as seconds for the fighters, were also guilty of an offence. In line with the previous authorities on these issues, these convictions were upheld.

The defendants who had been spectators in the crowd that had been watching the prize-fight had originally been convicted on the basis that their voluntary presence at an illegal activity was sufficient to prove that they had encouraged it to take place and therefore had aided and abetted it. In setting aside the convictions, a majority of the Court (8–3) held that mere presence at an illegal activity was not sufficient of itself to constitute aiding and abetting the crime to take place. Their presence at the contest could only constitute evidence that the defendants *may* have been aiding and abetting the unlawful prize-fight by watching it; to secure a conviction against them, it was still necessary to prove that the defendants had actively encouraged or assisted the unlawful fight to have taken place.

The court was unanimous in holding that prize-fights were illegal, that the participants in prize-fights commit criminal assaults with every punch thrown and that anyone who actively encourages the fighters, or who assisted with the organisation of the fight, is guilty of aiding and abetting the assaults committed by the fighters. In coming to these conclusions, a variety of explanations were given to explain why prize-fighting itself was a criminal activity.

Firstly, it was considered that where the blows were intended or likely to cause physical injury, then a criminal assault had been committed. As prize-fights were usually contests that were fought until one of the participants was physically incapable of continuing, injury was at least highly likely if not actually intended. This was contrasted with blows struck in the course of sparring contests where it was assumed that there was no intent to cause harm, only to exhibit one's skill, and little or no likelihood of causing harm to an opponent because of the safety rules and precautions that were in place.

Secondly, that assaults of this nature were breaches of the peace, particularly where a crowd of spectators was watching the event. Prize-fights were referred to as being disorderly exhibitions that were mischievous on many obvious grounds. Nobody is allowed to consent to injuries being inflicted on them where they are likely to be productive of a breach of the peace as it is not in the public interest to cause violent disturbances in the name of sport or entertainment. Therefore, prize-fights are criminal assaults that are incapable of being rendered lawful by the consent of the participants because they have the potential to incite violence in others.

Thirdly, the harm inflicted on the participants had the potential to be of such a high degree that it was not in the public interest to allow prize-fights for the protection of those taking part in them. As Matthew J pointed out at p.547, 'The fists of trained pugilists are dangerous weapons which they are not at liberty to use against each other.' By highlighting the similarities between the fists of trained fighters and weapons, the court was drawing a distinction similar to that which could be drawn between fencing and duelling. Both activities involve the use of swords, but the aim of the former is a test of skill based on a scoring system, whereas the aim of the latter is to inflict injury and/or death. Likewise, where fists are used in a controlled environment with a scoring system and safety procedures in place, then the event is a bout of lawful sparring, but where the aim is to inflict injury, and where there is an attendant risk of death, then the punches thrown are unlawful assaults.

7.2.1.3 An alternative approach – the reasonableness of the rules of the game

The approach of the English courts is in contrast to that used by the courts in the USA following a decision of the New York State Supreme Court.

▶ *People v Fitzsimmons* (1895) 34 NYS 1102

The defendant had killed his opponent by punching him during an exhibition of boxing. In directing the jury, the judge stated that where the rules and practices of the game are reasonable, are consented to by all engaged in the activity and are not likely to cause serious injury or death, then no offence is committed if the injury-causing blow is landed within those rules and practices. The focus of the New York court is on whether the rules and practices of the sport in question are reasonable; if they are, then all injury-causing contacts that occur during the playing of the game are lawful. However, where the rules and practices are not reasonable, then all contacts made are criminal.

In *Fitzsimmons*, the rules of boxing under which the event took place were considered to be reasonable and therefore no criminal assault that could form the basis of the manslaughter charge had been committed. Had the event been a prize-fight as defined by the English courts, then the court may have held that the rules of the game were unreasonable and that manslaughter had been committed by the defendant. This is a much simpler approach to the determination of the legality of an activity and would have allowed English law to have developed incrementally in a more structured manner than it has when confronted by some of the limited rules fighting sports that are currently popular.

7.3 The legal status of modern fighting sports

By the 1880s, a clear distinction had been drawn between lawful sparring and unlawful prize-fighting. The challenge for the law would be to see how it would respond to the emergence of professional fighting sports, particularly with the increasing popularity of professional boxing and later the evolution of hybrid and mixed-discipline sports; post-*Coney*, the only fighting sports specifically referred to as being lawful activities were sparring, wrestling and fighting with single-sticks or cudgels. Two arguments are at the centre of this debate. Firstly, some commentators have argued that as modern fighting sports in general, and boxing in particular, have never been declared lawful as part of the *ratio decidendi* of a case, then these, too, are unlawful activities.

In response to this claim, the lack of case law on the legality of fighting sports would appear in reality to suggest that most of the more common disciplines are lawful activities because of their longstanding judicial and Parliamentary acceptance . In the light of the many comments made by the appellate courts on the accepted legality of boxing over the years, it has been assumed that these activities are lawful until declared otherwise. Further, where appropriate analogies can be drawn, the exemption for fighting sports must extend beyond the three activities named in *Coney*, though how far is not entirely clear. This lack of judicial and Parliamentary analysis also means that there is no framework provided for determining whether a new sport should or should not be lawful.

A second claim draws on Foster's statement of the law and argues that where professional boxing is concerned, as the participants are fighting for money, the bouts are in legal terms prize-fights and therefore unlawful. This argument also struggles to withstand closer scrutiny as it focuses unduly on the financial element of the bout at the expense of analysing the intentions of the fighters. It is in the context of arguments such as these that the legality of fighting sports must be examined.

7.3.1 The anomalous position of fighting sports

The almost unquestioning acceptance of the legally anomalous position of fighting sports is epitomised by the comments of Lord Lane CJ in *Attorney-General's Reference (No6 of 1980)* [1981] QB 715 in the context of a fight between two young men trying to settle an argument, where he stated at p.719:

> 'It is not in the public interest that people should try to cause … each other actual bodily harm for no good reason … [It] is immaterial whether the act occurs in private or in public; it is an assault if actual bodily harm is intended and/or caused. This means that most fights will be unlawful regardless of consent. Nothing which we have said is intended to cast doubt upon the accepted legality of properly conducted games and sports … [This apparent exception] can be justified as … needed in the public interest.'

Thus, 'properly conducted sports' are exempted from the normal operation of the law of assault because it is accepted as being in the public interest to protect and encourage such activities. No further explanation is provided beyond this, but also no limits are put on the sports to which the exemption extends. Presumably, if similar reasoning to that used in *Fitzsimmons* is applied, then other established and properly conducted sports, such as the Olympic sports of judo and taekwondo, are also protected by the exemption. Although participants in sports such as these, and many others besides, are undoubtedly covered by this exemption, there is nothing in the case law that justifies definitively such a conclusion.

This was reiterated in *R v Brown* [1994] 1 AC 212, the leading case on the general application of consent in the criminal law, where Lord Mustill regarded an intellectually satisfying account of the immunity of boxing as being impossible to achieve. Instead, his Lordship stated simply that boxing is a special situation which stands outside the ordinary law of violence because society chooses at present to tolerate it.

The Law Commission's analysis in its two consultation papers on consent also failed to provide a convincing analysis of the legality of fighting sports. In *Consent and Offences against the Person* (LCCP No 134, 1994), the Law Commission stated that the immunity of boxing from the criminal law was so firmly embedded that only Parliamentary intervention could change its legal status. In respect of other fighting sports the Commission again thought that legislation was the most appropriate means of clarifying the legal position of these activities.

In its follow up paper, *Consent in the Criminal Law* (LCCP No 139, 1995), the Law Commission recommended that a scheme should be established under the auspices of what is now UK Sport that would 'recognise' lawful sports. If injury were inflicted during a recognised sport the conduct would be lawful, but if the same harm were caused during an unrecognised sport, then a criminal assault would be committed. As the consultation papers have not been acted on, and the proposed scheme was never developed into a workable set of criteria, they provide little further guidance on whether or not participation in a fighting sport is actually lawful. The intellectually satisfying justification for the immunity of fighting sports from the criminal law remains elusive.

Without a binding precedent to justify the legality of fighting sports, and in the absence of a convincing theoretical justification for the exemption extending beyond the activities referred to in *Coney*, the suggestion remains that sports whose object is to inflict harm rather than to score points in a test of skill should be illegal. In particular, the legality of modern professional boxing has been questioned by a number of academic commentators on the basis that it bears a greater resemblance to unlawful prize-fighting than to the lawful sparring referred to in *Coney*. It has been argued that a combination of over-hyped grudge matches, the emphasis on the knockout punch and the lack of protection for the main target area (the head) and that because injury is an integral and necessary part of participation, these points all demonstrate that professional boxing is about fighting until one party can no longer physically continue rather than being a test of skill based on point-scoring. In other words, professional boxing is the modern equivalent of prize-fighting and should be illegal. In contrast, amateur boxing, with its low number of short rounds, the requirement to wear head guards and its emphasis on point-scoring, is the true inheritor of the exemption afforded to sparring.

This argument is, of course, refuted by those who see boxing as the noble art of self-defence and professional boxers as its elite exponents. Those in favour of boxing remaining a lawful activity point out that even in the professional arena, most bouts are decided on points, not by a knockout. Moreover, the training undergone by all boxers, but particularly by professionals, means that they are able to dodge or cushion the impact of the blows struck, have to wear padded gloves and can be forced to retire by either the referee or their seconds if it appears that they are physically unable to continue to defend themselves. In other words, although a knockout is the most decisive way to secure victory, professional boxing is still a test of skill, strength, stamina and ability, as was sparring and as is amateur boxing.

Despite the lack of specific appellate authority, the legality of boxing was confirmed where contests were conducted in accordance with a set of rules that had been designed to measure the comparative skill of the fighters.

▶ *R v Roberts* (unreported) **Central Criminal Court (London), 28 June 1901**

The defendants were charged with manslaughter following the death of Roberts' opponent in a fight organised in accordance with the rules of the National Sporting Club, which in turn were based on the Marquis of Queensberry's Rules. The remaining defendants included the seconds at the fight, the referee, the timekeeper and the manager of the National Sporting Club on whose premises the contest took place. The prosecution argued that the rule that awarded the contest to a participant whose opponent could not resume fighting after having been knocked down for a count of ten seconds encouraged boxers to attempt to knock each other out. If this was the case, the fight was unlawful as its outcome was to be decided on the basis of the ability of one of the participants to continue fighting as opposed to their skill and ability at boxing. The defence argued that the ten-second rule was there to protect the safety of participants by preventing them from fighting when they were concussed and therefore unable to protect themselves properly. In directing the jury, the judge stated that if they believed that the contest was carried on with the intention that one of the parties should fight until the other gave in because of injury or exhaustion then they had been acting criminally. However if this was a case of fighting in accordance with rules that were designed to measure the comparative skill of the participants, not simply to enable them to fight until one or other of them was physically unable to continue, then this was a lawful sporting contest.

The jury found the defendant boxer not guilty of manslaughter on the basis that the participants had not intended to fight until one or other of them was physically incapable of continuing. Instead, the fight had been to determine who was the more skilful according to the number of points awarded by the referee. Further, the injury appeared to have been caused by the deceased's head hitting the ropes around the edge of the ring, not from a blow landed by the defendant and was an accident that had occurred in the course of a lawful sporting contest. As the primary liability of the defendant boxer could not be established, the cases of secondary party liability against the remaining defendants also failed as there was no crime committed for them to have aided and abetted.

Thus, where the aim of the fight is to determine who is the more skilful exponent of the noble art rather than to batter the opponent into submission or unconsciousness, then the fight is a lawful sporting contest. Although it could be argued that some professional boxing matches place too great an emphasis on the knockout blow, the further judicial acceptance of its legality in cases up to and including *Brown* indicate clearly that both professional and amateur boxing, and by analogy other 'properly conducted sports', are exempted from the criminal law. Furthermore, these sports will continue to benefit from this protection unless and until they are declared by Parliament to be otherwise.

7.3.2 Properly conducted sports

In the absence of a definitive list of lawful sports, some link needs to be found between the various decisions that will indicate how and why a fighting sport will be considered to be a lawful activity. For this to occur, it would appear that the most important criterion is that the sport be 'well-organised' or 'properly conducted.' Although there is no explanation of what is meant by these terms, certain basic requirements can be identified as being necessary in the sport's administration. For example, they will need to be contested according to a predetermined set of rules, where each contest is overseen by appropriately qualified referees or judges and possibly organised under the auspices of an appropriate NGB and/or ISF.

The necessary level of organisation will go beyond the drafting of the playing rules and administering fixtures to include the drafting of safety rules and protocols, including the provision of medical staff and facilities where appropriate. Where these are not provided, the governing body of the sport or the organiser of the event may not only find themselves guilty of organising an illegal event where they have aided and abetted the commission of criminal assaults and breaches of the peace, they may also be liable in negligence to any participant injured during the course of the bout (*Watson v British Boxing Board of Control* [2001] QB 1134, Court of Appeal, chapter 5.4.1.1.2). If these safeguards are in place and there is some inherent worth in the sport that justifies its protection as being in the public interest, usually that it is a test of strength, skill and dexterity and not just the infliction of violence and pain for the purposes of entertainment, then it is likely that the sport will be found to be a lawful activity. In the cases of boxing and other high-profile, universally-recognised sports, there is little doubt that their levels of organisation and conduct are sufficient to ensure that they will continue to be lawful activities for as long as society sees fit to tolerate them.

The position of less well-organised or newly-emergent disciplines is less clear. Their lack of an agreed set of playing rules or their inability to secure an appropriate level of medical support could mean that participation in such sports is significantly more dangerous than it is in the richer, higher-profile and more established sports. For example, despite its popularity as a participation sport, none of the major forms of kick boxing have ever been recognised by UK Sport for funding purposes. One of the main reasons for this is that there is no universally recognised governing body within the UK that oversees the sport. This means that the sport cannot be recognised as an activity by UK Sport as there is insufficient agreement on what the sport actually entails, no unified set of rules and no single entity in charge of regulating the activity. This lack of agreement makes it difficult to argue that the sport is properly conducted.

Mixed Martial Arts competitions have attracted a significant amount of controversy in recent years because of their apparent lack of rules. These events pit exponents of different fighting disciplines against one another and therefore require a limited set of rules to ensure that fighters from different traditions can compete against one another (below, Hot Topic). It is possible that competitions of this kind are lawful as they are based on what are generally recognised as lawful sports rather than being completely unregulated brawls. Provided that each contest has a pre-defined set of playing rules and appropriate safety protocols and medical support in place, it is difficult to see how it could be declared unlawful just because it is new to the UK and distasteful to some. The key to an activity's legality rests on whether or not it can demonstrate that it is properly conducted. For example, adherence to a clear set of rules or guidelines created for MMA-style events by a well-respected regulatory body, such as the New Jersey State Athletic Control Board's 'Mixed Martial Arts Unified Rules of Conduct', would tend towards an assumption that the event is lawful.

The requirement that a fighting sport must be properly organised ensures that there is in place at least a basic set of criteria against which its legality can be judged. The courts are then able to apply what they consider to be appropriate public interest arguments to prevent the emergence of any unnecessarily violent activities that they feel are masquerading as lawful sports. The Law Commission suggested that a validating body, perhaps UK Sport, would be able to accredit sports as lawful to avoid further litigation on this subject. In other countries (for example, Australia), this function is performed by the state. However, since the Law Commission's proposals were put forward, there have been no further developments on such a scheme. Regardless of the actual legal status of emergent and/or less-organised fighting sports, the reality is that they are protected by the participants on a day-to-day basis. The factual consent of these participants and their desire to ensure the continuation of their chosen discipline ensures that it is extremely unlikely that legal action will be taken by any of them against anyone else connected with their sport except in the most extreme of cases.

7.4 Justifying the legal status of fighting sports

When seeking to justify their views on the legal status of fighting sports, a wide range of public policy, legal and jurisprudential arguments are frequently referred to. What follows is not an attempt to provide a definitive proof that one side of the argument is more convincing than the other. Instead, it provides a basis upon which a justification for either point of view can be built. The focus of this discussion is the legal status of boxing rather than all fighting sports. Its traditional and well-established place within British sporting culture and its centrality to legal and medical debates on whether fighting sports are acceptable activities mean that boxing can be used as a benchmark against which the legality of other sports can be judged.

The starting point of any analysis of this area has to be that regardless of one's personal views on the matter, boxing is lawful. The twin bases for this claim are the judicial comments on the accepted legality of boxing referred to above and the failed attempts by Parliament to outlaw professional boxing that have taken place on several occasions over the past 50 years. If the Supreme Court considers that an activity, if properly conducted, is legal, then it can be assumed that it is, at least for the time being. Furthermore, if Parliament considers it necessary to debate the possibility of outlawing certain forms of boxing, then it can be assumed that the activity is lawful and will continue to be so until sufficient numbers of MPs vote to implement a ban.

7.4.1 The public policy arguments

A wide range of public policy arguments have been put forward to justify both sides of the argument about whether boxing should be a lawful activity. Although there is an element of validity contained in most of them, none deliver the decisive blow for either side.

7.4.1.1 Boxing should be lawful because it is a sport

Although the appellate courts have stated that 'properly conducted sports' are lawful activities, a simple statement that boxing is a sport is not sufficient for it to gain legal acceptance. As has already been discussed (above, 7.3.2), there appears to be a series of criteria that must be fulfilled before an activity can be considered to be a properly conducted sport; a simple declaration that it fulfils these is not sufficiently legally robust to justify that status without more. Although being a properly conducted sport enables boxing to clear the first hurdle to becoming a lawful sport, it still relies on the goodwill of Parliament and the courts for its continued protection.

7.4.1.2 Boxing should be lawful because it promotes fitness

It is undoubtedly true that the training regimes undertaken by boxers create extremely fit and healthy athletes. However, it is the training rather than participation in the sport that promotes health and fitness; actual participation in a boxing bout can be seriously detrimental to a boxer's health because of the blows received to the head and body. If fitness were the sole justification, then only training to box, rather than actually boxing, can be justified as being in a person's best interests.

7.4.1.3 Boxing should be lawful because it instils discipline

There are several facets to this argument. Firstly, the physicality of the training regime ensures that a boxer must exhibit a high degree of self-discipline by turning up for sessions, not drinking or smoking and generally looking after their physical well-being, otherwise they will not be physically or mentally prepared to fight in the ring. Secondly, it teaches boxers to be disciplined in the use of their fighting skills and encourages them not to use violence in any other setting except the boxing ring. Thirdly, it is often argued that the discipline and self-respect instilled by the training regime and camaraderie of the boxing club has prevented some young boxers from pursuing a life of crime. As with the previous argument, these arguments struggle to justify why boxing, rather than the training regime that boxers follow, should be lawful.

7.4.1.4 Boxing should be lawful because it offers financial security

This much-used justification, that boxing enables people from poor backgrounds to work their way out of poverty, is one that has little evidence to back it up. Although many of the world's most successful boxers have come from poor backgrounds, and those who become successful are usually financially secure for life, the vast majority of boxers make comparatively little money from participation in the sport. An opportunity to earn substantial sums of money is undoubtedly available to all boxers, but the reality is that very few are ever able to take full advantage of it.

7.4.1.5 Boxing should be lawful because it is popular

It has often been stated in the courts that what is of interest to the public is not necessarily in the public interest. Thus, just because an activity is popular does not automatically mean that it will be, or even ought to be, lawful. Boxing is not only popular but is important in economic terms, providing employment to many boxers, coaches and an entire supporting industry. Although it would be difficult and controversial to outlaw the sport because of its entrenchment within the UK's sporting and social fabric, Parliament has not always shied away from banning popular activities that it no longer considers to be socially acceptable, as was the case with some shooting sports and fox hunting. Popularity alone is not enough to guarantee the continued legality of boxing.

7.4.1.6 Boxing should be lawful because it is traditional

As with the previous point, the longevity and traditions of a sport are not enough to guarantee its legality. Both shooting sports and fox hunting can trace their roots back many centuries, though both have been regulated and/or outlawed by statute on the basis that their traditional position in British sport could no longer be justified as being in the public interest.

7.4.1.7 Boxing should not be lawful because it is too dangerous

Perhaps the strongest argument against the continuing legality of boxing is the growing weight of medical evidence about its inherent dangers. This may sound obvious, considering that this is a sport where points are scored for punching an opponent, but the difficulty that the medical profession has encountered has been creating an evidence base for some of its claims. In particular, until comparatively recently, it had been difficult to prove a specific link between boxing and chronic brain injury, which is the cumulative brain damage caused by repetitive blows to the head over a prolonged period of time. This kind of harm is distinguished from acute brain injury which is caused by individual traumatic blows to the head, such as the knockout punch.

Despite the specific risk of serious harm associated with boxing, serious injury and death are inherent dangers of participation in many sports. To single out boxing is to fail to take into account the risks associated with participating in these other sports, the measures taken by boxing to make it as safe as is reasonably practicable and that the inherent dangers of boxing are known to all boxers in advance of entering the ring. The risk of serious injury alone is not sufficient justification for outlawing boxing.

7.4.1.8 Boxing should not be lawful because it encourages violence

In direct contrast to the claim that boxing enables people to control their violent tendencies and only to let off steam inside the ring is the argument that training people to box encourages them to use violence in other less-regulated contexts. There is no definitive evidence that proves which of these claims is true, and it is possible that to some extent and for different people, both are. Without the necessary proof, this argument alone cannot justify outlawing boxing.

7.4.1.9 Boxing should not be lawful because it encourages gambling

There is little doubt that boxing is a sport that is heavily gambled upon and that this has always been the case. One of the main reasons for the outlawing of prize-fighting was the fear of outbreaks of public disorder that often occurred because of disagreements over the settling of gambling debts. However, the growth in sports betting in recent years and the much greater degree of social acceptance of gambling in general means that this argument is now rather outdated. If gambling was to be a key determinant in the legality of sporting activities, then other sports would be at a greater risk of being banned than boxing.

7.4.1.10 Boxing should not be lawful because it creates public disorder

As with the previous argument, this claim is outdated to a great extent. One of the reasons for outlawing prize-fighting was the potential for crowd disorder. Although outbreaks of crowd violence do occasionally occur, they are by no means as frequent and are not of the same scale as those which used to occur at prize-fights. If this were a genuine reason for outlawing a spectator sport, then football would be at much greater risk of being banned than boxing.

7.4.1.11 Summary of the public policy arguments

Whether individually or collectively, each of these claims have been used to explain why boxing either is or is not in the public interest. Although they can help to justify claims for either position, none of them provide a conclusive or robust explanation for what the legal status of boxing ought to be. As Lord Mustill observed, the best explanation would appear to be that boxing is lawful for the present because society chooses to tolerate it.

7.4.2 The legal arguments and R v Brown

In the wide-ranging discussions of the law of consent in *R v Brown*, the five members of the House of Lords provided a number of explanations for why an activity might be considered to be unlawful. As with the public policy arguments above, none provide a definitive explanation of how to determine the lawfulness of an activity, and the disparate views of their Lordships mean that none of these arguments can be said to form the ratio of the case. However, an analysis of them provides an insight into how the courts might approach the question of the legality of boxing.

7.4.2.1 The extent of the injuries caused is unknown in advance

This claim goes to the heart of the question of consent. It is argued that if a person does not know the extent of the harm that will be caused to them prior to contact being made with them, then they cannot know to what it is that they are consenting. In boxing, when a fighter is punched, it is impossible for them to know in advance whether they will be bruised, cut or concussed, suffer a serious facial injury or perhaps even die. If they are unaware of the precise nature of the harm that will be caused to them then, so the argument goes, they cannot provide a valid consent to its occurring.

The law of consent is supposed to enable a person to permit another to make specific contacts with them without the interference of the criminal law. In most cases (for example, where a person consents to undergo a surgical procedure), consent to the act being performed on them will necessarily mean that they have consented to a specific harm being caused to them. In contact sports in general and fighting sports in particular, the nature of the interpersonal contacts between the participants means that it is impossible to know the outcome of any specific contact in advance; at best, a range of potential outcomes can be speculated on.

Use of this argument to justify outlawing boxing is somewhat disingenuous. Under the criminal law, it is the contact that one consents to, not its consequences. If the contact is lawful, then all of the harm flowing from it will, of necessity, also have to be lawful. Thus, as boxers consent to be being hit by punches that are thrown within the rules of the sport, the full range of potential outcomes, all of which are possibilities known to the participants in advance, are lawfully inflicted. If, however, a punch is thrown outside of the rules or after the bell has rung to indicate the end of a round, then the punch itself is not consented to and all injury that flows from it is unlawful.

7.4.2.2 There is insufficient regulation of the causing of serious injury

The British Medical Association (BMA) has been a long-time opponent of the legality of boxing, especially the professional format. In particular, it is concerned that sufficient steps to prevent serious injury, specifically serious cumulative brain injury, are not taken by the boxing authorities. The BMA claims that as the unprotected head is the primary target in boxing, serious brain injury is the inevitable outcome of participation in the sport and that it should therefore be banned. Alternatively, if boxing is to be allowed to continue as a lawful activity, then the BMA suggests amongst other proposals removing the head from the target area.

The response of the boxing fraternity is that all reasonable steps have been taken to ensure that the sport is as safe as it can be without destroying its very essence. The requirements that boxers wear padded gloves, fight for a pre-determined number of rounds with breaks in between and have assistants present ringside who can provide advice and first aid and doctors who can provide more specialised medical assistance mean that the boxing match itself is as safe as it can be. The boxer's seconds and the referee can bring the fight to a premature end if they feel that the boxer is no longer able to defend himself and pre-fight medical checks and regular brain scans all ensure that professional boxers are as well-protected as it is possible for them to be without significantly changing the rules and nature of the sport.

The two views expressed here go to the very heart of the argument about the legal status of boxing. There is no doubt that boxing has the potential to cause serious injury, brain damage and death. Post-*Watson*, the BBBC has overseen a sport that is probably as safe as it can get. For the time being, that appears to be sufficient to ensure the continued legality of the sport.

7.4.2.3 There is a potential for the cross-infection of blood-borne diseases

In *Brown*, the House of Lords was concerned that where an activity could create an open wound and where close interpersonal contact also occurs, there is an increased risk of the transmission of blood-borne disease from one participant to another. The combination of facial cuts and grappling that frequently occur in boxing could therefore be of concern to the courts. A combination of pre-fight medical checks to ensure that boxers are not carrying infectious diseases that can be transmitted in this manner and in-fight medical treatment to stop any bleeding that does occur means that the risk of cross-infection is very low. As with the previous argument, the analysis of whether the risk of harm or infection is an acceptable one will determine the law's response to the legality of the activity. It would appear that at present, the steps taken by the governing bodies of boxing ensure that the risk is low enough for the sport to maintain its lawful status.

7.4.2.4 The activity promotes a cult of violence in society

The House of Lords was also concerned that if violent activities were capable of being consented to, then this would create a society in which the use of violence would be normalised and therefore resorted to more frequently. The lack of conclusive empirical evidence on this point makes it almost impossible to rely on this argument alone when determining whether or not boxing should be lawful (above, 7.4.1.8). The ethos inculcated into boxers is that fighting should only take place in the ring, not outside of it. Further, those watching a boxing match are rarely incited to commit acts of violence themselves. Alternatively, those who consider all fighting to be unjustifiable and that fighting for sport and entertainment purposes encourages the use of violence in the wider society, feel that there is a strong justification for outlawing boxing. Until such a link can be either proved or disproved however, this remains an unconvincing point to justify either side of the argument.

7.4.2.5 Summary of the legal arguments

As the leading case on consent, *Brown* is of paramount importance to the discussion of the legality of boxing and other fighting sports. The difficulty that it presents, however, is its factual context: *Brown* concerned the legality of sado-masochistic homosexual activity, not fighting sports. The judgments of the majority in the House of Lords demonstrate clearly their moral disapproval of conduct of this kind and their determination to find reasons for outlawing it. Boxing was mentioned only when their Lordships noted the existence of certain exempted activities; its exemption was neither justified in detail nor seriously questioned. As has been shown, the same arguments that were used to justify the illegality of sado-masochism can be used to justify outlawing boxing; however, robust counter-arguments can also be put forward to explain why boxing is different, why these arguments do not apply to boxing and why its continuation as a lawful activity is in the public interest.

7.4.3 The jurisprudential arguments

The search for Lord Mustill's 'intellectually satisfying' justification for the legality of boxing is a difficult one. Perhaps the most under-explored field that could provide such an explanation is jurisprudence. The theories that underpin the reasons why the law regulates certain forms of conduct should at least provide the foundations upon which a justification could be built. However, the cases on consent have avoided any real engagement with legal theory and have instead focused on less well-developed public interest and public policy arguments.

7.4.3.1 Liberalism

English law is founded upon the general principles of liberalism. All activities are lawful unless declared to be illegal by Parliament or the courts and state intervention in a person's private life is only justifiable to prevent non-consensual harm being caused to other people. For the state to intervene, it would have to be proved that either the consent of the participants was invalid or that harm beyond that which had been consented to had been inflicted on the participants. Therefore, as no Act of Parliament or decision of the Supreme Court has ever outlawed boxing, and because the only people likely to be physically harmed are the participants who have given their full, free and informed consent to participate in the sport, boxing is lawful.

It has been argued that harm is caused to the wider society by the glorification of violence inherent in boxing and because it is a degrading spectacle to watch fighting for the purposes of sport and entertainment. Moral repugnance is not the kind of harm that liberal theory is concerned with; that is the central tenet of legal moralism. Unless those who seek to have boxing outlawed can prove a specific link between the existence of boxing and an increased use of violence in society as a whole, then the kind of harm that liberalism would allow the state to step in to regulate has not been caused.

Liberalism best explains the current legal status of boxing and the law's reluctance to change that on behalf of a vocal and well-organised minority. It places a premium on the consent of the participants and justifies the legality of boxing as a sport on the basis that the boxers' consent to fight according to the rules of the sport has been given validly. If the state were to consider that boxing could no longer be tolerated as being in the public interest, then it would be difficult to justify such regulation on liberal grounds.

7.4.3.2 Paternalism

Paternalism is often used to justify the introduction of protective legislation. The basis of the theory is that where people fail to look after their own safety adequately and suffer preventable harm as a result, then the state should intervene and force safe practices to be observed by everybody. Anyone who fails to adhere to the imposed safety regime created by Parliament will then be guilty of a criminal offence. The requirement to wear seatbelts in cars is a classic example of paternalistic legislation; if people will not make themselves safe by wearing seatbelts voluntarily, then the state will force them to be worn or will impose a criminal sanction for the failure to do so (Road Traffic Act 1988 ss.14 and 15). On occasion, the courts have also justified their decisions on paternalistic grounds; Stephen J in *Coney* argued that prize-fighting should be outlawed because the severity of the injuries caused to the participants could not be justified. Building on these arguments, the BMA has consistently argued that boxers need protecting from themselves and that they should not be allowed to subject each other to the risk of such serious injury as can be caused when boxing.

Any legislation introduced to outlaw boxing would almost undoubtedly be based on paternalistic justifications. If the body of evidence linking boxing with cumulative chronic brain injury, rather than acute traumatic harm, continues to grow, then the basis for the state to intervene and regulate the sport by requiring a higher level of protection for the boxers, for example, by changing the target area and banning blows to the head or by outlawing boxing altogether, becomes much firmer. Without such evidence, it is difficult to justify banning boxing whilst allowing other dangerous activities to continue and it is difficult to justify introducing paternalistic legislation that overrides UK law's generally liberal legal tradition and the participants' specific and validly-given consent to box.

7.4.3.3 Legal moralism

The final theoretical standpoint that is relied on by some of those who are seeking to outlaw boxing is legal moralism. In accordance with this theory, the state is justified in introducing legislation to regulate spheres of activity on the basis of upholding community morality; if the majority of citizens consider that an activity is morally repugnant, then state intervention is justified to regulate or outlaw it.

The unfashionableness of legal moralism as a theory of state intervention comes more from its potential to justify oppression by the majority of the populace of any group that is 'different', for no other reason than distaste rather than for its specific application to boxing. At present, there is undoubtedly not enough widespread distaste of or moral repugnance felt towards boxing to justify banning it on these grounds. Furthermore, liberal theorists would argue that no amount of distaste could ever justify state intervention without specific identifiable harm being caused to someone other than the participants. However, legal moralism has been behind Parliamentary responses in the past, including the passing of the Firearms (Amendment) Act 1997 that led to shooting sports becoming more heavily regulated, and in some cases unlawful, activities. The next death in the ring will undoubtedly lead to these arguments being debated once again.

7.4.3.4 Summary of the jurisprudential arguments

Only three theories of state regulation have been discussed in brief here as they are the ones most frequently called upon when the legality of boxing is debated. Of the three, liberalism probably best sums up the current attitude of both Parliament and the courts to boxing: that as long as only consensual harm is caused to the participants, then there is no justification for state intervention to regulate a 'properly conducted' sport such as boxing. If state intervention were ever to be justified, then a paternalistic approach based on medical evidence that society should no longer allow injuries of such severity to be caused in the name of sport would appear to be the most appropriate. Legal moralism will continue to feature in the moral panics that follow all serious incidents and deaths that occur in the ring. Although it is unlikely that boxing will be banned on the basis of such intolerance, as has been seen with some shooting sports, it is not completely impossible for this to occur.

7.4.4   Conclusion

All of the legal, public policy and theoretical arguments are, to a greater or lesser extent, relevant to a coherent justification of the legal status of boxing and all other fighting sports. However, none of them can be said to provide a definitive, objective and intellectually satisfying justification for their being tolerated by the law. The responses of Parliament, the courts and society appear at present to favour a liberalist approach to boxing. Any change in the legal status of boxing would need justifying on clearly defined theoretical and evidential bases. It would appear that the current legal status of boxing is safe until either there is a significant groundswell of opinion in favour of banning it, or until there is sufficiently clear evidence of the lasting harm caused to boxers through participation in their chosen sport. On an individual level, it is important to be aware of all of the issues that need to be taken into account and that can be used to justify a more personal position on the status of all fighting sports, not just boxing. The focus of any future discussions is likely to be on the degree of injury caused to the participants either because too much harm appears to be being inflicted on them for the purposes of entertainment or because the apparent lack of safety protocols means that the sport is not being properly conducted.

Hot topic ...   # The legal status of mixed martial arts

Of the many new and increasingly popular forms of combat sport that have emerged in recent years, one category stands out as being more controversial than all the others: mixed martial arts (MMA). MMA is becoming a generic term for all sports that have limited rules or which advertise themselves as being 'no holds barred'. The aim of these modern hybrid sports is to enable inter-disciplinary contests to take place where exponents of different fighting traditions compete against one another without undue restriction on their individual skills.

For such contests to take place, the applicable rules need to be pared down to a minimum so that wrestling holds, punching, martial arts throws and kicking are all allowed. This enables, for example, an exponent of karate to take on a boxer. The rules of the various forms of MMA are, in reality, safety rules. These ensure that any moves, holds or blows that are intended to cause serious injury or which are particularly dangerous are banned; for example, eye-gouging and blows to the windpipe and the back of the head and the breaking of fingers and toes are almost always considered to be unlawful moves.

The controversy surrounding these sports is that to some viewers they appear to be little more than unregulated brawls where the infliction of pain and injury is the main goal of the bout; the publicity surrounding many of these events does little to dispel this concern. To others, however, this is a contest between two highly-trained athletes where each is trying to demonstrate that their particular discipline, or disciplines as many are proficient in more than one martial art, and their skill as a fighter is more effective than their opponent's. The difficulty for the law and for legal commentators is to determine whether MMA and related activities can justifiably claim that they are deserving of the same exemption that is afforded to more traditional British combat sports such as boxing and wrestling.

The first difficulty that these activities encounter is that simply calling an activity a sport, whether it is a generic name like MMA or a trade name such as Ultimate Fighting Championships or Cage Wars, does not mean that the activity will be legally recognised as a sport. Therefore, to be able to

benefit from the same exemption from the criminal law that boxing enjoys, it must also be properly conducted and in the public interest to allow participation in these kinds of sporting activities.

Secondly, there is a lack of a universally-accepted, standardised set of rules. This makes it almost impossible to determine whether participants in different events are actually competing in a sport rather than simply fighting. Thirdly, there is no single licensing authority, governing body or international federation that oversees these activities that can enable a standard set of rules and safety protocols to be developed. Fourthly, this lack of standardisation, coordination and administration leads some groups to claim that this is brutality masquerading as sport, that MMA events are not properly conducted sporting contests and that all MMA bouts are therefore unlawful and criminal.

Much of this unease comes from the hype surrounding many MMA contests. Describing a contest as 'no holds barred' where 'anything goes' in 'a competition to find the hardest man in the world' does little to allay the fears of those who consider these contests to be, at best, a modern incarnation of prize-fighting and, at worst, little more than unregulated brawling. When these concerns are coupled with images of fighters bleeding, nursing fractures and being carried unconscious from a caged ring, the case against MMA appears to be a strong one.

However, the counter-arguments are equally robust. Firstly, a set of rules, exemplified by the New Jersey State Athletic Control Board's *Mixed Martial Arts Unified Rules of Conduct*, have become the standard for most high-profile limited-rules fighting contests. These are the legal requirements that any contest must adhere to in order to stage an event in the

American states where MMA is recognised as being a lawful activity and they have been adopted by many other countries and fight organisers worldwide. Thus, a set of rules and safety requirements overseen by an independent body is emerging.

Secondly, although there is no governing body structure in place, the contests themselves are still well-organised or properly conducted. The difference between how sports are traditionally organised and how MMA is currently administered differ only in that most MMA bouts are run by purely commercial entities rather than by domestically, regionally or internationally recognised governing bodies that fulfil administrative, licensing and commercial roles. Further, professional boxing has experienced so many schisms over the years that its multiple world championship sanctioning bodies can hardly be said to provide a template of good governance for other fighting sports.

Thirdly, as these events are based upon fighting disciplines that are already generally recognised as being lawful, then MMA as a concept should also be lawful. If this were not the case, then where a fighter competed against someone trained in the same discipline as he or she was, all contacts would be lawful; but where they competed against someone who was trained in a different discipline, then the entire fight would be unlawful. There appears to be no logical justification for why this should represent the law's response to inter-disciplinary bouts that occur under the umbrella of MMA.

Fourthly, the chances of lasting serious injury are arguably lower than in more traditional sports such as boxing. In MMA, the entire body, not just the head and torso, is the target area. This ensures that there are much fewer blows to the head and therefore a much lower risk of being caused either chronic or acute brain injury. The majority of MMA contests are decided by a hold resulting in a submission rather than retirement through injury or concussion. Where injury does occur, it is usually to a part of the body that can heal rather than to the brain. Thus, although the associated imagery may make some bouts seem more violent than they are, the organisers can make a strong claim for MMA being less dangerous than boxing.

Finally, if the main issue is that a sport must be properly conducted to enable it to take advantage of the exemption afforded to boxing, then each individual event organiser's rules and medical procedures ought to be examined to determine whether or not they reach appropriate standards of administration and safety. Provided that it has sufficient rules in place that are robustly enforced by independent referees, that necessary safety and medical protocols are in place and are followed and that an appropriate level of ringside medical assistance is provided, then it becomes easier to draw an analogy between 'properly conducted' MMA contests and 'properly conducted' boxing bouts.

Many of the policy and theoretical arguments used against boxing are equally valid against MMA. Moreover its apparent glorification of the fight itself can make contests appear more violent than skilful. However provided that similar standards of safety are adhered to, then arguably it is a sport that can be at least as safe as boxing as it places so much less emphasis on the blows to the head that so concern the BMA. Until there is an agreed set of rules and perhaps a governing body MMA will continue to face criticism. If MMA as a whole, and its dominant commercial event organisers in particular can develop measures to ensure the quality and integrity of their competitions and the safety of the competitors over the glorification of violence, then it will not only survive the legal, moral and policy challenges thrown at it but may even find its way into the mainstream of British sport.

Summary

7.1 Historically, fighting sports needed to be protected by the law to ensure that the citizenry could be trained to be fit and able to defend the realm. As warfare evolved from hand-to-hand combat to more mechanised means of fighting, the learning of these skills became less important. In place of the training regimes that prepared people for war, activities such as boxing began to evolve into the modern forms of combat sports that we can see today. As this evolution took place, it fell to the courts to determine which forms of fighting, if any, should be protected by the law and which should not.

7.2 Eventually, the courts determined that only those fighting sports that were tests of skill were lawful activities that could be organised, watched and participated in without fear of prosecution. However, those sports that were more a test of how long a person could endure a physical battering were criminal assaults: anyone organising or actively encouraging participation in one of these unlawful prize-fights was guilty of aiding and abetting the criminal assaults perpetrated by the fighters on one another (*R v Coney*). When establishing the legality of a specific activity, the court must look to the aim of the organisers and the fighters, not just the form of the fight, to determine whether its true object is a test of skill or a fight until one or other of the participants is physically unable to continue.

7.3 *R v Roberts* established that fighting for sport that took place according to a pre-determined set of rules that were designed to measure the skill of the protagonists and that provided them with safety systems that could minimise the degree of harm suffered by them was not a criminal activity. Despite occasional attempts by Parliament to outlaw boxing, particularly in its professional form, the Law Commission stated that boxing and other similarly regulated fighting sports are, and should remain, lawful activities until such time as society no longer chooses to tolerate them.

7.4 There is a wide range of legal, jurisprudential, social, medical and policy arguments that attempt to justify the current legal status of combat sports or why their current status should be changed. It is important to be aware of these in order to be able to justify a position on whether or not sports of this kind should continue to be tolerated by the law.

Further reading

Anderson, *The Legality of Boxing* (2007, Routledge Cavendish)

Bettinson and Tristram, *The National Sporting Club past and present* (1902, Sands and Co) available at: http://openlibrary.org/details/nationalsportin00trisgoog

Cooper and James, 'Entertainment – the painful process of rethinking consent' [2012] 3 *Criminal Law Review* 188

Grill, 'The normative case of paternalism' (2007) 13(4) *Res Publica* 441

Law Commission, *Consent and Offences against the Person*, LCCP No 134 (1994, HMSO) paras 10 and 35–47

Law Commission, *Consent in the Criminal Law*, LCCP No 139, (1995, HMSO) paras 12–13 and appx C

Marwick, 'Harming consent' (2002) 8(2) *Res Publica* 157

Foster, *Crown Law* (1762) 260, quoted in Williams, 'Consent and public policy' [1962] *Criminal Law Review* 74

Gendall, 'The sport of boxing: freedom versus social constraint' [1997] *Waikato Law Review* 5

Gunn and Omerod, 'The legality of boxing' (1995) 15(2) *Legal Studies* 181

Sithamparanathan, 'Noble art of self-defence or unlawful barbarism?' [2002] *Entertainment Law Review* 183

Links to relevant websites can be found at www.palgrave.com/law/james2e

Part III

Stadiums, spectators and the law

Chapter 8

Liability for dangerous premises and dangerous events

Key terms

- **Occupier** – the person or body having sufficient control over premises to ensure that they are safe to use by those invited on to them.
- **Visitor** – a person who is invited on to the occupier's premises and who has permission to be there.
- **Trespasser** – a person who is on the occupier's premises without their permission or who is acting in excess of the original permission granted to them.
- **Private nuisance** – an unlawful and continuing activity that unreasonably interferes with the claimant's right to quiet enjoyment of their own property.
- **Public nuisance** – an activity that materially affects the reasonable comfort and convenience of a section of the community but which causes special damage to the claimant above and beyond that suffered by their neighbours.
- **Injunction** – an order of the court requiring the defendant either to stop doing something (prohibitory injunction) or to do something in a particular manner (mandatory injunction).

8.1 General tortious liability of organisers and hosts of sports events

The potential liability of those who organise sporting events and manage sports facilities is extremely wide. Injuries can be caused to the participants and spectators because of the state of the premises, to the spectators because of the management of the facility, or to neighbours and passersby by things, usually balls, being hit out of the playing area or stadium. The causes of action that can be relied on by claimants are equally diverse, including breach of contract, negligence, occupiers' liability and nuisance.

As spectator sports grew in popularity throughout the Victorian era, event organisers became aware of the need to construct facilities in which the competitions could take place. These new venues served two main purposes: firstly, to demarcate the playing area from the onlookerss and secondly to regulate entrance to the event, thereby facilitating the ability to charge spectators to watch the fixture. Later, facilities such as seating were provided to spectators who were willing to pay a premium to watch an event in comfort. One recurring feature of the early cases is the poor quality of the stadiums and grandstands that were constructed to host major sports events and the lack of appropriate regulation of these venues. This chapter will focus on the civil law remedies available to those caused harm at a sporting event.

8.1.1 Historical background

Before the development of the modern law of negligence in *Donoghue v Stevenson* [1932] AC 502 and the passing of the Occupiers' Liability Acts in 1957 and 1984, actions against the organisers of sporting events were particularly complex.

▶ *Francis v Cockrell* (1870) LR 5 QB 501, Court of Exchequer Chamber

The claimant was injured following the collapse of a temporary grandstand at the 1866 Cheltenham Races. The defendant, with others, had engaged a competent independent contractor to construct the grandstand, which enabled those who paid an entrance fee of five shillings to gain a better view of the races. The grandstand had been built negligently and collapsed, injuring the claimant.

The Court held that there was a contract between the claimant spectator and defendant organiser that allowed the claimant entry to the grandstand. This contract included an implied term that the grandstand was reasonably fit for the purpose of watching the races but did not cover unseen or unknown defects that could not reasonably be discovered. However, because the independent contractor had acted negligently in the construction of the grandstand, the defect that led to its collapse could not be considered to be unseen or unknown as a reasonably competent constructor would have identified it. Therefore, the implied term that the grandstand was fit for its purpose was breached, even though there was no fault on the part of the defendant-organiser.

Two of their Lordships also held that the defendant owed two tortious duties to the claimant. The defendant had discharged his first duty, to employ a reasonable and competent independent contractor, but breached the second, to provide a reasonably safe place from which to watch the race meeting.

Although some of the reasoning behind this case has been superseded by s.2(4) of Occupiers' Liability Act 1957 (OLA 1957), which would require the claimant to seek relief from the constructor if similar facts were to arise today, it still sets the scene for the cases that followed and for how spectators would continue to be treated in the future.

This apparent disregard for spectator safety was reinforced when a grandstand collapsed at Blackburn Rovers Football Club's home ground, Ewood Park. In *Brown v Lewis* (1896) 12 TLR 455, the directors of the club were held personally liable in negligence for the injuries caused to the claimant. Their breach of duty was the failure to engage a competent independent contractor to carry out work on the grandstand. This finding meant that each of the individual directors had to pay a proportion of the claimant's compensation. Rather than leading to an improvement in stadium safety or a change in the law regulating major events, the case resulted in the majority of professional sports clubs incorporating to ensure that in future the club, rather than its directors, would be liable in a similar situation (see further, chapter 9.1.1).

Over time, the law evolved to impose duties for the benefit of sports participants as well as the spectators. *Gillmore v London County Council* [1938] 4 All ER 331 held that the defendant council owed a duty of care to the claimant who was taking part in a physical training course on its premises. The duty was to ensure that the flooring on which the activity was taking place was reasonably safe for this purpose. As the lesson was taking place on a highly-polished dance floor, instead of in a purpose-built sports hall, the flooring was too slippery for the participants to maintain their footing. When the claimant slipped and injured himself, the defendant was liable for conducting an activity in an unsafe environment.

These cases show that as the law of negligence was developing generally, it was also developing specifically to ensure that those who were organising sports events, or who ran sports facilities, were doing so safely. Although the vast majority of actions will now be based on the Occupiers' Liability Acts 1957 and 1984, these early cases illustrate how the law was to develop and are relevant still in the limited circumstances where the Acts do not apply.

8.2 The Occupiers' Liability Acts 1957 and 1984

The OLA 1957 partially codifies this area of the law and in particular defines the duty of care owed by an occupier of premises to its visitors. The OLA 1984 deals specifically with situations where the claimant is a trespasser on the premises as opposed to someone who has permission to be there. As a preliminary to any claim, it must be established that the injury was caused by the state of the premises and that the defendant was the occupier of those premises at the time the injury occurred. It must then be determined whether the claimant was a lawful visitor with permission to be on the premises or was a trespasser on the premises without, or in excess of, the occupier's consent.

8.2.1 Liability for occupancy or liability for the activity

The preliminary factual investigation must establish whether the harm was caused because of the state of the premises or the nature of the activity taking place on them. Where the harm is caused because of the state of the premises, the cause of action is for the breach of the duty imposed on an occupier by s.2(2) OLA 1957 (below, 8.2.5). For example, the injuries caused in *Gillmore* were because of the inappropriate and unsafe nature of the flooring where the activity took place; if similar facts were to reoccur today, the claim would be made under the OLA 1957. However, where the injury is caused as a result of the activity taking place on the premises, then the only cause of action open to a claimant will be in negligence.

▶ *Poppleton v Trustees of the Portsmouth Youth Activities Centre* [2008] EWCA Civ 646

The claimant was an inexperienced rock climber who was using an artificial climbing wall operated by the defendants. He had not asked for, nor had he been offered, training or instruction on the use of the climbing wall and had not seen, nor had his attention drawn to, a sign prohibiting jumping from the wall and climbing on the roof beams. In trying to emulate a more experienced friend, the claimant jumped from the wall and attempted to grab hold of one of the roof beams, from where he intended to drop on to the safety matting below. He lost his grip midway through his attempt, somersaulted in the air and landed on his neck, rendering him tetraplegic.

It was held that as the claimant's injury was caused by his unsafe use of the climbing wall, not because the climbing wall itself was unsafe, the only claim that he could make was that he had been negligently trained or supervised by the defendant; the OLA 1957 was not engaged. The defendant had not breached its duty to provide a safe climbing facility; the accident was caused by the claimant running an obvious risk of injury by acting in a manner wholly inappropriate to his level of experience.

8.2.2 The premises

'Premises' is given a wide meaning and includes not only land and any permanent or movable structures on it, but also vessels, vehicles and aircraft (s.1(3)(a) OLA 1957). The width of the definition is important as it will extend to all sporting premises of whatever nature including temporary structures, such as the grandstand in *Francis v Cockrell*, and movable structures such as goalposts, as was the cause of the claimant's injuries in *Hall v Holker Estate Co Ltd* [2008] EWCA Civ 1422 (below, 8.2.5.1). Although there has not been any litigation on the point to date, the Act would also appear to cover participants who are injured whilst travelling in any vehicle, including cars, yachts and planes that are being used for racing.

8.2.3 The occupier of the premises

Perhaps surprisingly, the 'occupier' of premises is not defined in either of the Acts; s.1(2) OLA 1957 states specifically that reference to the previous common law should be made to determine the identity of this central character. An occupier is someone who has sufficient control of the premises to enable them to discharge the common duty of care owed to visitors under s.2(2) OLA 1957 (below, 8.2.5); they must be in a position to ensure that the premises are reasonably safe to be used by their visitors.

The most obvious occupiers of the premises will be the owner or tenant who is in possession of them. However, if another person is in day-to-day control of the premises, for example, because they have been hired to a third party, then the operator or organiser of the event can also be the occupier. In certain circumstances, it is possible for more than one person to be the occupier of the same premises. The fluidity of the concept provides the claimant with the best opportunity to identify the person or persons who were actually in control of the safety of the premises and to bring their action against any or all of them as appropriate (*Wheat v E Lacon and Co Ltd* [1966] AC 552).

8.2.4 Visitors and trespassers

The final preliminary issue is to determine whether the claimant was a lawful visitor to the premises or a trespasser on them. This point is key to the rest of the claim as it determines whether the action will be brought under the OLA 1957 or the OLA 1984. As with 'occupier', neither 'visitor' nor 'trespasser' are defined in the Acts.

A visitor is a person who has been invited on to the occupier's premises for a specific purpose, or who has the occupier's consent to be on them. Such permissions can be granted either expressly or impliedly by the occupier. Express permission would include where the participants have paid to use a sports facility (for example, the claimants in *Roddie and Roddie v Ski Llandudno Ltd* [2001] PIQR P5 had paid to go down a concrete toboggan run) or where spectators have paid an entrance fee to watch a sports fixture (*Murray v Harringay Arena LD* [1951] 2 KB 529) (below, 8.2.5.4.1). Implied consent would include where the occupier has allowed an activity to take place without specifically granting permission to the claimant or where the activity has been tacitly encouraged (*Hall v Holker*) (below, 8.2.5.1).

A trespasser is a person without the requisite permission to be on the premises, or someone who is acting in excess of their original permission. The former is what most people would consider to be a trespasser, a person on someone else's property without their permission (*Ratcliffe v McConnell* [1999] 1 WLR 670) (below, 8.2.6). The latter definition enables a person to change their status from being a lawful visitor to an unlawful trespasser by doing something, or by going somewhere, that is not permitted. This, and a number of related issues, were analysed in *Tomlinson v Congleton Borough Council* [2003] UKHL 47 (below, 8.2.6). By diving into a lake contrary to an express prohibition on swimming, the claimant's classification as a visitor to the defendant's park changed to his being a trespasser as he was doing something that he was not permitted to do on the premises. Thus, his claim was tried under the OLA 1984, not the OLA 1957.

8.2.5 Occupiers' Liability Act 1957

Once it has been established that the claimant is a lawful visitor to the premises, then the common duty of care is owed to them by the defendant-occupier.

> ▶ **Occupiers' Liability Act 1957 s.2(2) – the common duty of care**
>
> The common duty of care is a duty to take such care as in all the circumstances of the case is reasonable to see that the visitor will be reasonably safe in using the premises for the purposes for which he is invited or permitted by the occupier to be there.

As a codified version of common law negligence, it is a duty to take only reasonable steps to ensure that the visitor is safe; it is not a standard of absolute safety. As with negligence, the degree of safety provided will depend on the type of activity taking place and greater care must always be taken where children are concerned.

The OLA 1957 contains specific reference to ways that the common duty of care can be discharged and to defences that an occupier can raise to any claim made against them. Firstly, in s.2(4)(a) OLA 1957, the duty is discharged where a warning has been given that is sufficient to enable the visitor to make themselves reasonably safe. Consideration of this provision is often relevant where the claimant has been injured whilst swimming. Secondly, in s.2(4)(b) OLA 1957, the defendant is absolved from liability where they have chosen competent independent contractors to carry out works on the premises. Thus, if *Francis v Cockrell* were to occur today, the claimant would have to bring their action against the constructors of the grandstand, subject to the common duty of care being imposed by virtue of s.5(1) OLA 1957. Thirdly, s.2(5) OLA 1957 states that the occupier will not be liable for harm caused by risks willingly run by the claimant. This will include the inherent risks associated with dangerous activities, for example, losing control of a toboggan on a downhill run, as in *Roddie v Ski LLandudno*.

8.2.5.1 Participants v. Occupiers – establishing a claim

An occupier will be liable for the injuries caused to a sports participant where the injury has been caused by the dangerous state of the playing arena or the equipment that is used to play the game in question.

▶ *Hall v Holker Estate Co Ltd* [2008] EWCA Civ 1422

The claimant had been playing football with his son and one of his son's friends when his foot became entangled in the net of the goal. As he fell to the ground, the goal posts, which had not been adequately secured, fell on to him, and the crossbar hit him in the face, causing injuries to his teeth and jaw. The defendant was aware that from time to time, the pegs that should have secured the goalposts to the ground were removed by users of the campsite on which the football pitch was situated and that as a result, the goalposts were not as safe as they should have been.

The Court of Appeal held that where an occupier allows or encourages an activity to take place on its land and/or where it provides the equipment for such an activity, it must ensure that both the playing area and the equipment are reasonably safe for the purposes of playing the game in question. This will require the occupier to carry out risk assessments of the facilities and to ensure that the equipment is properly maintained. An occupier will only be able to avoid liability in circumstances such as these where it can prove not only that there is an adequate system in place for inspecting the facilities and eliminating any dangers but also that this system was being implemented effectively. As the defendant was aware that the pegs securing the goalposts were often missing, the common duty of care was breached by the failure to take proactive steps to remedy this dangerous situation.

In *Sutton v Syston RFC Ltd* [2011] EWCA Civ 1182, the claimant dived to score a try during a training game of touch rugby. As he landed, his knee came into contact with a wooden peg that had been used as a boundary marker for the cricket pitch with which the club shared facilities. At trial, the judge found for the claimant on the basis that different standards of care were imposed on the inspection of different parts of the pitch on the basis that when playing touch rugby, a player was much more likely to go to ground in the goal area and therefore a more thorough inspection of that part of the pitch should have taken place. In allowing the defendant's appeal, the Court of Appeal held that it was wrong to impose a variable standard in this manner. As the defendant club had carried out an inspection of the pitch at a reasonable walking pace to look for glass, concrete, large stones and dog waste, it had discharged the common duty of care in s.2(2) Occupiers' Liability Act 1957 by acting in accordance with the guidelines for pitch inspections laid down by the sport's governing body, the Rugby Football Union.

Despite this finding, the case remains on the borderline in terms of the defendant's liability because the rugby club *knew* that cricket had been played on the pitch a few days earlier. This issue of 'dual usage' was not fully explored at trial or on appeal and, as negligence is assessed in all relevant circumstances, this particular circumstance appears to have been overlooked by both courts; this wooden peg was not a random piece of debris, such as a stone or piece of glass, but something that the cricket club would have used every time that they played and, therefore, could have been looked for specifically. Instead, the trial judge unnecessarily complicated the case by applying a variable standard of care for difference parts of the pitch; if he had concentrated on the relevant circumstances rather than on this variable standard, a different result may have been reached. Further, the efficacy of the RFU's guidelines was not interrogated by either court, which mirrors the approach in *Simms v Leigh Rugby Football Club Ltd* [1969] 2 All ER 923, where the defendant was held not liable for the injuries caused to a player sliding into a concrete post that had been positioned adjacent to the pitch in accordance with the Rugby Football League's guidelines. NGBs should be aware that they need to be able to justify their risk assessment procedures in order to defend themselves from possible actions in the future; where the club is found to have acted reasonably by following the guidelines, the originating NGB may be liable for not having a sufficiently robust justification for their content. It should ensure that the guidelines' effectiveness is assessed regularly and reviewed in the light of any new pattern of injury that is occurring despite, or because of, its recommendations.

8.2.5.2 Participants v. Occupiers – defences

As with negligence at common law, the main defences to claims under the OLA 1957 are voluntary assumption of risk and contributory negligence (see further, chapter 4.6.2). Voluntary assumption of risk is specifically restated in s.2(5) OLA 1957, and the role of warnings in bringing the claimant's attention to any risks of injury is defined in s.2(4)(a) of the Act.

8.2.5.2.1 Voluntary assumption of risk and inherent dangers

> ▶ **Occupiers' Liability Act 1957 s.2(5) – voluntary assumption of risk**
>
> The common duty of care does not impose on an occupier any obligation to a visitor in respect of risks willingly accepted as his by the visitor (the question of whether a risk was so accepted to be decided on the same principles as in other cases in which one person owes a duty of care to another).

The key point here is to determine whether the risks to which the claimant was exposed can be said to be inherent in the activity, and therefore of necessity run by him or her, or are because of a particular problem with the premises on which the activity was taking place. For example, it is an inherent risk of playing football that goalkeepers might collide with the goalposts and be caused serious injury. However, they would not expect the goalposts to fall on them during the course of play. The former is an inherent risk willingly run by the injured player; the latter is neither an inherent risk of playing football nor one that is willingly run by goalkeepers.

When determining whether a claimant has willingly run the risks inherent in an activity, the court must perform a balancing act that weighs the risk of harm to which the participants were exposed against the nature of the activity in which they were involved. For example, in *Tysall Ltd v Snowdome* [2007] CLY 4196, the claimant was injured whilst tobogganing at an indoor snow centre. She claimed that there was insufficient time for those in her group who were following her down the slope to take evasive action and avoid colliding with her once she had fallen from her toboggan. The court held that the element of risk inherent in sports such as tobogganing is often part of the reason why participants engage in such activities. The inherent risks, such as falling off, have to be weighed against the nature of the activity, including that this was a group social event involving a number of friends, the gravity of the injury sustained and the social value of the exercise. To make the activity safe so that this injury could not have occurred would have compromised its nature to such an extent that either the group could not have participated together at the same time or would have removed the 'thrill' element of participation. Thus, following the briefings on safety and how to use the toboggan, the claimant had willingly run the inherent risks of the activity by taking part in it with her friends.

In *Grimes v Hawkins* [2011] EWHC 2004, the court provided very clear guidance on the role of voluntary assumption of risk where a person has been injured by diving into water. The claimant had been granted permission to use the defendant's pool by the defendant's daughter, along with a number of others. The group were swimming in and jumping, bombing and diving into the pool, which was approximately 9m in length and 4.5m in breadth with a depth of between 0.88m and 1.72m. There were no warning signs around the pool indicating depth or prohibiting diving, as there is no requirement for signs of this nature around a pool on private premises. After swimming for about 30 minutes, the claimant got out and then dived back in from about halfway along the length of the pool at a diagonal angle towards the deep end, coming into contact with the floor of the pool and suffering tetraplegia as a result.

The judge held that there is always a risk in diving into any pool; the safety of the diver depends on their technique, the angle of entry and the body of water being dived into. As a result, it is well known that diving always carries with it a risk of injury, particularly to the head and neck, if the dive is executed badly or is carried out in water that is too shallow. None of the foregoing requires any kind of specialist knowledge and the claimant, who was an experienced swimmer, was aware of these risks. As this was an ordinary domestic swimming pool that was well lit and free from hidden hazards so that the slope from the shallow end to the deep end could be clearly seen, the risk of injury was one that was inherent in diving and, therefore, voluntarily run by the claimant.

8.2.5.2.2 Warnings

The OLA 1957 also establishes the circumstances in which occupiers will be able to avoid liability by providing warnings to their visitors.

▶ **Occupiers' Liability Act 1957 s.2(4) – *discharging the common duty of care***

In determining whether the occupier of premises has discharged the common duty of care to a visitor, regard is to be had to all the circumstances so that …

(a) where damage is caused to a visitor by a danger of which he had been warned by the occupier, the warning is not to be treated without more as absolving the occupier from liability, unless in all the circumstances it was enough to enable the visitor to be reasonably safe.

The simple provision of a warning is unlikely to discharge the common duty of care; telling someone to be careful or installing a sign proclaiming only that there is 'Danger' will rarely be sufficient. The warning must be in sufficient detail to enable the visitor to make themselves safe or to enable them to make an informed decision that the risk is one that is worth running in the circumstances. In *Roddie and Roddie v Ski Llandudno*, the Court of Appeal held that the warnings provided throughout the length of the toboggan run reminding users to brake as they turned into corners were sufficient to have discharged the common duty of care. Firstly, the warnings brought the inherent risks of the activity to the notice of the claimant by highlighting that it was dangerous to go too fast round the corners. Secondly, the warnings enabled the claimant to make himself reasonably safe by reminding him to apply the brakes at appropriate points during his descent. Only if the toboggan or the track were defective would a claim under the OLA 1957 have been sustainable. Where warnings of a real risk of harm are not provided, there will be a breach s.2(2) OLA 1957. In *Phee v Gordon* [2011] CSOH 181, the risk of golf balls overshooting the 18th green and hitting those walking behind it towards the seventh tee was known to the defendant. In finding the defendant liable, the court held that occupiers must proactively assess risks, not assume that they will not happen simply because the risk had not previously eventuated.

8.2.5.2.3 Contributory negligence

Under s.1(1) Law Reform (Contributory Negligence) Act 1945, a defendant can seek a pro-rata reduction in the amount of compensation payable where the claimant has contributed by his own fault to the injuries that he has suffered (see further, chapter 4.6.2.2). This provision enables the court to balance the negligence of the defendant against the claimant's own carelessness and ensures that claimants cannot abdicate all responsibility for their own safety.

There are many cases involving injuries of varying degrees occurring at swimming pools, with one of the more unusual being *Greening v Stockton-on-Tees Borough Council* (unreported) Court of Appeal, 6 November 1998, where the claimant swam into the edge of a swimming pool and was caused facial injuries as a result. He claimed that the edge of the pool was not clearly visible because of the murkiness of the water and the inadequate depth of the contrasting line of tiling that delineated the pool's edge. In establishing the primary liability of the defendant, the Court held that both of these factors contributed to the claimant's inability to see the edge of the pool sufficiently clearly. The Court also held that there were two factors that should have alerted the claimant to the possible dangers of swimming in this pool and that he should have taken greater care of himself whilst he was in it. Firstly, as this was an irregularly shaped 'deck level pool', where the water is at the same level as the edge of the pool, he should have paid greater attention to his position in relation to its edge. Secondly, that as he was aware of the murkiness of the water (he claimed to have been unable to make out his own feet in only 95 cm of water), he should again have been paying greater attention to his whereabouts in the water. His failure to notice the edge of the pool and his taking an additional unnecessary stroke contributed significantly to the cause of the accident and his damages were reduced by 50 per cent.

This case highlights clearly that even where the occupier has provided a potentially dangerous facility, the claimant cannot ignore the dangers that have been created. The greater the degree of knowledge of the dangers exhibited by the claimant, the greater the chance that the court will find either that they have contributed to the cause of their own injuries or that they have willingly run the risk of being injured whilst using the defendant's premises.

8.2.5.3 Spectators v. Occupiers – establishing a claim

To bring an action under the OLA 1957, the claimant must be able to prove either that their injuries were caused by the state of disrepair of the premises or that they were unsuitable for hosting the kind of event that was taking place. Where there is a fault with the fabric of the venue, liability will be relatively easy to establish. In *McDyer v*

Celtic Football and Athletic Co Ltd (No 1) 2000 SC 379, a piece of timber that had been used as part of the framework from which banners were hung became dislodged and fell onto the claimant. Although the case was brought under the similarly worded s.2(1) Occupiers' Liability (Scotland) Act 1960, the principle that it establishes is the same; injuries caused by defects in the stadium which make it unsafe for the purposes of viewing an event will be the responsibility of the occupier.

The distinction between occupancy and activity liability was not so clear-cut in *Cunningham v Reading Football Club Ltd* [1992] PIQR P141, where the claimant, a police officer on duty at a professional football match, was injured by a piece of concrete thrown at him by one of the spectators. It could be argued that the claimant was not injured by the state of the premises but by the activity that was occurring on them; in this case, an outbreak of crowd violence. However, the case was approached on the basis that the premises taken as a whole were not reasonably safe for the police to carry out their duties effectively. In coming to this conclusion, the court took into account that spectator disorder of this specific kind was reasonably foreseeable because pieces of concrete had been thrown by fans at the defendant's stadium on a previous occasion four months earlier. The football club's awareness of this danger, especially in the light of assurances given by it to the Football Association that measures would be taken to correct this problem, and its failure to take any such action meant that the stadium was not reasonably safe for the purposes for which the claimant had been invited into it. Thus, once the defendant is aware of the specific danger, it must take specific steps to negate it or be held in breach of duty.

Defendants must also ensure that any risk assessment or licensing inspection undertaken addresses the needs of all users of the premises. In *Fenton v Thruxton (BARC) Ltd* (unreported) County Court (Basingstoke), 12 December 2008, the occupiers of a motor racing track were held not to have discharged the duty owed to spectators at a race meeting by relying on a safety inspection carried out by the NGB of motorcycle racing in the UK as this only addressed the safety of the competitors and race officials present at the event. A risk assessment that had been aimed at the safety of spectators would have identified the specific danger that led to the death of the deceased and enabled the occupier to take the necessary remedial action (below, 8.4.2).

8.2.5.4 Spectators v. Occupiers – defences

There are two categories of defences that can be raised by an occupier of sports premises: that the harm was caused by an inherent risk of the sport and/or that the spectator has voluntarily run the risk of being injured and that the occupier has excluded its liability under s.2(1) OLA 1957. It must be noted that the ability of an occupier to rely on s.2(1) OLA 1957 has been limited significantly by s.2(1) Unfair Contract Terms Act 1977 (UCTA 1977).

8.2.5.4.1 Inherent and voluntarily run risks

The occupier of premises will not be liable for injuries caused by the inherent risks of watching a sporting event, providing that they have taken reasonable care to ensure the safety of the spectators. It must be remembered that the duty under the OLA 1957 is only to ensure that the premises are reasonably safe; it is not to insure against all harm absolutely.

In determining what steps, if any, should have been taksen by the occupier to discharge this duty, a balance must be struck between spectator safety and spectator culture. For example, a spectator at a cricket match would not be able to claim for injuries caused by a cricket ball being hit for six runs into the crowd as it is an inherent risk of the game that the batting side will attempt to score as many runs as possible, which includes hitting sixes. The balance that has to be struck is between making the spectators reasonably safe and allowing them to view the game unhindered, against making them absolutely safe by erecting netting and posts that could stop the balls from entering the crowd but which may obstruct their view of the game. Thus, it is reasonable to provide no protection to spectators at a cricket game beyond their sitting at an appropriate distance from the action.

The closer to the action that a spectator is positioned, and the faster moving or more dangerous the game is, may mean that a greater degree of protection should be provided by the occupier.

> ▶ *Murray v Harringay Arena LD* [1951] 2 KB 529
>
> The claimant was watching an ice hockey match from a front row seat along the side of the rink. He was hit in the face by a puck that had unintentionally been hit out of the playing area and was caused a serious eye injury. In balancing spectator safety against spectator culture, it was considered necessary at the time to provide protective netting at the ends of the rink behind the goals to prevent mishit attempts to score from entering the crowd on a frequent basis, at high speed and with the potential to cause serious injury. However, it was not considered to be necessary to install similar netting down the sides of the rink because of the infrequent, low velocity and accidental nature of the puck entering the crowd at this point and further, because the netting would have unreasonably and unnecessarily obstructed the spectators' view of the action.
>
> It was held that there was no duty to protect spectators from the incidental risks of watching the sport in progress and that the claimant had willingly run a risk of injury that was reasonably foreseeable to any spectator by choosing to sit where he did. As occupiers only have to provide a reasonably safe environment, not one that is absolutely safe, the claim was dismissed.

Murray demonstrates that as long as a risk assessment has been carried out, and the decision regarding the level of protection can be justified rationally, then the defendant may be able to escape liability. Different protections will be required for different sports based on the nature of the sporting activity taking place, the expectations of the spectators and the risk of something leaving the playing area and entering the crowd. It is also important to note that changes in perceptions of what is reasonably safe can and do change over time; what was acceptable in some of the older cases would not be considered to be reasonably safe today.

8.2.5.4.2 Exclusions of liability

> ▶ *Occupiers' Liability Act 1957 s.2(1) – extent of occupier's ordinary duty*
>
> An occupier of premises owes the same duty, the 'common duty of care', to all his visitors except in so far as he is free and does extend, restrict, modify or exclude his duty to any visitor or visitors by agreement or otherwise.

This extraordinarily wide-ranging section appears to allow occupiers to avoid owing the common duty of care altogether if they can impose a sufficiently specific exclusion of liability on their visitors. This is precisely what happened in *White v Blackmore and Others* [1972] 2 QB 641 in respect of injuries caused to a spectator at a stock car racing event. However, the ability to disclaim liability in these circumstances is now significantly restricted.

> ▶ *Unfair Contract Terms Act 1977 s.2(1) – negligence liability*
>
> A person cannot by reference to any contract term or to a notice given to persons generally or to particular persons exclude or restrict his liability for death or personal injury resulting from negligence.

Under s.1(1)(c) UCTA 1977, negligence includes the common duty of care, thereby limiting severely what had become a significant loophole in the OLA 1957's protections. These provisions of UCTA 1977 apply only to business liability, which is defined in s.1(3) as being where the harm is caused in the course of business or on premises occupied for the purposes of the business. Thus, wherever sport is conducted as a business, the occupier will be unable to exclude liability for personal injury that is caused as a result of a breach of the common duty of care.

From a practical perspective, unless the injuries are caused during informal sports or games, or where the use of the land is gratuitous, then liability cannot be excluded. Where the sporting event is not organised in the course of a business, then liability can only be excluded by a clearly-worded exclusion clause that is brought to the attention of the spectator prior to their entry to the event.

8.2.6 Occupiers Liability Act 1984

Occupiers do not only owe a duty of care to the visitors who are permitted to be on their premises; they also owe a limited duty to trespassers who are on their premises without permission, or in excess of the permission that was initially granted to them. This is particularly important as it is possible for a visitor to become a trespasser by going somewhere on the premises, or by doing something on them, that they are not supposed to. If it is established that the claimant was in fact a trespasser, then the claim must be brought under the OLA 1984 instead of the OLA 1957. Before a claimant can rely on the protection of s.1(4) OLA 1984, three preconditions must be satisfied.

> ▶ *Occupiers' Liability Act 1984 s.1 – duty of occupier to persons other than visitors*
>
> (3) An occupier of premises owes a duty to another (not being his visitor) in respect of any [risk of their suffering injury on the premises by reason of any danger due to the state of the premises or to things done or omitted to be done on them] if –
> (a) he is aware of the danger or has reasonable grounds to believe that it exists;
> (b) he knows or has reasonable grounds to believe that the other is in the vicinity of the danger (in either case, whether the other has lawful authority for being in that vicinity or not); and
> (c) the risk is one against which, in all the circumstances of the case, he may reasonably be expected to offer the other some protection.
> (4) Where, by virtue of the section, an occupier of premises owes a duty to another in respect of such a risk, the duty is to take such care as is reasonable in all the circumstances of the case to see that he does not suffer any injury on the premises by reason of the danger concerned.

The duty in s.1(4) OLA 1984 is often referred to as the 'common duty of humanity' in that it is the lowest level of protection that anyone on the occupier's premises would expect to receive. The very nature of sports facilities, particularly for swimming, will often mean that some element of danger is associated with them and that the occupier will be aware of this danger; in reality, the danger will often be an integral component of a facility such as a swimming pool, climbing wall or motor racing track. Although these preconditions may be relatively easily satisfied, the corollary is that the duty imposed under s.1(4) OLA 1984 can often be easily discharged by a warning or notice of the dangerous nature of the premises, provided it fulfils the requirements of s.1(5):

> 'Any duty owed by virtue of this section in respect of a risk may, in an appropriate case, be discharged by taking such steps as are reasonable in all the circumstances of the case to see that he does not suffer injury on the premises by reason of the danger concerned.'

In *Ratcliff v McConnell and Others* [1999] 1 WLR 670, the Court of Appeal held that because of the obvious danger associated with diving into the shallow end of an outdoor swimming pool, the claimant had willingly accepted the risk of harm, in this case tetraplegia, under s.1(6) OLA 1984. It was also noted that the protections and warnings provided by the college about the pool would have been sufficient to discharge the duty owed under the OLA 1984. The pool was surrounded by walls and fences of at least 2.2m in height, there was a prohibition on the use of the pool between 10 pm and 6.30 am situated at the entrance to the pool and there was a substantial notice in red lettering on a white background identifying its shallow end.

▶ *Tomlinson v Congleton Borough Council* **[2003] UKHL 47**

The defendant was the owner and occupier of a country park and lake that were used as a leisure facility. Members of the public were permitted to use the park for recreational purposes but were specifically prohibited by prominent signage from swimming in the lake. Ignoring this prohibition, the claimant ran down to the water's edge and dived in. At this point, the water was extremely shallow, and he hit his head on the bottom of the lake, fracturing his neck, and was rendered tetraplegic as a result. Firstly, it was held that as his actions were in direct contravention of an express prohibition of the occupier, he was a trespasser from the point that he entered the water and that, therefore, he was owed the duty of care under s.1(4) OLA 1984 and not the more extensive duty under s.2(2) OLA 1957. Secondly, that under s.1(5) OLA 1984, the duty was discharged by providing warnings discouraging the defendant from incurring the risk. Thirdly, and in the alternative, the risk of injury from diving into water of unknown depth was so obvious as to have willingly accepted by the defendant, s.1(6) OLA 1984. Thus, although it is technically possible for a claimant to bring an action under the OLA 1984, their chances of success are likely to be low.

There is a clear distinction between the duties owed by an occupier under the two Acts. The OLA 1957 ensures that where the occupier has permitted a person to be on their premises for a specific purpose, they must take positive steps to make them safe for the purpose of the visit. The OLA 1984 requires only that the occupier take reasonable steps to see that the trespasser does not suffer harm from a known danger. For example, if an occupier invites people to swim on their premises, he must ensure that the area is safe for them to do so. Where an occupier does not want people to swim on his premises, they need only take steps to ensure that this is made clear to anyone who is present on them and to provide a warning of any known dangers. There is no need to warn of specific hidden dangers if a complete ban on swimming is in place, as was the case in *Rhind v Astbury Water Park Ltd* [2004] EWCA Civ 756. Thus, the positive duty owed to those with permission to be on the premises is replaced by a negative duty to avoid causing harm to those without the requisite permission to be there.

8.3　Nuisance

The aim of the tort of private nuisance is to protect a person's right to enjoy their own property without undue interference. Such a claim cannot be brought under the Occupiers' Liability Acts as the claimant must be physically present on the defendant's land to benefit from the protections of those statutes. Where sport is concerned, private nuisance ensures that the organisers of a sporting event, or those with a legal interest in the land on which an event is taking place, do not produce an unreasonable level of noise or cause physical damage to the neighbouring properties. An action could lie in public nuisance where a section of the community is affected by an activity but the claimant has suffered harm above and beyond that caused to other affected properties. Although difficult to prove and requiring the permission of the Attorney-General to bring the case, public nuisance actions can be of assistance to physically-injured claimants in certain limited circumstances.

The aim of nuisance claims will depend on the nature of the inconvenience suffered and the means by which it was caused. Where the interference is by noise, the claimant will usually seek an injunction to stop the activity or reduce its frequency. Where physical harm is concerned, the claimant will want both an injunction to stop the activity and compensation for the harm caused. In balancing the reasonableness of a defendant's conduct against the rights of the claimant to enjoy their property without interference, the court can decide that the defendant should be allowed to continue their activity, or that the activity be allowed to continue but that compensation be paid to the claimant to reflect the reduction in the value of the claimant's property, or that the activity be restricted in some way or stopped altogether.

8.3.1　Private nuisance

Private nuisance is where the defendant has created an unlawful and continuing interference with the claimant's use or enjoyment of their land, that has caused damage to the claimant's legal interest in the land and which is, on balance, unreasonable. An action in private nuisance can only be brought by a claimant who has a legal interest in the affected land, usually as either the owner or tenant of a neighbouring property (*Hunter v Canary Wharf Ltd* [1997] AC 655).

An interference is continuing where it is repeated sufficiently frequently; where it only happens occasionally, it is not 'continuing'. This is one of the reasons why *Bolton v Stone* [1951] AC 850 (below, 8.4.4) had to be brought in negligence rather than nuisance. The interference with the legal interest can be either direct or indirect. A direct interference will be where the defendant's conduct has caused physical harm to the claimant's land by, for example, hitting a ball on to it. Indirect interference is where there is no physical harm caused but the claimant's enjoyment of his land is interfered with by, for example, excessive noise.

In determining the reasonableness of the defendant's conduct, and therefore whether or not it is a nuisance, the court will take into account the type of interference, the locality in which it takes place, its duration, its public utility, the sensitivity of the claimant's land and whether the defendant was acting deliberately to annoy the claimant. The most common complaints from neighbours of sports facilities are that their property is being physically damaged by things exiting the stadium or that the noise is so excessive that they cannot live peacefully in their homes.

8.3.1.1 Physical injury

Where direct physical harm is caused to the claimant's land, an actionable nuisance will almost always have occurred. However, that does not mean that the activity causing the harm will be forced to stop.

▶ *Miller v Jackson* [1977] QB 966

This case has become a benchmark for discussions on whether or not an activity is a nuisance and is famous for Lord Denning MR's robust defence of village cricket as an integral part of the social fabric of a community. The claimant bought a house on the edge of a village green where cricket had been played by the local club for over 70 years. His back garden was separated from the playing field by a fence 1.8m in height. His complaint was that balls were being hit from the green on to his property, interfering with his right to enjoy his property and damaging his house on a regular basis. The club had increased the height of the fence to 4.5m, which had prevented the vast majority, but not all, of the balls from being struck onto his land, but the claimant did not consider this to be an acceptable solution.

The Court of Appeal was left with the difficult task of balancing the competing interests of the householder and the cricket club in reaching an appropriate solution. On the one hand, the type of interference, direct physical harm, was one that would usually be prohibited by an injunction; on the other was the public interest in allowing the cricket club to continue to play where it had done for over 70 years. The majority of the Court held that playing cricket on this piece of land was a nuisance as there was a degree of inevitability associated with the risk of balls being hit on to neighbouring properties and causing them physical harm. It was further held that the defendant cannot avoid liability by arguing that the claimant had placed himself in danger by moving into a house adjoining the pitch. It is not a defence to say that the claimant has 'come to the nuisance'; either the activity was a nuisance or it was not, and in this case it was.

However, in determining the appropriate response to this nuisance, the Court took into account the character of the neighbourhood, the social utility of the activity and the conduct of the parties. Firstly, it is to be expected that part of the character of rural villages is provided by having sports and other activities taking place on their greens. By purchasing a property overlooking the cricket ground, the claimant was not 'coming to the nuisance' but buying into the character of the village as a whole. This included that activities in general, and cricket in particular, would take place there. Secondly, the greater interest of the local community in maintaining the cricket club as a focal point of the village's life should take precedence over the occasional hardship caused to an individual householder. Thirdly, the club had paid for a higher fence to be installed, which had eliminated most of the harmful shots, but the householder was not prepared to accept any inconvenience whatsoever. In other words, by accepting the benefit of overlooking the green, the claimant also had to accept the burden of the activities taking place on it. Thus, compensation was awarded to reflect the claimant's past and future inconvenience.

8.3.1.2 Excessive noise

The noise created by certain sports, particularly motorsports, has been the focus of a number of cases over the years. Key to determining the existence of a nuisance in these cases will be the level of noise, its regularity and the character of the area where the activity is taking place. In *Stretch v Romford Football Club Ltd* (1971) 115 Sol J 641, an injunction was granted to prevent speedway events from taking place at Romford FC's football ground. Although fixtures only took place for two hours, once each week from May to October, the amount of noise generated was held to be so far in excess of that which occurred at football matches held at the same venue as to constitute an unreasonable interference with the club's neighbours' quiet enjoyment of their property. The speedway club was banned from competing in Romford from the end of that season's competition.

In contrast to *Stretch v Romford*, a judicially-imposed compromise saw the activities of the Cotswold Motor Boat Racing Club restricted rather than stopped altogether.

▶ *Kennaway v Thompson* [1981] QB 88

The Club had expanded its activities, including organising power boat races and water skiing sessions, without restriction until the amount of noise became unbearable to local residents. Each race day was preceded by practice days, and water skiing took place at every available opportunity. This meant that the lake was in use by high-powered boats from 9 am until dusk on most days, and especially on weekends, from March to November each year. The Court of Appeal held that the Club's use of the lake was unreasonable and imposed an injunction on it, limiting the number and type of race days per year, enforced gaps among each of these race days and limited the number of boats that could be involved in water skiing at any time. These limitations balanced the rights of local residents to enjoy the benefit of living in a peaceful lakeside environment against the Club's right to continue its activities in a responsible manner.

Similar reasoning could be applied to noxious fumes and smells emanating from a stadium. This is most likely to occur in respect of motorsports and was one of the lines of argument put forward in *Stretch v Romford*, although it was rejected by the Court. The success of such a claim would again focus on the character of the neighbourhood; the more residential the area, the less likely that interferences of this kind will be acceptable.

In *Lawrence v Fen Tigers Ltd* [2012] EWCA Civ 26, the Court held that the character of a neighbourhood can change following planning permission being granted to a noisy activity, in this case, a motorsports circuit. Once racing was permitted, what previously could have been a private nuisance became a lawful activity because of the changed character of the area, where noise had become 'a defining feature of the locality.' It would appear that residents will have to challenge proposals for building such facilities at the planning stage, not after they have begun operating.

8.3.2 Public nuisance

The tort of public nuisance has two discrete forms. The more common of the two versions is where the defendant's activity materially affects the reasonable comfort and convenience of a section of the community, but the claimant suffers special damage above and beyond that suffered by everyone else. The second version is where a series of individual private nuisances are amalgamated into one generic public nuisance. Although not commonly used, partly because the action must be brought by the Attorney-General on behalf of the injured party, it can provide additional protections to the neighbours of sports facilities.

Public nuisances include unlawful acts or omissions which endanger the lives, safety, health or comfort of a section of the public, or by which the public is obstructed in the exercise of some common right, for example, using the highway. Unlike claims for private nuisance, the claimant does not need to possess a legal interest in the land to bring the claim; whereas private nuisance protects the claimant's interests in their land, public interest protects the public in general from annoyance.

8.3.2.1 Special damage

Castle v St Augustine's Links Ltd (1922) 38 TLR 615 exemplifies the case where the claimant has suffered harm above and beyond that suffered by the rest of the public. The defendant was aware that golf balls were occasionally hit on to a busy road adjacent to its course. Thus, the class of affected members of the public extended to anyone who drove down this particular road. The claimant was the driver of a car who was blinded by a golf ball that had been hit from the defendant's course and which went through his windscreen. The claimant had, therefore, suffered above and beyond other members of the affected group; he had suffered a specific personal injury, whereas the other road users had suffered only the risk of personal injury.

8.3.2.2 Amalgamated private nuisances

Where a section of the community is affected by the same activity, then public nuisance can be established on the basis of amalgamating the individual private nuisances that are occurring. In *East Dorset District Council v Eaglebeam Ltd and Others* [2006] EWHC 2378 (QB), the defendants operated a motocross course in a large park. The noise this generated interfered with local residents' right to enjoy their own premises, particularly as it prevented them from being able to use their gardens peacefully in the summer. Despite the alterations that had been made by the defendant to his course in an attempt to abate the nuisance, the noise was still considered to be of a sufficient level of interference to constitute a public nuisance.

8.4   Actions in negligence

There are several situations where an action in negligence survives either alongside of or instead of a claim under the Occupiers' Liability Acts. Despite the Acts not applying in these cases, the duty owed by the defendants has been held to be coextensive with the common duty of care (*Craven v Riches and Others and the Knockhill Racing Circuit Ltd* [2001] EWCA Civ 375). From a practical perspective, this means that there will be no difference in how the case is argued and its ultimate outcome will be the same whether the action is brought under the OLA 1957 or the common law. As with any claim in negligence, it must then be established that a breach of the duty owed caused the claimant's injuries (see further, chapter 4)

8.4.1 Participants v. organisers

Where the claimant's harm is not caused by the state of the defendant's premises but by the nature of the activity taking place on them, then the action must be brought in negligence. In *Poppleton v Trustees of the Portsmouth Youth Activities Centre* [2008] EWCA Civ 646 (above, 8.2.1), the claimant alleged that in failing to train him before allowing him on to the climbing wall, to supervise him whilst he was taking part in the activity, to warn him of the dangers of leaping from the wall in the way that he did and to inform him that the matting would not save him from injury in all cases amounted to a breach of the duty of care owed to him. The Court of Appeal held that the defendants were only under a duty to warn the claimant about dangers that were not obvious; the other duties would only have been engaged where training was requested and carried out negligently. As his injuries were caused by his voluntarily running an obvious risk by leaping from the wall in the way that he did, his claim failed. In contrast, in *Pinchbeck v Craggy Island Ltd* [2012] EWHC 2745, the claimant was being instructed by the defendant's employees on how to use a climbing wall but had not been warned not to jump from it under any circumstances, even by a controlled jump. Again, there was no action under the OLA 1957 as there was nothing wrong with the wall itself; only an action in negligence was sustainable. On this occasion, liability was established, but the claimant was found to have been contributorily negligent because of the obvious risk in jumping from the wall and her damages were reduced by one-third.

In several cases, the courts discuss negligence and occupier's liability at the same time, making no clear distinction as to which cause of action is ultimately at issue. As the duties owed to the claimant are the same, this is not a significant problem; the main difficulty that these cases raise for the reader is that by combining the discussions in this way, the courts will often avoid identifying who is the occupier.

Where the distinction is not made specifically, organisers of an event, as opposed to occupiers of the premises, owe a duty to take reasonable care to ensure that the event is run in such a way that it is reasonably safe in all the circumstances for the claimant to participate in it (see also, chapter 5.4.1.1.1). In *Craven*, there was nothing wrong with the state of the racing track, only with the way that the first defendants had organised the event. They were under a duty to ensure that they had designed out any unnecessary dangers, which they had attempted to do by limiting the number of motorcyclists who were on the track at any one time and by grouping together those who would be riding at similar speeds. The duty was breached by their failure to enforce this grouping. Thus, when the claimant unexpectedly came across two riders who were travelling at a significantly slower speed, his being forced to brake suddenly and lose control was held to have been caused by the presence of riders who should not have been on the track at the same time as he was. Although he was found to have been contributorily negligent, because of his failure to keep a proper lookout for other track users, the defendant was liable for failing to organise a reasonably safe event.

8.4.2 Spectators v. organiser

As with participants, where the injury is caused as a result of the activity taking place on the premises, rather than their state, then an action can only be brought in negligence. In *Fenton v Thruxton (BARC) Ltd* (above, 8.2.5.3), the NGB was liable in negligence for the death of a spectator for conducting a safety inspection that focused only on the potential risks posed to competitors and officials from the operation of the race track. As danger caused to the spectators by things leaving the track at high speed was reasonably foreseeable, the inspection should also have addressed the safety concerns of this group of users.

8.4.3   Spectators v. participants

The opportunities for participants to cause injury to the spectators at a sporting event are somewhat limited. In most cases where injury can be said to have been factually caused by the participant, it will be the occupier or organiser who will actually be at fault for allowing the incident to have occurred (*Murray v Harringay Arena*) (above, 8.2.5.4.1). A duty of care is undoubtedly owed by the participant to the spectators at the event; the only question is the precise content of that duty. The problems in this area of the law stem from *Wooldridge v Sumner* [1963] 2 QB 43 and the obsession of some commentators with attempting to introduce a standard of reckless disregard into the law of negligence (see further, chapter 4.4.2.3). These discussions distract attention from the Court of Appeal's important analysis of how the determination of the defendant's breach of the duty of care requires the court to examine the case in the context of all of its relevant circumstances.

▶ *Wooldridge v Sumner* [1963] 2 QB 43

The claimant was injured when a rider temporarily lost control of his horse during a demonstration event at the Horse of the Year Show. The rider had taken a bend at speed and had lost control of his horse on entering the straight part of the track. He collided with the claimant, who had been standing at the edge of the arena taking official photographs of the event, as the photographer attempted to move out of the horse's direction of travel.

The duty of care identified by the Court was that a competitor should use reasonable care and skill in performing the manoeuvres necessary for participation in the sporting event. In determining whether this duty had been breached, the court held that it was important to take into consideration the nature of the event, that horses can be unpredictable and can be difficult to control and that the participant would be going all out to win the competition.

The Court also held that mistakes and errors of judgement can and do occur in the heat of competition and that when going all out to win an event, a participant will usually have little or no regard for the safety of the event's spectators. In this situation, the rider had only been doing what was expected of him and his loss of control was simply an inherent risk of competitive horse riding. Therefore, there was no breach of the duty owed by him to the claimant.

In going all out to win, it is possible that the participant may make errors of judgement or exhibit lapses of skill. As anyone who has ever played competitive sport is aware, it is impossible to get everything exactly right all of the time; this dynamic unpredictability is part of what makes sport the spectacle that it is. Such errors or lapses when made in the heat of competition are not negligent; they are simply an integral part of sport.

It was further added that participants are entitled to expect that the spectators will have some knowledge of the risks and dangers inherent in the sport that they are watching. Depending on the sport concerned, that might mean that in attempting to win an event, the competitor need have little or no regard for the safety of the spectator;

the safety of the spectators is a concern of the occupier and/or organiser of the event, not the participants in it.

After *Caldwell v Maguire and Fitzgerald* [2001] EWCA Civ 1054 (see further, chapter 4.4.1.2), it is now possible to propose a modernised version of the law that combines the imposition of the duty from *Wooldridge* with the 'negligence in all the circumstances' approach that the judges in both of these cases preferred; that a competitor in a sporting event owes a duty to take all the care that is objectively reasonable in the prevailing circumstances of the contest to avoid the infliction of reasonably foreseeable injury on those present as spectators. Perhaps the most important circumstances to be considered are that the competitor will be, or at least should be, concentrating on their performance, not the safety of the spectators, and the spectators should not be on the playing surface. Taking all of this into account, it will only rarely be the case that a competitor will have acted with a sufficient degree of carelessness to be individually responsible for the injuries caused to a spectator.

8.4.4 Passersby v. organisers

Organisers of sporting events must also ensure that harm is not caused to their neighbours. This includes those who are passing by when an event is taking place. Where the injured person is off the organiser's premises and cannot therefore use the Occupiers' Liability Acts, and the incident is a one-off, or is so infrequent that it cannot constitute a course of conduct constituting nuisance, then the claimant's only option will be an action in negligence.

> ▶ *Bolton v Stone* [1951] AC 850
>
> The claimant was struck on the head by a cricket ball that had been hit out of the local ground. The ball had been hit with considerable force and had travelled over a fence that was 2.1m high, situated 71m from the wicket, before hitting the claimant who was standing outside of her house about 91m from where the ball had been hit. The evidence suggested that there had not previously been a shot of this magnitude at this ground but that on perhaps six occasions over the previous 28 years, a ball had been hit on to the road in front of the claimant's house, but never as far as on this occasion. Nuisance could not be established as there was insufficient regularity of recurrence to establish a course of conduct, so discussion centred on whether the defendant had acted negligently in their organisation of cricket matches at this ground. The House of Lords held that the duty was to take care to prevent reasonably foreseeable harm from occurring, not all harm. As this incident was not reasonably foreseeable, only an improbable possibility, there was no breach of duty.

The House of Lords concluded that there was no negligent conduct on the basis that the duty owed by the cricket club, which was to prevent balls from being hit into the adjacent road but only in so far as there was any reasonably foreseeable risk of that happening, was not breached. Although it was foreseeable as a possibility that a ball might be hit out of the ground and that, as a result, it was foreseeable as a possibility that a ball might hit and injure someone outside of the ground, such an outcome was not sufficiently probable to establish liability in negligence. In this case, the probability of the ball being hit out of the ground was extremely low; when this was coupled with the probability of one of the balls that was struck out of the ground hitting a passerby on a little-used path, the risk of injury was considered to be so low that it would not be contemplated by the reasonable person. Therefore, there was no need to guard against such an improbable outcome.

This can be contrasted with *Lamond v Glasgow Corporation* (1968) SLT 291, where a pedestrian was hit on the head by a golf ball that had been hit from a course on the defendant's land. Although there was no evidence of any previous accident of this kind occurring, the fact that around 6,000 shots each year were hit over the fence behind which the claimant had been walking should have put the defendant on alert that it was reasonably foreseeable that at some point, someone would be injured by one of the shots.

8.5 Outdoor and adventure sports

In general, the normal rules relating to occupiers' liability, negligence and nuisance will apply to the organisers of outdoor and adventure sports in the same way as they would to those organising any other sport. There are, however, two situations where variations on the normal operation of the law occur. The first is in respect of activity centres providing instruction to children and the second is the modified duty of care owed to those who are exercising their right to roam over access land.

8.5.1 Activity Centres (Young Persons' Safety) Act 1995

Following the Lyme Bay canoeing tragedy (see further, chapter 6.2.7.2), the government reviewed the provision of adventure and outdoor activities to young people with a view to making them better regulated. Section 1 Activity Centres (Young Persons' Safety) Act 1995 creates a licensing regime that applies to all people who wish to provide facilities for adventure activities and s.2(1)(a) makes it an offence to provide instruction, leadership or facilities to those who are under the age of 18 unless a valid licence is held.

The aim of the legislation is to ensure that those providing adventure activities to young people are suitably qualified to lead or instruct the activity in question in an attempt to make provision safer for the participants. Where an adventure activities provider is in breach of this legislation, an action will still have to be brought either on the basis of negligent instruction or organisation, or a breach of the duty owed under the Occupiers' Liability Acts if compensation is to be secured.

8.5.2 Access land

There has been much debate over the extent and meaning of rights of access for recreational purposes to the wilder parts of the countryside. The 'right to roam' was until recently unknown in English law. The National Parks and Access to the Countryside Act 1949 created a framework of access agreements and orders allowing access to national parkland for open-air recreation. The Countryside and Rights of Way Act 2000 allows even greater rights to the public over access land, as defined in s.1 of the Act to include all registered common land, any land over 600m high and any other land designated as such under the Act.

These two provisions have enabled walkers, mountaineers and others engaged in outdoor and adventure sports to have much greater access to land throughout the country. Section 60 National Parks and Access to the Countryside Act 1949 and both s.2 and sch.2 Countryside and Rights of Way Act 2000 contain a number of restrictions on the right to roam. These restrictions are there to ensure that the right is exercised responsibly and does not cause damage to the land or to the plants and livestock that are farmed on it.

Section 1(4) OLA 1957 specifically excludes those on access land from being treated as visitors, meaning that the duty of care owed to those exercising their right to roam is the 'common duty of humanity' found in s.1(4) OLA 1984 (above, 8.2.6). The duty owed to those using access land has had a further gloss put on it by s.1A OLA 1984 to ensure that an undue burden is not placed on occupiers. In particular, s.1A(b) OLA 1984 provides that in determining the nature and extent of the duty owed by an occupier, regard must be had to the importance of maintaining the character of the countryside, including any features of historic, traditional or archaeological interest that are on it. Thus, occupiers must ensure that known dangers are brought to the attention of the users of access land but that the duty must be interpreted sympathetically in the context of the character of the land and its environment.

Hot topic …   # Subjecting motorsports to the law

Almost all of the UK's major participation and spectator sports have attracted the interest of the law over the last 25 years. The various forms of motorsport have not only helped to blaze that early trail in *Wilks v Cheltenham Home-guard Motor Cycle and Light Car Club*[1971] 1 WLR 668, where it was held that a competitor could go all out to win rather than focus on the safety of the watching spectators, but have helped to develop and extend the law of tort as it applies to sporting activities. Motorsports of all kinds, and at all levels of participation, have been subjected to an incredibly wide range of legal actions covering everything from participation in, and consumption of, the sports to their organization and commercial exploitation. Perhaps this is not surprising; motorsports are highly competitive, potentially dangerous and noisy, and they create noxious emissions, have multiple layers of regulation and, at the elite levels, are extremely commercialized. This makes motorsports one of the most interesting groups of activities for legal examination.

The dangers of engaging in motorsports are obvious; the vehicles are travelling at high speeds in an environment where there are many hazards, including other vehicles, barriers that are in place to protect the spectators and the potential for mechanical malfunction and driver error. Despite, or perhaps because of this, motorsports are amongst the most popular of spectator sports. The cases examined so far have included incidents arising out of informal track days (*Wattleworth*), competitive speedway (*Stretch*), motocross (*Stanley*), motorbike racing (*Fenton*), rallying (*Stratton*), hill scambles (*Wilks*) and powerboat racing (*Kennaway*); in later chapters, Formula 1 will make an appearance in the regulation of commercial contracts (*Force India Formula One Team* Ltd v *Ethiad Airways PJSC and Aldar Properties* see further, chapter 11.3.1) and intellectual property (the Lotus litigation, see further, chapter 13.2.1).

The range of legal actions that have challenged the organization of motorsports events is equally diverse. Occupiers of race tracks have been accused of not having effective safety barriers in place (*Wattleworth*) and failing to carry out adequate risk assessments to ensure the safety of the spectators (*Fenton*). It has even been argued that a television company's positioning of a camera on a curb-stone contributed to a claimant's loss of control of his classic racing car (*Green v Sunset and Vine Productions Company and others* [2010] EWCA Civ 1441). Although this claim failed on the facts, it was pointed out that the lack of any adequate risk assessment being carried out to determine whether it was appropriate for the camera to be located at that part of the track was extremely bad practice. Further, organisers of race meetings have been found negligent by failing to provide marshals of a sufficient level of competence (*Stanley*).

Most recently, however, has been a series of cases that have been brought by occupiers of premises that are adjacent to, or in the neighbourhood of, motorsports tracks. Despite being an inherent part of racing high-powered vehicles, those who have had the quiet enjoyment of their property interfered with by what they see as excessive engine noise, and potentially smells, have attempted to have these activities closed down. The courts have not always taken a consistent approach to what is and what is not an acceptable level of noise that can be created by motorsports. *Stretch* said that none was allowed in a residential environment and banned the activity altogether, whilst in *Kennaway*, a judicially-designed compromise that reduced the number of noisy days whilst allowing the club to continue to operate its business activities was imposed.

Again, in apparent contradiction, the court in *East Dorset* held that despite numerous changes to track design and improvements in noise reduction, the operation of the motocross track affected a sufficient number of people in a locality to be held a public nuisance, even though the applicant Council had granted planning permission for the track to be built. The alternative approach in *Lawrence* was that once planning permission to hold motorsports events had been granted, it had the impact of changing the character of the neighbourhood to such an extent that what previously would have been noise amounting to a private nuisance was now held to be one of the defining features of the area and not actionable.

These contradictions in approach, coupled with the inherent dangers of the sports in question and their innate inability to be anything other than noisy, ensures that the law will play a regular role in the resolution of motorsports disputes. As claimants continue to search for the deepest pockets or the best insurance policy, occupiers, organizers, inspectors, risk assessors, NGBs and ISFs will continue to face allegations of negligence and mismanagement. However, the judicial reluctance to simply ban these activities, and the decision in Lawrence in particular, demonstrate that motorsports will continue to receive protection from the law, provided that the appropriate safety and regulatory measures are in place.

Summary

8.1 The duties owed by the occupiers of sports stadiums and the organisers of sports events were originally governed by the law of contract and the tort of negligence. These two branches of the law still have a role to play in the protection of people affected by the holding of a sports event, though many of these cases will now fall under the Occupiers' Liability Acts.

8.2 An occupier owes visitors a duty to take reasonable care to ensure that the premises are reasonably safe for the purposes of the visit (OLA 1957 s.2(2)). Further, an occupier owes trespassers a duty of care to ensure that they do not suffer any harm from known dangers that the occupier has reasonable grounds to suspect that trespassers will come into contact with (OLA 1984 s.1(3)). Both of these duties can be discharged by providing warnings that there is a specific danger present on the premises or where the visitor/trespasser has voluntarily run the risk of harm being caused to them by the danger.

8.3 Private nuisance protects a landowner's right to enjoy the use of their property without unreasonable interference by others. This tort is most commonly used by people who live close by sports venues to control the noise (*Kennaway v Thompson*), the objects (*Miller v Jackson*) and potentially the odours (*Stretch v Romford*) emanating from them.

8.4 Where a claimant is injured at or in the proximity of a sports venue, but they do not fall under the protection of the Occupiers' Liability Acts or private nuisance, then they will have to resort to an action in negligence. The versatility of this tort means that it can be used in a variety of unusual circumstances, such as *Bolton v Stone* and *Wooldridge v Sumner*.

8.5 Following *R v Kite*, the Activity Centres (Young Persons' Safety) Act 1995 introduced a licensing regime for the providers of sporting and outdoor adventure activities to young people. The Countryside and Rights of Way Act 2000 defines more clearly the 'right to roam' and provides greater access to the wilder parts of the UK for sport and leisure purposes.

Further reading

Steele, *Tort Law: text, cases and materials* (2nd edn, 2010, Oxford University Press) chs 10 and 12

Bale, *Sport, Space and the City* (2001, The Blackburn Press)

Lewis and Taylor (eds), *Sport: Law and Practice* (2nd edn, 2008, Tottel) ch D5

Anderson, 'Countryside access and environmental protection: an American view of Britain's right to roam' (2007) 9(4) *Environmental Law Review* 241

James and James, 'Spectator safety and the liability of governing bodies' [2009] 4 *Sports Law Administration and Practice* 1

McArdle, 'The enduring legacy of reckless disregard' (2005) 34(4) *Common Law World Review* 316

Norris, 'Duty of care and personal responsibility: occupiers, owners, organisers and individuals' (2008) 3 *Journal of Personal Injury Law* 187

Wallinga, 'Effusa vel deiecta in Rome and Glasgow' (2002) 6(1) *Edinburgh Law Review* 117

Links to relevant websites can be found at www.palgrave.com/law/james2e

Stadium disasters and spectator safety

Background and context (9.1)
- Cheltenham Races, 1866 and Ewood Park, Blackburn, 1894 (9.1.1)
- Ibrox Park, Glasgow, 1902 (9.1.2)

Empire Stadium, Wembley and the Shortt Report, 1923–24 (9.2)
- Empire Stadium, Wembley, 1923 (9.2.1)
- The Shortt Report, 'Report of the Departmental Committee on Crowds' (9.2.2)

Burnden Park, Bolton and the Moelwyn Hughes Report, 1946 (9.3)
- Burnden Park, Bolton, 1946 (9.3.1)
- The Moelwyn Hughes Report, 'Enquiry into the Disaster at Bolton Wanderers' Football Ground on the 9th March 1946' (9.3.2)

Creating the conditions for further disasters (9.4)

Ibrox Park, Glasgow and the Wheatley Report, 1971 (9.5)
- Ibrox Park, Glasgow, 1971 (9.5.1)
- The Wheatley Report, 'Report on Crowd Safety at Sports Grounds' (9.5.2)
- The Safety at Sports Grounds Act 1975 (9.5.3)

Valley Parade, Bradford and the Popplewell Reports, 1985–86 (9.6)
- Valley Parade, Bradford, 1985 (9.6.1)
- The Popplewell Reports (9.6.2)
  - The Popplewell Interim Report, 'Committee of Enquiry into Crowd Safety and Control at Sports Grounds' (9.6.2.1)
  - The Popplewell Final Report, 'Committee of Enquiry into Crowd Safety and Control at Sports Grounds' (9.6.2.2)
  - The Fire Safety and Safety of Places of Sport Act 1987 (9.6.2.3)
  - Football Spectators Act 1989 (9.6.2.4)
  - The impact of the Popplewell Reports (9.6.2.5)

Hillsborough Stadium, Sheffield and the Taylor Reports, 1989–90 (9.7)
- Hillsborough Stadium, Sheffield, 1989 (9.7.1)
- The Taylor Interim Report, 'The Hillsborough Stadium Disaster' (9.7.2)
  - The Football Association (9.7.2.1)
  - Hillsborough did not have a valid safety certificate (9.7.2.2)
  - Sheffield Wednesday Football Club (9.7.2.3)
  - The recommendations (9.7.2.4)
- The Taylor Final Report, 'The Hillsborough Stadium Disaster' (9.7.3)
- The legacy (9.7.4)

Chapter 9

Stadium disasters and spectator safety

Key terms

▶ **Terraces** – stepped concrete or wooden standing areas at sports grounds.
▶ **Stands** – seated areas at sports grounds, also referred to as 'grandstands'.

9.1 Background and context

British sport, and football in particular, has suffered a series of major disasters leading to the deaths of hundreds of spectators. The responses from the governments of the time have often been minimal; although poor practices were identified and recommendations made, very little was done to improve the conditions in which sport was watched live. In this chapter, the causes of the major UK sporting disasters and the Parliamentary and sporting responses to them are examined in order to understand how the catastrophic events of the 1980s happened and why they were preventable.

In the late Victorian era, attending live sports events became a popular pastime with dedicated venues built throughout the country to host contests of all kinds. Many of these were permanent stadiums, and they or their successor buildings rank amongst some of the most iconic buildings in the world. Others were of a more temporary nature with grandstands built specifically to watch an individual event. Regardless of whether the stadium was of a temporary or permanent nature, the disasters that subsequently unfolded can generally be explained by one of two reasons: the negligent construction of the building used to watch the event, or mismanagement of the crowd once it was on the premises.

9.1.1 Cheltenham Races, 1866 and Ewood Park, Blackburn, 1894

In *Francis v Cockrell* (1870) LR 5 QB 501, the organisers of the 1866 Cheltenham Races were held liable to an injured spectator for being in breach of contract by failing to provide a safe place from which to watch the event; the injuries were caused by the collapse of a temporary grandstand that had been constructed negligently by an independent contractor. Thirty years later, in *Brown v Lewis* (1896) 12 TLR 455, the directors of Blackburn Rovers Football Club were held personally liable in negligence for the injuries caused to the claimant by the collapse of another temporary grandstand. The directors' breach of duty was their failure to engage a competent independent contractor to carry out work on the grandstand (see further, chapter 8.1.1).

Despite the potential for serious injury or death being caused to countless thousands of sports spectators around the country, these two incidents appear to have been treated as no more than unfortunate accidents. Perhaps this was because the numbers involved were comparatively low and their injuries comparatively minor. Whatever the reason for the complacency, there was no inquiry into how or why these grandstands had collapsed, there were no discussions of applicable safety standards that should have been adhered to and there was no mention of the need for a regulatory or licensing regime to be created.

9.1.2 Ibrox Park, Glasgow, 1902

Eight years later, at Ibrox Park, Glasgow the UK's first major sporting disaster provided the ideal opportunity for Parliament and the NGBs to investigate stadium safety and create a new set of standards for sports venues. They failed to take it, setting the scene for almost a century of ineffective responses to the needs of spectators.

> ▶ *Ibrox Park, 5 April 1902*
>
> The first Ibrox disaster occurred during the first fully professional international football match between Scotland and England. A section of the newly erected wooden terracing collapsed, leaving a gaping hole through which hundreds of spectators fell around 15 metres to the ground below. 25 people were killed and over 500 injured as a result of the poor construction of this part of the stadium. Despite the fatalities and the large number of injuries caused to spectators, no public inquiry into its causes was held. The official explanation was that the only statutory authority for ordering such an investigation at the time was the Fatal Accidents Inquiry (Scotland) Act 1895, which applied only to deaths caused during the course of the deceased's employment. As none of those who died were working at the stadium, it was claimed that there were no grounds for ordering a public inquiry into the disaster.
>
> Unusually, however, the contractor responsible for the terrace's construction was prosecuted for culpable homicide (the Scottish equivalent of the English offence of manslaughter) on the basis that he had substituted an inferior quality of wood that was weaker than the one specifically contracted for (*R v McDougall*, (unreported) High Court of Justiciary (Glasgow), 28 June 1902). McDougall was eventually acquitted on the basis of a lack of evidence, leaving yet another sporting disaster being registered as an unfortunate accident rather than resulting in a greater degree of safety being provided to those who had paid to watch the event.
>
> Although McDougall was prosecuted for having used substandard materials for the construction of the terracing, two other factors that could have been investigated by an appropriately constituted public inquiry may have contributed to the stadium's collapse. The first was the design of the terrace's structural framework, which appears not to have been adequately supported, causing it to become unstable. The second, and one which became a recurrent theme of subsequent official inquiries into stadium disasters, was that there was no accurate measure for calculating the maximum capacity of either the stadium as a whole or its individual terraces. Capacities, it appears, were calculated by no more scientific a basis than how many people could be fitted on to the terrace. Thus, the sheer weight of people on Ibrox's western terracing could have had a significant impact on both the cause and the scale of the disaster.

These early disasters were caused in the main part by the inadequate and/or negligent construction of the stadiums in which the sporting event was taking place. However, at both Ewood Park and Ibrox Park, one contributing factor appears to have been the mismanagement of the crowd that allowed too many people on to a structure that was not strong enough to support the spectators' combined weight. The lack of any inquiry into the causes of these incidents demonstrated the lack of regard in which sports fans were, and would continue to be, held by the authorities.

9.2 Empire Stadium, Wembley and the Shortt Report, 1923–24

The next major incident occurred at the newly constructed Empire Stadium, or Wembley Stadium as it became known, during the 1923 FA Cup Final. This incident and the genuinely disastrous events that happened at Burden Park, Bolton, in 1946 (below, 9.3) are of particular importance because they were the first of the sporting disasters to be followed by governmental inquiries. The main distinction between these two incidents and those that had gone before is that their sole cause was the mismanagement of the event itself rather than the negligent construction of either of the stadiums.

9.2.1 Empire Stadium, Wembley, 1923

Often referred to as the 'White Horse Final' because a policeman on a white horse has gone down in popular history as the man who single-handedly controlled the fans on the pitch and averted a major disaster, the events at Wembley provided the ideal opportunity for the government to develop an effective licensing regime for sports grounds.

> ▶ *Empire Stadium, 28 April 1923*
>
> The Empire Stadium at Wembley was completed only days before the 1923 FA Cup Final took place between Bolton Wanderers and West Ham United. The FA had decided that the vast majority of spectators would be admitted to the ground on payment of an admission fee at the turnstiles. Unfortunately, the public interest in attending the inaugural game at the new stadium was grossly underestimated and the authorities were totally unprepared for the volume of people who turned up. The stadium had an official capacity of 126,000, though this had not been calculated scientifically despite the events at Ibrox in 1902. Estimates of how many people actually gained entry to the Final reach as high as 300,000.
>
> The ground was full over an hour before kick-off, however, people continued to arrive in ever greater numbers expecting to be able to pay at the turnstiles. To alleviate the pressure on those who were being crushed immediately outside of the ground, large numbers of spectators were admitted onto terraces that were already full. As further crushes developed inside the now overcrowded stadium, spectators were forced to escape from the terraces on to the pitch and the track surrounding it. Fortunately, there were no perimeter fences in place. Around 900 spectators suffered minor injuries with 22 being treated in hospital.

Despite the scale of the incident and the obvious mismanagement of the crowd at the new stadium the Home Secretary, William Bridgeman did not order a full public inquiry as he considered that the police had dealt with the situation effectively and appropriately. He did, however, constitute a Committee of Enquiry with a remit to examine 'abnormally large crowds at special occasions.' It was not the Committee's aim to establish fault for what had happened at Wembley but to examine how a repeat of what had happened there could be avoided.

9.2.2 The Shortt Report, 'Report of the Departmental Committee on Crowds'

The Committee of Enquiry made a series of recommendations that it felt would make events of this magnitude much safer in the future. These included creating self-contained terraces with individually and scientifically calculated maximum capacities, which should be fed by specific and more efficient turnstiles that channelled spectators through dedicated entrances directly on to the standing areas.

It also recommended that more stringent fire precautions should be installed at all stadiums as wood continued to be an important building material. From a management perspective, the Committee recommended that the police should be in overall control of law and order and that a named officer should be in command of all crowd safety and crowd control measures on the day. Further, trained stewards who had stadium-specific knowledge should be in place to assist with the management of large crowds, particularly where the spectators were at an unfamiliar venue. It was also recommended that, in future, entrance to popular events such as the FA Cup Final should be by advanced purchase tickets only.

With hindsight, each of these recommendations seems to be grounded very much in common sense and would have been an efficient, cheap and effective means of controlling large crowds safely. The Committee considered it to be unnecessary for either national or local government to administer a formal framework of regulations to ensure safety at sports venues because the governing bodies of sport were capable of establishing a system that would be effective in their own sport. This conclusion was reached despite the FA's refusal to attend the Committee's hearings or to engage with the discussions that followed the publication of its proposals. Instead, somewhat naively, the Committee considered that the threat of the imposition of the licensing scheme that it had outlined in the final paragraphs of the Report, which could be implemented should the governing bodies continue to fail to take safety issues seriously, would lead to the necessary improvements in practice.

The Shortt Report was never debated in Parliament, and only one of its proposals was ever implemented: from 1924, tickets to all FA Cup Finals had to be bought in advance. It was clear from its findings that poor organisation and mismanagement of the event had caused the overcrowding and injuries at the Cup Final. Instead of learning from the events at Wembley and imposing basic safety standards that could have prevented each of the following disasters, the lasting image is of a large but well-behaved crowd being controlled by single policeman on a white horse.

9.3 Burnden Park, Bolton and the Moelwyn Hughes Report, 1946

The disaster that occurred at Burnden Park provided Parliament with a further opportunity to review the safety and management procedures at major sports events; its failure to do so led directly to the disasters of the 1970s and 1980s.

9.3.1 Burnden Park, Bolton, 1946

The Burnden Park disaster unfolded in circumstances bearing an eerie similarity both to those that led to the overcrowding at Wembley in 1923 and those that would occur 43 years later at Hillsborough.

▶ *Burnden Park, 9 March 1946*

Bolton Wanderers were playing at home to Stoke City in an FA Cup quarter-final tie. In much the same way as the police and football authorities had failed to gauge the popular interest in the 1923 FA Cup Final, so they failed to take into account a number of factors that helped to swell the numbers hoping to get in to see the game at Burnden Park. This was a tie involving two of the biggest clubs in the country at the time in the first FA Cup competition after the end of the Second World War; the weather was unseasonably good and a large number of spectators turned up in the hope of watching one of the most popular British footballers of all time, Stanley Matthews. Furthermore, as this was only a quarter-final tie, an entrance fee could be paid at the turnstiles, encouraging spontaneous attendance amongst a number of people who might not otherwise have turned up.

It is estimated that around 85,000 people gained entry to a ground that had a previous highest recorded attendance of fewer than 70,000 spectators. Predictions of the likely crowd size were based on the fact that Burden Park had not hosted a crowd in excess of 45,000 during the preceding season and so just as in 1923, the police and stadium operators were totally unprepared for the huge crowds that turned up. The stadium was closed around 20 minutes before kick-off, but many thousands gained entry to the terraces by climbing over walls, breaking through fences and coming in through an open exit gate.

As the crowd surged forward when the teams took to the field, two of the crush barriers on one of the terraces collapsed under the sheer weight of numbers pushing against it. In the resulting crush, 33 people died and over 400 were injured. Within a few weeks, an inquiry chaired by Moelwyn Hughes J had been commissioned by the Home Office.

9.3.2 The Moelwyn Hughes Report, 'Enquiry into the Disaster at Bolton Wanderers' Football Ground on the 9th March 1946'

The Moelwyn Hughes Report began by condemning the Shortt Report for being anaemic and failing to address the needs of football spectators by allowing the football authorities to regulate themselves on issues of safety. It then went on to explain that neither Bolton Wanderers FC nor the police were at fault for the disaster because they had taken proper steps to control the crowd on the day.

The Report then made several specific criticisms of the general framework of safety within which football clubs operated. In particular, it was critical of there being no scientific calculation of a ground's maximum capacity. This was compounded by there being no means available to those who were in charge of crowd safety for establishing precisely how many spectators were inside the ground. Thus, there were no means of knowing how many spectators could be accommodated safely inside the stadium nor when this number had been reached. Further, there was no effective means of closing the turnstiles when the stadium was full, enabling many people to climb over them when informed that the stadium's capacity had been reached.

Moelwyn Hughes' recommendations went far beyond those of the Shortt Report and refused to accept that the football authorities were capable of regulating themselves where spectator safety was concerned. The central coordination of crowd safety, the fixing of capacities for each specific part of a ground and the counting of spectators into each of those parts were again recommended as essential elements of ensuring that too many people were not herded into too small a section of the stadium. The Report specifically recommended that a licensing regime operated by local councils should be created by statute. If a stadium did not meet the standards and procedures required to make spectators safe, then a licence would not be granted and football matches could no longer be played at that ground.

Once again, none of the proposals were acted on by the government of the day. The licensing regime was considered to have the potential to place too great a financial and administrative burden on local authorities whilst the clubs and governing bodies of football were concerned that the cost of making their grounds as safe as the proposals required were prohibitively high. Thus, once again, the government opted for football in particular, and sport in general, to operate under an ill-defined system of self-regulation, despite the FA's failure to take a lead on safety issues post-1923.

9.4 Creating the conditions for further disasters

In an unrelated Parliamentary debate following the publication of the Shortt Report, Oswald Mosley MP accused those who had attempted to gain entry to the stadium after the gates had been closed, of acting like hooligans. Although not supported by other Members of the House of Commons and reprimanded by the Speaker for his comments, it highlights that there has always been a small but vociferous group that considers the spectators themselves to have been a prime cause of the deaths and injuries. In deciding that the licensing regime proposed in the Moelwyn Hughes Report should not be implemented, the government pointed out that no legislation could prevent accidents that were caused by spectators who had entered the stadium illegally. Although this statement is true where deliberate vandalism is concerned, it fails to take into account that the purpose of the licensing regime was to ensure that stadiums were constructed and managed in a way that ensured that it was easier to control and regulate the large numbers of people who were trying to gain entry to them. The anticipated result of such a regulatory scheme would have been that fewer spectators would attempt, or be able, to enter stadiums illegally in the manner that had been seen at both Wembley and Burnden Park.

Throughout the 1960s, the increased focus on crowd disorder hid the fact that many stadiums had become dilapidated and unsafe, exacerbating the problems that had already been identified by the disasters of 1902 and 1946 and the near miss in 1923. Stadiums and those attending the games at them were now viewed through a 'hooligan lens'. The overriding concern was no longer about making spectators safe but about controlling the anti-social behaviour of the hooligan minority. This change of focus, coupled with the failure to develop an effective safety regime, led to a situation where all of the previously identified problems were still in existence, but policing tactics and stadium design (for example, the introduction of perimeter fencing) were aimed at preventing rival fans from coming into contact with each other or getting on to the pitch.

Three further government reports on football were commissioned during the 1960s: the Chester Report of 1966 examined the administration of football and the means by which the game could be developed for the public good, and the Harrington and Lang Reports of 1968 and 1969, respectively, focused on the issue of crowd disorder (see further, chapter 10). All three reports made recommendations about the need to ensure that spectator facilities were both adequate and safe, though crowd safety was not their primary focus. The Harrington Report also noted that improved facilities at stadiums may make it easier for the police and clubs to control crowd disorder, but importantly acknowledged that the costs involved in stadium development meant that it was unlikely that clubs would voluntarily improve their own safety arrangements.

Conflating the issues of spectator safety and crowd disorder in this way ensured that the focus of the discussions in this area became confused. On the one hand, much greater importance was placed on the need to combat the growing threat posed by crowd disorder than on the need to make what were becoming increasingly outdated and dangerous stadiums safe. On the other, spectator safety and crowd disorder were seen as being inextricably linked; if crowd disorder could be eliminated, spectators would once again be safe almost regardless of the state of the premises in which they were watching the game. This change in focus ensured that the circumstances became ripe for yet another major disaster at a football stadium.

9.5 Ibrox Park, Glasgow and the Wheatley Report, 1971

Whilst the focus of the government, police and football authorities turned to football hooliganism, football stadiums continued to be mismanaged and increasingly unsafe places to visit. The second major Ibrox disaster finally resulted in legislative intervention that created the first licensing framework for sports grounds.

9.5.1 Ibrox Park, Glasgow, 1971

The precise cause of the second Ibrox disaster is unclear, however, a combination of poor stadium design and mismanagement of the crowd undoubtedly contributed to the scale of the tragedy.

> ▶ *Ibrox Park, 2 January 1971*
>
> In the 89th minute of a Glasgow derby between Rangers and Celtic football clubs, Celtic scored to take a one-nil lead. A minute later, with almost the last kick of the game, Rangers equalised. As the Rangers fans on Stairway 13 surged forward, one or more people appear to have lost their balance and fallen. With no crush barriers to stop the flow of people down the stairs, those who had fallen not only were crushed but caused others to fall and be crushed themselves. Sixty-six people were killed and 145 were injured on a stairway that had been the cause of three similar incidents over the previous ten years, including having caused two deaths in almost identical circumstances in 1961.
>
> Many reports of the disaster suggest that large numbers of Rangers fans had started to leave the stadium after Celtic had taken a late lead in the game. They go on to say that when Rangers equalised, these fans attempted to return to the terraces to celebrate and that their pushing against the flow of fans trying to leave the stadium caused someone to fall, and the subsequent disaster to occur. The Wheatley Report, the official inquiry into the disaster, denies that this can have occurred as the bodies of those killed and injured were all facing in the same direction: towards the pitch. Thus, it appears that it was the unrestricted surge of spectators down the stairway towards the pitch that caused someone to fall, not people pushing against one another. Once again, stadium design had played a key part in the events.
>
> Stairway 13 stretched from the bottom of the terrace at pitch-side to the top of the terrace at the back of the stadium. It formed an unbroken series of stairs for its entire length, except for three small landings the width of about five stairs. Although there were handrails dividing the stairway into seven lanes, there were neither crush barriers nor changes in the

direction of the lanes that could break up the flow of people. This meant that once the surge began, there was nothing to slow it down or stop it until the people at the front reached the bottom of the stairway or somebody fell. As with previous disasters, the lack of any means of calculating the capacity of a terrace and the lack of effective monitoring of the exact numbers of people in any area of the stadium meant that too many people were trying to use a badly designed stairway at the same time.

9.5.2 The Wheatley Report, 'Report on Crowd Safety at Sports Grounds'

The aim of the Wheatley Report was not to establish blame for the disaster but to investigate current standards of crowd safety. The Report did note that lessons had not been learned from the previous three incidents on Stairway 13 and that there was no clear or adequate division of responsibility for crowd safety between the club and the police. This in turn led to a situation where crowd safety fell between the spheres of responsibility of the bodies best placed to ensure that the stadium was, in fact, safe for the spectators. In *Dougan v Rangers Football Club Ltd* 1974 SLT (Sh Ct) 34, Rangers were held liable in negligence for the death of one of the spectators, with the club's failure to ensure that the stadium was reasonably safe being central to the claim.

The Wheatley Report not only made a series of recommendations, it pre-empted the complaints that would be made against them and sought to justify why its proposals should become law. The Report's main proposal was that all sports grounds, and in particular all major football grounds, should be subject to a licensing system. The justification for this was that if a club were charging an admission fee from the spectators, then it owed them a duty of care to ensure that they were reasonably safe. It was therefore necessary to impose certain standards on these stadiums and to ensure that these were observed, as self-regulation had clearly failed.

The proposed licensing system was not a new idea; it was first mooted in the Shortt Report in 1924. Furthermore, the identification of a duty of care being owed by the stadium owners or occupiers to their spectators is simply a restatement of the duty of care found in s.2(1) Occupiers' Liability Act (Scotland) 1960 (the equivalent Scottish duty to that found in s.2(2) Occupiers' Liability Act 1957 (see further, chapter 8.2.5)). The novelty in the proposal was that criminal liability should follow from a breach of the safety regime proposed to ensure that these minimum standards were actually achieved.

9.5.3 The Safety at Sports Grounds Act 1975

The Safety at Sports Grounds Act 1975 (SSGA 1975) enacted the proposed licensing system. Further guidance on how to design and build a safe stadium was provided by the *Guide to Safety at Sports Grounds*, more usually referred to as the Green Guide. Section 1(1) enabled the Home Secretary to designate any sports stadium that held more than 10,000 spectators as requiring a safety certificate before events could be held there. During the intervening years, this figure has been reduced to 5,000 spectators for football grounds but remains at 10,000 for all other sports (Safety of Sports Grounds (Accommodation of Spectators) Order 1996/499). The safety certificate is issued by the local authority in which the ground is located (s.1(3)) and by s.2(1) can contain any terms and conditions that the authority considers to be necessary or expedient to secure the reasonable safety of the spectators.

The SSGA 1975 was only to apply to 'sports stadia' not 'sports grounds'. Under s.17(1) of the Act, a sports ground was any place where sports or other competitive activities took place in the open air and where accommodation was provided for spectators that consisted of artificial structures or natural structures that had been artificially modified for the purpose. A sports stadium was a sports ground where the accommodation provided for spectators wholly or substantially surrounded the area used for the activities taking place on it. Thus, the Act was originally aimed at places where major team sports events were played, not for example horse racing courses, motorsports tracks or sports grounds used by lower league teams.

In addition to this requirement, under s.10, the local authority can issue a prohibition notice preventing any event from taking place at any sports ground, not just those that are designated under the Act, where it considers that the stadium as a whole or a particular part of it poses a serious risk of harm to spectators. The failure to secure a safety certificate and breach of the terms of either a safety certificate or a prohibition notice are offences under s.12.

From 1 January 1977, the Act applied to the major English and Welsh football grounds, Wembley Stadium and the international rugby stadiums at Twickenham, Murrayfield and in Cardiff. Since then, by means of what have become annual updates to the legislation, most professional sports grounds have now been added to the list. This includes all professional football, rugby and cricket grounds and the larger grounds used in most other major sports. However, the licensing regime created by the SSGA 1975 did not initially promote the culture of safety that was its aim. Firstly, the inspections carried out by the local authorities were not as thorough as had been originally intended. Secondly, because of concerns about the cost to clubs of meeting any conditions imposed on their grounds the Act did not apply to lower division football grounds for another eight years. This simple concession led directly to the disaster at Bradford City's ground, Valley Parade.

9.6 Valley Parade, Bradford and the Popplewell Reports, 1985–86

The end of the 1984–1985 football season saw three very different disasters unfold. At Valley Parade, Bradford City's home ground, a fire broke out in the wooden main stand, leading to 56 deaths and many hundreds of injuries. On the same day, at Birmingham City's stadium, St Andrew's, a fan was crushed to death when a wall collapsed on him during widespread violent disorder involving City supporters and fans of their opponents, Leeds United. Two weeks later, a riot at the European Cup Final between Liverpool and Juventus at the Heysel Stadium, Brussels, resulted in 39 deaths and hundreds of people being injured.

The combined reactions to these three tragedies could not have been more confused. Where the fire at Valley Parade was a classic case of a disaster based on stadium mismanagement and a failure to recognise the need to secure spectator safety, the fatalities in Birmingham and at Heysel were caused by crowd disorder descending into full-blown riots. The disaster at Heysel had the additional complicating factor of occurring in a stadium completely unfit for the game being played at it. Under normal circumstances, three separate inquires would have been appropriate because of the very different underlying causes of the deaths at each of these venues. Instead, a single Committee of Enquiry was convened under the chairmanship of Popplewell J with a remit to investigate issues of both crowd safety and crowd control. Although both safety and control were relevant at all three of these disasters, the focus of much of what followed, particularly of the government of the time, was on how to eradicate football hooliganism.

In an attempt to unpick the two lines of investigation that were pursued by the Committee, which although closely linked are separate and distinct problems for stadium operators, only the issues related to spectator safety will be examined here; those relating to spectator disorder, including analyses of the disasters at St Andrew's and Heysel, are examined in Chapter 10.3. In this way, it is possible to focus on the important conclusions drawn by the Popplewell Report on stadium safety that have been, to a certain extent, lost in the panic to promote the anti-hooligan agenda.

9.6.1   Valley Parade, Bradford, 1985

The Bradford fire was caused by an unfortunate coincidence of events. The failure to acknowledge the importance of spectator safety in an old wooden stadium was a key factor in this avoidable tragedy.

▶ *Valley Parade, 11 May 1985*

During the last game of the 1984–85 football season, a fire broke out underneath the main stand at Valley Parade. The direct cause of the fire was the ignition by a discarded match or cigarette of around 20 years' worth of rubbish that had accumulated in a void under the largely wooden stand. The shape of the structure caused the fire to intensify rapidly, with temperatures reaching 1000°C. The entire stand was completely ablaze within five minutes of the first sighting of flames appearing under the stand, killing 56 people and injuring hundreds more. Old newspapers dating back to 1968 were found in the debris of the disaster, demonstrating quite clearly the club's failure to keep its stadium safe to the extent that spectators were paying a premium entrance fee to sit on top of what was known to be a fire hazard. The scale of the disaster was exacerbated by the club locking most of the exit gates during the course of the game so that many people who might otherwise have survived were trapped at the back of the stand and unable to escape.

Bradford City had been made aware of the existence of this fire risk on at least two previous occasions. In 1980, a Principal Inspector of the Health and Safety Executive (HSE) had visited the ground to investigate a complaint that one of the concrete terraces had become unsafe. In the course of his inspection, he noticed that there had been a build up of rubbish in the void under the main stand and that this had constituted a fire risk. This was reported to the club in a letter outlining issues to which further consideration should be given to improve health and safety.

In 1984, a chartered engineer from the Engineering Department of the West Yorkshire Metropolitan County Council (WYMCC), who was also a member of the Council's Safety Team that was responsible for conducting licensing inspections for sports grounds designated under the SSGA 1975, noticed and reported the same risk of fire to the club whilst inspecting the condition of the main stand's roof. He also noted that those using the main stand should be able to exit it in the case of an emergency in two and a half minutes, a speed that he did not at that time consider to be possible. His report to the club pointed out that these were health and safety considerations that would need to be addressed should Valley Parade ever require to be designated under the SSGA 1975.

Although both of these inspections drew attention to the precise risk that eventuated, their main aim was to examine issues in other parts of the ground. In neither of the reports to the club was the risk of fire prioritised nor was the club required to do anything more than 'consider' how this could be addressed. Despite the clear concerns of the inspectors, the lack of forcefulness in the tone of the two reports led to the risk of fire in the main stand never being addressed by the club.

In *Fletcher and others v Bradford City Association Football Club (1983) Ltd, Health and Safety Executive and West Yorkshire Metropolitan County Council*, (unreported) High Court (QBD) (Bradford), 23 February 1987, compensation for injuries caused to spectators and police who were injured in the main stand and for dependency by relatives of those who had died in the fire was sought. Bradford City was found to be in breach of the common duty of care owed under s.2(2) Occupiers' Liability Act 1957 (see further, 8.2.5) because it had failed to provide premises that were reasonably safe for watching football matches. This was specifically evidenced by its failure to address the clear risk of fire that had been drawn to its attention by the two inspections and its lack of any evacuation plan and because the exit gates at the back of the stand were both locked and unmanned.

WYMCC was found liable in negligence for its failure to investigate a known fire risk more fully. Following the inspection by one of its officers in 1984, WYMCC should have utilised its powers under one of two Acts. Firstly, for the purposes of the Fire Precautions Act 1971, WYMCC was identified as the relevant Fire Authority. Under this Act, WYMCC had the power to investigate premises to ensure that people using them were adequately protected from the risk of fire. Under s.10, the Council had the power to apply to the Magistrates' Court for an order to close or restrict the use of the ground where it was satisfied that the risk of fire was so serious that it could no longer continue to be used in its current state. Further, under the emergency procedure contained in s.10 SSGA 1975, WYMCC could apply to the Magistrates' Court for a prohibition notice to prevent the use of Valley Parade if it was considered that the risk to the safety of the spectators was too great; as already noted above, this provision applies to all sports grounds whether or not they are designated. The court held that once a copy of the WYMCC's engineer's report had been forwarded to the Chief Fire Officer in 1984, no reasonable Fire Officer could have failed to realise the gravity of the risk posed by the rubbish that had accumulated in the void under the main stand.

The HSE was cleared of having acted negligently by failing to require the club to take immediate steps to eliminate the risk of fire. Although the initial report in 1980 had identified the risk posed by the build up of rubbish in the void under the main stand, and subsequent reports had failed to follow up on whether the club had taken any remedial action, this was considered to be only an error of judgement on the part of the Inspector. The prioritising of other safety issues above the fire risk was not so careless as to be a failure to utilise the HSE's powers under the Health and Safety at Work Act 1974. Thus, liability was apportioned between the first and third defendants so that the club was two-thirds responsible, and WYMCC one-third.

The indirect causes were more varied and included the club and police viewing the crowd and its behaviour through a hooligan lens and the ongoing governmental failure to take spectator safety seriously. By focusing on the potential for crowd disorder, Bradford City had exacerbated the risk of harm from fire by removing the fire extinguishers from the stand because they were concerned that they would be used as missiles by hooligans. Furthermore, most of the exit gates at the back of the grandstand, where many of the bodies were found piled up and having tried to escape, were locked shortly after the game began to ensure that entry to the stadium was easier to control. The justification for this decision was that if the gates were left unlocked, then people would either try to get into the stadium for free or undermine the club's segregation policies; no thought was given to the possibility that the spectators may need to escape from a dangerous situation. Fortunately, the club had not installed the perimeter fencing that many other clubs had; otherwise, the death toll could have been considerably higher.

The failure of any government from 1924 onwards to enforce an effective safety regime on sports grounds compounded the problems at Valley Parade. The Shortt Report had recommended that more stringent fire safety regulations be applied to sports grounds in 1924, but the government had preferred to rely on the governing bodies of sport regulating their own members' safety. Following the second Ibrox disaster, the government decided that the SSGA 1975 would not apply to Third and Fourth Division clubs because of the cost of implementation and monitoring. Thus, if the recommendations of a 60-year-old report had been implemented or the 1975 Act taken seriously and applied to all sports grounds, then this disaster could not have happened as Valley Parade would have been closed for failing to meet the relevant safety criteria.

9.6.2 The Popplewell Reports

Popplewell J authored two reports on the disasters that took place in 1985. The Interim Report, which focused on the events at Bradford and Birmingham, was published in July 1985. It ensured that at least some recommendations could be made prior to start of the 1985–86 football season that August. The Final Report, published in January 1986, contained an analysis of the events at Heysel and further consideration of a number of the issues that had been raised in the Interim Report.

9.6.2.1 The Popplewell Interim Report, 'Committee of Enquiry into Crowd Safety and Control at Sports Grounds'

Popplewell made 25 recommendations and a further eight provisional recommendations that were to be considered further in the Final Report. In respect of safety, the main recommendations were that police and stewards should be trained in evacuation procedures and that stewards should also receive fire-fighting training, that new permanent stands should not be made of combustible materials and that all sports grounds should have adequate and suitable exits, including exits in perimeter fencing. Several additional, though weakly phrased, proposals suggested that there should be a greater degree of consultation between clubs and the emergency services in devising major incident plans, that a local registration system be established to monitor sports grounds and that the *Green Guide* should be followed more explicitly by stadium owners. These proposals were eventually developed into the criteria that are applied by the Sports Grounds Safety Authority (formerly the Football Licensing Authority) when determining whether or not to grant a licence to a football stadium (below, 9.6.2.4).

Immediate legislative action was taken on one of the Report's provisional recommendations: from 9 August 1985, the football grounds of all clubs in the top four English divisions and the Scottish Premier League and all major rugby league grounds became designated sports grounds that required a safety certificate in order to hold a sports event (Safety of Sports Grounds (Association Football Grounds) (Designation) Order 1985/1063 and Safety of Sports Grounds (Rugby Football Grounds) (Designation) Order 1985/1064).

9.6.2.2 The Popplewell Final Report, 'Committee of Enquiry into Crowd Safety and Control at Sports Grounds'

After further consideration of the efficacy of the regulatory framework for spectator safety and how best to control disorderly crowds and a specific analysis of the Heysel disaster, Popplewell J's Final Report contained 15 specific recommendations to the government. Of these, ten referred to issues concerning spectator safety (the remaining five concerned issues of crowd control, see further chapter 10.3.). The Report makes it clear from the outset that responsibility for the safety of the spectators lies with the club, whilst responsibility for law and order is the primary concern of the police.

The most important of these recommendations were implemented in primary and secondary legislation that was produced over the 18 months following the publication of the Final Report. Firstly, having already designated all English Third and Fourth Division football grounds and all First and Second Division Rugby League grounds (9.6.2.1), the Safety of Sports Grounds (Designation) Order 1986/1296 added all major rugby union, cricket and athletics grounds to the licensing regime governed by the SSGA 1975. The age and state of repair of most stadiums in all parts of the UK was a clear indication that any subsequent disaster could occur at any sports stadium, not just a football ground.

9.6.2.3 The Fire Safety and Safety of Places of Sport Act 1987

The Fire Safety and Safety of Places of Sport Act 1987 enacted the most important of the remaining recommendations on spectator safety from the Final Report. The distinction between sports stadiums and sports grounds was abolished by amending s.17 SSGA 1975, ensuring that any premises where sport took place outdoors and accommodation was provided for 10,000 or more spectators would now be covered by the Act. The simple justification for this amendment was that a sports ground that was only partially surrounded by dangerous spectator accommodation was just as likely to cause death and/or serious injury as a dangerous sports stadium.

The lack of any adequate safety regime and the failure of sports governing bodies to self-regulate effectively on matters of safety had led to many smaller sports grounds providing particularly dangerous accommodation to their spectators. Parts II and III of the Fire Safety and Safety of Places of Sport Act 1987 provided that all stands that were wholly or partly covered by a roof, with a capacity of 500 spectators or greater and that were located in sports grounds that were not designated under the SSGA 1975 should be individually designated. Thus, the safety framework originally anticipated by the Wheatley Report was finally brought a step closer to reality.

Part IV of the Fire Safety and Safety of Places of Sport Act 1987 created a licensing framework for indoor sports premises. Although these provisions have subsequently been replaced by the Licensing Act 2003 in England and Wales, the 1987 Act ensured that local councils would now be in control of licensing all sports premises, regardless of size and whether the sporting event was taking place indoors or outdoors. By placing responsibility for licensing on one body in this way, it was anticipated that councils would be able to take an overview of the most effective way of licensing all sports premises and develop a high degree of expertise in matters of safety at sports events.

9.6.2.4 *Football Spectators Act 1989*

The Final Report recommended that improvements be made to the procedures by which licences were issued to designated sports grounds and that annual inspections be carried out as an integral part of the licensing procedure. Although the recommendation applied to all sports grounds, a new licensing procedure was only established for designated football grounds. The Football Licensing Authority (FLA) was established by s.8 and sch.2 Football Spectators Act 1989 (FSA 1989) with its powers further defined in s.13. These powers are now discharged by the FLA's successor body, the Sports Grounds Safety Authority (SGSA).

On 12 July 2011, the Sports Grounds Safety Authority Act 2011 received its Royal Assent and converted the FLA into the SGSA. This is no simple cosmetic change as the powers of the SGSA are significantly wider than those of its predecessor. The SGSA will continue to inspect all professional football grounds, as did the FLA, and it is anticipated that this aspect of its work will remain its core function. The main operational difference is that the SGSA will also be able to provide advice to a range of bodies other than professional football clubs. In future, it will be able to advise Ministers on issues relating to stadium safety (s.2), local authorities and stadium operators hosting sporting events other than professional football matches (s.3) and foreign governments, international organisations and other bodies whose functions, activities or responsibilities concern the safety of sports grounds (s.4). Where the consent of the Secretary of State is secured, the SGSA can charge the commissioning body for the advice given under ss.3 and 4.

The thinking behind the creation of the SGSA is twofold. Firstly, the expertise developed by the FLA should be capable of being shared amongst a wider constituency of potential users. The FLA was unique in its powers and knowledge and, as a result, could play an important role in advising other sports about stadium safety. Secondly, by being able to charge for the services not related to professional football in this country, it will be able to contribute to its own running costs and therefore reduce the financial burden that its functions place on the Department for Culture, Media and Sport. Provided that its newly created revenue-raising functions do not detract from its core business of ensuring the safety of professional football stadiums, the establishment of the SGSA should help to address the lack of specialist safety advice available outside of football.

9.6.2.5 *The impact of the Popplewell Reports*

The Popplewell Reports intended to create a more effective and more uniform approach to spectator safety at all sports grounds. The creation of what is now the SGSA has gone a long way to achieving that aim in respect of football stadiums. Having noted that many operators of sports grounds that were not designated did not take the recommendations of the Green Guide sufficiently seriously, it is perhaps strange that the Final Report recommended that its provisions should remain only a voluntary code without any further explanation. However, that the government of the time was prepared to take swift and, in the context of previous failures to act, dramatic action following the publication of the Final Report is testament to the forcefulness of the main recommendations made by Popplewell J. Unfortunately, during the passage of the FSA 1989 through Parliament and therefore before the creation of the new licensing regime, events once again overtook the legislative action that was being taken.

9.7 Hillsborough Stadium, Sheffield and the Taylor Reports, 1989–90

The worst British sporting disaster to date occurred when 96 people were crushed to death on the terraces at Hillsborough during an FA Cup semi-final between Liverpool and Nottingham Forrest. The striking similarities with the disaster at Burnden Park in 1946, reflected in the opening comments of Taylor LJ at para.19 of *The Hillsborough Stadium Disaster (Final Report)*, demonstrate starkly that these events would never have happened if spectator safety had been taken as seriously as it ought to have been:

> 'It is a depressing and chastening fact that mine is the ninth official report covering crowd safety at football grounds. After eight previous reports and three editions of the Green Guide, it seems astounding that [96] people could die from overcrowding before the very eyes of those controlling the event.'

Despite the recommendations of these eight previous reports, four of which specifically focused on spectator safety, three on crowd disorder and safety and one on the lack of effective leadership and administration of football, the Hillsborough disaster occurred at what had been assumed to be one of the safest grounds in country. It also occurred at a time when the focus of the police was almost entirely on crowd disorder and preventing acts of hooliganism. Despite the recommendations contained in the two Popplewell Reports, safety was not high on the agenda of the main contributors to the Hillsborough disaster. In its immediate aftermath, Taylor LJ was appointed to head an inquiry whose remit was to examine the causes of the deaths and to make recommendations on creating more effective systems of spectator safety and crowd control. The Interim Report focuses specifically on the events of 15 April 1989 and the recommendations to be implemented before the start of the next football season. The Final Report was a much more wide-ranging analysis of how football spectators and football grounds could be made safer.

The focus of this section is the impact of the disaster on stadium safety and Hillsborough's position at the end of a long period of inaction on the part of Parliament, the football authorities, the clubs and local authorities in the face of specific recommendations from the reports and inquiries commissioned over the previous 66 years. There were many other controversial aspects of the disaster: the use of the stadium gym as a temporary morgue, the misinformation supplied to the press by the police match day commander, Chief Superintendant Duckenfield, the presumption of the coroner that all of the victims had died by 3.15 pm and his use of generic rather than individual inquests, the editing of the first hand accounts of many of the officers who were on duty at the stadium by South Yorkshire Police's solicitors, the decisions of the House of Lords restricting who could claim for Post-Traumatic Stress Disorder as a result of witnessing the disaster and its aftermath and the lack of coordination of the various investigating authorities into the disaster leading to the failure to prosecute those in command on the day.

In 1997, the newly-elected Labour government announced that Stuart-Smith LJ was to conduct a scrutiny of the evidence that had not been available to, or was not presented at, previous enquiries or investigations. Its purpose was to establish whether a further judicial inquiry, or coronial inquest, or prosecution should be ordered; it was not to be a further inquiry into stadium safety after the implementation of Taylor LJ's recommendations. Stuart-Smith LJ's conclusion was that there was no basis for ordering a reopening of any of the previously-examined issues, despite his finding clear evidence of police misconduct and a concerted attempt to deflect blame for the disaster from the police on to the spectators. In contrast to the political, media and public reception of the Hillsborough Independent Panel Report (HIPR) in 2012, the response to Stuart-Smith's report was muted and resulted in no further Parliamentary, governmental or police action (below, Hot Topic).

9.7.1 Hillsborough Stadium, Sheffield, 1989

The Hillsborough disaster could have happened at almost any major English football stadium. Their general state of disrepair and the unrelenting focus on crowd disorder saw a disaster unfold that, in the light of the findings of the previous official enquiries, should not have occurred.

▶ *Hillsborough Stadium, 15 April 1989*

The direct cause of the deaths at Hillsborough was the chronic overcrowding of pens three and four in the middle of the Leppings Lane terraces, directly behind the goals. This overcrowding was, in turn, caused by mismanagement of the stadium itself and entry into it on the day. Firstly, although the entire standing area was recorded as having a maximum capacity of 10,100 spectators, no individual capacity had been calculated for each of the six pens into which the terrace had been divided. Secondly, as the seven turnstiles servicing the terrace did not feed directly into specific pens, there was no means of monitoring effectively exactly how many people were in each individual pen. The Shortt Report had recommended as early as 1924 that steps be taken to ensure that adequate means of counting spectators into each part of the ground were installed at all major sports grounds.

Thirdly, the police operated a policy of allowing the spectators to 'find their own level' as a means of determining when a pen was full. By this method, the police assumed that when a pen became uncomfortably full, spectators would use one of the emptier pens instead. Thus, instead of managing entry onto the terraces pro-actively, the police allowed events to unfold before them unchecked. Fourthly, the police failed to notice, when it should have been obvious to them, that pens three and four had become dangerously overcrowded. Fifthly, they failed to take any effective action to alleviate the crushing by barring further entry to pens three and four or allowing those at the front of the pens to escape onto the pitch and into the less crowded areas of the Leppings Lane terracing.

Finally, in response to the crushing that had begun to occur outside of the stadium after CS Duckenfield's refusal to delay the game's kick-off, an emergency exit gate, Gate C, was opened, and 2,000 further spectators were allowed entry onto the Leppings Lane terraces. The layout of the ground channelled the entirety of this large group of spectators into the already overcrowded pens three and four, to which the police had failed to block entry and redirect spectators to the emptier pens. The volume of spectators in the pens, followed soon after by a surge forwards, caused a number of crush barriers to collapse and many people to be crushed to death as bodies piled on top of those who had fallen. Further crushing occurred at the front of the terrace against the perimeter fencing as the mass of bodies pushed down the slope towards the pitch. It was only after some spectators got through the fencing and onto the pitch to talk to the players that the police became aware of the gravity of the situation and the match was abandoned.

Taylor LJ was clear that although there were other contributory causes, the main reason for the disaster was the failure of senior police officers to manage the crowd both outside and inside the stadium and the breakdown of effective policing on the day. In particular, he criticised the performance of CS Duckenfield for failing to draft an effective Operational Order, for failing to notice the overcrowding in pens three and four, which were clearly and dangerously overfull from about 2.30 pm, for perpetrating 'a blunder of the first magnitude' by failing to foresee the consequences of opening Gate C, for failing to show effective leadership and for freezing in the face of the unfolding disaster. Taylor LJ's damning conclusion that the overwhelming cause of the disaster was the fault of the police goes significantly further than any of the previous enquiries had done in specifically apportioning fault. It also provided him with the justification for insisting that his recommendations be acted upon rather than being filed away.

9.7.2   The Taylor Interim Report, 'The Hillsborough Stadium Disaster'

Having identified the police as the main cause of the disaster, chapters 16–22 of the Interim Report explain how its scale was compounded by a series of indirect causes attributable to many other actors. Taylor LJ identified an institutionalised lack of care for the safety of spectators amongst each of the organisations that should have been acutely aware of the danger that old, and in many cases decrepit, stadiums posed to those who paid to use them and an over-concentration on the threat posed by spectator disorder.

9.7.2.1 The Football Association

The FA was criticised for choosing Hillsborough as an appropriate venue for a match of this magnitude. Although the previous year's semi-final between the same two clubs had been held there, complaints had been made by both that the ground was neither suitable nor big enough to host the game again; these complaints were ignored. Although not causative of the disaster of itself, the choice of venue was a significant contributory factor. The FA had no specific criteria against which a stadium could be judged to be suitable to host a game of this importance, a fact mentioned in the Final but not the Interim Report. If the FA had inspected the ground or had required production of the ground's safety certificate (below, 9.7.2.2), then the game would not have been awarded to Hillsborough. This failure to have any objective criteria for determining the suitability of a ground to host this game led the FA to choose Hillsborough when it should not have done so.

9.7.2.2 Hillsborough did not have a valid safety certificate

The importance of demanding a copy of the safety certificate is that Hillsborough did not have one that was currently valid. According to the Interim Report, Sheffield City Council had been 'inefficient and dilatory' in the performance of its duties to inspect and license football grounds under the SSGA 1975. The failure of the Council to inspect and amend the safety certificate following alterations to the ground that had been made in 1981 and 1985 was a serious breach of duty. If an inspection had been carried out, it would have found numerous breaches of the Green Guide and problems with the siting and physical condition of the crush barriers, some of which were seriously corroded around their base. Further criticism was made of the informality with which the Safety Advisory Group, the body responsible for ensuring that the ground was safe enough to be awarded a safety certificate, operated. If an inspection had been made, then the safety certificate could have been withheld until appropriate changes to the stadium had been made. The failure of the Council to undertake its duties with sufficient vigour led to Hillsborough being chosen to host a game that, legally, should not have been played there.

9.7.2.3 Sheffield Wednesday Football Club

As part of its ongoing safety consultations with the police, Sheffield Wednesday Football Club had undertaken a number of developments to Hillsborough and was also aware of the need to make further alterations to the stadium. The club retained a consultant engineer who in 1985 had recommended that each of the six pens on the Leppings Lane terrace be completely separated from the others. To enable the effective monitoring of the number of spectators in each pen, it was also recommended that each pen have at least four dedicated turnstiles to enable safe entry into the ground. Following the fire at Valley Parade, the club had to make alterations to other parts of the ground to ensure that it complied with the recommendations of the Popplewell Reports, leaving the engineer's recommendations ignored on the basis of cost. The failure to implement these recommendations left the club and the police unable to know precisely how many people were in each pen at any one time, causing massive overcrowding to occur in a very short period of time. The poor layout of the ground, accompanied by poor signposting inside it, meant that entry into pens three and four appeared to be the only choice for those entering the Leppings Lane terraces.

Further, the club operated and could view the CCTV images of the terraces and knew exactly how many spectators had gone through the turnstiles. Thus, although it did not know how many people were in each pen, the club was aware of the total number of people on the terrace as a whole and so should have been in a position to alert the police of the uneven distribution in the pens. For these reasons, the club was at fault under the Occupiers' Liability Act for failing to provide a reasonably safe stadium for spectators paying to watch the game.

9.7.2.4 The recommendations

The Interim Report rebutted suggestions that the emergency services, including the South Yorkshire Ambulance Service (SYAS), the fire brigade and the St John's Ambulance Brigade were in any way to blame for delays in attending the ground or treating the injured. It did point out that there had been insufficient cooperation between the police and the other emergency services and recommended that more effective major incident planning be undertaken in the future, but that this would not have prevented the disaster from occurring. The HIPR revisited this issue and was much less forgiving of the SYAS and its failure to play a more active role in the creation and implementation of an effective disaster management plan that could have prevented at least some of the deaths from occurring.

The Interim Report's recommendations were for immediate implementation, where possible before the start of the next season, with the aim of preventing overcrowding and crushing on terraces and generally improving safety procedures at football grounds. The vast majority of the recommendations had been made, in one form or another, in one or more of the previous eight government-commissioned reports. The only radical difference with the recommendations in the Interim Report was that Taylor LJ insisted that they be implemented.

The recommendations ensured that there would need to be an upgrading of the quality of accommodation provided for spectators, an overhaul of the licensing procedure for all sports grounds, better training for, and planning by, the police and stewards and clearer coordination among the various emergency services. The first group of recommendations were to ensure that the specific conditions that gave rise to the Hillsborough disaster could not occur again. Firstly, all self-contained pens were to have individually-set maximum capacities that were calculated in accordance with the Green Guide; this maximum was then to be reduced by 15 per cent to improve the margin of safety. Secondly, on entry into the stadium, spectators must be counted into each pen and a means to shut down turnstiles and close off pens that were full would have to be employed. Finally, to enable easy escape from these pens, all perimeter fencing must have a clearly-marked emergency exit which should remain open for the entire period during which spectators were using it.

It was then recommended that an immediate review of all safety certificates take place as a matter of urgency and that an Advisory Group consisting of representatives of the Council, the club and the emergency services be established for each stadium. Having reviewed the safety certificates already issued, these should then be reviewed and, where necessary, renewed each year. In particular, the Interim Report recommended that all crush barriers be inspected as soon as possible because of the serious state of disrepair of those that had collapsed at Hillsborough. Thus, the procedure outlined in the Safety at Sports Grounds Act 1975 was finally being forced into a coherent framework for determining the safety or otherwise of major football grounds.

In addition to these major recommendations, clubs were required to review entry rates through their turnstiles to determine whether more should be installed, or the capacity of a part of the ground should be reduced. Additionally, the information provided to spectators on tickets and around the ground was to be improved. The police and stewards were to be trained in crowd safety and how to identify whether overcrowding was occurring, and a major incident plan was required to ensure that all organisations attending a disaster should know the relevant chains of command, lines of communication and roles which they were supposed to fulfil.

There was no real need for any new legislation to implement these recommendations as they were either instances of best practice that could not be rationally contradicted or could be enforced by imposing conditions on a stadium's safety certificate. For the first time, all interested parties were willing to engage with the recommendations of a Committee of Enquiry.

9.7.3   The Taylor Final Report, 'The Hillsborough Stadium Disaster'

Taylor LJ's final report focused on improving spectator control and crowd safety more generally; it was not to revisit the issues concerning the disaster itself. As the Football Spectators Act 1989, which contained the framework for the implementation of many of Popplewell J's recommendations, had made its way onto the statute books during the course of the Hillsborough inquiry, Taylor LJ also took the opportunity to revisit the efficacy of some of its provisions.

In the course of the opening chapter, Taylor LJ identified an institutional failing on the part of every group of people who were associated with football to take spectator safety seriously. He criticised the long line of governments that had failed to implement the recommendations of previous Committees of Enquiry and the football authorities for failing to show any leadership to the clubs on issues of safety. The clubs were criticised for failing to provide adequate facilities to spectators and for spending large sums of money on player transfers and wages instead of upgrading their stadiums. The police were criticised for being too focused on the potential of a minority of fans to create disorder at the expense of guaranteeing the safety of the majority of well-behaved fans. The players were criticised for their on-field conduct and for inciting over-exuberant celebrations in the crowd. And the fans were criticised for a culture of turning up to games late and for often having taken too much drink. This last comment was tempered following Taylor LJ's visiting grounds in the UK and abroad and empathising with the fans wanting to spend as little time as possible in grounds that were outdated and unsafe and which provided few adequate facilities to improve the match day experience.

The Final Report made it clear that very little that was being proposed was new as almost all of the proposals could be found in the reports of the previous enquiries. Conversely, it also made it clear that not all of the previous proposals were workable; for example, the criticisms of the proposed Football Membership Scheme, recommended by Popplewell J and enacted in ss.2–7 Football Spectators Act 1989, led to it never being implemented (see further, 10.3.5.3). Finally, the Rreport stated clearly and unequivocally that if further disasters were to be avoided, then its recommendations needed to be implemented and not ignored.

Perhaps the most controversial recommendation was that all designated football stadiums provide only seated accommodation for spectators by the start of the 1999–2000 season. The Football Spectators (Seating) Order 1994/1666 imposed this recommendation as a condition of receiving a licence to host a football match at a designated stadium for all clubs in the Premier League and what is now the Football League Championship from the start of the 1994–95 season. Each season, any club promoted to the Championship has added to its licence a condition that only seated accommodation be provided for, or used by, spectators at its home ground. The aim of this condition is to make spectators at football matches more comfortable, to remove the boisterousness of the terraces and to enable easier identification of troublemakers by using their seat number as an identifier. It is also a reflection that Taylor LJ, like others before him, felt that the football authorities and clubs were no longer capable of managing standing areas safely.

The recommendations concerning the need to conduct more effective inspections as part of the licensing procedure reinforced those put forward three years earlier by Popplewell J. Taylor LJ provided further detail for the framework created by the FSA 1989 by, for example, recommending that an advisory group be established for each designated football stadium. This group, comprising representatives from the local authority, the police, the fire and ambulance services and the club's safety officer, and all other aspects of safety at football grounds are now overseen by the SGSA.

The remaining recommendations improved best practice; those that have become legally binding have usually done so as a result of being included as a condition of a licence being awarded. Detailed recommendations were made about how terracing should be made safer, about the counting of spectators and the filling and monitoring of pens and particularly that exact capacities should be set for each section. Further technical advice was given regarding fencing, gates and exits, ensuring that spectators could no longer be trapped in stadiums from which they needed to escape. Clubs were urged to improve their stadiums generally and in particular to provide better information to all users and better stewarding to ensure that all spectators could be safe. They were also directed to pay more attention to the *Green Guide*, which was to be updated in the light of the findings of the inquiry. Finally, specific training on most aspects of the policing of a football game was recommended, as was the need for a greater degree of coordination among the various emergency services and the clubs.

Although this summary provides only a brief overview of the recommendations made in the Final Report, it highlights that its aim was to ensure that a disaster such as occurred at Hillsborough could not happen again. Each group of recommendations, even if acted on individually, could feasibly have prevented the disaster from occurring as they would have prevented the overcrowding in pens three and four, allowed emergency access to the pitch, ensured that those in charge were competent to oversee the safety of the crowd and, if the disaster still occurred though in more limited circumstances, provided the victims with significantly more effective emergency medical treatment.

9.7.4 The legacy

After nine official reports and many hundreds of deaths and injuries, the combined impact of the disasters at Valley Parade and Hillsborough finally produced the changes in spectator safety, at least at football grounds, that had originally been envisaged in the Shortt Report. The legislative, policy and procedural changes that have been implemented have made British football stadiums amongst the safest in the world. The SGSA/FLA has ensured that the recommendations in the *Green Guide*, though still not mandatory, are implemented unless there are exceptional reasons for them not to be. The threat of having a stadium, or part of it, closed to the public has been sufficient to ensure compliance with a licence's conditions, and the major incident and evacuation plans ensure that the effects of any unfolding disaster will be minimised.

Hot topic ... **The ongoing impact of the Hillsborough disaster**

Twenty-three years after the Hillsborough disaster, the publication of the Hillsborough Independent Panel Report (HIPR) brought the details of the day and its aftermath back into the public consciousness with almost as much force as when it originally happened. The Panel was established in 2010 with the remit to oversee the full public disclosure of all relevant documents concerning the disaster and manage the process of their disclosure; it was chaired by the Bishop of Liverpool, The Right Reverend James Jones.

The Panel examined and made public over 450,000 pages of documents, with the majority of headlines focusing on South Yorkshire Police's attempts to cover up their role in causing the disaster and the coroner's still unexplained

decision to find that all 96 deaths had occurred before 3.15 pm on 15 April 1989 when around half of those who eventually died were still alive at that time. Where the response to the publication of Stuart-Smith LJ's *Scrutiny* was, at best, muted, despite his having found evidence of the doctored police statements, the reaction to the publication of the HIPR was in many ways unprecedented. Prime Minister Cameron apologized on behalf of the country for the state's delay in responding to calls for justice. The leader of the opposition, David Milliband, apologized on behalf of his party and its failure to take more appropriate action following the publication of the *Scrutiny* that it had commissioned. Further apologies followed from the South Yorkshire Police, South

Yorkshire Ambulance Service, Sheffield City Council, Sheffield Wednesday Football Club and the Football Association. Although not all of these apologies can be read as acceptances of blame, they were, at the very least, admissions that the organisations had in some way contributed to the unfolding disaster or the way that its aftermath was handled.

For the first time, it was generally accepted that the fans were not at fault for the disaster and that the primary cause was the incompetence of the senior police officers and their management of the stadium. Specific criticisms were aimed at almost every other body that had a role to play on the day, and in particular Sheffield Wednesday, Sheffield City Council and the combined emergency services and their failure to implement an appropriate disaster-management response. The conduct of the police in trying to blame the fans for the disaster was singled out for particular criticism, especially as the sophistication of the cover up and accompanying campaign of misinformation came to light.

Hillsborough is already one of the most important events in English legal history. The Football Spectators Act 1989 and Football (Offences) Act 1991 can both trace their origins to the Taylor Report. The subsequent litigation included a clarification of the circumstances in which a life support machine can be switched off (*Airedale NHS Trust v Bland* [1993] 2 WLR 316) and the development of the test for determining whether a witness of a traumatic event can claim for psychiatric harm (*Alcock and others v Chief Constable of South Yorkshire Police* [1991] UKHL 5). Procedural firsts included the use of mass or generic inquests instead of each deceased having their own hearing, the *Scrutiny of the Evidence*, the establishment of the Independent Panel and the creation of the Football Licensing Authority.

The future is likely to hold equally important legal landmarks. The Attorney-General has already applied to the High Court to have all 96 inquests reopened in the light of the evidence contained in the HIPR. This, in turn, will allow for greater scrutiny of the post-disaster conduct of the emergency services and whether or not any of the deceased could have been saved. The Director of Public Prosecutions has commenced a review of the evidence in order to determine whether charges of manslaughter can be brought against the senior officers in charge of match day operations now that it has been accepted that the statements relied on to make the original decision not to prosecute had been altered substantially. Finally, the IPCC is conducting a wide-ranging investigation into all officers who were on duty on the day to determine who was involved with the cover-up and whether or not charges of perjury and perverting the course of justice can be brought against anyone. The scope of the investigation may require changes to its powers to enable it to interview and punish retired officers; alternatively, it may liaise more closely with the Crown Prosecution Service to ensure that everyone involved is punished appropriately. As the search for the truth draws to a close, the apportionment of responsibility begins, and the impact of Hillsborough will continue to be felt for many years to come.

Summary

9.1 The early disasters were usually caused by the defective construction of the sports grounds. Despite the high-profile nature of these incidents, and in particular the numbers of casualties and fatalities, the government took no steps to regulate the organisation and management of major sporting events.

9.2 The events at Wembley led to the first governmental Committee of Enquiry into safety at sports grounds. The wide-ranging recommendations of the Shortt Report, if implemented, could have prevented the disasters that followed.

9.3 The Burnden Park disaster should have provided the government with sufficient evidence that some kind of formal regulation of sports grounds was required. For reasons of cost, the licensing regime proposed in the Moelwyn Hughes Report was rejected by the government, leading directly to the disasters of the 1970s and 1980s.

9.4 The increase in football-related disorder in the 1960s changed the focus of discussions from spectator safety to crowd control. This, in turn, led to resources being diverted from providing safe accommodation for spectators to identifying and containing potential troublemakers.

9.5 The second Ibrox disaster, which was very clearly not caused by crowd disorder, finally forced the government to introduce a much-needed and long overdue licensing regime. However, its lack of application to lower division grounds and its piecemeal application by local councils led directly to the disasters at Valley Parade and Hillsborough.

9.6 The three disasters of 1985 caused a confused response from the government. The fire at Valley Parade should have focused government attention on spectator safety and the need

Summary cont'd

to update unsafe football grounds. However, these events were overshadowed by the riots in Birmingham and at Heysel. The Popplewell Reports proposed a wide range of responses to the regulation of football stadiums and football crowds that, unfortunately, had not yet been implemented when Hillsborough occurred.

9.7 Hillsborough provided the final wake-up call for the government, the police and everyone connected to football. Although directly caused by police incompetence and mismanagement of the crowd on the day, the subsequent review of all aspects of stadium design and safety management has resulted in much safer accommodation being provided to football spectators.

Further reading

Guide to Safety at Sports Grounds (5th edn, 2008, HMSO)

Moelwyn Hughes J, *Enquiry into the Disaster at Bolton Wanderers' Football Ground on the 9th March 1946*, Cmnd 6846 (1946, HMSO)

Popplewell J, *Committee of Inquiry into Crowd Safety and Control at Sports Grounds (Interim Report)*, Cmnd 9585 (1985, HMSO)

Popplewell J, *Committee of Inquiry into Crowd Safety and Control at Sports Grounds (Final Report)*, Cmnd 9710 (1986, HMSO)

Shortt, *Report of the Departmental Committee on Crowds*, Cmnd 2088 (1924, HMSO)

Taylor LJ, *The Hillsborough Stadium Disaster (Interim Report)*, Cm 765 (1989, HMSO)

Taylor LJ, *The Hillsborough Stadium Disaster (Final Report)*, Cm 962 (1990, HMSO)

Wheatley, *Report on Crowd Safety at Sports Grounds*, Cmnd 4962 (1972, HMSO)

Darby, Johnes and Mellor (eds), *Soccer and Disaster* (2005, Routledge) chs 1–4

Shiels, 'The Ibrox Disaster of 1902' [1997] *Juridical Review* 230

Shiels, 'The fatalities at the Ibrox Disaster of 1902' [1998] 18(2) *The Sports Historian* 148

The Hillsborough Disaster

Hartley, *Exploring Sport and Leisure Disasters: a socio-legal perspective* (2001, Cavendish Publishing) chs 6 and 8

McMillan, *The Hillsborough Football Disaster: context and consequences*, ebook, http://www.hfdinfo.com/

Scraton, *Hillsborough – The Truth* (2nd edn, 2002, Mainstream Publishing)

Stuart-Smith LJ, *Scrutiny of Evidence Relating to the Hillsborough Football Stadium Disaster*, Cmnd 3878 (1998, HMSO)

Rt Revd Jones, Bishop of Liverpool, *Hillsborough Independent Panel Report* (2012, TSO)

Links to relevant websites can be found at www.palgrave.com/law/james2e

Background and context (10.1)

Government inquiries into crowd disorder, 1967–84 (10.2)
- The Harrington Report, 1967 (10.2.1)
- The Lang Report (10.2.2)
- The McElhone Report, 1976 (10.2.3) — Criminal Justice (Scotland) Act 1980 ss.68–77 (10.2.3.1)
- Department of the Environment Working Group Report, 1984 (10.2.4)

St Andrew's, Birmingham, Heysel Stadium, Brussels and the Popplewell Reports, 1985–86 (10.3)
- St Andrew's, Birmingham, 1985 (10.3.1)
- Sporting Events (Control of Alcohol) Act 1985 (10.3.2)
- The Popplewell Interim Report (10.3.3)
- Heysel Stadium, Brussels 1985 (10.3.4)
- The Popplewell Final Report (10.3.5) — Criminal Justice and Public Order Act 1994 s.60 (10.3.5.1); Criminalising disorderly conduct at sports grounds (10.3.5.2)
- European Convention on Spectator Violence (10.3.6)

Crowd disorder and football hooliganism

Hillsborough Stadium, Sheffield and the Taylor Reports, 1989–90 (10.4)
- The Football (Offences) Act 1991 (10.4.1)
- Criminal Justice and Public Order Act 1994 ss.166 and 166A (10.4.2)
- Recommendations for amending the Football Spectators Act 1989 (10.4.3) — The National Membership Scheme (10.4.3.1); Exclusion Orders (10.4.3.2)

General legislation applicable to disorderly crowds (10.5)
- Public Order Act 1986 (10.5.1) — Public Order Act 1986 ss.1–5 (10.5.1.1); Public Order Act 1986 ss.17–19 (10.5.1.2)
- Other relevant legislation (10.5.2) — Criminal Justice and Public Order Act 1994 s.68 (10.5.2.1); Criminal Damage Act 1971 (10.5.2.2); Violent Crime Reduction Act s.27 (10.5.2.3); Offensive Behaviour at Football and Threatening Communications (Scotland) Act 2012 (10.5.2.4); Payment for police services (10.5.2.5)

Football Banning Orders (10.6)
- Football Spectators Act 1989 s.14A (10.6.1)
- Football Spectators Act 1989 s.14B (10.6.2)
- The effect of being subject to a Football Banning Order (10.6.3)

Crowd disorder and football hooliganism

Key terms

▶ **Council of Europe** – a transnational body whose primary aim is to create a common democratic and legal area throughout the whole of Europe, ensuring respect for its fundamental values: human rights, democracy and the rule of law.
▶ **Police spotters** – police officers assigned to identify potential troublemakers at specific football clubs, who often travel with fans and liaise with the UK Football Policing Unit.

10.1 Background and context

Crowd disorder has long been associated with sporting events and was one of the main reasons for the criminalisation of prize-fighting at the end of the nineteenth century (*R v Coney and others* (1881–82) 8 QBD 534) (see further, chapter 7.2.1.2). However, it is the particularly violent form of disorder that occurs at football matches that has attracted the majority of academic, media, political and police attention. Commonly referred to as 'football hooliganism', this category of crowd disorder is perceived to be both more organised and more widespread than that seen at other sporting events. Since the 1960s, football hooliganism and the means to control those engaged in it has been a particular focus of the government, the police and the football authorities. Throughout the 1970s and 1980s, as supporters of the England national team, rather than supporters of domestic club sides, ran riot throughout continental Europe, it was the disorder associated with the England team that created many of the headlines and drove the subsequent policy initiatives.

The only substantive recommendation made by either the Shortt or Moelwyn Hughes Reports was that the police should be in overall control of law and order in and around football stadiums. Improving crowd behaviour was seen as a natural corollary of making the spectators safer. The government inquiries of the 1960s had a more specific focus on spectator disorder. Despite this change of focus, spectator safety and crowd control continued to be examined as though they were integral parts of the same phenomenon; in reality they are very different issues with very different causes. With hindsight, conflating them can now be said to have been one of the biggest mistakes made by the various governments that commissioned the inquiries as the focus on controlling the potential for crowd disorder at the expense of spectator safety led in part to the disasters at Valley Parade and Hillsborough. This chapter examines the effectiveness of the legal and governmental responses to football-related disorder.

10.2 Government inquiries into crowd disorder, 1967–84

The 1960s saw a dramatic increase in the incidence of football-related disorder. Where previous outbreaks of violence had apparently occurred spontaneously, these new incidents had an element of organisation about them. Away fans developed deliberate strategies to infiltrate and take over the favoured terraces of the home team's fans;

home fans strategically ambushed away fans on their way to or from the stadium. The police also became aware that some of those involved had begun to carry weapons. The focus of the violence was, in general, the stadium and the streets around it, though disorder could also break out at motorway service areas and railway stations where groups of fans came into contact with each other. The growing concern over this increase in football hooliganism caused the government to commission three reports into crowd disorder in 1967, 1969 and 1984, and the Scottish Office to commission its own study in 1976.

10.2.1 The Harrington Report, 1967 – 'Soccer Hooliganism: A Preliminary Report'

The Harrington Report was prepared for the Minister of Sport following the rise in football-related disorder that occurred in the early 1960s. It identified the growth in violent conduct, the use of weapons and obscene chanting as the most commonly occurring forms of disorder without examining their causes in any detail. The report suggested measures that could be taken to control football crowds more effectively, but as its title implies, this preliminary report was to pave the way for a more detailed examination of football-related disorder by the following year's Lang Report (below, 10.2.2).

The Harrington Report made two main suggestions to improve effective crowd control. Firstly, that ground facilities should be improved to a nationally-approved minimum standard; by providing better accommodation for spectators, it was assumed that crowds would be easier to control, and outbreaks of hooliganism prevented. The report explained that this could only be achieved by imposing legislatively-defined minimum standards of safety and amenity on stadium owners because without such coercion, clubs had preferred to spend their money on the purchase of players and on their wages rather than on the ground improvements that had been recommended previously in the Shortt and Moelwyn Hughes Reports.

Secondly, the Harrington Report suggested that more responsibility should be placed on clubs for the behaviour of their own spectators both within the stadium and whilst travelling to and from games. Instead of abdicating responsibility for fans' conduct to the police, the report considered that the most effective solution to the problem of football-related disorder would be to punish clubs that failed to control their own fans' behaviour. The failure of English football clubs to accept this responsibility led instead to the police seeking, and eventually being granted, much greater powers over football spectators, though no immediate legislative action was taken following the report's publication.

10.2.2 The Lang Report – 'Crowd Behaviour at Football Matches: Report of the Working Party 1969'

The Lang Report drew on the experiences of the previous governmental inquiries and on its own new research. It identified that the causes of football-related disorder were complex and often due to a combination of social, physical and management factors. The report produced 23 recommendations that were aimed at improving the surveillance, control and punishment of football hooligans. However, despite the perceived importance of football hooliganism as a social problem that needed to be addressed, none of the recommendations of the Lang Report were acted upon by the government or football authorities at the time.

To improve the surveillance of crowds and the quality of evidence gathered, it was recommended that CCTV cameras be installed and used as a means of identifying those who were involved in the disorder. This recommendation was finally taken up by clubs after the Popplewell Reports were published (below, 10.3.3) and, together with the now ubiquitous filming of football crowds, has become a standard means of collecting football-related intelligence.

In order to control access to stadiums more effectively, it was recommended that ticketing policies be made more robust by monitoring advance sales and segregating opposing fans. It was also recommended that spectators should be prevented from entering the playing area. Although it was noted that alcohol played a part in outbreaks of disorder by making spectators more quarrelsome and providing them with missiles in the form of empty bottles, no recommendations were made about how this problem could be addressed. Finally, it was recommended that those convicted of football-related offences be prevented from attending future games, the first time that some sort of football banning order was seriously considered.

Most of these recommendations have now become law following the Wheatley, Popplewell and Taylor Reports. However, the Lang Report's emphasis on the development of a more cooperative approach to crowd control, bringing together the football authorities, the clubs, the police and the fans, saw its recommendations become aspirations to best practice rather than legal requirements.

10.2.3 The McElhone Report, 1976 – 'Report of the Working Group on Football Crowd Behaviour'

Crowd disorder was also becoming a significant feature of football matches in Scotland. The McElhone Report was commissioned by the Secretary of State for Scotland and focused specifically on disorder at Scottish matches. The Report's 52 recommendations covered much of the same ground as had the previous inquiries, however it stands out as being the first that led directly to legislative intervention.

In common with previous reports, the McElhone Report recommended that ground improvements would make crowd control easier and would attract a greater cross-section of society to attend games. In particular, the report considered that if more women and children were to attend matches held in better-quality accommodation, then the overall behaviour of the crowd would improve. It also repeated previous recommendations that more severe punishments be handed down to hooligans as a deterrent to them and others who may be tempted to engage in football-related disorder.

In order to reduce the opportunity for clashes inside the stadium, the report recommended that rival fans be segregated from each other. Moreover, to increase the effectiveness of this segregation, it was recommended that fences be erected to a height of not less than 1.8m to prevent spectators from accessing the playing area and areas in which opposing fans were accommodated. In proposing ways of reducing crowd disorder, the report was inadvertently creating the circumstances in which spectator safety could be compromised.

One innovative recommendation was that clubs should improve engagement with their local community by, for example, providing players to conduct coaching sessions at nearby schools and clubs. The aim of this recommendation, reflected in clubs' 'Football in the Community' programmes, was designed to promote a club's responsibility for its fans and the fans' responsibility for the maintenance of the club's reputation by forging stronger ties between the two. None of these recommendations, whether being made for the first time or being repeated and updated for, in some cases, the fifth time, had sufficient impact on the government to result in legislative action.

10.2.3.1 Criminal Justice (Scotland) Act 1980 ss.68–77 – control of alcohol at sporting events in Scotland

The only Parliamentary response was to the McElhone Report's recommendations on alcohol. At the time, Scottish football clubs did not have licenses to sell alcohol inside their stadiums, leading to a culture of spectators drinking before the game began and bringing their own drink with them into the ground. This led not only to drunkenness amongst the spectators but to a ready supply of missiles that could be thrown at opposing fans or players. Part V Criminal Justice (Scotland) Act 1980, which was subsequently amended by the Sporting Events (Control of Alcohol) Act 1985 and has now been replaced by Part II Criminal Law (Consolidation) (Scotland) Act 1995, introduced a package of criminal offences to restrict the consumption of alcohol by football spectators in Scotland.

The Act criminalises the possession of alcohol on public transport or in private vehicles capable of carrying more than eight passengers on the way to a designated football game. The operator of a public service vehicle or driver of a private vehicle is guilty of an offence by allowing alcohol to be carried in their vehicles. It is also an offence to carry alcohol into a football stadium, to have a container capable of carrying liquids in one's possession inside the ground and to be drunk at, or whilst trying to gain entry to a football match. Similar provisions were not enacted for the rest of the UK and in 1984 were specifically rejected as unnecessary by a Department of the Environment Working Group (below, 10.2.4). Part V Criminal Justice (Scotland) Act 1980 did, however, form the template for the Sporting Events (Control of Alcohol) Act 1985, which was passed in the immediate aftermath of the fatalities at Birmingham and Heysel.

10.2.4 Department of the Environment Working Group Report, 1984 – 'Football Spectator Violence'

Following high-profile incidents of disorder at England matches, in particular those held in Luxembourg and France during the qualifying rounds for the 1984 UEFA European Nations Championships, the Department of the Environment commissioned a further report on spectator disorder. Its proposals sought to restrict the opportunities for disorder through the better organisation of the sport as a whole and through more effective planning and preparation for disorder at high-risk games. In contrast to the McElhone Report, it found that there was no evidential basis for the claims that there was a link between alcohol and disorder. The Working Group rejected the need for legislation comparable to the Criminal Justice (Scotland) Act 1980 on the further ground that it would cause unnecessary financial hardship to the majority of clubs where disorder was not a problem.

Thus, despite the similarity of both the findings and recommendations made by the Harrington, Lang, McElhone and Department of the Environment Reports, the only legislative action taken to improve the effectiveness of crowd control in the UK was to regulate the possession and consumption of alcohol at and on the way to football matches in Scotland. None of the reports made their recommendations with the same degree of forcefulness that had led to the enactment of the Wheatley Report's recommendations in the Safety of Sports Grounds Act 1975 (see further, chapter 9.5). Despite the lack of Parliamentary intervention at the time, almost all of what were then considered to be the more politically or financially controversial recommendations have been enacted subsequently.

10.3 St Andrew's, Birmingham, Heysel Stadium, Brussels and the Popplewell Reports, 1985–86

In contrast to the fire at Valley Parade, Bradford, the two other football disasters of 1985 were caused primarily by spectator disorder, not just the state of the premises or the mismanagement of the event. The Popplewell Reports examined all three disasters and made recommendations concerning how both spectator safety and crowd control could be improved in the future. In this section, the incidents at St Andrew's and Heysel will be examined and the recommendations concerning crowd control discussed.

10.3.1 St Andrew's, Birmingham, 1985

On the same day as the fire at Bradford, a 15-year-old boy was killed, and 20 others injured when a wall collapsed at St Andrew's Stadium, Birmingham.

▶ *St Andrew's, 9 May 1985*

Serious disorder had begun in the centre of Birmingham on the morning of the match and continued throughout the game. The police had been continually bombarded with missiles, including pieces of concrete and bricks that had been dislodged from the fabric of the stadium. There had been a pitch invasion by both sets of fans at half-time, and disorder continued throughout the match.

At the end of the game, as most spectators were leaving the stadium, others continued to fight and throw things at each other. A surge of spectators pushed against a wall that divided the back of the stadium from the car park, causing it to collapse, killing one person. There was no indication that the wall was structurally unsound or that it had collapsed for any other reason than excessive force being applied to it. The only explanation given for the surge of spectators against the wall was that it was part of the ongoing disorder between the two sets of fans, though those crushed by the wall were simply passersby who were not involved in any violent conduct.

10.3.2 Sporting Events (Control of Alcohol) Act 1985

Before the publication of the Popplewell Reports and in time for the start of the 1985–86 football season, the government decided that it needed to take action against what it saw to be drink-fuelled hooliganism. Although the previous year's Department of the Environment Report had recommended that there was no need to restrict access to alcohol at football grounds in England and Wales, the government disagreed. The Sporting Events (Control of Alcohol) Act 1985 enacted a framework for the control of alcohol at designated football matches based on the Criminal Justice (Scotland) Act 1980. Thus, possessing alcohol whilst travelling to a designated football match on public transport or in a private vehicle capable of carrying more than eight passengers became offences, as did permitting another person to possess alcohol in such vehicles under ss.1 and 1A.

Moreover, attempting to gain entry to a designated football ground whilst drunk and being drunk or possessing alcohol or possessing a container capable of holding liquid whilst in a designated football ground were criminalised under s.2 of the Act. As with the Scottish legislation this latter provision was passed to prevent bottles and cans from being used as missiles. Section 2 also bans sales of alcohol in sight of the pitch to prevent spectators from staying in a bar and drinking whilst watching the game. Thus, Parliament took the pro-active step of preventing entry to football matches for spectators who were drunk (though no definition of 'drunk' is provided), preventing entry into the ground when possessing alcohol and preventing the consumption of alcohol in sight of the game; a complete prohibition on the consumption of alcohol inside the stadium was not considered appropriate on financial grounds despite its apparent potential to create serious disorder.

10.3.3 The Popplewell Interim Report – 'Interim Report of the Committee of Inquiry into Crowd Safety and Control at Sports Grounds'

The Interim Report's recommendations on crowd control were aimed at improving the police's ability to conduct effective surveillance of large and potentially disorderly crowds and criminalising specific types of conduct most commonly associated with football hooliganism. To improve police surveillance, it was recommended that closed-circuit television cameras (CCTV) should be installed at all major football grounds so that those who were engaging in violent conduct could be more easily identified and eventually prosecuted. The practical benefits to the police and the consequent reduction of disorder inside the ground that was observed where CCTV had been installed meant that this recommendation was implemented by clubs without the need for further legislative intervention.

The Interim Report also recommended that the introduction of a national membership system be investigated so that football spectators could be more easily identified and later banned if they were involved in disorder. It was also hoped that away fans could be prevented from attending all matches. Under this proposal, attendance at football matches would only be granted to members of the home club who had been vetted by it in advance. As an incentive to good behaviour, their membership could be revoked if they were convicted of an offence of football-related disorder. By preventing away fans from attending a game, it was hoped that the opportunity for clashes between rival fans would be removed and that therefore football-related disorder would be eradicated. This proposal was developed further in the Final Report but was ultimately rejected as unworkable by the Taylor Report (below, 10.4.3).

Finally the Interim Report recommended that throwing missiles and chanting obscene and racial abuse at sports grounds should be specifically criminalised. The Interim Report identified that many injuries were caused by the throwing of missiles at other spectators and the police and that such conduct was often the precursor to more serious disorder between rival groups of spectators. By making the throwing of a missile an offence, the need to prove intent to harm another person and/or their property is removed, thereby making it easier to secure a conviction.

The aim of criminalising obscene and racial chanting was to reduce the amount of anti-social behaviour at football matches, to improve the overall conduct of the spectators and to remove the possibility of retaliatory disorder on the part of those who had been abused. Both of these proposals were examined further in the Final Report before being enacted in the Football Offences Act 1991 (below, 10.4.1).

10.3.4 Heysel Stadium, Brussels 1985

Just over two weeks after the Bradford fire and the collapse of the wall at St Andrew's, the events at the Heysel Stadium during the European Cup Final between Liverpool and Juventus changed the focus of attention from spectator safety in outdated sports grounds to the need for better and more effective control of disorderly and violent football crowds.

▶ *Heysel Stadium, 27 May 1985*

The build up to the final had seen sporadic outbreaks of violence both within and outside of the stadium. This grew worse as the opposing fans began by throwing missiles at each other, and ended with a riot during which a large group of Liverpool fans attacked a group of Juventus fans in the neighbouring pen. The direct cause of the Heysel disaster was an aggressive charge by a group of Liverpool fans into an adjoining section of the ground that was populated predominantly by Juventus fans. As the Juventus fans tried to escape the threat of an imminent attack, they became trapped against a wall that separated the end of the terrace from one of the stadium's entrance corridors. As the pressure against the wall mounted, it collapsed, causing many fans to fall and many more to pile on top of them; as a result, 39 spectators were crushed to death, and over 400 were injured.

Heysel occupies a controversial place in the history of stadium disasters involving British football clubs; the disaster was clearly and obviously caused by a riot involving a large group of people intent on committing violence. That the direct cause of the resulting deaths was not the physical state of the stadium nor the failure to manage the safety of the spectators inside the ground distinguishes it from the disasters discussed in Chapter 9. What is less frequently examined is that the scale of the Heysel disaster was exacerbated by a poor-quality stadium, mismanagement of the crowd on the day and a lack of any appropriate licensing procedures.

Had Heysel been located in England, it is unlikely that it would have satisfied the safety requirements of the Safety at Sports Grounds Act 1975. The concrete steps that formed the terracing were decaying and pieces were easily broken off and used as missiles; lengths of piping that had been left at the back of the terracing were also used as missiles and weapons when the violence broke out. Further, the pens dividing the terraces were separated only by insubstantial plastic-coated wire, which was easily torn down. Thus, the physical condition of the ground was not safe enough to host a match of this size and importance and helped to create the circumstances in which the disorder could arise and then escalate.

Despite the best intentions of the organisers, segregation of the opposing fans was not maintained. Neutral zones of terracing were placed between the Liverpool and Juventus fans so that there would be some considerable distance between them, thereby minimising the opportunities for disorderly interaction. Tickets for these zones were supposed to be restricted to Belgian nationals purchasing them from the stadium's ticket office. In reality, the majority of these tickets were purchased by Juventus fans, resulting in a complete breakdown in segregation at one end of the ground. This was compounded by a misunderstanding in the division of roles between the two police forces on duty at the match. The lack of one overall commander in charge of policing on the day left the local police on duty inside the ground whilst the more highly-trained and better-equipped riot police were based back at their barracks on standby in case disorder broke out. When rioting did begin, these specialist officers found it difficult to cross the city quickly because of the weight of traffic making its way to the stadium.

Finally, neither the Belgian state authorities nor UEFA, which had chosen Heysel to host its showpiece final, had any criteria against which to judge the appropriateness of a stadium to stage a game of this magnitude. Heysel was chosen because it was a large stadium that hosted international football games; therefore, it was assumed that it was also capable of hosting the European Cup Final.

The choice of stadium and mismanagement of the crowd by both the police and event organisers created the conditions in which a riot could occur. This is not to detract from the fact that the disaster was caused by violence and disorder carried out by a sizeable minority of spectators, some of whom were armed and some of whom had gained access to the ground illegally. What it highlights is that where organisational and operational protocols are either not in place or not adhered to, the conditions in which disorder may occur can be exploited by those intent on acting violently, all of which had been highlighted by the UK government's reports into spectator disorder.

10.3.5 The Popplewell Final Report – 'The Final Report of the Committee of Inquiry into Crowd Safety and Control at Sports Grounds'

Popplewell J's Final Report examined the Heysel Stadium disaster in detail before analysing in more depth some of the issues that had been raised in the Interim Report. Of the 15 final recommendations, five related to crowd control. Despite a wide-ranging review of the sociological, criminological, historical and legal literature on football hooliganism, the Final Report was unable to explain why people became involved with football-related disorder. Although the causes of the disorder could not be identified definitively the Final Report does propose a series of preventive measures that should be taken to reduce its incidence in the future. The main proposals covered the need for the police to have extended powers to stop and search football spectators, the creation of new offences that covered specific forms of disorder and the creation of a national football membership scheme; separately, the forerunner of Football Banning Orders, the Exclusion Order, was introduced by s.30 Public Order Act 1986 (below, 10.4.3.2).

10.3.5.1 Criminal Justice and Public Order Act 1994 s.60 – police powers of stop and search

One of the main concerns of the Committee was that the police were unable to carry out effective searches of spectators before they entered a football ground. Under the s.1(3) Police and Criminal Evidence Act 1984, the police were only able to search a person or vehicle where there were reasonable grounds for suspecting that stolen property or offensive weapons would be found. The police knew that some spectators carried weapons, but not who. As s.1(3) does not provide a general power to search unless there were reasonable grounds for suspecting that a specific individual was carrying a weapon, a search could not be carried out. The Final Report recommended that the police be given an unfettered power to stop and search anyone entering or trying to enter a football ground.

At first, the government did not consider this general power to be appropriate. However, s.60 Criminal Justice and Public Order Act 1994 enacts the Final Report's recommendation but in an even wider form than that proposed, as it is not just applicable to football spectators. Section 60 enables the police to stop and search any person or any vehicle where a police officer of the rank of Inspector or above reasonably believes that incidents of serious violence may take place and that it is expedient to use this power to prevent them from occurring or where there are reasonable grounds for suspecting that dangerous instruments or offensive weapons are being carried without good reason. Authorisations under s.60 have become commonplace at football matches, not so much as a means of preventing football-related disorder but to gather intelligence about football spectators, despite this not being one of the justifications for sanctioning the use of these powers; the intelligence gathered from fans during the stop and search is frequently used in applications for Football Banning Orders under s.14B Football Spectators Act 1989 (below, 10.6.2).

10.3.5.2 Criminalising disorderly conduct at sports grounds

Both the Interim and Final Reports considered the need for specific offences to be enacted to control commonly-occurring types of disorderly conduct at football matches. The final recommendation was that a generic offence of disorderly conduct at a sports ground should be created that would criminalise a range of anti-social behaviour. The specific concerns of the Committee were the throwing of missiles, obscene and racial chanting and pitch invasions.

The Final Report acknowledges that the investigation and enforcement of crimes such as these would be difficult when large numbers of people may be committing the same offence at the same time. However it was also considered that the new offence could create a significant deterrent to engaging in disorderly conduct; the symbolic effect of the legislation and its use against a few offenders may be enough to stop others from joining in. Before being able to enact a criminal offence based on this recommendation, the Taylor Report's more specific recommendations for enacting three separate offences of throwing missiles inside a stadium, engaging in indecent and/or racial chanting and encroaching on to the pitch without lawful excuse led to the passing of the Football (Offences) Act 1990 (below, 10.4.1).

10.3.6   European Convention on Spectator Violence

A further and less well-known legal instrument that was created as a direct response to the events at Heysel is the Council of Europe's 'European Convention on Spectator Violence'. The aims of the Convention mirror those of each of the governmental reports discussed here: to prevent and control spectator violence on the one hand and to ensure the safety of spectators at sports events on the other. The Convention was signed and ratified by the UK on 19 August 1985 and came into force on 1 November of that year, however, its terms are not legally binding on the UK Parliament, though there is a high degree of coincidence between the terms of the Convention and the statutes enacted and policies pursued by all UK governments since 1985.

The Convention seeks to standardise the approaches of European governments towards the policing and control of potentially disorderly crowds, to improve cooperation and knowledge sharing among law enforcement agencies, to improve standards of stadium safety and to educate fans about the cultures and customs of their opponents. In respect of each of these issues, the UK has been at the forefront of legal and policy developments.

Although most police forces now routinely exchange information on potential risk spectators, cross-border policing and judicial cooperation were at their highest profile during the 2006 FIFA World Cup in Germany, where uniformed English police spotters patrolled with their German colleagues in the cities where England played. This enabled the English police to identify potential troublemakers, monitor their behaviour and take appropriate action to diffuse situations that could escalate into violence. Further, representatives of the Crown Prosecution Service travelled to Germany to ensure that anyone arrested for a football-related offence could have a Football Banning Order imposed on them on their return to the UK. Cooperation between the English and German authorities in these ways ensured that disorder was kept to a minimum and that where it did happen, it was punished in the same way that it would have been had it occurred at a game in England.

10.4 Hillsborough Stadium, Sheffield and the Taylor Reports, 1989–90

As the main cause of the Hillsborough disaster was mismanagement of the crowd on the day (see further, chapter 9.5), the majority of the Taylor Reports' recommendations naturally concerned spectator safety. However, the Final Report also proposed the creation of four new criminal offences and made suggestions concerning the efficacy of Parts I and II of the recently-enacted Football Spectators Act 1989. The Popplewell Reports had identified three specific forms of anti-social behaviour that were often the precursor to more serious outbreaks of disorder: throwing missiles, chanting obscene and/or racialist abuse and going on to the field of play without a reasonable excuse. In his final report, Popplewell J had recommended that a generic offence of disorderly conduct at a football match be enacted to cover each of these three types of conduct.

Taylor LJ reviewed this proposal and the operation of the Public Order Act 1986, which had come into force after the publication of the Popplewell Reports. He concluded that none of the existing offences or the generic crime proposed by Popplewell J adequately covered these three specific acts.

10.4.1 The Football (Offences) Act 1991

The Football (Offences) Act 1991 enacted these recommendations by creating three new football-specific offences rather than one of disorderly conduct at a sports ground. The behaviour covered by these offences does not fall easily within existing general provisions as the *mens rea* required for crimes of assault and public disorder might not be present when simply chanting or throwing things. Further, behaviour of this kind was often the precursor to incidents of more serious disorder. The throwing of missiles could escalate through retaliatory missile-throwing to a full-scale riot; the verbal abuse of an opposing team's players or spectators could likewise lead to a violent reaction in those seeking to defend those being abused and running on to the pitch was often the final act before a confrontation between opposing sets of fans. If this kind of conduct could be stopped at as early a stage as possible, it was argued, then the incidence of serious disorder inside stadiums could be reduced significantly. Thus, the proposed offences sought to close genuine loopholes in the law.

Under s.2, it is an offence to throw anything at or towards the playing area or any other area where spectators or other persons are without lawful excuse. Although obviously aimed at the throwing of objects such as coins, bottles and pieces of masonry, it is drafted widely enough to include any object.

Section 3 creates the offence of indecent or racialist chanting. There is no definition of 'indecent' however, it is clear from the tone of the Final Report that any abusive and/or crude chanting was considered to be unwelcome at football matches. 'Racialist' is defined as including threatening, abusive or insulting words aimed at a person's colour, race, nationality, ethnic or national origins. A specific person does not have to be the target of the chanting; the offence is committed if the chanting is, in fact, indecent or racialist. In *DPP v Stoke-on-Trent Magistrates' Court* [2003] EWHC 1593 (Admin), the High Court held that a chant of 'You're just a town full of Pakis' directed at Oldham Athletic FC fans by Port Vale FC fans was racially abusive despite a finding that there were no persons of Pakistani, Asian or black origin in the crowd or on the playing field. A loophole in the original Act, that this offence could only be committed if the chanting were engaged in by two or more persons, was closed by a later amendment; the s.3 offence can now be committed by one or more people chanting indecent or racial words.

Finally s.4 makes it an offence to go on to the playing area or any area adjoining the playing area without lawful excuse, making running on to the pitch a criminal offence unless it is to escape from a dangerous or disorderly situation. The police have generally avoided prosecuting the occasional over-exuberant celebration, but where threatening behaviour has been directed at players, match officials, club employees or other spectators, a prosecution will usually follow (*R (on the application of White) v Blackfriars Crown Court* [2008] EWHC 510 (Admin)) (below, 10.6.1).

Each of these three crimes can only be committed at a designated football match. This has been extended on three occasions since 1991 and now includes all matches where at least one of the teams involved is a member of the Football Association Premier League, the Football League, the Football Conference, the Scottish Football League or the League of Wales or is a team that represents a territory or country or whose home ground is situated for the time being outside of England and Wales; games in the FA Cup, excluding qualifying and preliminary rounds are also included, (Football (Offences) (Designation of Football Matches) Order 2004/2410). This leaves the rather strange situation that where, for example, a sports ground hosts both football and rugby games, the Act applies when a football match is being played, but not when a rugby match is played. Despite the cogent justification for the creation of these new offences, they are only rarely used by the police to prosecute football-related disorder (below, 10.5).

10.4.2   Criminal Justice and Public Order Act 1994 ss.166 and 166A – regulating ticketing touting

The fourth offence recommended by the Final Report was that the unauthorised sale of tickets to a designated football match, or ticket touting, should be criminalised. The justification for this proposal was that ticket touting can create disorder in two specific ways. Firstly, it can lead to the breakdown in segregation of the opposing fans as the tout is unlikely to pay much attention to the allegiance of the purchaser. If opposing fans are to be kept apart so that they cannot fight with each other inside a football ground, then ticket touting could seriously undermine this basic crowd-control tactic. Secondly, the act of selling can create disorder amongst the prospective purchasers, either through creating a crowd of prospective purchasers or because of disputes over price.

Ticket touting was eventually made a criminal offence at designated football matches by s.166 Criminal Justice and Public Order Act 1994 (see further, chapter 13.4). In its current form, s.166(a) defines a sale as being unauthorised where it is concluded without the written consent of the match organiser, ensuring that any sale not conducted by an authorised ticket agent is a crime. Under s.166(2)(aa), 'selling' is given a particularly wide meaning to include offering to sell a ticket, exposing a ticket for sale, making a ticket available for sale by another, advertising that a ticket is available for purchase and giving a ticket to a person who pays or agrees to pay for some other goods or services or offering to do so. This wider meaning of 'selling' was enacted in the light of activities undertaken by touts to avoid being caught simply selling or offering to sell tickets under the more basic original definition of the offence. In *Brown v Inner London Crown Court* [2003] EWHC 3194, a three-year Football Banning Order was held to be reasonable and proportionate to prevent a professional ticket tout from operating near football grounds because of the risk of disorder created by his activities.

In 2007, in response to the growth in unauthorised ticket sales taking place online, s.166A was added to the Criminal Justice and Public Order Act 1994 to impose criminal liability on Internet service providers (ISPs) in certain limited circumstances. An ISP is not liable simply for hosting or enabling unauthorised sales to take place on its service; it will only be liable in one of two specific situations. Firstly, when it is aware that the information supplied to it by a user contains material that contravenes s.166. Secondly, when having become aware that information on its service contravenes s.166, it fails to remove it or disable access to it expeditiously. Thus, only where an ISP has specific knowledge that a specific individual is selling tickets on its service without the authorisation of the primary rights holder will an offence be committed. From a practical perspective, this means that unless a specific unauthorised sale is brought to the attention of the ISP, which is often done by the primary rights holder, and it takes no action to remove it from its service, no offence is committed.

10.4.3 Recommendations for amending the Football Spectators Act 1989

The Final Report also reviewed the Football Spectators Act 1989 which had enacted some of the key recommendations of the Popplewell Reports. Two aspects in particular were analysed in some depth: the National Membership Scheme and the means by which exclusion and restriction orders, the forerunners of Football Banning Orders (below, 10.6), could be made more effective.

10.4.3.1 The National Membership Scheme

The aim of the National Membership Scheme was to restrict entry to designated football grounds to people who held valid membership cards. The card would contain information including the name, address, photograph, club and national allegiance of the member and would have to be presented when purchasing tickets and when attempting to gain entry to a stadium; anyone who was ineligible to hold a membership card, including anyone who had been the subject of an Exclusion or Restriction Order, would not be able to purchase tickets to designated football matches. It was hoped that the restrictions on membership and the ability of the Authority to monitor and exclude members would break the connection between violent disorder and football.

Taylor LJ reviewed the scheme and identified three specific concerns with it that he thought would make it unworkable and potentially dangerous. Firstly, he considered that checking the membership cards at the turnstiles would slow down entry into the stadium to such an extent that congestion and crushing outside of the ground would be exacerbated. The inadequate technology of the time was considered to pose greater problems than it would solve and for this reason alone should be abandoned. Secondly, it was observed that since the introduction of CCTV cameras at designated football grounds, most violence and disorder took place outside of the stadiums. Therefore, restricting access to the ground to known hooligans would not prevent disorder inside the stadium as this had already been reduced to a minimum. Thirdly, the impact on police resources would be too great as each turnstile would require at least two officers to be on duty in case a banned person were to attempt to gain entry to the ground. Thus, instead of recommending the implementation of the National Membership Scheme, which had been included in ss.2–7 Football Spectators Act 1989, the Taylor Report recommended that further and more restrictive conditions should be added to the Exclusion Orders imposed on those convicted of football-related disorder; the National Membership Scheme was eventually removed from the Act by sch.5 para.1 Violent Crime Reduction Act 2006.

10.4.3.2 Exclusion Orders

A court's ability to impose an Exclusion Order on a person convicted of a football-related offence had been introduced by s.30 Public Order Act 1986. Its aim was to prevent violence or disorder at or in connection with football matches by banning the person subject to it from entering every designated football ground in England and Wales for a minimum of three months.

Taylor LJ's concern was that these orders were not being imposed often enough on conviction and where they were, there was no effective means of enforcing them. He proposed that Attendance Centre Orders should be attached to Exclusion Orders so that anyone subject to a ban would have to attend a specific place during the time that a football match involving the team supported by the subject was taking place. Alternatively, it was recommended that the subject of the order should be electronically tagged so that their whereabouts on match days could be monitored remotely. Although these recommendations were not followed, they promoted the debate that led to the development of Football Banning Orders into the much more extensive preventive measure that is in place today. This new banning regime, coupled with improved surveillance technology that enables its restrictions to be monitored and enforced much more effectively, has ensured that being banned from a ground and specific areas around it is more easily policed than Taylor LJ might have imagined at the time (below, 10.6).

10.5 General legislation applicable to disorderly crowds

There is no legal definition of 'football hooliganism' and no crime of being a 'football hooligan' in English law. Anyone who is accused of being involved in football-related disorder will be charged either with an offence under one of the football-specific pieces of legislation mentioned above or with one of a relatively small number of criminal offences. In sports other than football, only the general criminal offences discussed below will be available to the prosecutor.

Despite the wide range of offences with which a person involved with spectator disorder could be charged, the annually released Home Office's statistics on football-related arrests and banning orders show that football fans are arrested for comparatively few crimes. In general, around half of all arrests are for offences under the Public Order Act 1986, in particular, the offences of public disorder under ss.4 and 5. A further third are for alcohol-related offences under the Sporting Events (Control of Alcohol) Act 1985. Only ten per cent of all arrests are for offences under the Football (Offences) Act 1991, with the remainder being for a range of crimes including ticket touting, breaching a Football Banning Order, assault and criminal damage. Where these offences are committed 24 hours before kick-off or 24 hours after the end of a regulated football match, they are categorised as 'football related', and a Football Banning Order can be imposed on the defendant (below, 10.6).

10.5.1 Public Order Act 1986

The Public Order Act 1986 (POA 1986) consolidated and updated the law on disorderly conduct. Its Parliamentary progress was also influenced, albeit at the last minute, by concerns raised in the Popplewell Reports. The offences created by the POA 1986 cover almost all conduct that could be considered to be acts of hooliganism and is regularly relied on by the police and the CPS to secure convictions against those involved with disorder at all sports fixtures.

10.5.1.1 Public Order Act 1986 ss.1–5 – riot, violent disorder, affray and public disorder

Sections 1–5 POA 1986 create a hierarchy of offences that vary in their seriousness, depending on how many people are involved in the disorder and the nature of the conduct in which they are engaged. The most serious of these offences, riot, is defined in s.1 POA 1986. Riot occurs where 12 or more people who are present together use or threaten unlawful violence as part of a common purpose. If their conduct is such that it would hypothetically cause a person of reasonable firmness present at the scene to fear for their personal safety, then each of the people using or threatening to use unlawful violence is guilty of riot. The persons involved in the riot do not have to threaten unlawful violence simultaneously, nor does a person of reasonable firmness actually have to be present at the scene of the disorder for the offence to be committed. Although many instances of sports-related disorder could constitute riot, the offence is rarely used to prosecute suspected hooligans. The difficulties associated with proving that a minimum of 12 people each had the same common purpose, particularly where not all of them have been prosecuted, means that offenders are more likely to be charged with violent disorder or affray under ss.2 and 3 POA 1986, respectively.

Violent disorder is defined in almost exactly the same way as riot but requires only three people to be using or threatening to use unlawful violence. Affray can be committed in the same way as violent disorder but by one person acting alone. The only difference between these two offences and riot, apart from the minimum numbers required to be involved with the disorder, is that riot requires proof that the people involved were acting with a common purpose when using or threatening to use unlawful violence, whereas violent disorder and affray do not. Thus, to secure a conviction for riot, it must be proved that, for example, 12 or more people were acting with a common purpose of attacking the supporters of the opposing team. However, to secure convictions for violent disorder or affray, the people involved may each be motivated by different reasons for acting with unlawful violence; for example, one is involved in a fight with someone against whom he has a longstanding grudge, another in threatening violence towards opposing spectators and another in committing criminal damage. As long as their conduct taken as a whole would cause a person of reasonable firmness to fear for their personal safety, the offences are committed. It is also possible, and often appropriate, for conspiracy to commit one of the POA 1986 offences to be charged as a means of preventing the disorder from arising in the first place, *R v Gornall and others* [2011] EWCA Crim 1402.

Although almost all incidents of sports-related disorder could constitute at least one of the offences under ss.1–3 POA 1986, it is more likely that anyone engaged in this type of conduct will be arrested and charged with an offence under ss.4, 4A or 5 POA 1986 because of the comparative ease of proving that one of these crimes has been committed. In particular, the ability of the prosecution to rely on a police officer's evidence that they were put in fear, harassed, alarmed or distressed by the defendant's conduct makes these offences much easier to prove.

Each of these three offences is committed where a person uses threatening, abusive or insulting words or behaviour towards another or who displays to another person any writing or makes any sign to them which is threatening, abusive or insulting; it must be noted that there are ongoing Parliamentary discussions about removing the word 'insulting' from s.5 POA 1986 as it is considered inappropriate by some to criminalize such a low level of disorderly conduct (see Strickland, *"Insulting words or behaviour": section 5 of the Public Order Act 1986*, SN/HA/5760). The difference between the offences is in the intent of the defendant when using or displaying the words or signs and its impact on the other person. For an offence under s.4 POA 1986, the defendant must have had the intent to cause another person to believe that immediate unlawful violence would be used against them or against somebody else, or that their behaviour would provoke others to use immediate unlawful violence, or that it is likely that such violence would be used or provoked. Under s.4A, the defendant must intend only that their conduct would cause another person harassment, alarm or distress, whilst under s.5 it is only necessary for the conduct to have taken place within the hearing or sight of someone likely to be caused harassment, alarm or distress.

Almost all disorderly conduct and much that is simply part of fan culture at football games could be caught by one of these three offences. As it is not necessary to show that the target of the threats or abuse was, in fact, threatened or caused harassment, alarm or distress, it is possible for the police to claim that they were the ones who were put in fear that violence would be used or provoked, or that they were harassed, alarmed or distressed by the defendant's behaviour. This ability of the police to give evidence that they were the victims of the disorderly conduct, rather than opposing spectators or players, has made the offences under ss.4, 4A and 5 powerful tools with which to control spectators. Perhaps the most important outcome of committing these minor public order offences is that if the disorderly conduct is found to be football-related, then a Football Banning Order must be imposed on conviction (below, 10.6.1).

10.5.1.2 *Public Order Act 1986 ss.17–19 – inciting racial hatred*

The offences under ss.18 and 19 POA 1986 criminalise a range of racist behaviour and can be used to control racism at any sports fixture including football. These offences are drafted more widely than the offence of indecent or racialist chanting under s.3 Football

(Offences) Act 1991 because they cover individual instances of racial abuse, not just those that are repeated, as is required for the s.3 offence, and are generally applicable rather than being restricted to regulating incidents that occur at designated football matches.

The s.18 offence is committed by a person who intends to stir up racial hatred by using words or behaviour or by displaying written material, which is abusive, threatening or insulting. The offence under s.19 is committed by publishing or distributing material of the same kind. The offences are also committed where, having regard to the surrounding circumstances, racial hatred is likely to be stirred up by the defendant's conduct. Racial hatred is defined in s.17 POA 1986 as being hatred against a group of persons defined by reference to colour, race, nationality, citizenship or ethnic or national origins. Thus, the offences will cover abuse spoken or shouted by spectators, written signs or banners containing racist comments, and leaflets, pamphlets or other printed material that incites racial hatred. These POA 1986 offences are rarely charged, because of the comparative difficulty in securing a conviction, compared to the ease with which s.3 Football (Offences) Act 1991 can be established.

10.5.2   Other relevant legislation

Outside of the football-specific legislation and the offences contained in the POA 1986, the majority of arrests at sports fixtures are for assault, aggravated trespass and criminal damage. The various assault offences with which a person could be charged are the same as those that can be committed by sports participants (see further, chapter 6). The remaining offences are outlined below.

10.5.2.1 *Criminal Justice and Public Order Act 1994 s.68 – aggravated trespass*

Although originally introduced to prevent certain forms of industrial action that had been prevalent in the 1980s and to control the rave scene of the early 1990s, s.68 Criminal Justice and Public Order Act 1994 (CJPOA 1994) can also be used to prosecute pitch invasions in sports other than football (where s.4 Football (Offences) Act applies). The offence is committed by a trespasser who intimidates, obstructs or disrupts anyone who is carrying out or is about to carry out a lawful activity on the land or on adjoining land. A further offence is committed under s.69 CJPOA 1994 where a trespasser fails to leave the land having been required to do so by a police officer. Aggravated trespass is wide-ranging enough to cover any situation where a spectator runs on to the playing area whilst a game is in progress, or where damage is caused to the playing area, or where ground-staff are prevented from preparing or maintaining any part of the stadium.

10.5.2.2 *Criminal Damage Act 1971*

The final category of crimes that are likely to be committed by those engaged in sports-related disorder is criminal damage. The basic offence of criminal damage is committed where the defendant intentionally or subjectively recklessly damages any property belonging to another person (s.1(1) Criminal Damage Act 1971 (CDA 1971)). The aggravated offence is committed where the defendant intentionally or recklessly endangers the life of another person by damaging or destroying property (s.1(2) CDA 1971). If either of these offences is committed by fire, then the offence is charged under s.1(3) as arson. There are further offences of threatening to destroy or damage property under s.2 and possessing items with the intent to destroy or damage property under s.3 of the Act. Any harm caused to the fabric of the stadium, the playing area or even the clothing of another person present at a sports match can constitute criminal damage.

10.5.2.3 Violent Crime Reduction Act s.27 – alcohol-related disorder directions

The introduction of s.27 Violent Crime Reduction Act 2006 has provided a uniformed police officer with the power to direct an individual to leave a designated locality for a period not exceeding 48 hours if it is believed that their presence is likely to cause or contribute to the occurrence, repetition or continuance of alcohol-related crime or disorder and that such a direction is necessary for reducing the likelihood of such crime or disorder in that locality for the period of the order. This new power has been used extensively, and often unlawfully, as a means of preventing football spectators from attending football matches.

Many police forces have used their powers under s.27 as a means of targeting pubs where away fans have congregated and insisting that they return home without watching the match. The justification for using s.27 in this manner is that the spectators have met in a pub, are drinking before going to a football match and are likely to become involved in alcohol- and football-related disorder. Following *R (on application of Lyndon) v Chief Constable of Greater Manchester Police,* (unreported) High Court (QBD) 15 November 2008, it has been clarified that before a direction to disperse can be given, each person present must be individually assessed in terms of their risk of causing alcohol-related disorder; the mere fact that a person has been drinking is insufficient grounds for directing them to leave an area. Further, the locality from which they must leave must be specifically drawn to their attention; police cannot ban a person from 'Greater Manchester' nor can they require them to 'go home'.

Despite this and other similar decisions, police forces around the country still use s.27 in this manner. In addition, the fact that a spectator has been directed to leave a locality is often recorded on their police profile and (often incorrectly) used as evidence of disorderly behaviour when applying for Football Banning Orders under s.14B Football Spectators Act 1989 (below, 10.6.2).

10.5.2.4 Offensive Behaviour at Football and Threatening Communications (Scotland) Act 2012

In response to what is perceived to be the ongoing problem of sectarian abuse at and around Scottish football matches, the Offensive Behaviour at Football and Threatening Communications (Scotland) Act 2012 has introduced the offence of engaging in offensive behaviour at a football match. The primary aim of the Act is to criminalise singing, chanting and offensive behaviour that targets groups across the sectarian divide, though its actual impact is potentially much wider than that.

Under s.1(1), the offence of engaging in behaviour that is likely to incite public disorder, including threatening or offensive conduct, is created. In particular, s.1(2) defines offensive behaviour as expressing hatred of or stirring up hatred against an individual or a group of persons based on their religion or a social or cultural group with a perceived religious affiliation. This ensures that abuse aimed at a group of football fans either because of their religious persuasion or the assumption that they are of a particular religious persuasion because of the team that they support is a criminal offence. Further, s.1(4)(a-g)criminalises offensive behaviour based on a person or group's colour, race, nationality or citizenship, ethnic or national origins, sexual orientation, transgender identity and/or disability. In each of these cases, the proposed offence is only committed where the offensive behaviour is likely to incite public disorder.

By ensuring that this conduct is specifically criminalised in an individual offence, the intention is that it will be easier to secure convictions against those who engage in this type of behaviour. To date, there have been no convictions under this controversial Act.

10.5.2.5 Payment for police services

A long-running dispute between football clubs and police forces around the country has been identifying who should be responsible for policing at and around football matches. In *Harris v Sheffield United Football Club Ltd*[1988] QB 77, it was held that the provision of officers at football matches is not an integral part of the police's duty to maintain law and order but constitutes 'special police services' above and beyond normal policing duties that should be paid for by the home club in accordance with s.15(1) Police Act 1964.

This has been clarified in *Leeds United Football Club v West Yorkshire Police* [2013] EWCA Civ 115, where payment was claimed for policing a footprint around the stadium that included the stadium itself, car parks, a bus station and the public highways. The Court of Appeal held that the club was only liable to pay the charge for 'special police services' provided on land that they owned or utilised on match days, for example, car parks. Policing of the public highway and public land fell within the normal constabulary duty to keep the peace and did not constitute 'special police services' for which a charge could be levied.

10.6 Football Banning Orders

Since the introduction of Exclusion Orders in the POA 1986, a comprehensive framework for banning people who have been involved in, or are suspected of being involved in, football-related disorder has been developed and is now contained in the Football Spectators Act 1989 (FSA 1989). This regime has been amended and revised on a number of occasions over the years, most significantly by the Football (Offences and Disorder) Act 1999 and the Football (Disorder) Act 2000, and is considered to be one of the most effective tools for controlling football hooliganism. Despite these claims, disorder still occurs, and controversy continues to surround the use of Football Banning Orders (FBOs) as a means of controlling spectator behaviour.

10.6.1 Football Spectators Act 1989 s.14A – Football Banning Orders on conviction

The sentencing court must address three issues before imposing an FBO on a football spectator. First, it must be established that the defendant has committed a relevant offence. Secondly, the offence must be football-related. Thirdly, there must be reasonable grounds for believing that the imposition of an FBO on the defendant will help to prevent violence or disorder at future regulated football matches. If these conditions are met, then s.14A requires the court to impose an FBO on the defendant in addition to any punishment handed down unless the judge provides reasons for not doing so.

According to sch.1 FSA 1989 a relevant offence is any crime of violence or disorder, or which is alcohol-related, that is committed at or in connection with or on the way to or from a regulated football match and which occurs within 24 hours of the game's kick-off or within 24 hours of its end. A regulated football match now has the same meaning as a designated football match and includes any game where one of the teams is a member of the Football Association Premier League, the Football League, the Football Conference, the Scottish Football League or the League of Wales or is a team that represents a territory or country, or whose home ground is situated for the time being outside of England and Wales; games in the FA Cup, excluding qualifying and preliminary rounds, are also included, (Football Spectators (Prescription) Order 2004/2409).

The meaning of 'football-related' has been clarified further by the courts. In *R v Doyle and others* [2012] EWCA Crim 995, whether an offence was 'related to football matches' was held to include situations where the 'tribalist nature' of football supporters had contributed to the violence or disorder in question. This confirms the reasoning in Court's earlier decision in *R v Parkes and Cartwright* [2010] EWCA Crim 2803, where supporters of Wolverhampton Wanderers (Wolves) and West Bromwich Albion (West Brom) had clashed at a pub in Wednesbury that was frequented by West Brom fans. The defendant Wolves fans argued that as the match that they had been due to watch had been cancelled and as the two teams in question had not been playing each other that day, this incident was not football-related; it was just a fight between two groups of young men. The Court held that as the Wolves fans were only in the pub because they knew that it was frequented by West Brom fans and taking into account the long history of enmity between the fans of the two clubs, this was clearly a football-related incident and the trial court had correctly imposed FBOs on the defendants. In contrast, in *R v Doyle*, it was held that the behaviour of the defendants was not football-related just because they were returning from a football match. The trigger for the disorder was the consumption of alcohol, not football, and so the offences committed were not football-related.

Where there are reasonable grounds for believing that the imposition of an FBO on the defendant will help to prevent violence or disorder at future regulated football matches, the court *must* impose an order in addition to any sentence that it has handed down. If the defendant was sentenced to a period of imprisonment, then the FBO must be in place for between six and ten years; where a non-custodial sentence is imposed, it must be in place for between three and five years. The prosecution will ask for an FBO to be imposed as a matter of course where a relevant offence has been committed, and in the vast majority of cases, this will be granted. In *R v Boggild and others* [2011] EWCA Crim 1928, however, it was reiterated that it is not compulsory for an FBO to be imposed following a conviction for a football-related offence. Although one will usually be imposed in such circumstances, the judge can refuse to do so, provided that he gives reasons for his decision. On this point, *R v Allen* [2011] EWCA Crim 3076 is clearly wrong; the judge maintains a limited discretion on whether or not to impose a FBO but must justify a decision not to.

In *Boggild*, the trial judge thought that it was inappropriate to impose an FBO on the defendants because they had already been banned from attending regulated football matches for one year as a condition of their bail, had been convicted and sentenced to a range of punishments including suspended terms of imprisonment and community orders and had, as a result of their experiences, learned the appropriate lessons. Further, the judge did not believe that any of the defendants would be involved acts of football-related disorder in the future and that, therefore, FBOs were not necessary in this case.

Despite these cases, it is unnecessary to prove that the defendant has a propensity to violence. In *R v Hughes*, [2005] EWCA Crim 2537, the defendant had thrown one punch at an opposing spectator and was convicted of affray under s.3 POA 1986; he had no previous football-related convictions. As s.14A FSA 1989 requires only that a person has been convicted of a relevant offence, which Hughes had been, and that the court was satisfied that the imposition of the FBO would help to prevent disorder at future football matches, which it was, the FBO had been imposed correctly.

Similarly, the court can take into consideration the general deterrent effect, not just its individual impact, when imposing an FBO on a defendant. In *R (on the application of White) v Blackfriars Crown Court* [2008] EWHC 510, a three-year FBO was imposed on White after he pleaded guilty to running on to a football pitch, contrary to s.4 Football (Offences) Act, and committing a common assault on the referee. In dismissing his appeal, Richards LJ stated that although this was an isolated incident on the part of the defendant, the imposition of the FBO was a warning to other fans not to run on to the pitch and assault referees and was therefore capable of helping to prevent violence or disorder at future regulated football matches.

This group of cases highlight that the impact of a FBO can be twofold; first, it prevents the specific defendant from engaging in similar conduct for the period of the ban and secondly, it acts as a general deterrent to all football spectators, warning them of the likely outcome of behaving in this way. They also have the potential to extend significantly the number of incidents that can be classed as football-related. For example, fights in pubs where regulated football matches are being shown on television would now appear to be football-related and a FBO could be imposed on a defendant to deter others from engaging in similar incidents of disorder. Although not what was originally intended by the legislation, it captures the kinds of disorder that the police are keen to control in connection with football matches.

10.6.2 Football Spectators Act 1989 s.14B – Football Banning Orders on complaint

Under s.14B FSA 1989 a Chief Officer of Police or the Director of Public Prosecutions can apply for a FBO to be imposed on a person without the need to secure a conviction for a football-related offence against them. Where it can be proved that a spectator has at any time caused or contributed to any violence or disorder, whether in the United Kingdom or elsewhere, and the court is satisfied that there are reasonable grounds for believing that making an FBO would help to prevent violence or disorder at or in connection with any regulated football matches, the spectator *must* be made the subject of an order.

▶ *Gough v Chief Constable of Derbyshire [2002] EWCA Civ 351*

Where the subject of an FBO under s.14B appealed against its imposition on the basis that he had never been proved to have engaged in football-related disorder, the Court of Appeal justified the imposition of the order on the basis that FBOs are preventive, not punitive; therefore, there is no need to prove that the conduct has occurred, just that the order will prevent it from occurring in the future. As this is a civil application under s.14B FSA 1989, hearings are not subject to the normal rules of evidence or procedural safeguards required of a criminal trial. Although it was stated that a court should be satisfied to a standard approaching the criminal standard of beyond reasonable doubt before imposing an FBO, much of the evidence submitted is not of a sufficient quality to go before a criminal court. Thus spectators who have never been convicted of a football-related offence can be banned from attending football matches for a similar length of time to those who are guilty of a relevant offence.

Where a spectator is thought to be a member of a 'risk' group, or involved with football-related disorder, their conduct will be monitored by police spotters with a view to compiling a 'profile' of their disorderly conduct. This will include any evidence collected during a s.60 Criminal Justice and Public Order Act 1994 stop and search, evidence that they have been directed to disperse under s.27 Violence Crime Reduction Act 2006, video evidence filmed at games and eyewitness accounts that the spectator has associated with others known to engage in football-related disorder.

The adding together of all these seemingly trivial pieces of evidence means that an FBO can be imposed on a person who has not been proved to have been involved in any criminal activity but is only suspected of being a hooligan. Evidence of having caused or contributed to any violence or disorder can be provided by producing a person's previous football-related convictions, or any non-football-related convictions for violence or disorder, or on the basis of their police profile, even where they have not been convicted of any relevant offence themselves. Thus, even though there may not be sufficient evidence to secure a conviction against a spectator, they can still be the subject of a FBO for a period of three to five years, following a successful application under s.14B. The use of this controversial provision is being challenged more frequently by respondents to s.14B applications, and as a result the law is slowly being clarified. In particular, the use of a higher standard of proof approaching that of the criminal standard, instead of the normal civil standard of proof on the balance of probabilities, and better-quality evidence are now being demanded by courts rather than FBOs being issued as a matter of course (below, Hot Topic).

10.6.3 The effect of being subject to a Football Banning Order

All FBOs, whether imposed under ss.14A or 14B, contain a series of relatively standard conditions in an attempt to prevent those to whom they apply from being involved in future incidents of football-related disorder. Firstly, each FBO will ban its subject from entering every regulated football ground in the UK. This will include an exclusion zone around the banned person's home football ground on match days and may also involve a ban from going to specific pubs where fans congregate before a match.

Secondly, it will ban the subject from travelling abroad when England and Wales are playing matches away from home. Thirdly, it will ban the subject from travelling when either the FIFA World Cup Finals or UEFA European Nations Cup Finals are taking place. Fourthly, a travel ban will be imposed on the subject if their team is playing away from home in an international club competition. Furthermore, if any English club team is playing against a team or in a country that is considered to be high-risk in terms of the potential for crowd disorder, then everyone who is subject to an FBO will be banned from travelling regardless of their club allegiance.

Under s.14C FSA 1989, the various travel bans are in place from five days before the game until the end of the relevant match or, where an international finals tournament is taking place, from a minimum of ten days before the date of the first game until the end of the final match. To ensure that the ban is enforceable, the subject must surrender their passport to a named police station five days before the game or ten days before tournament begins.

Finally, under s.14J FSA 1989, the breach of any of the conditions contained in a FBO is an offence. Where a person is found guilty of breaching the conditions of an FBO, the offence is a relevant offence for the purposes of s.14A, enabling the court to impose a new FBO on them. Following the decision in *Gough*, FBOs containing these conditions are not in any way punitive but are merely a means of protecting the public from football-related disorder.

Hot topic ... The legal and evidential problems associated with pursuing Football Banning Orders on complaint

The imposition of Football Banning Orders under s.14B Football Spectators Act 1989 remains one of the most controversial aspects of the regulation of football fans and the disorder presumed to be associated with them. In particular, there are concerns over the ways that evidence is collected in order to make applications under s.14B, that s.14B is being used instead of prosecuting known football hooligans, that there is ongoing confusion over the applicable standard of proof and questions about the legality of the entire process persist.

The evidence presented to the court to demonstrate that the respondent is a 'risk supporter' is often collected through the misuse of police powers and is of little probative value. For example, the stop-and-search powers under s.60 Criminal Justice and Public Order Act 1994 are supposed to be used to search for weapons or to determine whether or not the stopped person is about to engage in a specific incident of serious disorder which the police are trying to prevent; they are not

supposed to be used to collect information about spectators on the off chance that they might at some indeterminate point in the future be engaged in a random act of spontaneous football-related disorder. Further, s.27 Violent Crime Reduction Act 2006 requires an individual risk assessment to be carried out on each individual; it should not be used to disperse a pub full of boisterous football fans. And in neither case is the fact that a person has been stopped and searched or directed to leave an area proof that they are involved in football-related disorder.

The ease and speed with which s.14B applications can be made appear to have contributed to the drop in the number of prosecutions for football-related disorder in recent years. Not only is it a quicker procedure, it is cheaper for the police to apply for an FBO under s.14B than it is to prosecute for an offence and then make a request under s.14A, leading to some known hooligans receiving a three-year FBO instead of being found guilty of a football-related offence.

There is also ongoing concern that all parties involved in s.14B applications, including both the police and judiciary, are unsure of the appropriate standard of proof required to determine whether or not an FBO should be imposed. As a civil order, it should technically be decided on the balance of probabilities; however, in Gough it was held that because FBOs impose serious restraints on the freedoms usually enjoyed by citizens, a standard approaching that used in criminal cases, proof of the need for imposing an FBO beyond reasonable doubt, should be used. This alternative standard, part way between the civil and criminal, is widely misunderstood by judges and can lead to FBOs being imposed where there is insufficient evidence to justify banning the spectator.

In Gough, the spectators who were the subject of FBOs also claimed that the procedure used was unlawful as it constituted the imposition of a punishment when it had not been proven that they had committed a crime, contrary to Art.7 European Convention on

Human Rights and Fundamental Freedoms. The Court of Appeal neatly sidestepped this argument by stating that FBOs are preventive, not punitive, in their nature because their aim is to protect society from football-related disorder, not to punish the subject of the order. The jurisprudence of the European Court of Human Rights has regularly stated that the effect of the order, not its form, is the key to determining whether or not it is a punishment. To ban a person from watching live football for between three and five years and to prevent them from travelling abroad for, in some years, up to three months of the year certainly has the appearance of a punishment and has yet to be explored fully by the appellate courts (R v Hughes). The impression given is that FBOs are generic punishments imposed on suspected football hooligans rather than being specifically targeted at known troublemakers.

The s.14B procedure can subvert the normal criminal process. Instead of collecting evidence on suspected football hooligans with a view to prosecuting them, the current tactic appears to be to collect only enough evidence to secure an FBO against them. The current approach to imposing FBOs is not sufficiently robust and successful challenges will increase as more spectators become aware of the problems inherent with the current scheme.

Summary

10.1 Violence and disorder have been occurring at sports fixtures for many years. It is important to distinguish the causes of disorder from issues affecting spectator safety, a distinction not clearly made by either the government or the football authorities.

10.2 Despite government concerns about the increasing number of violent incidents occurring at football matches, both in the UK and when some English fans travelled overseas, very few steps were taken to control spectator conduct. The four reports that were published between 1967 and 1984 did little more than identify that hooliganism had become a problem; the only legislative response was to control the consumption of alcohol at football matches in Scotland (ss.68–77 Criminal Justice (Scotland) Act 1980).

10.3 The fatalities at St Andrew's and Heysel resulted in a piecemeal rather than a coordinated legislative response to football-related disorder. The use of CCTV became a commonplace surveillance tool, the Sporting Events (Control of Alcohol) Act 1985 regulated the consumption of alcohol at football matches in England and Wales and the police were granted increased powers of stop and search by s.60 Criminal Justice and Public Order Act 1994. Further proposals made in the Popplewell Reports were amended, developed or dropped post-Hillsborough.

10.4 As part of its review of all aspects of crowd management, the Taylor Reports recommended a number of new criminal offences. The Football (Offences) Act 1991 criminalises throwing missiles, indecent and racial chanting and running on to a football pitch without lawful authority; ticket touting was made an offence under s.166 Criminal Justice and Public Order Act 1994, and the comparatively ineffective Exclusion Orders were replaced by the much more stringent Football Banning Orders. The proposed National Membership Scheme was dropped as being technologically unworkable at the time and likely to cause more disorder than it would prevent.

10.5 The Public Order Act 1986 can be used to prosecute most disorderly conduct that occurs at all sports fixtures. The police most frequently resort to charges under ss.4, 4A and 5 as it is relatively easy to identify someone who has been harassed, alarmed or distressed by the disorderly conduct. The Offences Against the Person Act 1861 and the Criminal Damage Act 1971 are used to control the more extreme cases of disorder. There is evidence of a growing use of s.27 Violent Crime Reduction Act 2006 as a means of preventing groups of spectators from attending games. In Scotland, the Offensive Behaviour at Football and Threatening Communications (Scotland) Act 2012 has been introduced to regulate offensive and sectarian abuse.

Summary cont'd

10.6 Football Banning Orders, whether imposed on conviction under s.14A Football Spectators Act 1989 or on complaint under s.14B, are now a standard response to football-related disorder. They constitute severe restrictions on the subject's freedom of movement and in particular, their ability to attend or be in the neighbourhood of designated football stadiums on match days. Despite claims of their effectiveness as a control mechanism, over a thousand new orders are issued each year, demonstrating that the police are yet to reach the root cause of the problem.

Further reading

Greenfield and Osborn, *Regulating Football* (2001, Pluto Press)

Herring, *Criminal Law: text, cases and materials* (5th edn, 2012, Oxford University Press) chs 6 and 11

Pollard, Parpworth and Hughes, *Constitutional and Administrative Law: text and materials* (4th edn, 2007, Oxford University Press) ch 11

Deards, 'Human rights for football hooligans' (2002) 27(6) *Entertainment Law Review* 765

Goodall, 'Tackling sectarianism through the criminal law' (2011) 15(3) *Edinburgh Law Review* 423

Hamilton-Smith et al, 'An evaluation of Football Banning Orders in Scotland' (Scottish Government Social Research, 2011)

James and Pearson, 'Football Banning Orders: analysing their use in court' (2006) 70(6) *Journal of Criminal Law* 509

Pearson, 'Qualifying for Europe? The Legitimacy of Football Banning Orders 'on complaint' under the principle of proportionality' (2005) 3(1) Entertainment and Sports Law Journal, online

Pearson, 'Contextualising the Football (Disorder) Act: proportionality under the hammer' in Greenfield and Osborn (eds), *Readings in Law and Popular Culture* (2006, Routledge)

Pearson and James, 'The Legality and Effectiveness of Using Football Banning Orders in the Fight Against Racism and Violence at Sports Events' in Gardiner, Parrish and Siekmann (eds), *EU, Sport, Law and Policy* (2009, TMC Asser Press)

Tsoukala, *Football Hooliganism in Europe: Security and Civil Liberties in the Balance* (2009, Palgrave Macmillan).

Government Reports

Chester, *Report of the Committee on Football* (1968, HMSO)

Department of Environment Working Group, *Football Spectator Violence* (1984, HMSO)

Harrington, *Soccer Hooliganism: A Preliminary Report* (1968, John Wright and Sons: Bristol)

Lang, *Crowd Behaviour at Football Matches* (1969, HMSO)

Law Commission Working Paper No.82, *Offences Against Public Order* (1982, HMSO)

McElhone, *Report of the Working Group on Football Crowd Behaviour* (1977, Scottish Education Department, HMSO)

Popplewell J, *Committee of Inquiry into Crowd Safety and Control at Sports Grounds (Interim Report)*, Cmnd 9585 (1985, HMSO)

Popplewell J, *Committee of Inquiry into Crowd Safety and Control at Sports Grounds (Final Report)*, Cmnd 9710 (1986, HMSO)

Links to relevant websites can be found at www.palgrave.com/law/james2e

The commercialisation of sport

Chapter 11

Regulating sporting relationships in English law

Key terms

- **Direct discrimination** – conduct that treats a person less favourably on the grounds of their possessing a protected characteristic.
- **Indirect discrimination** – conduct that appears to be objectively neutral but has a disproportionate and adverse impact on a person because of their possessing a protected characteristic.
- **Restraint of trade** – conduct that restrains a person from earning a living, is unreasonable as between the parties involved and is not in the public interest.

11.1 The changing nature of sporting relationships

Since the more formal organisation of sport began in earnest during the second half of the nineteenth century, there has been a dramatic shift in the balance of power that exists among the players, the clubs and the governing bodies. The dominant position of the NGBs has been gradually eroded, first by the rising financial power of their more successful club members and more recently by the rise of 'player power'. The impact of challenges to the authority and practices of some NGBs has been seismic; for example, when the Rugby Football Union refused to sanction payments to players so that they could be compensated for having to take Saturday mornings off work to play, a group of northern clubs considered themselves to be successful and powerful enough not only to challenge the authority of the RFU but to break away from it altogether to form what is now the Rugby Football League (see further, chapter 2.2.2).

As sport has become more commercialised, many of the relationships that exist within it have had to be re-evaluated. Litigation has been a key driver of the clarification, amendment or abolition of various practices that had become entrenched in sporting relationships. Practices that were considered to be normal within sport, but would never be contemplated as lawful in other industries, have been challenged, usually to the benefit of the players. Despite these changes the courts have always employed a degree of pragmatism in their approach to sports cases; just because the practice is unusual does not automatically mean that it will be declared unlawful. If a legally satisfying justification for the existence of the practice can be provided then the courts have shown a willingness to take into consideration that sport is different and have applied a more pragmatic and sports-friendly interpretation of the law (*Manchester City FC v Royle* (below, 11.2.2) and *Eastham v Newcastle United FC* (below, 11.4.2.4)). However, without such a justification, the courts have always been prepared to declare that the restrictive practices operated by NGBs, clubs, promoters and agents are unlawful. Alongside these developments, many NGBs have tried to reclaim the good governance initiative through the creation of specialist tribunals. For example, the Premier League Managers' Arbitration Tribunal has heard a number of cases that would ordinarily have been heard before the Employment Tribunal (below, 11.3.5).

11.2 Identifying and interpreting sports contracts

In contrast to the informality of the relatively recent past, sports contracts are now almost always evidenced in writing and will generally have to make use of a standard form or contain certain standard clauses that will have been negotiated between representatives of the players, the clubs and the NGB. This basic standard form contract will include terms that are applicable to all players of that sport and which provide a minimum level of protection for all parties. It will also invariably include terms that require the player to conform to the rules of the NGB and ISF, particularly the disciplinary and anti-doping procedures (see further, chapter 2.2.1).

11.2.1 Identifying the existence of a contract

As the majority of the terms included in sports contracts are either imposed on the parties by the NGB or ISF or are negotiated by the parties or their representatives, there is little scope for examining the basics of contract law at this stage. The contract is formed by a series of offers and counter-offers that are eventually accepted by the parties and which are evidenced in a written contract that was clearly formed with the intention to create a legally binding relationship. In the past, several high-profile football managers have famously declared that they have never signed a contract and that they were simply working on the basis of a gentleman's agreement entered into between themselves and their chairman. Although they may never have signed a formal written agreement, a legally enforceable contract of employment would have been in place between them and their club. The existence of the contract would have been implied on the basis of the course of dealings that had occurred between the parties.

This level of informality is unlikely to be acceptable to either the NGB, who will often now require the contract of employment to be registered with it, or the players, coaches, managers or clubs seeking to protect themselves by entering into more formal contractual relationships. For example s.P(7) Premier League Handbook requires all Premier League managers' contracts to be evidenced in writing and registered with the League's Secretary. All such contracts must also invclude the series of standard terms and conditions that are set out in Appendix 8 of the Handbook. More generally, where there is a history of contracts being evidenced in writing, it will be almost impossible for a claimant to establish that a binding agreement has been entered into where there is no such physical evidence (*Sports Network Ltd v Calzaghe* [2009] EWHC 480 (QB)). This growing level of formality can result in highly complex contractual arrangements in certain circumstances.

▶ *Leeds Rugby Ltd v Harris and Bradford Bulls Holdings Ltd* **[2005] EWHC 1591 (QBD)**

The complexity of the contractual relationships entered into by a modern professional sportsperson can be seen in the multiple agreements entered into when Iestyn Harris moved from playing rugby league for Leeds Rhinos to rugby union for Cardiff Blues and Wales. To enable this move to take place, four interlocking agreements were entered into by Harris, Leeds, Cardiff and the Welsh Rugby Union (WRU). Firstly, Leeds and Harris entered into an agreement that released him from his existing playing contract with Leeds. This contract also contained an option which would enable Leeds to re-employ Harris, should he wish to return to playing rugby league in the future. Secondly, Cardiff agreed to employ Harris as a professional rugby union player for four years. This contract contained a clause enabling Harris to unilaterally terminate the agreement after three years. Thirdly a tripartite agreement between the WRU, Cardiff and Leeds contained the terms of the transfer fee to be paid to Leeds. Fourthly a contract between the WRU and Harris contained the terms on which Harris would play for Wales if selected.

A dispute arose when, after three years of playing rugby union for Cardiff, Harris terminated his playing contract with them and entered into an agreement to play rugby league for Bradford Bulls. Leeds claimed that Harris was contractually bound to play for them for one season on his return to rugby league whilst Harris claimed that the terms of any such agreement were an unlawful restraint of trade. The court held that all four of the original contracts had been entered into validly and that their terms were sufficiently clear to be enforced. The court also held that although the contract between Harris and Leeds was a restraint on his ability to choose which club to play for, it was neither unreasonable nor an unlawful restraint of trade (below, 11.4.2). Therefore, Harris was in breach of contract by entering into an agreement to play for Bradford and Leeds was compensated for its loss of Harris' services.

In *Harris,* the initial problem was in identifying which contracts were enforceable between the various parties. The court stated that the entire contractual framework had to be examined, not just individual terms of individual contracts and in doing so was able to provide additional context to the agreements. Once the validity of the agreements was confirmed the next step was to interpret the effect of the applicable terms. In *Harris,* this was a relatively straightforward matter as the terms were clearly drafted. In other cases, the courts have followed a sports-friendly interpretation of contractual terms.

11.2.2 Interpreting the terms of the contract

Most issues of interpretation occur on breach or termination of the contract. Specific challenges made to contractual terms or the rules of an NGB that are claimed to be in restraint of trade or operating in a discriminatory manner are discussed separately (below, 11.4 and 11.5 respectively). Breach of contract is where one of the parties does not comply with the terms by which they have agreed to be bound. Where one party is in breach, the other can treat the contract as at an end and sue for compensation that will put them into the same financial position that they would have been had the contract been successfully completed. In sports cases, the breach will usually be quite straightforward: either the club will have sacked one of its employees, or one of its employees will be seeking to leave to work for another club. The issues of interpretation will determine who breached the contract, at what time and how much compensation will need to be paid. The courts have allowed a degree of flexibility into their interpretation of sports contracts, enabling a certain amount of pragmatism and the customs and conventions of sports employment to contextualise the decision-making process.

> ▶ *Manchester City Football Club Plc v Royle* [2005] EWCA Civ 195

The parties were in dispute over the amount of compensation to be paid after the claimant club had sacked Royle from his role as first team manager. On 1 June 2000 the parties had agreed that Royle would act as manager of Manchester City FC for a period of four years. The contract included a term such that if the club terminated the agreement before its end on 31 May 2004 it would pay Royle compensation amounting to 12 months' salary if it were in the Premier League at the time, and six months' salary if it was in the First Division; the amounts would have been £750,000 and £150,000, respectively.

On 19 May 2001, following their last match of the season, Manchester City finished 18th in the Premier League and were relegated to the First Division. Following a meeting with the club's chairman on 21 May, Royle was sacked and his contract was terminated. Royle argued that he was entitled to compensation at the Premier League rate because, as of 21 May 2001, the club was still a shareholder-member of the Premier League. The club claimed that as it had been relegated on 19 May, it was no longer a Premier League team and compensation was payable at the lower First Division rate.

The Court of Appeal held that the test to be applied when interpreting the contract was that of the reasonable person with knowledge of football. As such, a person would assume that a football club had been relegated to the league below at the end of the final game of the season, not on the transfer of its shareholding in the league of which it had been a member, then the compensation payable on termination of Royle's contract was at the First Division rate.

This sports-friendly approach is appropriate for two reasons. Firstly, it takes account of the way that a football season actually operates: relegation takes place on the last day of the season after the final league standings have been calculated. As Manchester City had finished 18th, any reasonable person with knowledge of football would consider that they were relegated on 19 May, two days before Royle was sacked. Secondly, the interpretation put forward by the defendant would have rewarded him for failure during the 2000–01 season; he had overseen the club's relegation to the First Division and should therefore be compensated at the lower level. The realities of modern sport and the litigation to which it gives rise have been taken into consideration not only in the cases coming before the national courts but also before the specialist tribunals such as CAS.

> ▶ *Mutu v Chelsea Football Club Ltd* CAS 2008/A/1644

Following an appeal to determine the circumstances in which a club could terminate a player's contract of employment, CAS confirmed the findings of a series of hearings that had taken place before itself, FIFA's Dispute Resolution Chamber (DRC) and the Premier League's Appeals Committee. Firstly, it acknowledged that Mutu had breached his contract of employment with Chelsea by testing positive for cocaine following a targeted drugs test conducted by the Football Association. Secondly, it acknowledged that under English Law Chelsea was entitled to accept Mutu's conduct as a repudiatory breach of contract and that it was entitled to treat the contract as terminated with immediate effect. Thirdly, it found that the DRC had adopted the correct approach when calculating the amount of compensation due to Chelsea as a result of Mutu's breach of contract. This required the DRC to take into consideration the relevant principles of English law, Art.22 FIFA Regulations for the Status and Transfer of Players and the specificity of sport.

CAS explained that this approach was appropriate for this dispute because, according to the contract itself, English law was applicable to all disputes arising from it. Furthermore the Regulations for the Status and Transfer of Players were incorporated into that contract by a term that required all relevant rules of FIFA to be adhered to. Finally it was noted that the jurisprudence of both the DRC and CAS allowed the 'specificity of sport' to be taken into consideration. Thus, when providing its reasons for the resolution of a dispute, the interests of not only the parties involved but the whole football community had to be taken into account. By acknowledging the need to consider the specificity of sport, both the DRC and CAS were able to take account of the impact that the decision to award Chelsea in excess of €17m would have on football, the signs that it would send out to players and clubs alike about drug taking and the importance of following proper procedures when terminating a contract of employment.

Reliance on a sports-specific analysis of this kind is likely to occur more frequently in the future as parties try to convince the courts and specialist tribunals before which they are appearing that it is not just the applicable law that should be taken into consideration when determining the outcome of their dispute but also the customs and conventions of their sport.

11.3 Conduct interfering with the performance of a contract

Where a contract has been validly concluded, it is unlawful for any other person to procure its breach or to interfere with its performance. Where sporting relationships are concerned this will usually occur where a third party who is unconnected with the contract seeks to lure one of the parties to move from one employer to another (below, 11.3.1) or in some other way actively prevent them from fulfilling the terms of their contract (below, 11.3.2). Further, a potential conflict of interest can arise in a contractual relationship where one of the parties acts in two or more roles that can influence how the contract is performed (below, 11.3.3). This kind of problem now occurs much more rarely than in the past and is only likely to occur where an NGB has inadequate regulatory safeguards in place.

11.3.1 Breach of contract

Despite the inherent complexity of sports sponsorship agreements, what was at issue in *Force India Formula One Team Ltd v Etihad Airways PJSC and Aldar Properties PJSC* [2010] EWCA Civ 1051 was a relatively straightforward issue of breach of contract. The defendants had entered into a three-year sponsorship agreement with the Spyker Formula One team. The agreement included terms that Etihad's name would be integrated into the team name and that Etihad would be the sole airline associated with the team. The defendants had the option to terminate the agreement if the team found an alternative source of sponsorship and could also terminate by written notice if the team owners were to commit a material breach of the agreement that had not been remedied within 10 working days of notification by the defendants.

Around four months later, the team was sold to the claimant, one of whose backers was the owner of the Indian airline, Kingfisher Airways. The claimant sought, and had approved, a change in the name of the team and included the Kingfisher logo in its new livery during the winter testing period. A further three months later, the claimant proposed to the defendant a change in the sponsorship fees. At this stage, the defendants claimed to terminate the agreement on the basis that the claimant was in breach of contract by sourcing alternative sponsors, changing the team name and incorporating the logos of a competitor into its livery.

The Court of Appeal found that there had been an accumulation of repeated, or continuing, breaches of contract by the claimant that could be treated as repudiatory by the defendants. In particular, the Court considered that the claimant's changing of the team's name and its incorporation of the Kingfisher Airways logo was part of a deliberate and clearly defined marketing strategy designed to undermine the defendants' sponsorship of the team. As the defendants had at no time acquiesced in the claimant's breaches, they were entitled to accept the conduct as a repudiatory breach and a termination of the agreement under common law.

Sports cases can have an additional complicating factor where they are heard in the first instance before a governing body's arbitration or disciplinary tribunal. Any punishment handed down by the tribunal, and ultimately upheld by CAS, must not prevent the guilty party from being able to earn an income that might enable them to pay any compensation due. In the *Matuzalem* litigation (*FC Shaktar Donetsk v Matuzalem Francelino da Silva, Real Zaragoza SAD and FIFA* CAS 2008/A/1519 and 1520 and *Matuzalem Francelino da Silva v CAS* Swiss Federal Tribunal 4A_558/2011 27 March 2012, see further, Hot Topic 3), the player had unilaterally breached his contract with FC Shaktar Donetsk by leaving to play for Real Zaragoza. FIFA's Dispute Resolution Chamber found that this was a unilateral termination of the playing contract without just cause in breach of Art.17 of its Regulations and awarded Shaktar Donetsk €6.8m in compensation. On appeal, CAS upheld the DRC's decision but increased the compensation to €11.9m, payable jointly and severally by Matuzalem and Real Zaragoza. This decision was later affirmed by the Swiss Federal Tribunal.

Once it became apparent that neither player nor club could pay the award, Shaktar Donetsk requested that FIFA ban the player from all football-related activity until the sum had been paid in full. This request was granted by FIFA and upheld by CAS; however, this time the Swiss Federal Tribunal did not uphold CAS's decision. It held that a ban of unlimited duration was unlawful because it restricted the player's economic freedom excessively by preventing him from earning an income that would enable him to pay the outstanding amount of compensation. Thus, there was nothing wrong in requiring the player to pay the compensation, but it was unreasonable to ban him indefinitely as this would prevent him from ever being able to make good on the payment.

11.3.2 Procuring a breach of contract

The tort of procuring a breach of contract occurs when a third party, A, intentionally induces one of the parties to a contract, B, to break any of the terms of their contract with the other party, C (*Lumley v Gye* (1853) 118 ER 749). In order for C to be able to make a claim for damages against A, C must be able to prove that: B has breached their contract with C; A knew that their conduct was interfering with an existing contract between B and C in such a way as to cause its breach; and that A intended by their conduct to cause a breach of the contract between B and C (*OGB Ltd v Allan* [2007] UKHL 21).

The most common situation where the procurement of a breach of contract may occur is when a professional football club, A, causes a player, B, to move from their existing club, C, following an unauthorised approach to the player by club A. Although there is very little litigation on this point, particularly as the rules governing unauthorised approaches to contracted players are now much more strictly defined and enforced by the football authorities, there is no reason why the tort would not be committed if it could be proved that player B had breached their contract of employment with club C in order to move to new employment with club A (*Middlesbrough Football and Athletic Co (1986) Ltd v Liverpool Football and Athletic Grounds Plc* [2002] EWCA Civ 1929).

▶ *Greig v Insole; World Series Cricket Pty Ltd v Insole* **[1978] 1 WLR 302**

In early 1977, World Series Cricket (WSC) entered into contracts with 34 of the world's leading cricketers. Its aim was to organise a series of private test matches and one day games that would be played primarily at venues in Australia but with the option to stage events in other countries should the opportunity arise. The contracts were not exclusive and were designed to run alongside each of the players' existing obligations, not to replace them.

On 26 July, shortly after news of these privately organised matches had broken the International Cricket Council (ICC), the ISF for cricket, announced a change in its rules so that any player who took part in or made themselves available to take part in an unauthorised cricket match after 1 October 1977 would be disqualified from playing ICC sanctioned Test Matches. The ICC then passed a resolution declaring that all matches organised by WSC between 1 October 1977 and 31 March 1979 were unauthorised cricket matches. On 5 August, the Test and County Cricket Board (TCCB), the NGB for cricket in the UK, announced that it intended to implement the decision of the ICC, dependent on the outcome of the challenges brought by the claimants. The TCCB also stated its intention to ban any player who had been disqualified in these circumstances by the ICC from playing county cricket for a period of two years following the last day of the unauthorised game in which they had played or made themselves available to play in. WSC challenged these rule changes on the basis that they acted as an inducement to the contracted players to breach their contracts with WSC by forcing them to play only in 'officially sanctioned' cricket matches. A group of the players also made challenges alleging that the rules acted as a restraint of trade (below, 11.4.2).

The High Court held that the ICC's rule change and the changes proposed by the TCCB were inducements to the players to breach their contracts with WSC. The finding was based on the defendants' knowledge of the existence of the contracts between the players and WSC, the timing of the introduction of the rule changes and their retrospective impact on the players. Taken as a whole, the defendants' conduct was specifically designed to apply pressure to the contracted players to withdraw from their obligations to WSC. As they were unable to provide any justification for the rule changes, the defendants were inducing the players to breach their contracts.

The key issue here is not the rule changes themselves but the timing of them. If such a rule had been in place before WSC had entered into agreements with the players, then WSC would have been guilty of inducing a breach of contract, not the cricket authorities. Alternatively, if the rule changes had been designed to come into force once the 34 players' obligations were fulfilled, then that, too, would not have been inducing a breach of contract, though may now attract the attention of the Competition Commission. The problem was that the rule changes were specifically designed to induce the players to breach their contracts not to promote the better organisation or administration of the sport. The current, legally-defensible version of the rule ensures that players can only play in authorised competitions, such as the Indian Premier League, whilst those who play in unauthorised events may find themselves banned from playing in some authorised events.

11.3.3 Unlawful interference with the performance of a contract

The tort of unlawful interference is committed where D deliberately interferes with the performance of a contract between E and F by unlawful means and with the intent to cause harm to the commercial interests of either E or F by such interference. The difficulty for any claimant trying to establish that this tort has been committed is the need to prove D's intention at two separate stages: the intent to act unlawfully and the intent to cause harm to the claimant by the unlawful act. These difficulties were highlighted in *Watson and Bradford City Association Football Club (1983) Ltd v Gray and Huddersfield Town Association Football Club Ltd* [1998] The Times, 26 November (see further, chapter 4.4.3.2).

Alongside the claim of negligence brought by Watson, Bradford City claimed that by injuring their player, the defendants had unlawfully interfered with the performance of his playing contract. The basis of Bradford City's claim was that Gray had intentionally caused serious injury to Watson by fouling him. As both players were professionals, Gray would have known that Watson was playing under a contract of employment with Bradford City. Therefore, any injury intentionally caused to Watson by Gray must, of necessity, have been accompanied by an intention to interfere with Watson's ability to perform the obligations defined in his contract of employment with Bradford City. Although Bradford's claim was dismissed on the grounds that Gray had acted only negligently, it demonstrates that in the most exceptional of cases, where it can be proved that a player, D, deliberately injured an opponent, E, the tort may be capable of being established by E's employer, F. The benefits of succeeding in a claim of unlawful interference are potentially huge, including recouping the costs of paying and rehabilitating an injured player and recruiting a replacement for the period of their injury.

11.3.4 Conflicts of interest in the contractual relationship

The opportunity for conflicts of interest to arise is becoming increasingly rare as contractual arrangements become more formalised and NGBs' regulatory procedures become more stringent. The most important development has been to prevent one party to a contract from acting in two or more roles in relation to its performance. For example, in *Watson v Prager* [1991] 1 WLR 726, one of the arguments put forward by the claimant boxer for why their contract should be set aside was that the defendant was unable to represent him effectively as the defendant acted as both his manager and the promoter of his fights. In his role as manager, the defendant was contractually obliged to use his best endeavours to negotiate terms and conditions that were as favourable as possible for the claimant; however, when acting as the promoter of the claimant's fights, the defendant would be trying to maximise his own personal profit from the event. Conflicts of interest of this nature are inherently unreasonable, despite the disputed terms being sanctioned by the British Boxing Board of Control, and therefore, the contract was unenforceable.

In football, an analogous situation developed where agents would act for both sides to a transaction, for example, the player and the buying club. The conflict arises here because the agent will be attempting to negotiate the best possible deal for the client-player whilst trying to reduce the outlay of the client-club. Regulation C of the FA's Football Agents Regulations now specifically prevents dual representation of this kind.

11.3.5 Constructive dismissal

Where the conduct of an employer undermines the ability of an employee to carry out their job effectively, the employee may be able to claim that they have been constructively dismissed. The employee's claim will be successful if they can prove that the employer's behaviour amounted to a fundamental breach of contract such that in essence, they have been sacked by being unable to carry out the job that they had originally agreed to carry out.

▶ *Keegan v Newcastle United Football Club Ltd* **Premier League Manager's Arbitration Tribunal, 2 October 2009**

During negotiations between the parties concerning the appointment of the claimant as the defendant's first team manager, the claimant understood that he was to have the final say on all matters relating to the transfer of players into and out of the club. On the basis of this understanding, the claimant agreed to take up the post from 16 January 2008. On 31 August 2008, contrary to the express wishes of the claimant, the club signed Ignacio Gonzalez. Over the next few days, the club made a series of public statements reaffirming that the final say on all transfers was Keegan's and that he was in charge of first team matters. On 4 September, after the parties had failed to resolve the matter of who was in charge of player transfers, the claimant resigned.

In the course of evidence, the club's witnesses admitted that the signing had been made for 'commercial purposes' as a favour to two South American agents, not to improve the playing strength of the first team squad. Moreover they admitted that the public statements made at the beginning of September concerning Keegan having the final say on all transfers had been part of a public relations exercise designed to reassure the fans, not a truthful statement that they intended to be bound by. The panel found that having the final say on transfers was a duty usually associated with football managers unless the parties agreed specifically to the contrary and that therefore signing a player against the claimant's express wishes was a fundamental breach of contract. The claimant was therefore entitled to treat himself as having been constructively dismissed and could accept the club's repudiation of the contract.

Whereas Keegan's case was heard before the Premier League Manager's Arbitration Panel, James McBride took a similar case of constructive dismissal before the Employment Tribunal (*McBride v Falkirk Football and Athletic Club* [2011] UKEAT 0058_10_1706). McBride had been employed to run the club's under-19 team. Following a dispute with the first team coach, responsibility for determining tactics and team selection was transferred from him to the Director of the Youth Academy, leading to McBride resigning his post. By unilaterally removing responsibility for such a key element of the job to another employee, the Tribunal held that the club was in fundamental breach of an express term of McBride's employment contract without his consent, that this was causative of his resignation and that constructive dismissal was established.

11.4 Restraint of trade

The purpose of the doctrine of restraint of trade is to ensure that a person or an organisation is not restricted in their ability to earn a living or make a profit. There are three stages to establishing that the doctrine has been infringed: firstly, the claimant must be able to prove that they have been, as a matter of fact, restrained from earning money from their chosen profession; secondly, the defendant must demonstrate that any restraint affecting the claimant's ability to work is reasonable and proportionate as between them; thirdly, if the defendant fails at the second stage, the claimant must then satisfy the court that the restraint is not in the public interest in the way that it operates (*Nordenfelt v Maxim Nordenfelt Guns* [1894] AC 535). However, the mere fact that a restriction exists does not mean that a restraint of trade has occurred. Where the restraint of trade is necessary and proportionate for the proper administration of a sport and it is in the public interest, it will be lawful.

11.4.1 Restraints affecting clubs

The restraints of trade that are capable of affecting sporting clubs are usually the result of the impact of the rules or decisions that have been incorporated into the club's contract of membership with the relevant NGB or ISF (see further, chapter 2.3.3). Where no contractual relationship can be established, the club may be able to invoke the court's supervisory jurisdiction to pursue a challenge (*Enderby Town FC v Football Association* [1971] Ch 591) (see further, chapter 2.3.2). The club will usually be seeking an injunction to stop the NGB from operating a rule in a specific way, or a declaration that the rule should or should not be applied in a particular way, or compensation for the harm caused by the adverse effects of the rule restraining the club from maximising its profits. The courts have long held that where an NGB is exercising monopoly power in this manner, it is within their jurisdiction to see that it is not abused (*Nagle v Feilden* [1966] 2 QB 633) (below, 11.5.2 and in the EU context, chapter 12.5).

> ▶ *Newport Association Football Club Ltd v Football Association of Wales Ltd* (unreported) **High Court (ChD), 12 April 1995**
>
> In 1992, the Football Association of Wales (FAW) took steps to establish a professional football league in Wales. Until that time, the more successful of the Welsh professional and semi-professional football clubs had competed in the English league structure. Having failed in its attempts to encourage all professional teams based in Wales to join the new league, the FAW passed a resolution that prevented any Welsh club from playing games at its home ground if it chose to remain playing in the English leagues. The only clubs that were exempted from this ruling were those already playing in the Football League or Football Conference at the time: Cardiff City, Swansea City, Wrexham and Merthyr Tydfil.
>
> The effect of this resolution was that Newport County was forced to play its home games 50 miles away in Moreton-in-Marsh, Gloucestershire. The club challenged the resolution as being in restraint of trade because by forcing it to play 'home' games so far outside of its normal catchment area, it was unable to attract enough supporters to make its continued existence viable. At trial, the judge accepted that this reduction in income was in fact a restraint on the club's ability to maximise its takings from attendance at the game, in accordance with the first part of the test established in *Nordenfelt*. As the FAW was unable to

provide a satisfactory explanation for the necessity of the rule or prove that the restraint was a reasonable means of protecting its own legitimate interests when balanced against those of the club, a declaration was granted to the club that allowed it to continue playing in the English league structure and to play its home games in Newport.

Newport County wanted to remain in the English league structure because of the possibility of being promoted back to the Football League with the higher financial rewards that are on offer there when compared to those which are available in what is now the Welsh Premier League. The FAW hoped that by forcing the more established Welsh clubs to play in the new league, the standard of play and rewards on offer would improve significantly. However, the resolution passed by the FAW was a disproportionate means of trying to create a truly national professional league. Therefore, the interests of the club in trying to maximise its earnings potential was considered to be more in need of protection than the FAW's desire to create a new league. In order for such a claim to succeed, the affected club must ensure that it challenges the rules by which it is playing in a timely and appropriate manner.

▶ *Stevenage Borough Football Club Ltd v Football League Ltd* **(1997) 9 Admin LR 109**

Having won the Football Conference at the end of the 1995–96 football season, Stevenage Borough FC challenged the Football League's refusal to promote it to the Third Division. The club's argument was that the requirement that it must satisfy the League's criteria on stadium capacity by 31 December 1995, over four months before it knew whether or not it would finish top of the Football Conference, was an unreasonable restraint of trade. The basis for this claim was that the criteria required a small club of modest financial means to expend large amounts of money speculatively on ground improvements that would only be necessary should it win the Conference. As the required stadium improvements would, in fact, have been completed before the start of the 1996–97 Football League season, the club argued that it should be promoted despite not having met the original deadline of 31 December 1995.

At trial, the judge found that the Football League had failed to justify why the deadline for the completion of ground improvements should be set at so early a date in the season. However, regardless of whether this criterion was an unlawful restraint of trade, the judge refused to grant the declaration on the grounds of delay, a decision which was upheld in the Court of Appeal. Both courts highlighted that the club had been aware of the League's stadium criteria well before the start of the 1995–96 football season and that it had sought clarification on them on a number of occasions. As a result, it could not challenge the rules by which the competition had been run after it had finished; any challenge to the lawfulness of the rules should have been made at the start of the season, not after its completion.

Although the judgment of the Court of Appeal was reserved on whether the criteria were being operated in restraint of trade, and the trial judge's opinion is in reality obiter, it seems likely that Stevenage Borough were correct in their arguments as the League changed the date by which the criteria must be met for the following season to 30 April 1997. However, neither court was prepared to allow the club to change the rules that had governed the competition retrospectively following completion of the competition as this would undermine the proper administration of the League. If all competitors have adhered to the applicable rules all season, they cannot be altered for the benefit of one participant after the last game has been played. A more timely challenge could have seen Stevenage Borough succeed in having the criteria changed and its being promoted.

11.4.2 Restraints affecting players

The same test to establish a restraint of trade applies to contracts, rules and decisions that affect players, however, the variety of ways in which a sportsperson's ability to earn a living can be restricted is significantly wider. The internationalisation of elite sport has led to fewer cases being decided on the basis of restraint of trade as many of the practices that operate as restrictions will have a European element and are therefore more likely to be challenged as infringements of the freedoms of movement protected by Arts.45 and 56 TFEU (ex Arts.39 and 49 ECT) or as anti-competitive practices under Arts.101 and 102 TFEU (ex Arts.81 and 82 ECT) (see further, chapters 12.2–4). Specific restrictions on a sportsperson's ability to compete that are based on sex, gender, race and disability discrimination are also examined separately (below, 11.5). Despite these developments, the common law doctrine of restraint of trade not has only played an important role in the development of national sports law, it has the ability to continue to do so in the future.

11.4.2.1 Restraints imposed by contract

Where a player has specifically agreed to be bound by a restriction, it is likely to be held to be reasonable in the way that it operates as between the parties. In *Leeds v Harris* (above, 11.2.1), one of the interlocking agreements entered into by the parties to transfer Harris to Cardiff Blues provided Leeds with the option of requiring him to play for it for one year, should the player decide to return to playing rugby league. Harris claimed that the agreement was void for being a restraint of trade, however the court held that this was a valid and enforceable contract that he had breached by signing a contract to play for Bradford Bulls. Although the option exercisable by Leeds was a restriction as it prevented Harris from playing for the club of his choice for a year, it was reasonable and proportionate in the circumstances because he had voluntarily entered into it on the basis of legal advice and was to be paid an appropriate salary.

Similarly in *Araci v Fallon* [2011] EWCA Civ 668, the defendant had entered into an agreement with the claimant that he would ride his horse Native Khan when asked to do so for a period on one year. The agreement also contained a negative obligation not to ride any other horse in any race when he had been asked to ride Native Khan. In other words, Fallon had agreed to limit his racing options to Native Khan, or if he were to choose not to race that horse when asked to, then he would have to sit out the race. At the Epson Derby in 2011, Fallon was asked to ride Native Khan but declined to do so in favour of racing a different horse in the same race. On appeal, the claimant was granted an injunction to prevent Fallon from racing in the Derby for a clear breach of his negative obligation not to ride a rival horse when he had been asked to ride Native Khan. Jackson LJ held that granting the injunction was neither oppressive nor unjust as the defendant had voluntarily entered into a lucrative arrangement that prevented him from riding any horse other than Native Khan in this race. He added that Fallon had brought this predicament upon himself by his own deliberate and cynical disregard of the contractual relationship into which he had entered; the contract was valid, binding and not in restraint of trade.

It is particularly important to ensure that contracts affecting young athletes at the beginning of their careers do not impose unreasonable and disproportionate burdens or restraints on them. In *Proactive Sports Management Ltd v Rooney* [2011] EWCA Civ 1444, the claimant attempted to enforce the terms of an image-rights agency contract that it had entered into with a 17-year-old Wayne Rooney. The contract granted the claimant the right to market Rooney's image rights exclusively, worldwide, for a period of eight years, for a 20 per cent commission on earnings.

The Court of Appeal found the agreement to be an unlawful restraint of trade. Firstly, it held that although the exploitation of his image rights was ancillary to his primary income stream as a professional footballer, any unlawful restrictions on his related earnings would be a restraint of trade. Secondly, the restrictions contained within the agreement were unreasonable and oppressive. In particular, the agreement was not one that conformed to industry standards; there was an inequality of bargaining power when taking into account the youth and lack of business experience of the player and his parents; they were not advised to take independent advice before entering into the agreement; the eight-year term was well-beyond the industry norm, would represent perhaps half of Rooney's entire career and was without any right of early termination; and that although the 20 per cent commission might be reasonable for a young player at the start of his career, it was unreasonable to expect such a high rate to be paid for such an extensive period of time.

11.4.2.2 *Restraints imposed by a rule of the NGB*

Many of the employment restrictions imposed on professional athletes are justifiable as being necessary for the proper administration of a sport by its NGB. For example, many team sports have a final date by which transfers of players between sides must be completed, or specific dates during which such transfers can be made. This is to protect the integrity of a competition by promoting contractual stability throughout the playing season.

However, where the restriction has been implemented specifically to prevent a certain type of conduct, then the timing of its introduction is all important. In *Greig v Insole* (above, 11.3.2), the passing of a resolution that had retrospective effect was held to be an unlawful restraint of trade. Greig had entered into a contract to play in a series of cricket matches organised by World Series Cricket Pty Ltd (WSC). At the time that he did, there was nothing in the rules of either the International Cricket Council (ICC) or the Test and County Cricket Board (TCCB) to prevent him from playing for a potential rival like WSC, if only because the cricketing authorities had never contemplated that such an event could happen. Once the ICC and TCCB became aware of WSC's plans, they passed rules that would mean that any player who was contracted with WSC would be banned from playing international and county cricket for two years following the date of the end of the last unauthorised game in which they had played or for which they had made themselves available.

This rewriting of the eligibility rules was held to be an unlawful restraint of trade because it had been deliberately designed to prevent the players from playing in 'unauthorised' forms of cricket. If the rule had been in place before Greig had entered into a contract to play for WSC, then he would have been aware of the impact of his choice and would have been aware that he would be banned for acting in the way that he had. However, at the time that he signed with WSC, there were no such rules in place, and there was no such thing as an 'unauthorised' cricket match. The ICC and TCCB could only change their rules by giving adequate notice to the players who had signed with WSC that the eligibility criteria would change at some point in the future. The retrospective effect of the ban is what caused the restraint to be unlawful. Most NGBs and ISFs now include prohibitions in their rules that prevent players from playing for a rival organisation or in unauthorised competitions.

In *Johnston v Cliftonville Football and Athletic Club and Irish Football League Ltd*[1984] NI 9, the Irish Football League's (IFL) regulations provided for a maximum signing-on fee of £120, maximum weekly wages of £12 and bonuses of £12 for a win and £6 for a draw; these maxima were incorporated into the claimant's contract, as were all other relevant IFL regulations. The claimant challenged these maxima as a restraint on his freedom to negotiate the best possible terms of remuneration, with the defendants attempting to justify them as a necessary means of preventing the league's richer clubs from signing up all of the best players. The Court held that in the absence of any proof of the defendants' claims, the defendants were unable to establish that these restrictions on earnings capacity were reasonable and proportionate. The legality of modern salary caps will be dependent upon the engagement of the players, usually through their union, in negotiations of the earnings limits. If these are unilaterally imposed, they are less likely to be found lawful restraints.

11.4.2.3 Restraints imposed by suspension from competition

Perhaps the most high-profile restriction on a person's ability to play, and therefore earn a living from sport, is when they are banned or suspended from being able to compete by their NGB or ISF. Suspensions are usually imposed on players following a breach of the NGB's rules and include bans for taking performance-enhancing and/or recreational drugs, using violence, illegal techniques or equipment, match-fixing and bringing the game into disrepute.

In *Gasser v Stinson* (unreported) High Court (QBD), 15 June 1988, the claimant was an athlete who had been banned from competing for two years by the International Association of Athletics Federations (IAAF) following a positive test for a performance-enhancing substance. She challenged the legality of the ban by claiming that it was an unlawful restraint of trade as it would prevent her from having the opportunity to compete for reward as a professional runner. The High Court acknowledged that as a matter of fact, a ban of this nature could act as a restraint of trade; however, it held that the two-year suspension imposed on Gasser in this case was reasonable and proportionate in order to protect the integrity of the sport from those choosing to cheat. Provided that doping bans conform with the WADA Code, their duration will be considered by the courts and CAS to be reasonable and proportionate. Where match-fixing is concerned, significantly longer bans of up to life for a first offence have been held to be lawful to protect the integrity of the sport (see chapter 6.4 and Hot Topic 6).

Clubs must also ensure that they follow reasonable, proportionate and appropriate procedures when disciplining players. An extreme example, which would be decided in the same way in England but as constructive dismissal, occurred recently in Switzerland, *Barea v Neuchatel Xamax SA* Swiss Federal Tribunal 137 III 303, 28 June 2011. Football club captain Barea refused to follow the team coach's instructions about using the offside trap in a match. He was immediately substituted and from then on required to train with under-21 team. This was considered to be a wholly disproportionate response to one instance of disobedience. Thus, where the body imposing the ban or suspension can provide a justification for its necessity and it is proportionate in that it is no more than is necessary for the proper administration of the sport and/or the protection of its integrity, then there is no unlawful restraint of trade (see further, chapter 12.1 for the position in EU law).

11.4.2.4 Restraints imposed by the operation of the transfer system

The transfer system, particularly as it has been operated in professional football, is a unique sporting arrangement. Instead of being able to resign and move to a new employer, many professional athletes must effectively ask their employer's permission to resign, see out the remainder of their contract or wait to be sold on to a new club. There are no notice clauses in most sports contracts, though Art.15 of FIFA's Regulations on the Status and Transfer of Players allows a player to move for 'sporting just cause' where they have been picked to play in fewer than ten per cent of the club's matches for no good reason. Such a situation would be unthinkable in any other industry.

Although any restrictive practices emanating from the operation of the transfer system are now likely to engage EU law, especially after *Bosman* and its progeny (see further, 12.2.1), common law restraint of trade remains a live issue. The ongoing attempts of both FIFA and UEFA to reinforce the transfer system mean that it is important to understand how these organisations have reacted to being challenged in the past.

▶ *Eastham v Newcastle United Football Club Ltd, the Football League Ltd and the Football Association* **[1964] Ch 413**

Prior to this case, professional football's transfer system operated in a markedly different way to how it does today. When a player came to the end of a fixed-term contract with their employing club, the club had four options: (1) offer the player a new contract; (2) place the player on the transfer list; (3) place the player on the retained list; or (4) allow the player to leave on a free transfer. If option (2) were pursued, the employing club let it be known that the player was no longer wanted and could move (on payment of an appropriate fee) to a new club. If option (3) were pursued, the club had to pay the player a reasonable wage of at least the Football League minimum. The employing club did not have to pick the player to play, for it nor did it have to sell him. In effect, it could pay him to do nothing and prevent him from playing for any other professional club.

During the 1959–60 football season Eastham, a Newcastle United player, asked his club's permission to be transferred; Newcastle refused. For the 1960–61 season, he was retained for a further year on his previous salary but did not sign a new contract, choosing instead to work outside of football. From 1961, he was to be paid the Football League minimum wage and kept on the retained list by Newcastle, unable to play professional football for any other club. Eastham argued that, taken together, options (2) and (3) operated as an unlawful restraint of trade by preventing him from moving to a new employer of his choice after his fixed-term contract had come to an end.

The defendants argued that charging a transfer fee enabled clubs to recoup the money that they had expended on training and developing players during their time with them. Moreover, they argued that the fees helped to redistribute wealth within the game by trickling money down from the richer buying clubs to the poorer selling clubs. Finally, it was argued that transfer fees helped to reinforce the competitive balance within the League by preventing clubs from hoarding the best players.

> The court rejected these claims and held that the 'retain and transfer' system as operated was an unlawful restraint of trade. The 'retained' element was immediately declared void, enabling Eastham to complete his move to Arsenal for an undisclosed fee. However, the judge thought that the transfer system on its own was justifiable because a player could appeal to the League's Management Committee against his club requiring an unreasonably high transfer fee and because it facilitated the circulation of both players and money throughout the game. He concluded that there was a restraint but not one that was either unlawful or as serious as that found in the combined 'retain and transfer' system.

It is important to note that this dispute took place after the expiry of the claimant's contract. He was not able to 'run down' his contract as players now do, because the club was entitled to place him on the retained list and prevent him from playing elsewhere. Thus, despite technically not being employed by Newcastle, the club was still able to influence where he could work next, including preventing him from working as a professional footballer altogether.

The transfer system which operated in Belgium that gave rise to the *Bosman* case was at least as restrictive as the pre-*Eastham* English system (see further, 12.2.1). The new rules put in place by the FA after *Eastham* meant that it was unlikely that a similar challenge would have been made in England; if a player was offered the same money or more than he had been on previously, and he rejected it, he could only move clubs if a transfer fee were paid. However, if he were offered less than he had been previously earning he could leave on a free transfer. What remains to be seen is whether in-contract transfer fees are lawful, particularly in cases where a player is unable to move to a new employer because the amount charged by their current club is seen by others as excessive.

11.5 Discriminatory behaviour

Sport is riddled with what would be considered to be discriminatory practices in almost any other context. The vast majority of sports practice a form of sex discrimination by preventing men and women from playing alongside of, and competing against, one another. Where quotas restrict the number of foreign nationals that can play in the same team, there is the possibility of race discrimination on the grounds of nationality. And in some circumstances, equipment and medication that would enable disabled athletes to compete alongside those without disabilities are considered to be unfairly performance enhancing and are banned (*Pistorius v International Association of Athletics Federations* CAS 2008/A/1480) (below, 11.5.4). Yet, in sport, such discrimination not only is often tolerated but is so culturally entrenched as to receive statutory backing.

Discrimination in sport can occur for any number of reasons. It can be blatant, such as the ban on allowing women to train racehorses prior to *Nagle v Feilden* [1966] 2 QB 633 (below, 11.5.2.1); it can be misguided paternalism, as has been seen by the reluctance to allow women to box professionally (*Couch v British Boxing Board of Control* (unreported) Employment Appeal Tribunal, 31 March 1988) (below, 11.5.2.2); it can be protectionist, as is seen in the rules governing nationality quotas (see further, chapter 12.2.1); and it can be culturally driven, as are many of the explanations for why men and women should not compete against each other. However, in many cases, discrimination has been justified as being both in the best interests of the sport and of those who play sport. Conduct amounting to discrimination is unlawful when practised by employers against employees, by organisations such as NGBs that have the power to confer qualifications or authorisations on a person or to provide them with vocational training and by providers of sports facilities and services.

11.5.1 Equality Act 2010

The Equality Act 2010 (EA 2010) came into force on 1 October 2010, replacing and consolidating each of the previous individually focused Acts that regulated discriminatory behaviour in the UK. Although providing a new framework for tackling discrimination, extending the range of protected characteristics of the person being discriminated against and standardising the terms used, the EA 2010 does not change significantly the way that the law will apply to sport. Until there is new interpretative case law, it should be assumed that previously decided cases still represent how the new law will be applied in similar situations and will be used here as examples of what would still be unlawfully discriminatory conduct.

The aim of the Act is to ensure that people are treated equally and, in particular, to outlaw generalisations about a person's competence to perform an activity being based on their possessing one of the protected characteristics. These have been extended by s.4 EA 2010 so that discrimination on the grounds of one or more of the following is now unlawful: age, disability, gender reassignment, marriage and civil partnership, pregnancy and maternity, race (including colour, nationality and ethnicity), religion and belief and sex and sexual orientation. Direct discrimination is defined in s.13 EA 2010 so that A discriminates against B if, because of a protected characteristic, A treats B less favourably than A treats or would treat others. This simplified definition is unlikely to change how the law previously operated; for example, the complete ban on women acting as licensed racehorse trainers simply because they were women was direct sex discrimination (*Nagle v Feilden*).

Indirect discrimination is given a standard meaning that, although not extending its definition, is more fully explained:

▶ **Equality Act 2010 s.19 – indirect discrimination**

(1) A discriminates against B if A applies to B a provision, criterion or practice which is discriminatory in relation to a relevant protected characteristic of B's.

(2) A provision, criterion or practice is discriminatory in relation to a relevant protected characteristic of B's if—

  (a) A applies, or would apply, it to persons with whom B does not share the characteristic,

  (b) it puts, or would put, persons with whom B shares the characteristic at a particular disadvantage when compared with persons with whom B does not share it,

  (c) it puts, or would put, B at that disadvantage, and

  (d) A cannot show it to be a proportionate means of achieving a legitimate aim.

Thus, indirect discrimination is where the criterion applied is objectively neutral but has a disproportionate and adverse impact on a member of a protected class. For example, UEFA's 'home grown player' rule could be considered to be indirectly discriminatory as the applicable criteria are much more easily fulfilled by players born and raised in the same country as the employing club than those born and raised abroad, despite the rule being drafted in such a way as to make it appear to be capable of being fulfilled by any person regardless of nationality.

Finally, s.195 EA 2010 contains the exceptions for sport that were found previously in ss.44 Sex Discrimination Act 1975, s.19 Gender Recognition Act 2004 and s.39 Race Relations Act 1976:

▶ **Equality Act 2010 s.195 - sport**

(1) A person does not contravene this Act, so far as relating to sex, only by doing anything in relation to the participation of another as a competitor in a gender-affected activity.

(2) A person does not contravene section 29, 33, 34 or 35, so far as relating to gender reassignment, only by doing anything in relation to the participation of a transsexual person as a competitor in a gender-affected activity if it is necessary to do so to secure in relation to the activity—
  (a) fair competition, or
  (b) the safety of competitors.

(3) A gender-affected activity is a sport, game or other activity of a competitive nature in circumstances in which the physical strength, stamina or physique of average persons of one sex would put them at a disadvantage compared to average persons of the other sex as competitors in events involving the activity.

(4) In considering whether a sport, game or other activity is gender-affected in relation to children, it is appropriate to take account of the age and stage of development of children who are likely to be competitors.

(5) A person who does anything to which subsection (6) applies does not contravene this Act only because of the nationality or place of birth of another or because of the length of time the other has been resident in a particular area or place.

(6) This subsection applies to—
  (a) selecting one or more persons to represent a country, place or area or a related association, in a sport or game or other activity of a competitive nature;
  (b) doing anything in pursuance of the rules of a competition so far as relating to eligibility to compete in a sport or game or other such activity.

These provisions provide additional detail that was not in the previous legislation but does not appear to change how it would apply to sport in practise. Until challenges to the rules and practices of NGBs are brought under the new Act, the scope of all of these redefined provisions is unclear. Although it is likely that they will not result in significant changes to the way that sport is governed, the Act ensures that NGBs will from now be expected to justify why different groups of athletes are treated differently.

11.5.2 Sex discrimination

The EA 2010 explicitly covers several different aspects of discrimination that can be grouped under the broad heading of sex discrimination: sex, sexual orientation, gender reassignment, pregnancy and maternity.

11.5.2.1 Sex discrimination

Nagle v Feilden remains the clearest example of direct sex discrimination. The claimant was an experienced racehorse trainer who had applied to the Jockey Club for a trainer's licence on a number of occasions. The Club consistently refused to grant her a licence even though it had been prepared to license her male employees. The Court of Appeal held that the Club's policy of not granting a licence to a person on the grounds that the applicant was a woman was unlawful and should be amended. Discrimination of this kind would now be unlawful under s.53 EA 2010 as the Jockey Club was a body that had the power to confer an authorisation on a person and had refused to do so solely on the grounds of the applicant's sex.

Under what is now s.29 EA 2010, it is unlawful to discriminate against groups of users of facilities and services. In *James v Eastleigh Borough Council* [1990] ICR 554, the defendant charged retired people a lower amount to use its facilities than those who were not retired. At the time, the retirement age for women was 60 but for men was 65. The differential charging policy was found to be discriminatory as between the ages of 60 and 65, men and women were charged different amounts solely on the basis of their sex.

11.5.2.2 Gender reassignment

Where a person has been issued with a gender recognition certificate, they must be treated for all purposes as being of their acquired gender. This would appear to mean that once a certificate has been issued, the person should be able to participate in sport without their original gender being disclosed. However, where a sport is gender-affected, a transgendered-person can be discriminated against where it is necessary for the purposes of securing fair competition and/or the safety of other competitors according to s.195(2)EA 2010, where the physical strength, stamina or physique of average persons of one gender would put them at a disadvantage to average persons of the other gender as competitors in events involving the sport.

The legislature appears to be concerned that male-to-female transgendered persons will be at a competitive advantage when compared to non-transgendered female participants and that the transgendered person will pose a risk of physical harm to the non-transgendered person. As with sex discrimination, the problem here is with the generalist approach to legitimising discriminatory rules and conduct rather than requiring the individual circumstances of each participant to be addressed on a case-by-case basis. The lack of litigation on this point leaves open the question of whether or not this will cause problems for transgendered persons hoping to participate in competitive sports in the future.

11.5.2.3 Pregnancy

In a development new to English law, it is now specifically unlawful to treat a person differently on the basis of their being pregnant. Under similar legislation in Australia, the Federal Magistrates' Court held that it was unlawful to prevent a woman from competing in a netball tournament because she was pregnant (*Gardner v All Australia Netball Association Ltd* [2003] FMCA 81).The clearly paternalistic rule was introduced to protect pregnant women from either hurting themselves or their unborn child by playing sport. Provided that the known risks of competing, including competing whilst pregnant, were either obvious or made clear to the athletes, the decision on whether or not to run the risk is the woman's; it is not for others to make the decision on her behalf. As a result, a pregnant woman is free to compete until she is physically unable to justify her place on the team.

11.5.2.4 The Caster Semenya Affair

Following her victory in the 2009 World Athletics Championships 800m final, doubts were aired publically about whether Caster Semenya was genetically female for the purposes of competing in IAAF sanctioned women's athletics events. Following a protracted investigation where rumour and innuendo have cast aspersions on her gender on the basis of her looks, the make-up of her chromosomes and the visual presentation of her genitals, on 6 July 2010 the IAAF declared that she was able to compete as a women with immediate effect but that the medical details of the investigation would remain confidential. This case raises a number of important issues that have not yet been addressed by either the relevant ISFs or the courts, including why women need to have their gender verified but men do not. Perhaps the least satisfactory outcome is that a young woman's privacy has been violated in the most extreme and personal manner by this investigation and that its final outcome does little to explain why she is no longer 'suspected' of not being female.

11.5.2.5 Applying the sports exemption

Despite one of the aims of the EA 2010 being to abolish discrimination on the basis of generalisations about the competence of one sex's ability to perform specific tasks, s.195 provides an exemption for sport that has precisely this effect. The aim of s.195 is twofold: it is supposed to protect women from being injured by larger, stronger men and to preserve competitive balance within sport by shielding women from having to compete against men. The exemption means that, for example, in heavy contact sports like rugby, separate competitions for men and women can be organised so that the greater 'physical strength and physique' of the average man will not cause unnecessary injury to the average woman. Furthermore, it enables separate competitions to be held in athletics, for example, where the 'stronger and faster' average man will usually put them at a competitive advantage when competing against the average woman.

Section 195 introduces precisely the kind of generalisation about the attributes of men and women that EA 2010 is trying to make unlawful. Its effect is to legitimise stereotypical assumptions about men's and women's sporting attributes rather than basing conclusions about eligibility to compete on merit; unusually for sport, in this situation, it is not how good you are that counts. The exemption, and its forerunner s.44 Sex Discrimination Act 1975, has proved to be culturally expedient and at least for now it appears to reflect societal attitudes towards sports participation. For many disparate reasons, in general, men and women appear to be happy to compete in separate events and in separate competitions.

To reflect its unusual position, the exemption has been interpreted narrowly by the courts in an attempt to limit its impact. Firstly, the exemption only applies to the participants in a sporting competition. In *British Judo Association v Petty* [1981] ICR 660, Petty had been denied the opportunity to referee national standard judo bouts between men despite being qualified to do so. The British Judo Association (BJA) justified its refusal on the grounds that women in general, rather than Petty in particular, did not have the necessary physical or vocal strength to be able to referee men's bouts. As the BJA did not provide any objective justification capable of demonstrating why a referee would need these attributes, it was held to have acted in a discriminatory manner. Further, the Employment Appeal Tribunal held that the BJA was unable to rely on the exemption as it only applied to competitors in a sporting event not to the match officials, as this latter group should not need to become physically involved with the participants during the course of a bout.

Secondly, the exemption only applies to prevent mixed-sex competitions, not those that involve members of only one sex. In *Couch v British Boxing Board of Control*, the claimant challenged the BBBC's decision not to award her a licence to box professionally in the UK. The BBBC claimed, amongst other things, that it was unsafe for women to box because their weight varies during the course of their menstrual cycle, making it impossible to determine which weight category they should fight in, and because women are accident prone and emotionally unstable when experiencing pre-menstrual syndrome. The BBBC also claimed that boxing was an unsuitable sport for women to compete in because of the lack of strength, stamina and physical stature of the average woman. The Tribunal held that as there was no evidence that Couch suffered from any of the medical conditions identified as problematic by the BBBC, there was no objective justification for denying her a licence to box professionally, and therefore the Board of Control had acted unlawfully. Furthermore, the Tribunal stated that the exemption only applies to prevent men and women from competing against one another, and as Couch only sought a licence to fight other women, she was not at a competitive disadvantage when compared to her prospective opponents.

Finally, there must be actual evidence of the participant being at a competitive disadvantage, not just an assumption that they are. In *Thompson v Professional Pool Players' Organisation* (unreported) Employment Appeal Tribunal, 11 March 1992, the PPPO was found to have acted unlawfully by repeatedly refusing to grant Thompson professional status. An argument that she was at a competitive disadvantage because of her stature when compared to male players was dismissed on the basis of her repeated victories against men in open competitions.

11.5.3 Race discrimination

It is unlawful to discriminate against a person on the grounds of their race, colour, nationality, ethnicity, religion or beliefs. As with other forms of discrimination, race discrimination can be committed either directly or indirectly. Direct discrimination in sport will often take the form of harassment of the affected person, whilst indirect discrimination, which will be much more difficult to prove, may be found in the rules of the NGB.

11.5.3.1 Discriminatory practices

Race discrimination in sport usually occurs by means of either harassment or victimisation, ss.26 and 27 EA 2010 respectively, both of which are generally applicable to all protected characteristics. Harassment is where the purpose or effect of the conduct is to violate the claimant's dignity or where an intimidating, hostile, degrading, humiliating or offensive environment has been created, s.27(1). Victimisation encompasses discriminatory treatment arising out of making use of the Act to challenge the behaviour of the discriminator, s.27(2). For example, in *Leeds Rhinos Rugby Club Ltd, Lance, Howes and Hetherington v Stirling* EAT 267/01, the Tribunal found that Stirling had been victimised by his club because it had failed to investigate properly his claims that racism had been a factor in the coach's decision not to select him for the first team. In *McCammon v Gillingham Football Club* ET/1100815/2011, the claimant succeeded with a claim of victimisation as his dismissal letter specifically stated that one of the reasons for his sacking was for making a 'protected allegation'; in this instance, that he had been treated differently to other players because of his colour.

A claim of harassment would now be possible in *Hussaney v Chester City Football Club and Ratcliffe* EAT 203/98, where the Tribunal found that a football manager had called a young player a 'black cunt' whilst he was out of the room. The alternative claim that Hussaney had been victimised by the club when it had failed to offer him a professional playing contract was not established on the facts as it was objectively justifiable on the evidence of the coaching staff that he was not good enough to play professional football.

11.5.3.2 Applying the sports exemption

A specific, limited exemption has been granted to sport to enable the proper administration of representative fixtures to take place. The exemption granted by s.195(6) serves two specific and distinct purposes. Firstly, it ensures that genuinely representative sports teams are not acting in a discriminatory fashion when applying their eligibility criteria. To insist that a person was born in a specific county, region or country is not race discrimination when the purpose is to pick a team to represent that county, region or country. Secondly, it enables an NGB to organise competitions to establish who the best player from a particular area is in a particular sport. For example, it is not race discrimination to insist that only British players take part in a British Championships where the purpose of the competition is to find the best British player. Outside of these two limited situations, discrimination on the basis of race is unlawful.

11.5.4 Disability discrimination

The EA 2010 builds on the protections first introduced to English law by the Disability Discrimination Act 1995. Section 15 EA 2010 defines disability discrimination as where a person A treats B unfavourably because of something arsing as a consequence of B's disability and A cannot show that the differential treatment is a proportionate means of achieving a legitimate aim. There is no explanation of what might constitute a 'legitimate aim', but it would appear to enable sports to prevent disabled athletes from competing against their able-bodied contemporaries in some circumstances. The justification for this would presumably be that disabled athletes need protecting from the physicality of their able-bodied opponents, or alternatively on the grounds put forward in *Pistorius*, that the aids used by disabled athletes to enable them to compete give them a competitive advantage over their able-bodied opponents. In both cases, however, NGBs should be put on alert that they will need to be able to prove that their rules are necessary, reasonable and proportionate when excluding groups of athletes from a competition on the grounds of disability; it should not be assumed automatically that to do so is lawful in all situations.

▶ *Pistorius v International Association of Athletics Federations* **CAS 2008/A/1480**

The applicant, a double amputee, sought to overturn the IAAF's decision to ban him from using 'Cheetah Flex-Foot' prosthetic limbs when competing against able-bodied athletes; there was no dispute that he could use them in Paralympic competitions. One of his grounds of challenge was that it was discriminatory of the IAAF to prevent him from using these prosthetics as without them he could not compete to the best of his ability against athletes who were not disabled. The IAAF argued that the prosthetics gave the user a mechanical and metabolic advantage over runners who were not using them, thereby giving Pistorius an unfair competitive advantage. CAS held that the scientific evidence relied on by the IAAF did not prove to the panel's comfortable satisfaction that the prosthetics provided Pistorius with the claimed advantage; therefore, there was no objective justification for the ban. In overturning the ban and allowing Pistorius to compete using these prosthetic limbs, CAS made clear that its decision related only to Pistorius and only to this particular design of prosthetic limb; any future developments in prosthetic technology would have to be re-tested to ensure that they did not provide the user with an unfair competitive advantage.

This line of reasoning is likely to be followed by the English Courts in their interpretation of what is a proportionate means of achieving a legitimate aim when making, or refusing to make, allowances for disabled athletes.

A failure to comply with a duty to make reasonable adjustments for a disabled person can also result in a finding of discrimination under ss.4A and 21 DDA 1995. An NGB does not have to take all steps necessary to enable a disabled person to compete in their competitions but if reasonable adjustments can be made it is discriminatory not to make them. For example in *PGA Tour Inc v Martin* 532 US 661 (2001) the Supreme Court of the United States held that it was reasonable to allow a disabled golfer to use a golf cart to enable him to play competitive golf at a professional level. The rules of the PGA Tour did not allow the use of golf carts as it considered that it was an integral part of the game of golf that the player be able to walk unaided around the course. Martin argued that as a result of his suffering from a degenerative circulatory disorder that obstructed the flow of blood from his right leg to his heart, he could only play golf at a professional standard if he were able to use a golf cart to transport him around the course. The Supreme Court agreed with Martin that as there was nothing in the Rules of Golf that required a player to walk the course as opposed to be transported around it in a cart, such a proposal was a reasonable adjustment that would enable him to compete as a professional golfer alongside able-bodied players as required by the Americans with Disabilities Act 1990. Again, a similar result would be likely under English law.

11.5.5 Age discrimination

Another new addition to the list of protected characteristics is age, meaning that a person should not be prohibited from engaging in an activity on the basis of either their youth or advanced years. However, s.13(2) states that a person does not discriminate against another where the potentially unlawful treatment is a proportionate means of achieving a legitimate aim. As with disability discrimination, there is no explanation of what might be a legitimate aim; however, where sport is concerned there are two potential justifications. At one end of the age spectrum, it would appear to protect junior age-group sport, enabling players of different ages (and as is currently presumed, size, strength, stamina, physique, skill and experience) to play against each other until they are more evenly and safely matched at adult/open levels of the sport. Further, it could also provide a justification for age-group competitions for older athletes in order to protect them from more physical younger opponents and to level the playing field in terms of athleticism.

11.6 The 'Football Creditors' Rule'

The case of *Re Portsmouth City Football Club (In Administration)* [2010] EWHC 2013 brought into sharp focus one of the more unusual rules that affects the creditors of an insolvent football club. Portsmouth had invested heavily in players and their wages in the four years up to 2010 but had failed to collect all of the relevant PAYE income tax, National Insurance and VAT payments due to Her Majesty's Revenue and Customs (HMRC). HMRC petitioned to wind up the club as these debts amounted to at least £24.5m, with a further £13.2m in dispute. Portsmouth went into administration in order to pay off some of its debts and avoid being wound up.

According to Rules E.25-45 Premier League Handbook, a club can only exit from administration by means of a Company Voluntary Arrangement (CVA). In order for the CVA to be approved by the Premier League, all 'football creditors' must be paid in full with non-football creditors having to accept only partial payment of the debts owed to them; similar rules are in place in other British football leagues. The rule effectively grants football creditors secured creditor status. The aim of the rule is to ensure that a club cannot continue to play in a competition when it owes to others in the same competition debts that it cannot repay as this would have the effect of putting the debtor club at a financial and competitive advantage over its football creditors.

Under Rule E.32, football creditors are defined as: other football clubs, the Premier League and related companies, any pension or life assurance scheme administered by or on behalf of the Premier League, the Football League and its related companies and the Football Foundation. If a club fails to pay these football creditors in full, it is expelled from the League. As a result of Portsmouth's administrators negotiating an approved CVA, all football creditors were paid in full from monies owed to the club by the Premier League as a result of broadcasting contracts entered into by the League, whilst all non-football creditors, including in particular HMRC, were to be paid 20p in the pound, or around £5m of the £24.5m acknowledged to be owed to it.

HMRC brought an action to have the CVA entered into by Portsmouth revoked on the basis that it was unfairly prejudiced by the football creditors rule. HMRC wanted the monies paid to the football creditors by the Premier League spread evenly amongst all of the creditors so that each would have had an equal share of the available assets. HMRC's application was refused by the court. Unless the court is satisfied that a better compromise agreement was available to the parties, then the only alternative is for it is to compare the CVA agreed by the creditors with there being no agreement at all. As no alternative had been proposed and agreed by the creditors, the only option with which the CVA could be compared was the liquidation of the football club. If this occurred, all contracts of employment would be cancelled and all creditors would have received 0.4p for every pound owed; i.e. HMRC would have received only £100,000. As this was clearly of no benefit to any of the creditors, this option was not considered appropriate by the court. Thus, HMRC had to settle for being paid 20 per cent of the debt owed to it, whilst the football creditors were paid in full.

Following this defeat, HMRC challenged the legality of the Football League's version of the 'football creditors' rule' in *Revenue and Customs Commissioners v Football League Ltd and Football Association Premier League Ltd* [2012] EWHC 1372. HMRC argued that the football creditors' rule was an unlawful attempt to contract out of the Insolvency Act

1986 requirement that all unsecured creditors be paid on a *pro rata* basis; the *pari passu* rule. The court declined to grant the declarations sought by HMRC on a technicality based on the way in which the assets of a club are distributed and the timing of any payments made by the Football League, as opposed to the debtor club, to football creditors. Further, it was held that this was no more than the exercise of the clubs' right to refuse to compete against an insolvent club unless their communal debts were met in full. It should be noted, however, that despite this apparent victory, the final paragraph of Richards J's judgment states that the result of the case should not be regarded as an endorsement of the League's approach to football creditors, leaving further challenges likely in the future.

Since these cases, HMRC appears to have been pursuing the tax liabilities owed by football clubs more aggressively and challenging the terms of CVAs more proactively. To date, the most high-profile casualty of this approach has been the liquidation of Rangers Football Club in 2012. It was estimated that Rangers owed HMRC around £50m and as a result was unwilling to sanction the CVA that would have seen them receive a significantly reduced sum. Such a hard-line approach is likely to be seen more frequently in the future.

Hot topic ... A move towards genuinely 'open' competition?

Many of the practices most closely associated with the organisation of sporting competitions can be seen as being inherently discriminatory and potentially unlawful. In particular, administrative rules that require separate teams, sports and competitions for participants on the basis of their sex, age and disability are ubiquitous. The underlying justifications for these rules are varied and include paternalistic notions of safety and appropriateness (sex discrimination), facilitating youth development (age discrimination), protectionism through nationality quotas (race discrimination) and a combination of any of the above (disability discrimination).

Regardless of the original purpose for introducing the particular rule, these restrictions are being challenged successfully with increasing regularity. Whereas age discrimination can probably be justified on the basis of protecting youth sports and facilitating a developmental environment in which young players can learn the game and acquire the skills necessary to play a particular sport, it is not so easy to continue to justify the sex and disability discrimination that is inherent in many sports.

Following the decision in *Pistorius v IAAF*, it has been accepted that a blanket ban on the participation of disabled athletes in 'open' competitions is not justifiable. Even more importantly, *Pistorius* and *PGA Tour Inc v Martin* have demonstrated that the use of equipment that enables a disabled athlete to participate in an 'open' competition without providing them with an unfair competitive advantage is acceptable. Although it will not always be appropriate, or even possible, for all athletes to compete against each other on a level playing field, as is demonstrated by the many different categories of Paralympic competition, these decisions have paved the way for a degree of openness not previously seen.

Despite these legal developments, it is still extremely rare for men and women to compete against each other as equals, especially at the elite levels of sport. Paternalistic arguments that women need protecting from bigger, stronger, faster men prevail to justify why women need their own competitions instead of allowing skill and ability to determine the appropriate level of competition in which a specific athlete should compete. In what is a typical response for a governing body, the International Ski Federation, at its Council Meeting of 3 November 2012, rejected Lindsey Vonn's request to participate in the Lake Louise leg of the men's World Cup on the very simple basis that one gender is not entitled to participate in races of the other and that exceptions will not be made. This failure to provide an intellectually satisfying and objectively justified rationale for separate competitions that is not based on stereotypical generalisations is what is likely to lead governing bodies to be challenged further in the future. In this instance, as skiing is a non-contact sport, it is even more difficult to justify separate competitions for men and women, especially as not all male skiers are of the same physical stature, making it extremely difficult to prove that athlete is at a competitive disadvantage to another simply because they possess different physical attributes.

Although there is no great clamour for all events in all sports to be completely open, there is no reason why a successful challenge to the segregation of men's and women's sport could not be made by a high-profile female athlete. Success in sport is rarely predicated on 'strength, stamina an physique' alone, leaving open the possibility of a claim being made by a female athlete who wants to test her skills against the best participants in her sport, not only the best women, instead of being told that she cannot do so because she is not big or strong enough to compete on a level playing field or that she is simply not allowed to. What governing bodies need to be capable of doing in order to protect themselves from future litigation is to develop a justification for why separate competitions are needed instead of assuming that they are, without providing adequate reasons.

Summary

11.1 During the course of the last century, there has been a shift in the balance of power in professional sport from the NGBs to the clubs and players. To a large extent, this has been driven by the increasing commercialisation of sport and the desire of players to earn their 'fair share' from the games in which they play. The changes that have occurred to practices that had long been accepted as normal within sport have often been driven by the outcome of specific legal disputes or occasionally by the threat of legal action.

11.2 Most contracts affecting professional sporting relationships are now clearly identifiable and a written copy of the document will often have to be lodged with the appropriate NGB. Although some contractual relationships have become extremely complex, the courts and the specialist tribunals hearing these cases have been prepared to provide sport-friendly interpretations to the disputed clauses to ensure that they operate appropriately in the sporting context which they inhabit.

11.3 Breaches of contract can occur in respect of any sporting contract. Overt interference with the performance of a contract has become increasingly rare in sport as a result of the greater regulation of such conduct by NGBs and ISFs. Its most common occurrence is where one club seeks to entice a player to breach their current contract of employment in order to join it. The increased formality of contractual relationships which more clearly define both parties' obligations, and the better administration of these relationships by the governing bodies leaves fewer opportunities for unlawful approaches to be made.

11.4 Both clubs and players can be subjected to restraints of trade that prevent them from being able to maximise their income. Any such restraints are unlawful unless they can be justified as being necessary, reasonable, proportionate and in the public interest. Although historically this was an important cause of action for protecting clubs and players, most actions that are in restraint of trade are now likely to have a European aspect that will engage EU law.

11.5 Conduct that discriminates against a person on one of the protected grounds identified in the Equality Act 2010, and in particular on the grounds of sex, race, age or disability, is unlawful if practised by an employer, such as a club, or a body responsible for granting qualifications and authorisations, like an NGB. Some limited exemptions exist within the legislation to allow single-sex sports and representative teams to be lawful despite the inherent discrimination

Summary cont'd

involved in their eligibility criteria, however, there is considerable scope for challenging these rules, should a move to greater openness of competition be desired by the public as a whole, and elite athletes in particular.

11.6 The football creditors rule has been introduced to ensure that any club going into administration pays all of its football-related debts first in order that participants in the same competition are not financially disadvantaged by one of the teams owing others money. This leaves other creditors receiving only a fraction of the money owed to them, whereas football creditors are paid in full. HMRC doubts the legality of this rule and has begun to challenge CVAs that do not treat all creditors equally.

Further reading

Beloff et al, *Sports Law* (2nd edn, 2012, Hart) ch 4

Jones and Dugdale (eds), *Clerk & Lindsell on Torts* (20th edn, 2010, Sweet and Maxwell) chs 25 and 26

Furmston, *Cheshire, Fifoot and Furmston's Law of Contract* (16th edn, 2012, Oxford University Press) chs 6 and 18

Lewis and Taylor (eds), *Sport: Law and Practice* (2nd edn, 2008, Tottel) chs D1–3

Harding, *Living to Play* (2004, Robson Press)

Pannick, *Sex Discrimination in Sport* (1983, Equal Opportunities Commission)

Gretton, 'The laws of the game' (2012) 16(3) *Edinburgh Law Review* 414

McArdle, 'Can legislation stop me from playing? The distinction between sport competitors and sport workers under the United Kingdom's sex discrimination laws' (1999) 2(2) *Culture, Sport, Society* 44

McArdle, 'One hundred years of servitude: contractual conflict in English professional football before *Bosman*' [2000] 2 *Web Journal of Current Legal Issues*, online

McArdle, 'Just one of the challenges of 21st-century life: Oscar Pistorius in the Court of Arbitration for Sport' (2008) 5(2) *Script-ed*, online

McCormack, 'Football creditors – a game of two halves?' (2011) 24(7) *Insolvency Intelligence* 105

Wolbring, 'Oscar Pistorius and the future nature of Olympic, Paralympic and other sports' (2008) 5(1) *Script-ed*, online

Links to relevant websites can be found at www.palgrave.com/law/james2e

Engaging EU law through sporting relationships (12.1)
- Jurisdiction of European Court of Justice to hear disputes (12.1.1)
- The European Court of Justice's jurisdiction to hear sports disputes (12.1.2)

Treaty on the functioning of the European Union Art.45 (ex Art.39 ECT) – freedom of movement for workers (12.2)
- The *Bosman* decision (12.2.1)
- The impact of the *Bosman* decision (12.2.2)
  - Requiring a training compensation fee instead of a transfer fee (12.2.2.1)
  - Receiving compensation for breach of contract instead of a transfer fee (12.2.2.2)
  - Buy-out and player release clauses instead of transfer fees (12.2.2.3)
  - The juridification of football (12.2.2.4)
- Extending the reach of Art.45 TFEU (12.2.3)

Treaty on the functioning of the European Union Art.56 (ex Art.49 ECT) – freedom to provide services (12.3)
- The *Deliège* decision (12.3.1)
- The impact of *Deliège* on English law (12.3.2)

Regulating sporting relationships in EU law

Treaty on the functioning of the European Union Art.49 (ex Art.43 ECT) – freedom of establishment (12.4)

Treaty on the foundation of the European Union Arts.101 and 102 (ex Arts.81 and 82 ECT) – competition law (12.5)
- Undertakings, associations of undertakings and the 'dual role' of sports authorities (12.5.1)
- The 'dual role' of sporting rules (12.5.2)
- Conduct protected from the scope of EU law (12.5.3)
  - Anti-doping regimes and disciplinary bans (12.5.3.1)
  - Preventing multiple ownership of clubs in the same competition (12.5.3.2)
  - Rules of a purely sporting nature (12.5.3.3)
- Future developments (12.5.4)

Regulating sporting relationships in EU law

Key terms

- **Direct effect** – where provisions of EU law are clear, precise and unconditional enough to be justiciable, they can be relied on by individuals as the basis of their cause of action before national courts.
- **Training compensation fee** – the fee payable by the new employing club to all those involved in training a young footballer each time the player moves club before their 23rd birthday.
- **Transfer fee** – the fee payable by a new employer to facilitate the release of a player from their current contract of employment.

12.1 Engaging EU law through sporting relationships

Making use of the protections now enshrined in the Treaty on the Functioning of the European Union (TFEU) to resolve sports disputes is a relatively new phenomenon. This is most easily explained by the fact that until comparatively recently, most elite athletes would have played out their entire career in their home country. The internationalisation of the sports employment market has not only seen many athletes now expecting to spend at least part of their career playing abroad but has led employing clubs to consider that there are no geographical boundaries to the catchment area from which they can draw their players. Where once clubs would have recruited from the areas surrounding the towns and cities where they are based, they now draw talent not just from the whole of Europe but from all over the world. As a result, the employment rights of many elite sports performers will engage EU law even if the specific relationship itself does not breach it.

EU law is engaged whenever the conduct of at least one of the parties to a dispute infringes the directly effective provisions that affect a person's protected rights. In particular, this means that the fundamental freedoms of movement created to enable the operation of the single European market and the competition law provisions of the TFEU are applicable to sports disputes. The recently acquired competence to act in respect of sport, as defined by Arts.6 and 165 TFEU (see further, chapter 1.5.3) creates an as yet unexplored potential for further increases in the scope of the engagement of EU law with sports disputes.

The development of European sports law has been relatively slow, piecemeal and reactive as no EU institution had the specific competence to act on issues relating to sport. Thus the evolution of European sports law has to be traced through the jurisprudence of what is now the Court of Justice of the European Union (CJEU) and the decisions of the European Commission on the applicability of EU law to sport. As so few sports cases have been heard by the CJEU, a problem compounded by the increasing number of cases being brought before sports own tribunals and CAS, it has taken around 40 years for the Court to produce a workable explanation of when and why EU law is engaged by a sports dispute.

This slow pace of development has been affected by the attitudes of all concerned with sport towards what is often seen as the intrusion of EU law into their relationships with each other. In the same way that NGBs appeared to assume that national law either should not apply to them, or if it did then it should apply differently and on their terms, it also appeared that the ISFs, and many of the players over whom they exercised control, assumed that EU law did not apply to them either. As a result, practices that are clearly contrary to EU law became entrenched in sport. This problem was further compounded by an entirely erroneous belief that because some major ISFs were based outside of the EU (for example, in Switzerland), then EU law was not applicable to their conduct. Provided that the conduct of an undertaking has an impact on the rights protected by the TFEU, then EU law is engaged whenever it affects events on EU territory.

Sports disputes engage EU law most frequently where a restriction is placed on the freedom granted to workers to move to another member state in order to take up an offer of work under Art.45 (ex Art.39 ECT), or on their freedom to establish in another member state under Art.49 (ex Art.43 ECT), or on their freedom to provide services in another member state under Art.56 (ex Art.49 ECT), or where there has been a breach of the competition provisions in Arts.101 and 102 (ex Arts.81 and 82 ECT) by either the use of a restrictive practice or the abuse of a dominant position in a specific market. Following *Deutscher Handballbund eV v Kolpak* (Case C-438/00) [2003] ECR I-4135 and *Simutenkov v Ministerio de Educacion y Cultura* (Case C-265/03) [2005] ECR I-2579, rights similar to those protected by the TFEU can in certain circumstances be relied on by citizens of countries with which the EU has Association Agreements and Agreements on Partnership and Cooperation. This enabled Kolpak, a Slovakian national and professional handball player (prior to Slovakia's accession to the EU in 2004), and Simutenkov, a Russian national and professional footballer, to rely on the employment and non-discrimination protections contained in their home countries' Agreements with the EU and not be treated as 'foreign' players under their ISFs' nationality rules.

12.1.1　The European Court of Justice's jurisdiction to hear disputes – making a reference under Art.267 TFEU (ex Art.234 ECT)

The usual procedure for seeking a preliminary ruling on the interpretation of the TFEU will be by invoking the jurisdiction of the CJEU under Art.267. Where a national court considers that such an interpretation is necessary for it to be able to pass judgment on the case before it, the national court may submit specific questions to the CJEU requesting it to clarify the meaning of the appropriate issue of EU law; if the disputed interpretation arises before the final court of appeal in a member state, for example, the Supreme Court in the UK, then the court must make an Art.267 reference.

Three important procedural issues must be noted at this point. Firstly, it is the national court, not one or more of the parties to the dispute, which makes the Art.267 reference. Secondly, the national court must provide the full legal and factual context to the CJEU so that it is in a position to give the appropriate general guidance on how the Treaty should be interpreted. If insufficient information is provided, the Court may not be in a position to show that it was, in fact, necessary to make the interpretations requested of it. Thirdly, the CJEU does not act as an appellate court when references are made to it under Art.267; its purpose is to provide authoritative interpretations of the TFEU that can then be applied in all courts throughout the EU, not just in the case currently before it. Thus, having answered the questions put to it in its preliminary ruling, the CJEU will return the case to the national court for a final ruling according to the law of the member state from which the reference originated (*Van Gend en Loos v Nederlandse Administratie der Belastingen* (Case 26/62) [1963] ECR 1).

12.1.2 The European Court of Justice's jurisdiction to hear sports disputes

Once it has been established that EU law is engaged by the dispute, it is then necessary to determine whether sport is an appropriate context in which EU law should be enforced.

▶ *Walrave and Koch v Association Union Cycliste Internationale* (Case 36/74) [1974] ECR 1405

The claimants were employed as pacemakers for cyclists in competitions organised by the UCI. Each cyclist had their own individual pacemaker with whom they worked as a team and even at world championship events it was not uncommon for each team member to be of a different nationality; here the claimants were Dutch, yet they usually worked with Belgian or German cyclists. In 1970, the UCI announced that from 1973, all pacemakers must be of the same nationality as the cyclists with whom they worked. As this rule change would reduce the pool of cyclists with whom they could work and their ability to earn a living from their chosen profession, the claimants challenged its compatibility with Arts.18, 45 and 56 TFEU (ex Arts.6, 48 and 59 TEEC) by claiming that they were being discriminated against on the grounds of their nationality.

In response to the questions posed by the Utrecht District Court, the CJEU made a number of rulings concerning the applicability of EU law to sporting relationships. Firstly, it held that Arts.18, 45 and 56 apply to the rules of collective regulatory bodies such as ISFs where they regulate participants' employment rights and their ability to provide their services to others. As this rule affected their right to work for, or provide services to, elite cyclists it was a restriction on the claimants' ability to earn a living. Secondly, it held that sporting relationships are subject to EU law only where they constitute an 'economic activity'. As the two claimants were both professional pacemakers who were paid for their work, the rule change clearly affected an 'economic activity' with which they were engaged. Thirdly, the CJEU held that where the rules of an ISF were concerned only with matters of a 'purely sporting interest' then EU law did not apply, even where the rules affected a person's economic interests. The Court explained that as the rule concerned the composition of a national representative team competing in the World Championships and was therefore nothing to do with economic activity, the rule was not subject to EU law, provided that it was limited to achieving only its proper object. In this case, the proper objective was the organisation of international representative competitive cycling events and the rule was therefore lawful.

The difficulty inherent in *Walrave* is that it required a trial court to distinguish between rules that have economic effects and those that are for purely sporting purposes, when in reality most rules will fall into both categories. In the intervening years, sport has changed dramatically so that it is unlikely that the CJEU would today hold that international representative sport is 'nothing to do with economic activity' and therefore outside of the scope of EU law. The increased commercialisation and internationalisation of much elite sport will mean that almost every dispute involving a professional athlete will be an 'economic activity' that will, at least on the face of it, engage EU law. Thus, although a similar outcome would be reached today, it would be on modified grounds that would focus on an examination of whether the rule was inherent in the proper organisation of the sporting competition in question.

▶ *Meca-Medina and Majcen v Commission* (C-519/04 P) [2006] ECR I-6991

The applicants were professional swimmers who had been banned for two years by their ISF, FINA, after having tested positive for the banned substance nandrolone. In the first instance, they complained to the European Commission that the anti-doping regime operated by FINA and the IOC was anti-competitive contrary to Arts.101 and 102 TFEU (ex Arts.81 and 82 ECT). Following the Commission's rejection of their complaint, they applied to the GCEU for an annulment of its decision under Art.263 TFEU (ex Art.230 ECT); this was also rejected.

On appeal, the CJEU began by stating, in accordance with *Walrave* and the decisions following it, that sport is subject to EU law when it constitutes an economic activity and that EU law is not engaged by rules that are of a purely sporting interest. It made the further point that where the participants are either employed or paid for their services, they are engaged in an economic activity. However, as it is often not easy to distinguish clearly between rules impacting on an economic activity and those that are of a purely sporting interest, trying to create such a distinction can be somewhat artificial and unhelpful as many rules and procedures of ISFs, including those establishing anti-doping regimes, fall into both categories.

Therefore, in circumstances where what appears to be a purely sporting purpose has at least an incidental economic impact, the relationship between the athletes and FINA can be subject to the provisions of the TFEU. To be lawful, FINA and the IOC would have to be able to demonstrate that their anti-doping procedures complied with Arts.101 and 102 TFEU. In order to do this, the CJEU held that the following must be taken into consideration: the overall context in which the rules were adopted; whether their objectives were legitimate; whether any restrictive consequences of the rules were inherent in the pursuit of those legitimate objectives; and whether their were a proportionate means of achieving those objectives. In this case, the overall objectives of the rules were to combat doping in order to ensure that the sport was conducted fairly, that equality of chance was safeguarded for the athletes, that their health was protected and that the integrity and objectivity of competitive sport and its ethical values were upheld.

To be lawful, both the definition of the offence of doping and the imposition of the penalties following any infringement of the rules had to comply with the provisions of the TFEU. The CJEU held that both the anti-doping regime operated by the IOC and FINA and the restrictions imposed on the applicants by means of a participation ban were inherent in the organisation and proper conduct of competitive sport and no more than was necessary to ensure a healthy rivalry among athletes. Further, as the claimants had not pursued the issue of the proportionality of their bans, it was held that the IOC and FINA had acted lawfully in their pursuit of a legitimate objective.

Meca-Medina has proved to be a controversial decision, with many ISFs seeing it as a direct attack on their autonomy. In making this complaint, however, it must be remembered that many major ISFs have been lobbying for some time for a complete exemption from EU law, so any decision that did not specifically serve their purposes was likely to be criticised by this group. In reality, the decision is more of a warning shot than a direct attack. The CJEU requires ISFs to explain why certain rules and procedures are necessary and proportionate for the proper functioning of their sports and is making them produce cogent evidence to back up the claims being made in support of their legality. For example, FINA provided scientific evidence to justify the level at which a positive test for nandrolone would be recorded in an athlete's urine sample, whilst the athletes could provide no evidence for why this level should be raised. FINA could therefore explain why this was not an arbitrarily-defined offence, whereas the claimants could not provide a robust explanation for why the rule needed to be changed.

There are three main criticisms that can be levelled at *Meca-Medina*. Firstly, there was no detailed examination of whether the IOC and FINA were undertakings for the purposes of competition law. In particular, the Court did not examine whether it was possible for bodies of this nature to be undertakings for some purposes but not for others and therefore whether EU competition law was the appropriate means of challenging FINA's rules in these circumstances; they can, as has now been clarified in *Motosykletistiki Omospondia Ellados NPID (MOTOE) v Eilliniko Dimosio* (Case C-49/07) [2008] ECR I-4863 (below, 12.5). Secondly, the CJEU failed to interrogate rigorously the proportionality of FINA's anti-doping regime. Instead of requiring FINA to establish that its restrictive though inherently necessary rule was proportionate, the Court refused to engage with this aspect of the analysis because the claimants had not brought their claim on this basis. In general, the party seeking to rely on a restrictive rule has to prove not only that it is inherent or necessary but also that it is proportionate in order for it to be found to be lawful; this central issue was left unexamined by the Court. Thirdly, the decision does not explain whether taking account of the 'specificity of sport' requires consideration of different issues in competition law cases from those that are relevant for challenges brought under the free movement provisions.

This last point could not be examined further in *Meca-Medina* because the CJEU did not have jurisdiction to hear the challenges made to the anti-doping rules under Arts.45 and 56 TFEU (ex Arts.39 and 49 ECT). Although there is a possibility of convergence in how the law will be applied in the future, there are at present two similar though distinct approaches for determining the legality of an ISF's rules and procedures under EU law. Challenges brought under the free movement provisions will generally be decided on the basis of whether the rule is necessary, proportionate and can be objectively justified, whilst anti-competitive behaviour will only be lawful where the beneficial effects outweigh its restrictive impact (below, 12.2 and 12.5, respectively). The subtle differences in approach will make it important for claimants to choose the most appropriate cause of action when challenging an ISF.

What *Meca-Medina* does confirm is that ISFs have only what Weatherill refers to as a 'conditional autonomy' to self-regulate; they are free to govern their own sports in the way that they see fit, provided that where they engage in or have an impact on an economic activity they comply with EU law or can prove that their conduct falls outside of its scope. The development of the concept of the 'specificity of sport' means that it is now not only rules that are of a purely sporting interest that fall outside of the scope of the TFEU, as was the case after *Walrave*; those rules which are necessary for the proper functioning of sport are also not subject to the Treaty's provisions.

Although EU law will generally be applicable to professionalised and commercialised sport, the *Staff Working Document* that was published alongside of the European Commission's *White Paper on Sport* (COM (2007) 391) states unequivocally that amateur sport is not to be considered exempt from the operation of EU law. In particular, the Commission expressed concern that discriminatory practices in sport could discourage workers from working in other member states if they were not allowed the same access to sport as the nationals of the country to which they were moving. In making these statements, the Commission acknowledges that sport is a social advantage and recognises its importance as a tool of social integration that should be protected by the principles of free movement.

12.2 Treaty on the functioning of the European Union Art.45 (ex Art.39 ECT) – freedom of movement for workers

The right of workers to move freely throughout the EU for employment purposes is secured by Art.45 TFEU. This enables workers to accept and take up offers of employment in any member state of the EU and to remain there for the purpose of working. It makes it unlawful to discriminate against a worker on the grounds of their nationality, ensuring equal access to employment and social advantages, equal pay for equal work and equality of treatment for all workers.

▶ *Treaty on the Functioning of the European Union Art.45*

1 Freedom of movement for workers shall be secured within the Union.
2 Such freedom of movement shall entail the abolition of any discrimination based on nationality between workers of the Member States as regards employment, remuneration and other conditions of work and employment.
3 It shall entail the right, subject to limitations justified on grounds of public policy, public security or public health:
   (a) to accept offers of employment actually made;
   (b) to move freely within the territory of Member States for this purpose;
   (c) to stay in a Member State for the purpose of employment in accordance with the provisions governing the employment of nationals of that State laid down by law, regulation or administrative action;
   (d) to remain in the territory of a Member State after having been employed in that State, subject to conditions which shall be embodied in implementing regulations to be drawn up by the Commission.

Despite the clarity of the wording of Art.45, sports authorities appeared not to appreciate that EU law in general and the free movement provisions in particular could apply to sporting relationships. From the early 1970s, a series of well-reported cases, including *Walrave*, had been heard before the CJEU, though the potential impact of EU law was largely ignored by the bodies at which these judgments were directed.

Following *Bosman* (below, 12.2.1) and *Deliège v ASBL Ligue Francophone de Judo and others* (Cases C-51/96 and C-191/97) [2000] ECR I-2549 (below, 12.3.1), a four-stage test has evolved to determine whether there has been breach of the free movement provisions. Firstly, the Court must begin by determining whether the rule in question is a restriction on a worker's freedom of movement under Art.45 TFEU, or a person's freedom of establishment under Art.49, or on their freedom to provide services under Art.56. Again, if the rule is inherent in the organisation and proper conduct of the sport or, following *Walrave*, is a purely sporting rule then it will fall outside of the scope of the Treaty. Secondly, if the rule is a restriction, it must be determined whether it can be justified objectively. Where a rule is directly discriminatory, it can only be justified on the grounds of public policy, public security or public health (Art.45(3) TFEU), which are rarely likely to apply to most sporting rules. Where a rule is indirectly discriminatory, or non-discriminatory, it can be objectively justified if its purpose includes the protection of the integrity of the competition and competitive balance, or the protection of athletes' health, or encourages the training and education of young athletes. Thirdly, the rule must be effective in promoting the objectives pursued. Fourthly, the rule must be a proportionate means of achieving the objectives. These last two stages ensure that the restriction is capable of achieving a legitimate objective and is an appropriate means of doing so.

12.2.1 The *Bosman* decision

It was not until the case of *Union Royale Belge des Sociétés de Football Association ASBL v Bosman* (Case C-415/93) [1995] ECR I-4921 that ISFs finally realised that some of the practices that they considered to be integral to the organisation of their sports were unlawful according to EU law. In terms of its public perception and impact, *Bosman* marks the true starting point of the development of European sports law, as it was through this case that EU law finally came to the attention not just of EU lawyers but of everyone connected with sport, including its administrators, clubs, the players and the fans.

From May 1988 to 30 June 1990, Bosman was employed as a professional footballer by RC Liège on a gross basic salary of BFr75,000 per month; with bonuses, his average monthly salary was BFr120,000. In April 1990, Liège offered him a new one-year contract for the following season at the league's minimum salary of BFr30,000 per month. Bosman rejected this offer and was transfer listed at a fee of BFr11,743,000, referred to by the Belgian Football Association (URBSFA) as compensation for training a player, and which had been calculated in accordance with its transfer regulations on the basis of his previous season's salary.

As no club was prepared to pay such a high fee for him, Bosman negotiated a move to US Dunkerque of the French second division, who agreed to pay him the equivalent of BFr90,000 per month and to pay Liège a training compensation fee of BFr1.2m in order to secure his services for the following season. At the end of this contract Dunkerque had the option to secure his permanent transfer by paying an additional BFr4.8m to Liège. Liège, however, had doubts about Dunkerque's solvency and failed to request the necessary international clearance certificate from the URBSFA, causing the contracts to lapse and Bosman to be left unemployed.

Bosman initially sued Liège, and the URBSFA for BFr100,000 per month for the period of time until he was able to find suitable alternative employment to that which had been offered to him by Dunkerque. In the course of the protracted litigation, UEFA was also joined as a defendant. Bosman's case eventually focused on two specific claims. Firstly, that the transfer system as operated in Belgium and sanctioned by UEFA was contrary to Art.45 TFEU (ex Art.39 ECT) as it restricted him from being able to take up an offer of employment in another member state.

Secondly, he argued that the '3+2' Rule operated by UEFA was also in contravention of Art.45. The '3+2' Rule, which had been introduced in July 1992 whilst the litigation was progressing through the courts, prevented a club from fielding more than three players who were eligible to play international football for a national association other than the one where their employing club was based. A further two foreign players could be fielded if they had played for five years continuously in the country in question, of which at least three years had to have been as a junior. Bosman argued that this rule limited the number of non-Belgian clubs that were able to employ him, as many would have already filled their foreign quota, and therefore it restricted his ability to work throughout the EU as a professional footballer.

The Belgian courts referred the following questions to the CJEU for a preliminary ruling:

Is Art.45 TFEU to be interpreted as:

1. prohibiting a football club from requiring and receiving payment of a sum of money upon the engagement of one of its players who has come to the end of his contract by a new employing club;
2. prohibiting the national and international sporting associations or federations from including in their respective regulations provisions restricting access of foreign players from the EU to the competitions which they organise?

The Court was unequivocal in holding that the demanding of a transfer fee by a former employer after the conclusion of a fixed-term employment contract was an obstacle to the freedom of movement for workers as it impeded and potentially prevented a professional footballer's ability to move to new club. Therefore, the rules providing for such payments were unlawful unless it could be shown that they were necessary and proportionate for achieving a legitimate objective.

UEFA and URBSFA advanced two main justifications for the existence of the transfer system. Firstly, they argued that it helped to maintain financial and sporting equilibrium among clubs. The CJEU accepted that this was a legitimate aim for a governing body to achieve but rejected the claim that the transfer system was an appropriate means of securing such an outcome. The operation of this transfer system did not preclude the richest clubs from securing the services of the best players, nor could it restrict their commercial activities to such an extent as to create a financial level playing field. Furthermore, as potentially less restrictive mechanisms, such as collective wage agreements, solidarity payments and the pooling and sharing of income, had not been investigated, the continuation of the transfer system could not be justified on the basis that it was necessary to promote competitive balance. In the absence of proof based on cogent evidence, the Court was unable to justify why such a clear infringement of Art.45 should be lawful on this basis.

Secondly, it was argued that transfer fees represented compensation for costs expended by a club on the training of a player. The CJEU again accepted that this was potentially a legitimate aim of the rules; however as there was no identifiable relationship between the compensation fees demanded and the actual costs involved with training a player, the transfer system was not necessary for the achievement of this aim. It was specifically noted that the transfer system operated in Belgium calculated the fee payable on the basis of the salary previously paid to the player not on the costs associated with training him. Only if a reasonable sum representing the actual training costs incurred by the club could be calculated objectively could a transfer system be justified. Therefore, question one was answered in the affirmative: a rule that requires the payment of a transfer, training or development fee to a previous employer to enable an out-of-contract player to move to a new employer is prohibited by Art.45 as being an obstacle to the freedom of movement of workers.

The CJEU was equally unequivocal that nationality quotas that restricted an EU citizen's opportunity to play for their employing club were obstacles to their ability to work unimpeded as professional footballers. Therefore, the '3+2' Rule was also unlawful unless it could be shown that it was a purely sporting rule falling outside of the scope of the Treaty or that it was necessary and proportionate for achieving a legitimate objective.

The CJEU was not prepared to accept that a nationality quota of the kind being operated by UEFA was a purely sporting rule that was necessary for the proper functioning of the game. Whereas nationality restrictions were inherently necessary for the composition of international representative teams, as per *Walrave*, the same arguments could not be used to explain the need for quotas at club level. In reaching this conclusion, the Court began its move away from the concept of providing exemptions for purely sporting rules by requiring instead that UEFA objectively justify the need for imposing nationality restrictions through the '3+2' Rule.

UEFA argued that there were three justifications for the existence of the Rule: that it helped to maintain the traditional link between a club and the country in which it was based; that it ensured that there was a sufficient pool of nationally qualified players playing in a country's top league to feed its national team and that it maintained a competitive balance between clubs by preventing the richest from acquiring all the best players. The Court again dismissed each of these claims. Firstly, it held that it is not necessary for the organisation of football that a club maintain a link with its home country, region or locality through the engagement of players from specific areas. Although it is justifiable to impose eligibility restrictions based on nationality for genuinely representative competitions, UEFA had not provided evidence of the need for a corresponding restriction at club level.

Secondly, it held that as a player could be selected to play for his national team whilst registered with a club based anywhere in the world, the Rule did not of itself create a pool of players eligible to compete for a national team. If players could be based at clubs outside of the country for which they would compete nationally, they should be able to play for any club within the EU without restriction.

Thirdly, the Court did not accept that the Rule was capable of maintaining a competitive balance between clubs. The richer clubs would still be able to recruit the best foreign players and would still have the ability to horde excess players by employing but not always playing them. They would also retain the ability to acquire the services of the best domestic players when their foreign quota was full. Therefore, question two was also answered in the affirmative: a rule that imposes restrictions on the ability of an employer to recruit employees that is based on their nationality alone is prohibited by Art.45 as being an obstacle to the freedom of movement of workers.

The CJEU's ruling in *Bosman* came as a shock not just to the football authorities but to the ISFs of all professional team sports. Despite *Walrave* having already served warning to ISFs that their rules could be subject to EU law, UEFA and its member associations still appeared to think that they could operate without interference from the courts on the basis that all of their rules would be covered by the sporting exception defence. *Bosman* demonstrates quite clearly that only rules that are necessary for the organisation of sport are completely exempt from the operation of EU law; all others will require an objective justification to explain why they should be lawful, something that UEFA was unable to provide to the Court.

Looked at from a contractual perspective, it seems absurd to think that it could be lawful for a club to demand compensation from the new employer of a former employee whose contract has ended. Like *Eastham* (see chapter 11.4.2.4), Bosman was technically no longer employed by his previous club but was unable to work elsewhere until a fee had been paid to them. Treating players as tradable assets rather than employees occurred in professional team sport for almost the entire twentieth century until *Bosman* brought sports employment more into line with the employment practices operated in other sectors. As a result of the Court's ruling, transfer fees can no longer be charged for out-of-contract players, though training compensation of a significantly lower level must now be paid when a player under the age of 23 moves clubs (below, 12.2.2.1). Further, discriminatory nationality quotas should not be used to restrict the number of EU players that a club can field or employ, despite recent moves to the contrary, unless they are capable of being objectively justified (below, Hot Topic).

The importance of the *Bosman* decision must not be underestimated. Not only was it a landmark ruling on the application of Art.45 but it marked a change in the relationship between sport and the EU. The CJEU made it clear that it would no longer tolerate such a flagrant disregard of EU law in such a high-profile activity without a robust objective justification, something that UEFA was unable to provide. The case also marks the beginning of the European Commission's much more proactive examinations of sports governance. After *Bosman*, ISFs could be under no illusion but that they were subject to EU law and that some of the practices that they considered to be inherent in the proper organisation of their sports were unlawful.

It also began a process of greater collaboration among ISFs when responding to EU initiatives and the juridification of the language of their interactions with EU institutions. For example, in 2008, the European sports federations responsible for basketball, football, handball, rugby and volleyball (FIBA Europe, UEFA, EHF, FIRA-AER and CEV), together with the International Ice Hockey Federation, presented a joint document, *Safeguarding the heritage and future of team sport in Europe*, to the European Council outlining measures that it felt should be protected from the unchecked operation of EU law (below, 12.4.4). The document discusses the definition of the specificity and autonomy of team sports, the protection and education of young players and the need for good governance, providing the platform from which perhaps the kind of justifications demanded of UEFA by the CJEU in *Bosman* may be developed in the future.

12.2.2 The impact of the *Bosman* decision

The *Bosman* decision is applicable to all professional sports, a point reflected by much of the subsequent case law. However, it has had its biggest impact on football, where a player 'doing a *Bosman*' is a frequent topic of conversation. Despite creeping into football's vernacular, FIFA and UEFA did not accept the judgment readily and since it was handed down, they have spent much of the intervening period attempting to find ways of limiting its impact.

12.2.2.1 Requiring a training compensation fee instead of a transfer fee

FIFA's Regulations on the Status and Transfer Players were introduced in 2001 following an agreement among the EU, FIFA, UEFA and FIFPRO, the International Federation of Professional Footballers' Associations, on how post-*Bosman* transfers should be administered. According to Art.20 FIFA Regulations, a 'training compensation fee' is payable to the club or clubs where a player was trained when they enter into their first professional playing contract and each subsequent occasion on which they are transferred until the end of the season during which they turn 23 years of age. This fee, which is calculated in accordance with Annexe 4 of the Regulations, is payable regardless of whether the transfer takes place during or at the end of the player's contract. By providing clubs with a means of calculating the fee payable, a more easily justifiable and considerably smaller sum is required to be paid in compensation to the training club for its work with the player. When read in conjunction with Art.21 FIFA Regulations concerning solidarity payments, which disperses a small amount of any future in-contract transfer fee to each club involved in the training of a player between the ages of 12 and 23, FIFA's aim is to ensure that the clubs responsible for finding, training and developing young players are compensated for their efforts where they are unable to reap the benefits of their work because the player has chosen to play elsewhere.

Art.20 reintroduces transfer fees for players under 23 years of age in the guise of a requirement that the new club pay compensation to the previous employer for having provided the player with training. As transfer, training and development fees were declared unlawful in *Bosman*, this restriction on a young player's freedom of movement as a worker needs to be justified objectively if it is avoid being found to infringe Art.45 TFEU. In *Olympique Lyonnais v Bernard and Newcastle United FC* (Case C-325/08), Advocate General Sharpston, although refusing to comment on the legality of Art.20 FIFA Regulations as not being relevant to the case before her, gave her opinion on the legality of a French law that covers a similar situation. In line with *Bosman*, she advised that a rule that requires the payment of a fee to the previous employer once the contract of employment is at an end is, in principle, prohibited by Art.45 TFEU. However, she stated that it may be possible to justify such a law by the need to encourage the recruitment and training of young professional footballers.

The Advocate General stated that where it is necessary to train *n* players in order to produce one who will be successful professionally, then the cost to the training club, and therefore the amount that it could recover in compensation from the next employer, would be the cost of training *n* young players. If the player rather than their new club were to be personally liable, the Advocate General considered that it was fair that only the individual cost of training them could be recovered. What she found unacceptable was that Olympique Lyonnais had calculated the amount of compensation due to them by reference to the salary that it had offered Bernard and not to the cost that it had incurred in training him.

The method of calculating the compensation due to a training club used by Advocate General Sharpston is strikingly similar to that used in Art.20 FIFA Regulations and supports the view of the football authorities that a club that has trained a player, but for whatever reason cannot convince them to stay and play for it, should be compensated for the effort that it has expended. Further, as Art.21 provides a mechanism for the redistribution of a part of any later in-contract transfer fee to the clubs responsible for training the player, FIFA appears to have demonstrated the importance of training young players and the cost involved in creating someone capable of playing sport professionally.

The CJEU affirmed the opinion of Advocate General Sharpston and held that Art.45 TFEU applies to sports employment relationships and that if such contracts create an obstacle to the freedom of movement of workers, then they will only be lawful if the restrictions contained within them are proportionate and in pursuit of a legitimate objective. A scheme that guarantees compensation to the club that provided training to a young player, in order to attain the legitimate objective of encouraging the ongoing recruitment and training of further young players, is not precluded by Art.45, provided that it is capable of achieving that objective and is no more than is necessary for its achievement.

In *Bernard*, the *jouer espoir* scheme operated in France did not satisfy these requirements as the compensation payable when signing for Newcastle United was based on the future salary that would have been paid to the player had he remained at Olympique Lyonnais rather than on the actual cost of training him over the previous three seasons. Thus, the reasoning in this case could explain the legality of FIFA's Regulations regarding the fees payable to clubs responsible for training young players under the age of 24 as the compensation payable is based on an approximation of the cost of the player's training, not the salary payable under his or her new contract.

12.2.2.2 Receiving compensation for breach of contract instead of a transfer fee

Where a player breaches their contract without just cause in order to join a new club, Art.17 FIFA Regulations defines how the compensation payable to the original employing club should be calculated. In *FC Shaktar Donetsk v Matuzalem Francelino da Silva, Real Zaragoza SAD and FIFA* CAS 2008/A/1519 and 1520 (see further, Hot Topic 3 and chapter 11.3.1), CAS stated that Art.17 did not give a player the right to unilaterally terminate their agreement but was instead the equivalent of a liquidated damages clause that defined the consequences of a player's breach of contract and the methodology to be followed when calculating the compensation payable. Thus, the law of the country where the previous club was based or the jurisdiction that has been chosen to govern any contractual disputes (in this case, Switzerland), the specificity of sport, the value of the player's services to FC Shaktar Donetsk, the status of the player, his standing at the club, his behaviour and the timing of his departure were all to be taken into account when calculating the amount of compensation payable.

On this basis, and taking into account the savings made in respect of the salary that Shaktar would not have to pay Matuzalem now he had moved to another club, the total amount payable was €11.9m. In the light of Advocate General Sharpston's opinion in *Olympique Lyonnais*, Art.17 is likely to be found lawful on the grounds of its being an objectively justifiable means of calculating the current value to a club of a player who has left it in breach of contract.

12.2.2.3 Buy-out and player release clauses instead of transfer fees

Mutually agreed in-contract transfers are in reality subject only to market forces. In some jurisdictions, clubs try to protect themselves to a certain extent by inserting player release clauses or buy-out clauses into the contract of employment, though these are not universally legal and if excessive could constitute a restraint of trade (see further, chapter 11.4). Art.21 FIFA Regulations requires a maximum of five per cent of the fee to be paid through the solidarity mechanism to the training clubs, but apart from this redistributive element, the fee is that which is negotiated by the parties. Where a player is out of contract, they can now 'go on a *Bosman*' once the contract is at an end; the player becomes an unattached free agent and is able to join any club that is prepared to employ them.

12.2.2.4 The juridification of football

It is possible, in the light of the creation of the FIFA Dispute Resolution Chamber and the ability of the parties to a football dispute to appeal to CAS, that cases such as *Matuzalem* may not be heard before national and European courts in the future unless the conduct conflicts with fundamental principles of law (see further, chapter 3). This formalisation and juridification of football's dispute resolution framework could be said to have been one of the most important developments to have been caused by the *Bosman* decision.

The case can also be said to have contributed significantly to the juridification of FIFA and UEFA's language and their approach to proposed developments within their sport. For example, UEFA's 'home grown players' rule reintroduces nationality quotas that were ostensibly outlawed by *Bosman*. The justifications for these restrictive practices are couched in EU law terms as being necessary and proportionate for the proper administration of football or are claimed to be purely sporting rules outside of the jurisdiction of EU law on the basis of the specificity and autonomy of sport (below, Hot Topic). Taken together with the newly established dispute resolution framework, these developments indicate the lengths to which the football authorities have gone in order to avoid the much-feared '*Bosman 2*' whilst highlighting the ways in which they continue to try to subvert the original decision.

12.2.3 Extending the reach of Art.45 TFEU

Since *Bosman* further challenges have been brought against what have long been accepted as common practices within the sports sector. In *Lehtonen v Federation Royale Belge des Sociétés de Basket-ball ASBL* (Case C-176/96) [2000] ECR I-2681, the legality of the transfer deadlines operated in European professional basketball were called into question. On completion of the national championships in Finland, Lehtonen, a professional basketball player and Finnish national, moved to Castors Braine in order to compete for it in the play-offs of the Belgian championships. The Belgian Basketball Federation operated two separate transfer deadlines: 28 February for transfers from clubs based within Europe, and 31 March for transfers from all other areas.

The CJEU held that transfer deadlines such as these are restrictions on the freedom of movement of workers because they create obstacles to a player's ability to take up employment elsewhere within the EU. However, they are objectively justifiable as necessary to protect the integrity of a sporting competition. The basis of this justification was that late-season transfers have the potential to change the competitive strength of an individual team disproportionately, thereby calling into question the comparability of results between all participants over the course of a season-long championship. In other words, it is a legitimate objective of a governing body to prevent a team from buying in better players at the last minute in order to distort the true picture of its performance over an entire season. Thus, a single transfer deadline was lawful but further justification was required for the operation of two separate deadlines that were based on a player's residency in order for the rule to be compatible with Art.45 TFEU. The more recent practise of using transfer windows as a means of securing contractual stability as well as the integrity of a competition would therefore appear to be objectively justifiable.

The use of salary caps in some sports could also give rise to claims that Art.45 has been infringed. Where a player is unable to play for a prospective employer who has reached the overall level of the cap, or has to accept a lower salary in order for the club to come within the cap's conditions, a clear obstacle to the player's right to free movement appears to have been raised. Using the 'specificity of sport' analysis introduced in *Meca-Medina and Majcen v Commission* (Case 519/04) [2006] ECR I-6991, the more obvious the restriction, the more robust the justifications will have to be in order for the practice to be declared lawful. For example, salary restrictions might be justifiable on the basis of securing the financial stability of a sport and therefore its future existence or the competitive balance of its competitions. Although the legality of any particular salary cap would depend on its definition and operation there is no reason why one that is appropriately drafted should not be found to be compatible with EU law.

12.3 Treaty on the functioning of the European Union Art.56 (ex Art.49 ECT) – freedom to provide services

Where Art.45 TFEU is used to protect the freedom of movement of workers or employees, Art.56 provides similar protection for those who provide their services for remuneration or who are self-employed. This enables individual athletes, rather than those who are employed to play team sports, to ply their trade anywhere within the EU without being discriminated against on the grounds of nationality.

> ▶ *Treaty on the Functioning of the European Union Art.56*
>
> [Restrictions] on freedom to provide services within the Union shall be prohibited in respect of nationals of member states who are established in a member state other than that of the person for whom the services are intended.

Art.56 prevents the creation of obstacles to a person who is ordinarily based in one member state from being able to provide their services elsewhere in the EU. One accepted corollary of the right to provide services is the right to receive them, which was explored extensively in *Murphy v Media Protection Services Ltd* [2007] EWHC 3091 and [2008] EWHC 1666 (see further, chapter 13.4.2). The interlocking agreements concerning the sale and broadcast of Premier League football matches were held to be in contravention of Art.56 because they prevented nationals of one member state (the UK) from receiving services from providers established in another (Greece).

12.3.1 The *Deliège* decision

Despite the high-profile and drawn-out nature of the *Bosman* litigation, ISFs failed to appreciate that other provisions of the TFEU might also apply to sporting relationships. As most athletes are either employees/workers or self-employed and therefore providers of services, the next natural extension of EU law to sport was that its rules and procedures could be subject to Art.56 TFEU.

> ▶ *Deliège v Ligue Francophone de Judo et Disciplines Associées ASBL, Ligue Belge de Judo ASBL (LBJ) and Union Européenne de Judo (UEJ)* **(Joined Cases C-51/96 and C-191/97) [2000] ECR I-2549**
>
> Deliège was an elite-level judoka who hoped to compete in the 1996 Atlanta Olympics. In order to achieve a high enough ranking to be invited to compete in Atlanta, she had to participate in a number of specific tournaments in the run-up to the Games. The UEJ had stipulated that at all 'Category A' ranking tournaments, each national federation, in this case the LBJ, could enter only seven judoka of each sex. This would enable each NGB to enter one person into each of the seven weight categories open to each sex. Where there was nobody of sufficient standing to participate in a particular category, additional judokas could be entered into any of the other weight divisions at the discretion of the NGB.

Despite being one of the highest-ranking judokas in her weight division, Deliège was not selected to compete at several Category A tournaments. In an attempt to facilitate her participation in the Paris International Tournament, she challenged the entry criteria of the UEJ and the selection criteria of the LBJ, claiming that their refusal to allow her to compete was an unlawful restriction on her freedom to provide her services as a judoka in another member state.

The CJEU began by stating that Art.56 TFEU (ex Art.49 ECT) was directly effective and could therefore be invoked against non-state bodies such as ISFs and NGBs, where the rules of such bodies were regulating employment. However, Art.56 would only be engaged where the athlete was performing an economic activity. The UEJ and LBJ both argued that as judo was an amateur sport Deliège could not be engaged in an economic activity and that as a result, there could be no breach of Art.56. The Court rejected this argument on the basis that Deliège had received grants from the state and had entered into personal sponsorship agreements with various corporations, both of which constituted the necessary remuneration to classify her activity as being economic in nature. Thus, as the criteria operated by the UEJ and LBJ together prevented her from being able to provide her services as a judoka at international tournaments, the rules were potentially an unlawful restriction contrary to Art.56.

However, the CJEU held that the selection and entry criteria operated by the defendants were inherently necessary for the proper administration of the sport and therefore fell outside of the scope of the treaty. The rules of the UEJ were inherent in the organisation of elite-level judo tournaments as it could not be expected that each national federation would be allowed to enter an unlimited number of competitors to any and every tournament; a limit of one person per weight division per NGB was an appropriate means of regulating the maximum number of entrants able to compete at an event. Moreover, unless the definition of the selection criteria used by the LBJ or their operation by it could be proved to have been in bad faith, which it could not, then decisions regarding how the members of a team should be selected were a matter for the appropriate national federation, not the Court.

Following the updated reasoning from *Meca-Medina*, the same outcome would be arrived at: the rules of the UEJ and LBJ both had the potential to create obstructions to an athlete's ability to move freely about the EU to provide her services, however, both sets of rules can be objectively justified as being necessary and proportionate for the proper administration of elite-level judo tournaments. Thus, whereas *Walrave* justified the use of restrictive practices on the grounds of nationality where the athletes were competing in international representative competitions, *Deliège* allowed restrictions to be imposed on the ability of individual athletes to compete in a tournament where to do so was necessary from an administrative point of view.

12.3.2 The impact of *Deliège* on English law

The leading English authority on Art.56 TFEU was *Edwards v The British Athletic Federation and the International Amateur Athletic Federation* [1998] 2 CMLR 363; however, in the light of both *Deliège* and *Meca-Medina*, *Edwards* now needs to be significantly revisited. Edwards had been banned from competing as an athlete for four years following the commission of a doping offence. The IAAF routinely allowed athletes to be reinstated after serving only two years of a ban if they were based in a country where a four-year ban was considered to be disproportionate and therefore unlawful, on the grounds that exceptional circumstances existed that would justify it commuting the punishment. After serving two years of his ban, Edwards applied to the IAAF for reinstatement, however, his application was rejected on the basis that there were no exceptional circumstances relevant to his case as a four-year ban was considered to be reasonable and therefore lawful in the UK.

Edwards applied to the High Court to have the decision of the IAAF ruled unlawful for being contrary to Art.56 TFEU. He argued that by allowing the ban to continue for a further two years, he was being prevented from providing his services as a professional athlete to tournament organisers when other EU nationals would have been automatically reinstated.

The Court then went on to hold that the IAAF's anti-doping rules and the bans imposed on athletes who had breached them merely regulated sporting conduct, not any economic activity. The basis of Lightman J's decision was that as the rules were designed to ban cheating by drug-taking, a practice which was banned to ensure that athletes competed on a level playing field, then this was a purely sporting rule that had only an incidental economic impact. After *Meca-Medina*, this can no longer be considered to be the correct approach; the anti-doping regime designed by WADA and implemented by most ISFs does have an impact on economic activity, but it is justifiable as necessary for the maintenance of the integrity of sporting competition and for the protection of athletes' health.

Further, Lightman J found that there was nothing unlawful in the IAAF imposing bans of different lengths on athletes from different countries. He stated that if there was no such body as the IAAF or if the IAAF left the punishment of athletes to its constituent member NGBs then differential punishments that were in accordance with the law of the country in which an NGB was based would be the norm. However, the judge's hypothetical reasoning misses the reality of the situation; the IAAF does exist and was, in fact, sanctioning punishments of differing lengths on athletes who had committed the same doping infringement on the basis of their nationality. Therefore, it is difficult to come to any conclusion other than that the IAAF was acting in a discriminatory fashion.

Finally, it was accepted by the Court without any significant analysis that a four-year ban for a doping offence was reasonable, justified and proportionate. In the light of the various revisions to the anti-doping rules operated by most ISFs and their adoption of the World Anti-Doping Code, it is extremely unlikely that a ban that is not in accordance with the Code would be considered to be a proportionate response to a doping offence. Thus, almost every aspect of the judgment is now open to question following the decisions in *Deliège* and *Meca-Medina*.

12.4 Treaty on the functioning of the European Union Art.49 (ex Art.43 ECT) – freedom of establishment

The third of the freedoms protected by the TFEU that is relevant to sport is the freedom of establishment under Art.49. The effect of Art.49 is twofold: it guarantees self-employed persons the right to take up and pursue activities in other member states and it provides undertakings with the right to set up businesses in any country in the EU. In both cases, establishment should be capable of being effected under the same conditions as would be imposed on nationals of the country where they seek to operate. Thus, it is unlawful to prevent or restrict the ability of either a person or a business that originated in one member state from operating from a base in another member state on the grounds of nationality.

There is no sports-related litigation on this point, although the possibility has arisen on several occasions. In the late 1990s, Wimbledon FC, which was established in England, and Clydebank FC, which was established in Scotland, both attempted to relocate to Dublin but remain playing in the English and Scottish leagues respectively. The Football Association of Ireland refused to sanction the moves and its decisions were enforced by the English and Scottish Football Associations. The two clubs could have argued that Art.49 TFEU enabled them to establish their business in another member state, in this case Ireland, and that to prevent them from doing so on the sole basis of where they were currently established was unlawful.

By analogy to the reasoning of the European Commission in *Royal Excelsior Mouscron/ UEFA* IP/99/965 9 December 1999, it is unlikely that an action under Art.49 would have succeeded in justifying the attempts by these two clubs to play their home games in another member state (below, 12.4.3.3). Mouscron, a Belgian football team with a small home ground, sought to play a UEFA Cup match in the nearest large stadium to where it was based in order to maximise its profits and increase spectator safety; the ideal candidate happened to be based in France. One of reasons ascribed to the Commission's decision to uphold UEFA's decision to refuse Mouscron permission to play a home game outside of Belgium was that the rule was necessary for the organisation of sporting competitions of this kind and was therefore outside of the scope of the competition law rules. It is likely that the decisions of both the FAI and UEFA would be found to be necessary and proportionate means of protecting the integrity of these sporting competitions and for their proper organisation in accordance with the European model of sport.

12.5 Treaty on the foundation of the European Union Arts.101 and 102 (ex Arts.81 and 82 ECT) – competition law

Fully developed claims that sports authorities have acted in breach of EU competition law have been comparatively rare to date. Although some of the leading cases have included assertions that a governing body has engaged in anti-competitive behaviour, including *Bosman*, *Lehtonen* and *Deliège*, few had provided a sufficiently detailed factual context on which the Court could base a preliminary ruling.

The main provisions defining EU competition law are found in Arts.101 and 102 TFEU. Article 101 prohibits agreements between undertakings and decisions made by associations of undertakings which have as their object or effect the prevention, restriction or distortion of competition within the EU. Article 102 prohibits a monopoly or market-dominating undertaking from taking an unfair advantage by abusing its dominant position. If either of these kinds of anti-competitive conduct affects trade between member states, then the undertaking is acting unlawfully.

Following *Meca-Medina* and *Motosykletistiki Omospondia Ellados NPID (MOTOE) v Eilliniko Dimosio (Case C-49/07) [2008] ECR I-4863*, and in line with the discussions in para.2.1.2 of Annex 1 *Staff Working Document* (SEC (2007) 935) published alongside the Commission's *White Paper on Sport* (COM (2007) 39 Final), whether or not a rule conforms with EU competition law can be determined by asking four questions. Firstly, is the collective regulatory body that is seeking to rely on the potentially restrictive rule an undertaking or an association of undertakings? Secondly, is the rule a restriction of competition contrary to Art.101(1) TFEU or an abuse of a dominant position under Art.102 TFEU? In answering this question the Court will examine the overall context in which the rule was adopted or produces its effects, the objectives behind the adoption and operation of the rule, whether the restrictions caused by the rule are inherent in the pursuit of those objectives and whether the rule is proportionate in light of the objectives being pursued. If the rule is inherent in the organisation and proper conduct of the sport, for example, because it protects the integrity of the competition, or protects athletes' health, or encourages the training and education of young athletes, or ensures the financial stability of the participating teams, then it falls outside of the scope of the Treaty. Thirdly, if the rule is a restriction, does it affect trade between member states? Fourthly, if it does affect trade within the internal market, can it be justified under Art.101(3) TFEU on the basis that its beneficial effects outweigh the restrictions that it imposes? For example, by Commission Decision of 23 July 2003, Comp/C-2/37.398 Joint Selling of the Commercial Rights to the UEFA Champions League, UEFA's proposal for selling the rights to its Champions League tournament was found to be a restriction under Art.101(1) TFEU (ex Art.81(1) ECT). However, this restriction was justified and therefore lawful, on the basis that it promoted economic efficiency and was of benefit to consumers (see further, chapter 13.4.1). Thus, any rule or practice that interferes with the operation of the sports market, from anti-doping and transfer rules to nationality restrictions and eligibility criteria, has the potential to be anti-competitive and therefore unlawful.

▶ *Treaty on the Foundation of the European Union Art.101*

1   The following shall be prohibited as incompatible with the internal market: all agreements between undertakings, decisions by associations of undertakings and concerted practices which may affect trade between member states and which have as their object or effect the prevention, restriction or distortion of competition within the internal market and in particular those which:
   (a)   directly or indirectly fix purchase or selling prices or any other trading conditions;
   (b)   limit or control production, markets, technical development, or investment;
   (c)   share markets or sources of supply;
   (d)   apply dissimilar conditions to equivalent transactions with other trading parties, thereby placing them at a competitive disadvantage;
   (e)   make the conclusion of contracts subject to acceptance by the other parties of supplementary obligations which, by their nature or according to commercial usage, have no connection with the subject of such contracts.
2   Any agreements or decisions prohibited pursuant to this article shall be automatically void.
3   The provisions of paragraph 1 may, however, be declared inapplicable in the case of:
   – any agreement or category of agreements between undertakings,
   – any decision or category of decisions by associations of undertakings,
   – any concerted practice or category of concerted practices,
   which contributes to improving the production or distribution of goods or to promoting technical or economic progress, while allowing consumers a fair share of the resulting benefit, and which does not:
   (a)   impose on the undertakings concerned restrictions which are not indispensable to the attainment of these objectives;
   (b)   afford such undertakings the possibility of eliminating competition in respect of a substantial part of the products in question.

▶ *Treaty on the Foundation of the European Union Art.102*

Any abuse by one or more undertakings of a dominant position within the internal market or in a substantial part of it shall be prohibited as incompatible with the internal market in so far as it may affect trade between Member States.

Such abuse may, in particular, consist in:
(a) directly or indirectly imposing unfair purchase or selling prices or other unfair trading conditions;
(b) limiting production, markets or technical development to the prejudice of consumers;
(c) applying dissimilar conditions to equivalent transactions with other trading parties, thereby placing them at a competitive disadvantage;
(d) making the conclusion of contracts subject to acceptance by the other parties of supplementary obligations which, by their nature or according to commercial usage, have no connection with the subject of such contracts.

Although the early sports litigation did not follow through on the competition law issues, recent case law has brought to the fore the potential scope of Arts.101 and 102 TFEU as ways of challenging the rules and decisions of sports authorities. At the same time as this potential extension has occurred, however, the development of the claim that a rule is justified as being necessary because of the 'specificity of sport' has gone some significant way to ameliorate the difficulties that this could cause.

12.5.1 Undertakings, associations of undertakings and the 'dual role' of sports authorities

In sport most NGBs and ISFs are undertakings for at least part of the time. Under their constitutions, it is also possible for them to be associations of undertakings. An NGB or ISF is an undertaking when it is engaged in economic activity, irrespective of its legal form or the way that it is financed (*Hofner and Elser* (Case C-41/90) [1991] ECR I-1979). Either body can also be an association of undertakings where it comprises members who are themselves undertakings; NGBs are usually associations of clubs, whilst ISFs are usually associations of NGBs. Not only can they be undertakings for the purposes of EU competition law, they can also act as monopolies in their fields of governance. As most sports have one NGB per country and one global ISF per sport, the circumstances by which sport is governed are inherently monopolistic in form. However, the mere existence of undertakings acting in concert or being a monopoly does not automatically mean that they are acting anti-competitively. Only where there is an abuse of that position that affects trade between member states will the conduct be unlawful.

The failure of the CJEU to examine whether FINA and the IOC were undertakings is one of the main criticisms of the decision in *Meca-Medina*, as only undertakings are subject to Arts.101 and 102 (above, 12.1.2). The variety of functions undertaken by sports bodies means that they are not always engaged in economic activity when governing their sport. On the one hand, they can be acting as a quasi-public regulatory body that grants the authority to compete in or host an event. On the other, they can be acting as private commercial organisations whose aim is to generate income by, for example, selling broadcasting rights or organising competitions. As sports authorities can have such disparate functions, it is important to be able to determine whether they are undertakings in respect of some of their activities but not in others, or whether once it has been established that they are engaged in some economic activity, they should be considered to be an undertaking in respect of all of their activities.

▶ *Motosykletistiki Omospondia Ellados NPID (MOTOE) v Eilliniko Dimosio* **(Case C-49/07) [2008] ECR I-4863**

Under Greek law, any body seeking to organise a motorcycling competition in Greece first had to secure authorisation from the Minister for Public Order. Part of this authorisation process required the consent of the national motor racing organisation, Elliniki Leskhi Aftokinitou kai Periigiseon (ELPA), which is the official representative in Greece of the ISF for motorcycling, the Federation Internationale de Motocyclisme (FIM). ELPA had two main roles: it acted as both the official regulator of motorcycling by authorising events and competitions run by other bodies and as a commercial entity that organised competitions in its own name.

MOTOE applied for authorisation from the government to run a motorcycle competition but failed to secure the necessary consent from ELPA, suffering financial losses of GDr5m as a result. MOTOE sued Greece under Arts.102 and 106 TFEU, arguing that the body to which the Greek state had granted these powers, ELPA, was abusing its monopoly position as the sole authorising body for motorcycling events by refusing to give its consent to a competition organised by a commercial rival.

MOTOE argued that ELPA was an undertaking on the basis that when it organised its own events and competitions it was engaging in commercially orientated economic activity. ELPA countered that as it was a non-profit-making regulatory body, it was not engaged in any economic activity and therefore could not be an undertaking.

To a limited extent, the CJEU agreed with both points of view; ELPA was a commercial entity engaging in economic activity when it organised its own events by reason of its entering into sponsorship and advertising agreements and insurance contracts; however, when acting purely as a regulator, it was not acting as an undertaking. This led the Court to identify a third alternative; ELPA was acting in a 'dual role' where its regulatory decisions, such as whether to grant consent to MOTOE's application, could be influenced by its own commercial imperatives, such as the need to limit the number of competitions that could act as direct competitors to its own events. Where an entity operated with this dual role, it was an undertaking for the purposes of EU competition law.

The next step was to determine whether ELPA was in a dominant market position. As MOTOE had no opportunity to apply to a body other than ELPA for permission to organise such an event, there was no substitutable or sufficiently interchangeable service provider and therefore the relevant market was defined as being the organisation of motorcycling competitions in Greece. Dominance is established where an undertaking is in such a position of strength in the relevant market that it is able to prevent effective competition and act to an appreciable extent independently of its competitors and consumers (*United Brands and United Brands Continentaal v Commission* (Case 27/76) [1978] ECR 207). By virtue of its structure and its control over the relevant market as the sole and state-sanctioned authorising body of such events, ELPA was found to be in a dominant position in the market for organising motorcycling competitions in Greece.

The final stage for determining a breach of Art.102 is to establish whether the undertaking is abusing its dominant position. If ELPA had been acting in bad faith when refusing to give its consent to MOTOE's application, a clear case of abuse of its dominant position would be established. However the Court went considerably further by holding that a breach of Art.102 could also be established where the rights granted to an undertaking by the state gave rise to a *risk* of an abuse of its dominant position. Thus, there was an assumption of anti-competitive behaviour that was based on the conflict of interest between ELPA's regulatory and commercial roles. As neither Greece nor ELPA could provide a justification for operating a decision-making process with no appropriate safeguards to minimise the opportunity for abuse, it was anti-competitive.

This decision appears to cause particular problems for NGBs and ISFs which are inherently monopolistic in their governance of sports. As many will also fulfil the 'dual role' referred to by the Court, there is a real possibility of their actions engaging EU competition law; however just because EU competition law is engaged does not automatically mean that it is also breached. The CJEU only found that the way in which ELPA fulfilled its dual role was anti-competitive, not that the concept of the dual role was automatically anti-competitive. Therefore, there is no immediate need for a sports body that fulfils a dual role to divest itself of its commercial activities; as was the case in *Meca-Medina*, where the conduct of an NGB can be justified objectively it can still be acting lawfully.

The power granted to ELPA to give or refuse its consent to MOTOE to organise a motorcycle competition was not subject to any restrictions or obligations to review. Furthermore the Greek government had not laid down any procedures that needed to be followed or any means of challenging ELPA's decisions. Thus, the power granted to ELPA was open to abuse, even if it had not actually been abused. To ensure the legality of the decision-making process, all decisions should be taken in accordance with objectively justifiable criteria, following a fair hearing where the applicant is able to present their own case, where reasons for the eventual decision are given and where there is an opportunity to appeal against it or to apply for some other form of review. If such a procedure is followed, then the opportunity for abuse is significantly reduced if not entirely negated.

The effect of *MOTOE* and *Meca-Medina* is to subject the conduct of most ISFs and NGBs to the possibility of scrutiny by EU competition law, particularly where professional and elite sport is concerned, as so many of them perform this dual role. However where their rules can be justified as necessary for the proper administration of their sport or where there is an appropriate review or appeals process in place, there will be no actionable infringement of Arts.101 and 102 despite their inherently monopolistic position. The development of the 'specificity of sport' argument will provide a significant degree of protection to the majority of activities engaged in by ISFs and NGBs. Provided that they can produce a sufficiently robust explanation for why their conduct should fall outside of the scope of the competition provisions, it is unlikely that they will have been acting unlawfully.

12.5.2   The 'dual role' of sporting rules

A related difficulty arises when trying to determine whether the disputed rule, practice or decision of an ISF or NGB is one that has an impact on economic activity or whether it has been implemented for a purely sporting purpose. Such a distinction is somewhat artificial and can be misleading as much of the conduct of these bodies can fall into both categories at the same time, especially where elite sport is concerned. *Meca-Medina* and *MOTOE* now require that the rules, practices and procedures of an ISF or NGB be examined in more detail in order to determine whether the sports authority has infringed Arts.101 or 102 TFEU.

In *Meca-Medina* the CJEU held that the mere fact that a rule appears to be purely sporting in nature does not automatically remove it from the scope of the treaty. In *MOTOE*, the Court elaborated on this reasoning by stating that this could be because the rule was fulfilling a 'dual role'. The anti-doping rules operated by FINA were not purely sporting because they also had an impact on economic activity by banning from competition any athlete who had tested positive for a doping offence. Therefore, the rules could only be lawful if they were inherent in the conduct and proper organisation of the sport. The anti-doping regime operated by FINA had been implemented to ensure equality among the participants, the uncertainty of results, competitive balance and the integrity of the competition. These objectives were held to be legitimate and therefore the rules adopted to achieve them were inherent in the proper organisation of international swimming championships. Moreover, the anti-doping regime implemented by FINA was proportionate because the rules creating it were no more than was necessary to achieve its sporting objectives. Thus, the anti-doping rules were not anti-competitive restrictions according to Art.101 TFEU. If an ISF is unable to prove that there is an inherent need for a rule, practice or decision, then it will instead have to claim that it is exempted under Art.101(3) TFEU.

12.5.3 Conduct protected from the scope of EU law

Post-*MOTOE*, the second and third stages of the test are much easier to establish because the disputed rule will almost inevitably restrict competition or be the exercise of monopolistic powers. As a challenge to a major sports body will as a matter of course have an impact on trade between member states, the key to establishing anti-competitive behaviour will be the determination of whether the beneficial effects of the conduct outweigh its restrictive impact.

The judgments of the CJEU and the decisions of the European Commission have established that what would otherwise be anti-competitive conduct in most other contexts can be justified as being necessary because of the 'specificity of sport'. In particular, where a rule has been implemented to protect the integrity of a sport, it will generally be held to be lawful if it is proportionate. It is also likely, because of the similarity of the tests used under both the competition and free movement provisions, that conduct which has been found not to breach Arts.45 and 56, such as in *Walrave* and *Deliège*, will also be found not to have infringed Arts.101 and 102.

12.5.3.1 Anti-doping regimes and disciplinary bans

Following *Meca-Medina*, it is unlikely that any anti-doping regime that is operated in accordance with the World Anti-Doping Code will be unlawful. Although clearly having an economic impact and the potential to be anti-competitive by banning athletes and teams from participating in major competitions, the CJEU held that anti-doping rules are both necessary and proportionate for the proper administration of sport. In particular the Court considered that the protection of the integrity of sports competitions, the maintenance of competitive balance between the participants and the protection of the health of the athletes were sufficient justifications for the legality of anti-doping rules.

It also held that banning those athletes who were found to have breached anti-doping provisions was necessary as a means of ensuring that the rules were complied with by the athletes at whom they were aimed. Provided that the bans are proportionate to the gravity of the particular doping infringement committed and the length of an athlete's career, it is lawful to prevent a person or team from competing in a sport for a specified period of time. Similar reasoning could be used to justify the legality of bans imposed for violent conduct and match-fixing.

12.5.3.2 Preventing multiple ownership of clubs in the same competition

In *ENIC plc/UEFA* IP/02/942 27 June 2002, the European Commission adopted a decision that upheld the legality of a UEFA rule that was designed to protect the independence of clubs from undue influence by one another when competing in the same competition and which is now found in rule A3 of the Regulations of the UEFA Champions League and Europa League competitions. The rule in question prevented: a club from owning or being involved in the management, administration or sporting performance of another club; a person from being involved in the management, administration or sporting performance of more than one club at a time; and two or more clubs from being under common control. For the purposes of the rule, common control was established where an individual or other legal entity held or could exercise a majority of the shareholders' voting rights or had the right to appoint or remove a majority of the members of the administrative, management or supervisory body of two or more clubs at the same time.

ENIC was an investment company that owned stakes of various sizes in six professional football clubs. When two of the clubs in which it had a major shareholding were drawn to play against each other in the UEFA Cup, UEFA stated that the lower-ranked of the two, according to its seeding system, would have to withdraw from the competition in accordance with its rules on the independence of clubs. ENIC complained to the Commission that this rule was anti-competitive as it restricted its ability to invest freely in European football clubs.

The Commission concluded that although the rule was a decision taken by an association of undertakings and could in principle engage Art.101, it was inherent in the organisation and proper conduct of sport because it was necessary for the protection of the integrity of its competitions. UEFA's concern was that where two or more clubs were controlled by the same person or body, that person or body could influence the outcome of the game between the two sides and, as a result, undermine the competitive balance of the particular game in question and the integrity of the results of the competition as a whole; UEFA was concerned about the possibility of match-fixing and this rule was a means of reducing the possibility of this practice occurring.

The rule was not only necessary, it was also a proportionate means of achieving this legitimate goal. Investors were not completely banned from owning stakes in more than one club; they were only banned from owning controlling interests in two or more clubs at the same time. As the UEFA rule did no more than was necessary to protect the uncertainty of the results in its competitions, it was a proportionate response to a legitimate concern and therefore was not a restriction on trade for the purposes of EU competition law.

12.5.3.3 Rules of a purely sporting nature

The Commission has also upheld the validity of requiring ties to be played on a 'home and away' basis. In *Royal Excelsior Mouscron* IP/99/965 9 December 1999 the owners of a football stadium in Lille, France complained that the UEFA decision to refuse the request of the Belgian football club Excelsior Mouscron to play its 'home' games in Lille was anti-competitive. The request had come about because Mouscron's home stadium was small and it wanted to maximise the profits it could make from a forthcoming UEFA Cup tie with the French first division side FC Metz. As the closest major stadium to Mouscron was in Lille, it sought permission to play its 'home' game there.

The Commission upheld the legality of the UEFA rule on the basis that this was an isolated situation that was unlikely to reoccur and that there was therefore an insufficiently serious interference with trade between member states to engage EU competition law. Thus, although the owners of the stadium in Lille had lost the opportunity to hire out their facility for a major European game the UEFA rule was considered to be of too small an impact on the operation of the internal market to infringe EU law.

A further reading of the decision has been that it was legitimate from a sporting perspective to require a club to play its 'home' fixtures at its own stadium unless there were compelling reasons for it not to do so. If the club is able to demonstrate that its request falls into one of the exceptions to the rule, then it is also legitimate for UEFA to require that its 'home' fixtures be played at a stadium within the territory of its NGB because football in Europe is organised along national lines according to the European model of sport. Thus, to require a Belgian club to play its home games at its own stadium, or, where appropriate, at an alternative stadium within Belgium, was a legitimate sporting requirement that was needed to ensure equality among clubs.

12.5.4 Future developments

Despite the concerns of the European ISFs, the CJEU and the Commission have been prepared to accept that sport is different and is deserving of some degree of protection from the unfettered application of EU law. Provided that the ISFs can demonstrate that their restrictive practices are necessary and proportionate for the proper organisation of sporting competitions, that they are there to ensure equality and competitive balance among participants, preserve the uncertainty of outcome and, overall, operate in a way that guarantees the integrity of sporting competition then their conduct will be lawful. However, both institutions are more concerned when the ISFs seek similar treatment for more overtly commercial practices.

In its 2008 document *Safeguarding the heritage and future of team sports in Europe*, the European Team Sports Federations identified 15 matters whose legal position it considered to be in need of further clarification. Each of these 15 issues falls into one of three broad groups. Four could be said to concern issues of a purely sporting nature: in-game rules and the structure of championships; rules relating to the organisation of sport according to the European or pyramidal model; solidarity mechanisms; and the use of alternative dispute resolution mechanisms. A further eight are rules that have the potential to restrict trade among member states but are capable of objective justification in certain circumstances: rules concerning player transfers and contractual stability; rules that protect and encourage attendance at, and participation in, amateur sport; rules concerning the composition of national teams and player release clauses; anti-doping and disciplinary rules; rules to promote the use of club licensing systems; rules preventing the common control of clubs in the same competition; rules promoting youth development and the recruitment of local players; and rules concerning financial stability. The final group appear to be issues that are much more commercial in nature but have a significant impact on the organisation of sport: the regulation of agents; the sale of commercial rights; and the protection of the integrity of results from the threat of match-fixing.

Of these issues, the Federations identified the training and education of young players, the need to introduce a licensing framework and associated monitoring body to ensure good governance among clubs and the regulation of agents as the matters requiring the most urgent attention. These three matters are likely to have been flagged as urgent in an attempt to prevent further litigation in these areas. Following *Meca-Medina* and *MOTOE*, rules concerning each of these three issues can, in principle, infringe Arts.101 and 102 TFEU by preventing players, clubs and agents from acting in ways that would allow them to maximise their earnings by forcing them to satisfy a range of non-sporting criteria before they can act in a certain capacity or are allowed to compete in certain tournaments. To be lawful, the Federations will have to provide objective justifications for the need to make rules that regulate these activities. By appealing to the European Council to request the Commission to work with them, the Federations are hoping to avoid the costly litigation of the past and to influence proactively the development of European sports law in the future.

Hot topic … Can nationality restrictions ever be legal?

After the decision in *Bosman* and its extension in *Kolpak* and *Simutenkov*, restrictions on the number of non-domestic (EU and associated nation) players that a club could field in any game were held to be unlawful. Since then, UEFA has reintroduced a player quota scheme in the club competitions that it organises (the Champions League and the Europa League) in the form of the 'home-grown players' rule, whilst FIFA proposed a similar system, the '6+5' rule, which has now been withdrawn.

Art.18 of the Regulations of both the UEFA Champions League and UEFA Europa League require that a club submit a squad list of 25 players from whom the team to play in these competitions will be selected. Of these 25, eight must be 'locally trained players', and of these eight, a minimum of four must be 'club-trained players', and a maximum of four must be 'association-trained players'. Club-trained players must have been registered for at least three years with the club for which they are now playing between the ages of 15 and 21, whilst association-trained players must have been registered for at least three years with a club or clubs affiliated to

the same national association as their current club, again between the ages of 15 and 21.

FIFA proposed that the starting 11 players of any professional football team must include a minimum of six players who are qualified to play for the national association to which their current club is affiliated, with the remaining five being able to come from anywhere else in the world. Substitutes could also come from any country, meaning that under current rules, it would have been possible for a maximum of eight of the 14 players who could play for a team in any game to be 'foreign' players.

UEFA claims that its rule is of a 'purely sporting interest' and therefore not capable of engaging EU law on the basis that it affects nothing more than the composition of a team. However, the reality is that this is a 'dual role' rule that, although having a clear sporting objective, also has an impact on economic activity, which is sufficient to engage Art.45 TFEU as was the case in *Bosman*. Following *Meca-Medina*, as the 'home-grown players' rule is a decision of an association of undertakings that has an impact on the operation of the employment market for

professional footballers, Art.101 TFEU is in principle also engaged. Therefore, further investigation of its legality is required.

Art.45 as interpreted by *Bosman* prohibits restrictions on the freedom of movement for workers on the grounds of nationality. The UEFA rule requires only that a player is 'locally trained' and applies irrespective of their nationality. It is therefore not directly discriminatory. However, as the condition is much more easily fulfilled by nationals of the country where a club is based, it is potentially indirectly discriminatory. The rule may appear to be neutral, but its effect has the potential to discriminate against the group of people who find it more difficult to comply with, in this case, the young foreign players who were trained abroad and who later want to move to a club established elsewhere in the EU. An indirectly discriminatory rule is lawful only if it can be objectively justified.

It is likely that, after *Meca-Medina* and *MOTOE*, infringements of both Arts.45 and 101 will be capable of being justified on broadly similar grounds. As both provisions are, in principle, infringed by the 'home-grown player' rule, the quality of the justifications put forward by UEFA must also be interrogated. UEFA claims that its rules promote competitive balance by spreading the available talent across a greater number of clubs and that they encourage the proper training and protection of young players.

The CJEU has long held that it is a legitimate objective of the rules of an ISF to seek to maintain a competitive balance between the participants in a championship and to ensure the uncertainty of results. The problem faced by UEFA, however, is that there is no proof that this rule can achieve these aims. There is still nothing to stop the richest clubs buying the best players in accordance with the quotas and nothing to stop them from hoarding excess players in order to stop them from playing for a rival, thereby perpetuating the imbalance that the UEFA is seeking to eradicate. The UEFA rule can be further undermined by a club deciding simply not to fill any of the eight places constituting its 'locally trained' quota. For example, a club could choose to name 17 world-class 'foreign' players on its squad list and still be able to compete in either of UEFA's tournaments. Thus, the rule appears from the outset to be neither necessary nor inherent in achieving competitive balance or securing the uncertainty of results.

It is also a legitimate objective of an ISF to have rules that both encourage and protect the development of young players. Again, however, there is no proof that the home-grown players rule can actually achieve this aim. There are a variety of problems faced by the UEFA rule. Firstly, it can be undermined by a club simply choosing not to name any players in the club-trained category, while allowing it to buy in four association-trained players and 17 foreign players. There is nothing in the way that the UEFA rule is drafted that forces a club to develop new players if it chooses not to. Secondly, it can be subverted by naming four academy players who have no realistic prospect of making it on to the field of play except in the most extreme of circumstances; if the players are not going to be exposed to playing at the highest level, it cannot be said to be developing their career by their sitting on the substitutes' bench. Thirdly, the rule might actually create the conditions in which the trafficking of young players can occur as clubs seek to bring in players at as young an age as possible to ensure that they can qualify as club-trained despite being qualified to play for a foreign international representative team. If young players need not be exposed to the highest levels of play as a result of this rule then there appears to be no justification for its implementing in the first place. Therefore, it is neither necessary nor inherent that young players will be developed by professional clubs as the rule cannot guarantee that a club's own youth system will be used as a supply of players for their first team or for selection in UEFA competitions.

The rules respectively proposed and implemented by FIFA and UEFA appear to be on uncertain legal ground. FIFA's proposal in particular appeared to be little more than an attempt to reintroduce the kind of directly discriminatory measure that was specifically declared unlawful in *Bosman* and would have been incapable of withstanding the scrutiny of either the European Commission or the CJEU; despite commissioning advice to prove its legality, FIFA eventually withdrew its proposal when it became clear that it would be declared anti-competitive if introduced. UEFA's 'home-grown players' rule appears to pay greater regard to the requirements of EU law, but there remain problems with whether it is a necessary and proportionate means of achieving what would otherwise be legitimate and protectable goals.

A solution may present itself to both bodies, should they decide to focus more on the training, education and protection of young players and on rewarding clubs for the operation of successful academies and their work in the community rather than on trying to reintroduce nationality quotas. If the restrictions based on nationality are challenged, it is possible that they will be found to infringe EU law. However, a justification for such quotas that can be based on the improvement of the all-round education of young athletes and the prevention of their exploitation in the labour market is likely to meet with the explicit approval of the institutions of the EU, provided that the rules are appropriately drafted. *Bernard* could be the starting point for any potential developments in this area.

Summary

12.1 Since *Walrave,* it has been held that sporting rules and relationships are capable of engaging EU law when they have an impact on an economic activity. In particular, where the rules and decisions of an ISF or NGB affect an athlete's ability to engage in gainful employment, it must be ensured that they do not infringe EU law. As the provisions of the TFEU have direct effect on sports bodies, an athlete is able to rely on a breach of its provisions as their cause of action before the national courts of the EU, however, this right has been restricted to some degree by the development of the 'specificity of sport' argument.

12.2 Art.45 TFEU guarantees the freedom of movement for workers to travel throughout the EU for employment purposes. *Bosman* interpreted Art.45 to mean that no restrictions can be placed on this fundamental freedom by requiring the payment of a fee to enable an athlete to join a new club after the expiry of their previous contract of employment or through the imposition of nationality quotas. An exemption has been granted to genuinely representative sporting competitions to enable regional and international tournaments to continue on the basis that they are not economic activities. Following *Meca-Medina*, it may be better to describe the restrictions created by the rules governing international sport as inherent in the proper organisation of such competitions rather than as an exemption. In order to determine whether a rule, decision or practice of a sports authority breaches the free movement provisions of the Treaty, the Court must address four issues. Firstly, is the conduct in question a restriction on a worker's freedom of movement under Art.45 TFEU? Secondly, if the rule is a restriction, is its use capable of being justified objectively? Thirdly, is the rule effective in promoting the objectives pursued? Fourthly, is the rule a proportionate means of achieving the objectives?

12.3 Art.56 guarantees a person established in one member state the freedom to provide their services in any other member state of the EU. It has the effect of extending the same protections to self-employed individual athletes as are guaranteed to athletes employed by clubs under Art.45. *Deliège* made it clear that there are no restrictions on a person's right to provide their services where they are necessary and proportionate for achieving a legitimate goal. The selection criteria operated by NGBs when picking national teams and the entry criteria operated by the organisers of elite level championships are both lawful because they enable international sport to be administered effectively. In order to determine whether a sports authority's rules, decisions or practices breach Art.56, the ECJ will follow the same four steps that it would when considering a breach of Art.45.

12.4 Art.49 enables undertakings to establish their business in any member state of the EU. There is no sport specific litigation on this issue to date, however, it would appear to be difficult for a club to argue that it should be free to relocate from one member state to another because of the way in which sport is governed and administered in the EU.

12.5 Arts.101 and 102 TFEU apply to the conduct of sports bodies where they are engaged in economic activity. As most ISFs and NGBs have 'dual roles' in respect of the governance of their sport, meaning that they perform both regulatory and commercial functions, their conduct will usually engage EU competition law at least in principle. As ISFs and NGBs are undertakings in their own right, and are associations of undertakings taking decisions that have an impact on the market in which they operate, many of their rules and decisions have the potential to infringe Art.101. As the pyramidal structure or European model of sport has the effect of creating jurisdictional monopolies, it is also possible for their decisions to constitute an abuse of a dominant position. Whether or not a rule conforms with EU competition law can be determined by asking four questions. Firstly, is the collective regulatory body that is seeking to rely on the potentially restrictive rule an undertaking or an association of undertakings? Secondly, is the rule a restriction

Summary cont'd

of competition contrary to Art.101(1) TFEU or an abuse of a dominant position under Art.102 TFEU? Thirdly, if the rule is a restriction, does it affect trade between member states? Fourthly, if it does affect trade within the internal market, can it be justified under Art.101(3) TFEU on the basis that its beneficial effects outweigh the restrictions that it imposes? Where the rules in dispute are necessary and inherent to the proper administration of sport, protect its competitive balance and/or the uncertainty of its results, then no breach of competition law will be established.

Further reading

Beloff et al, *Sports Law* (2nd edn, 2012, Hart) chs 4 and 6

Craig and De Burca, *EU Law* (5th edn, 2011, Oxford University Press) chs 21, 22, 26, 27

Lewis and Taylor (eds), *Sport: Law and Practice* (2nd edn, 2008, Tottel) chs B2 and 3

Parrish and Miettinen, *The sporting exception in European Union Law* (2008, TMC Asser Press)

Weatherill, *Cases and Materials on EU Law* (10th edn, 2012, Oxford University Press) chs 7, 13, 14 and 16

Majani, 'An excavation into the legal deficiencies of the FIFA "6+5 Rule" and the UEFA "Home-grown Players Rule" in the eyes of European Union Law' [2009] 1/2 *International Sports Law Journal* 19

Manville, 'The UEFA "Home-grown Player Rule" and the Meca-Medina judgment of the European Court of Justice' [2009] 1/2 *International Sports Law Journal* 25

Miettinen, 'Policing the boundaries between regulation and commercial exploitation: lessons from the MOTOE case' [2008] 3/4 *International Sports Law Journal* 13

Pijetlovic, 'Another classic of EU sports jurisprudence: the legal implications of Olympique Lyonnais v Olivier Bernard and Newcastle United FC (C-325/09)' (2010) 35(6) *European Law Review* 857

Rincon, 'EC competition and internal market law: on the existence of a sporting exemption and its withdrawal' (2007) 3(3) *Journal of Contemporary European Research* 224

Subiotto, 'The adoption and enforcement of anti-doping rules should not be subject to European competition law' (2010) 31(8) *European Competition Law Review* 33

Szyszczak, 'Competition and sport' (2007) 32(1) *European Law Review* 95

Van Rompey, 'Fair access to exclusive sports rights still a long shot in UK pay TV market' (2009) 14(4) *Communications Law* 118

Wathelet, 'Sport governance and EU legal order' in Gardiner, Parrish and Siekmann (eds), *EU, Sport, Law and Policy* (2009, TMC Asser Press) ch 4

Weatherill, 'The influence of EU law on sports governance' in Gardiner, Parrish and Siekmann (eds), *EU, Sport, Law and Policy* (2009, TMC Asser Press) ch 5

Weatherill, 'The *White Paper on Sport* as an exercise in "Better Regulation"' in Gardiner, Parrish and Siekmann (eds), *EU, Sport, Law and Policy* (2009, TMC Asser Press) ch 6

Weatherill, 'Anti-doping revisited – the demise of the rule of "purely sporting interest"'? (2006) 27(12) *European Competition Law Review* 645

Weatherill, 'Article 82 EC and sporting "conflict of interest": the judgment in MOTOE' [2009] 1/2 *International Sports Law Journal* 3

Links to relevant websites can be found at www.palgrave.com/law/james2e

Chapter 13 follows overleaf.

The fan as consumer and the commercial exploitation of sport

- The commercialisation and commodification of sport (13.1)
- The exploitation of intellectual property and merchandising rights (13.2)
  - Protecting team names (13.2.1)
  - Replica kits (13.2.2)
  - Protecting other merchandising rights (13.2.3)
    - Passing off (13.2.3.1)
    - Trade marks (13.2.3.2)
    - Scarves, badges and retro kits (13.2.3.3)
  - Ambush marketing (13.2.4)
- Regulating access to televised sport (13.3)
  - Collective sales and exclusive deals (13.3.1)
  - Live sport in pubs (13.3.2)
  - Protected events of national importance (13.3.3)
- Ticket touting and the regulation of secondary ticket sales (13.4)
  - The evolution of the secondary market (13.4.1)
  - Regulation by generally applicable criminal law provisions (13.4.2)
    - Fraud Act 2006 ss.2 and 3 (13.4.2.1)
    - Consumer Protection Regulations (13.4.2.2)
  - Regulation of specific instances of ticket touting (13.4.3)
    - Touting at designated football matches – Criminal Justice and Public Order Act 1994 s.166 (13.4.3.1)
    - Touting at the London Olympics 2012 – London Olympic and Paralympic Games Act 2006 s.31 (13.4.3.2)
    - Touting at the Glasgow Commonwealth Games 2014 – Glasgow Commonwealth Games Act 2008 s.17 (13.4.3.3)
  - Enforcing ticket conditions under the civil law (13.4.4)

The fan as consumer and the commercial exploitation of sport

Key terms

- **Commodification** – the repackaging and rebranding of an event or competition that creates a commodity that can be more easily marketed to the public.
- **Primary rights holder** – the owner of the commercial rights vested in an event, competition or product.
- **Ambush marketing** – the unofficial or unauthorised association of a product or service with an event in an attempt to undermine the marketing strategy of one or more of the event's official sponsors.

13.1 The commercialisation and commodification of sport

The commercialisation of sport has not only affected athletes, clubs and administrators but also has had a significant impact on the ways in which sport is now consumed by the fans. The quest for success both on and off the field of play has led in recent years to an unprecedented growth in the exploitation of commercial rights, with sports sponsorship, merchandising sales and the value of broadcasting rights all soaring. Whilst providing some elite athletes, clubs and competition organisers with access to additional income streams that dwarf what they previously could have expected to earn, it has been the fans who have bankrolled these commercial developments.

The commercialisation of sport is not just about replica kits and scarves; many clubs now sell a range of sportswear, leisurewear, gifts and even financial services. Nor is it just about the main television deals; some professional clubs now run their own TV channels and stream live games and highlights packages online and to mobile communications devices. Nor is it just about corporate hospitality and executive boxes; ordinary ticket prices have increased dramatically over the past 20 years, particularly in professional football and also since the introduction of all-seater stadiums, a development that is very much contrary to the predictions of Lord Justice Taylor in the aftermath of the Hillsborough disaster. The commercialisation seen in modern sport is about the creation of new income streams and the development of new markets in which to sell these products and services.

One integral aspect of this commercialisation has been the commodification of sport. This marketing phenomenon is where a valuable asset is repackaged and rebranded, turned into a more attractive commodity and sold back to the consumer as something new. Perhaps the most well-known example of this in British sport is the creation of the Premier League in 1992. A national professional football league had existed in England since 1888. After receiving a marketing and administrative makeover, the top division of English football was sold back to the public as the Premier League as though the previous era had not happened. One of the main differences to the fan is that what was once available for free on terrestrial television is now only available on subscription services.

The money involved with some of the more commercialised sports and events is huge: the sale of broadcast rights to the London Olympics in 2012 is estimated to have exceeded £2.5bn and the total value of the worldwide rights for the Premier League is now over £5bn. Either directly or indirectly, these sums are provided by the fans; it is the fan, now often referred to as simply a loyal consumer, who buys ever more varied merchandising, who subscribes to the various broadcast platforms and who buys the products of the corporate sponsors who aim at developing a relationship with them by associating themselves with their team, their sport or the event that they are attending.

This chapter analyses from a legal perspective the impact of the commercialisation of sport on the fan-consumer. It begins by examining intellectual property issues and how clubs, teams and event organisers protect their commercial rights from exploitation by others. Secondly, where subscription-based broadcasting of events is concerned, a range of methods have been tried by fan-consumers to find cheaper alternatives to paying the necessary fee to the official broadcaster, even if it means watching an event with a foreign commentary. Finally, as tickets to some events have become more difficult to acquire, a sophisticated secondary market in unofficial sales, or ticket touting, has developed The legality of these alternative markets has become increasingly contested as clubs and competition organisers seek to maximise their profits and protect their investments, whilst fans try to limit the exploitation of their finite financial resources.

13.2 The exploitation of intellectual property and merchandising rights

The sale of goods and services associated with a particular team, event or sport has become an important income stream for many sports bodies. It is through the sale of an ever-growing range of merchandise that many sports clubs in particular are able to meet the wage demands of their star players. However, as the primary rights holders have sought to exploit this new income stream ever more creatively, various secondary markets have evolved to provide fan-consumers with alternatives to officially-branded products. This section explores the situations in which the law has engaged with various practices to ensure that an appropriate balance is maintained between protecting the commercial rights of clubs and event organisers and ensuring that the fan-consumers are not unlawfully exploited.

13.2.1 Protecting team names

In 2011, two separate and distinct teams raced in the Formula 1 motor racing championship using the name 'Lotus'. Group Lotus, a long-established British manufacturer of sports cars, raced as Lotus Renault, GP and the 1Malaysia Racing Team raced as Team Lotus. In *Group Lotus plc v 1 Malaysia Racing Team SDN BHD* [2011] EWHC 1366, the High Court was asked to determine which of the two teams had the right to race as 'Lotus', an issue made all the more important because of the iconic nature of the Lotus name in motorsport and the accompanying brand recognition and merchandising rights that this would secure.

In 2009, Group Lotus had granted the defendant a five-year licence to race in Formula 1 as 'Lotus Racing'. The relationship ended acrimoniously and with a breach of contract in 2010 when the defendant failed to secure the exclusive right to use 'Lotus' on accompanying merchandising. The defendant then acquired the naming rights of the historic racing brand, 'Team Lotus' from a third party, who had in turn acquired the rights when the original racing team had gone into administration in 1994. Group Lotus claimed that it alone owned the goodwill vested in the name 'Lotus' and that nobody else could use that name on any sports or motor racing cars.

The High Court held that two separate and distinct companies had been created by the former racing driver Colin Chapman; Lotus Cars (now Group Lotus) to manufacture sports cars and Team Lotus to race in motorsports events. Over the years, each had generated goodwill in its own specific fields of operation and that as a result, both were able to use the word 'Lotus' within those fields; Group Lotus on sports cars, and Team Lotus on cars racing in motorsports events. Therefore, Group Lotus could not complain that there was a diminution of the value of its own goodwill or that there would be confusion in the eyes of motor racing fans when it entered a team in the Formula 1 championship for the first time in 2011. The parties have subsequently agreed that Group Lotus will race in Formula 1 as 'Lotus F1 Team', whilst the defendants have bought another iconic British sports car manufacturer and now race as Caterham F1 Team, ensuring that both are able to exploit commercially the history and status of the two famous marques.

13.2.2 Replica kits

The last 20 years have seen an unprecedented growth in sales of replica sports kits. Most major professional sports clubs in the UK generally now use at least one home kit and one differently-coloured away kit in any playing season; replica versions or reproductions of these kits, including shirts, shorts, socks and training outfits, are then made available for sale to fans. Each of these designs usually has a life of two seasons, enabling the clubs to bring out a new version of one or other of their kits every year. Some clubs have begun to register a third kit in yet another colour scheme, whilst others use modified versions of one or more of these kits when participating in specific competitions such as the UEFA Champions League and the Heineken European Rugby Cup. Within this market, the sale of replica shirts has become a cornerstone of many clubs' merchandising strategies.

The perhaps unusual starting point for legal discussion in this area is to determine whether the products in question are sports kit or leisurewear. In *Hudson Bay Apparel Brands LLC v Umbro International Ltd* [2010] EWCA Civ 949, the Court of Appeal was asked to examine, amongst a number of claims and counterclaims, whether the appellants were in breach of their licensing agreement with Umbro by manufacturing and marketing sportswear instead of leisurewear. Hudson Bay was licensed to produce 'off-field' apparel such as polo and tee shirts, pullovers, warm-up suits and rain suits sporting the Umbro 'double diamond' logo in the US; another company had the rights to sell on-field apparel.

Hudson Bay produced a range of 'pocketless soccer basics' that included shirts, shorts and tracksuits cut in the style and using colour patterns reminiscent of kits usually produced for on-field use. Further, in the marketing of these products, most of the models were pictured with footballs. In coming to the conclusion that this was on-field sports kit, not off-field leisurewear, the Court made specific reference to the images used in the adverts and the lack of pockets in the various products. This last point was considered to be important as under FIFA regulations, playing apparel must not contain pockets, therefore, if pockets had been added to the items, they could only have been used as off-field leisurewear. Thus, taken as a whole and based on the colour schemes, style and fabric used, the lack of pockets and the associated advertising campaign, the

Court held that these were items of sportswear designed to be used on the field of play, not items of leisurewear to be used off it.

As the market in replica kits continued to boom throughout the 1990s, the Office of Fair Trading (OFT) began an investigation into this specific market because all kits available for purchase in the UK appeared to be sold at the same price regardless of the team, manufacturer or retailer concerned. Its investigation into price-fixing and related concerted practices came to a head in more litigation involving Umbro.

▶ *JJB Sports plc v OFT; Allsports Ltd v OFT* [2004] CAT 17 and *JJB Sports plc v OFT* [2006] EWCA Civ 1318

JJB Sports (JJB), a national sportswear retailer, had become concerned about the pricing strategy of a rival store, Sports Soccer (SS), which was aggressively discounting replica football shirts with a view to securing for itself a larger share of the market. JJB was concerned about SS's reduction in the price of some of the most popular replica kits and in particular those of Manchester United FC, Celtic FC and the England national team. Each of these kits was produced by the same manufacturer, Umbro Holdings plc. In the course of its dealings with Umbro, JJB provided Umbro with information that led it to apply commercial pressure on SS in an attempt to persuade it not to reduce the price at which it sold replica football shirts below £40.

Following an extensive investigation by the OFT, it was found that JJB, Allsports and a number of other high street stores, together with Umbro and Manchester United, were guilty of price fixing and/or other concerted practices that distorted the market in replica football kits to the detriment of consumers, contrary to s.2 Competition Act 1998. It was found that prices were being maintained at an artificially high level throughout the sector and that competition among rival stores was stifled as a result. JJB and Allsports appealed against this finding to the Competition Appeal Tribunal, however, their appeals were rejected. JJB made a further unsuccessful appeal to the Court of Appeal.

The motives behind why the various companies involved in this litigation engaged in such an obviously illegal activity as price-fixing were varied. The six retailers were concerned about losing market share and profits in the event that one company, in this case Sports Soccer, decided to discount its prices significantly. Manchester United and the FA appear to have been attempting to maintain their status as 'premium brands' that were sold in proper sports shops, not by discount retailers or supermarkets. As Umbro would also hope that sales of its replica kits would encourage consumers to buy its performance wear, it too appears to have wanted to its goods to be sold at premium prices in reputable sports shops.

Although each of these concerns is legitimate from a purely commercial perspective, anti-competitive behaviour of this kind is unlawful and is severely punished. A brand can be protected from damage, but it cannot be isolated from legitimate competition in the market. The four companies who were fined the largest amounts all appealed against the punishments imposed on them ([2005] CAT 22). JJB Sports plc, Umbro Holdings Ltd and Manchester United plc eventually had their fines reduced to £6.7m, £5.3m and £1.5m, respectively whilst Allsports Ltd had theirs increased to £1.42m.

The OFT investigation into the replica kits market unearthed the lengths to which the parties involved were prepared to go in order to exploit this new revenue stream and to protect their own commercial interests. The result was an initial reduction in the price of shirts, followed by a degree of variation in the amount charged by different retailers for the kits of different clubs. Appendix 1 of the Premier League Handbook now specifically prohibits manufacturers of replica kits from imposing minimum sale prices on retailers. Although fan-consumers have received a degree of protection by the OFT requiring a greater degree of freedom to retailers to charge a genuinely competitive amount for replicas, the proliferation in the number of kits produced by some teams ensures that this income stream will continue to be a lucrative one for the foreseeable future.

13.2.3 Protecting other merchandising rights

Whereas the market for replica kits is relatively new, the market for products incorporating other symbols of allegiance are of much greater longevity. The wearing of hats and scarves in a particular team's colours or sporting its badge or crest has long been associated with fan culture. These items were seen as a means by which fans could express their support for their club rather than being products sold by it as part of an integrated merchandising strategy. As a result, the market was originally supplied by unofficial and unlicensed manufacturers and retailers; when clubs began to appreciate the true value of these markets, they began to take action to enforce their intellectual property rights in the symbols and signs that were most commonly associated with them.

The problem for many clubs was that these symbols were often unprotected. Most were not registered as trade marks, enabling unlicensed products to use them comparatively freely; those clubs which had gone through the registration process had rarely, if ever, adequately asserted their rights over their trade mark, effectively allowing the protection to lapse under ss.42 or 46 Trade Marks Act 1994. Further, actions for breach of copyright are difficult to sustain because of the problems associated with identifying the original author or current owner of the symbol. Where the oldest and most traditional symbols are at issue, copyright lapses 70 years after the end of the year in which its author died (s.12(2) Copyright, Designs and Patents Act 1988); where the author is unknown, copyright lapses 70 years after the end of the year in which the symbol was first made available to the public (s.12(3)). Thus clubs have been forced to resort to a variety of strategies to protect these valuable commercial rights from exploitation by unofficial competitors.

13.2.3.1 Passing off

The tort of passing off was originally developed to prevent one business from unfairly exploiting the goodwill and reputation of another (*Warnik v Townend* [1979] AC 731). Firstly, it must be established that the claimant owns goodwill in relation to its business, goods or services. Secondly, the defendant must have, in the course of its trade, made a misrepresentation that the goods or services that it supplies in a common field of activity are connected in some way to the claimant. Thirdly, there must be a real likelihood of confusion in the mind of the public that there is or might be a material connection between the defendant's goods and services and those of the claimant. Finally, there must be harm to the claimant's goodwill as a result of the defendant's conduct.

Now sometimes referred to as 'unfair trading' or 'unlawful competition', the tort is more widely defined and encompasses not only passing off, but also the situation where the unrestricted use by others of a company's goodwill or reputation so dilutes it as to render the original worthless or meaningless (*Vine Products Ltd v Mackenzie and Co Ltd* [1969] RPC 1). On the face of it, the tort enables clubs to prevent the sale of any unofficial merchandise where it can be proved that the manufacturer or retailer was either expressly or impliedly representing that their produce was in some way connected to the club by the use of words or symbols commonly associated with it.

There are two difficulties facing a primary rights holder seeking to bring an action for passing off. Firstly, it must prove that there has been an actual misrepresentation by the defendant, as opposed to a simple misuse of their trade marks or other related symbols. Only where the impression is given that the products in question are official will the claimant be able to prove this element of the tort. Secondly, it may be difficult for a claimant to prove that potential consumers were confused about the provenance of the products as they will usually be able to distinguish between what is and what is not officially licensed merchandise. Although the more modern form of the tort might be of some help if unfair trading practices could be established on the part of the defendant, one much more effective means of protecting the goodwill and reputation of a club and the use of its symbols and insignia will be by registering them as trade marks.

13.2.3.2 Trade marks

The Trade Marks Act 1994 enacted the Trade Marks Directive 89/104/EEC and created a new framework of protection for signs designating the trade origin of a product. Under s.1(1), a trade mark is defined as being any sign capable of being represented graphically and which is capable of distinguishing the goods or services of one undertaking from those of other undertakings. The registration of a trade mark provides the proprietor with an enforceable property right relating to its improper use under s.2(1). Thus, any infringement of the trade mark allows the proprietor to claim damages from the infringer, to request an injunction prohibiting them from further infringements, and under s.16, delivery up of any infringing goods in the possession of any person acting in the course of business.

▶ *Trade Marks Act 1994 s.10 – infringement of registered trade mark*

(1) A person infringes a registered trade mark if he uses in the course of trade a sign which is identical with the trade mark in relation to goods or services which are identical with those for which it is registered.

(2) A person infringes a registered trade mark if he uses in the course of trade a sign where because –

    (a) the sign is identical with the trade mark and is used in relation to goods or services similar to those for which the trade mark is registered, or

    (b) the sign is similar to the trade mark and is used in relation to goods or services identical with or similar to those for which the trade mark is registered,

there exists a likelihood of confusion on the part of the public, which includes the likelihood of association with the trade mark.

(3) A person infringes a registered trade mark if he uses in the course of trade in relation to goods or services, a sign which –

    (a) is identical with or similar to the trade mark, where the trade mark has a reputation in the United Kingdom and the use of the sign, being without due cause, takes unfair advantage of, or is detrimental to, the distinctive character or the repute of the trade mark.

(4) For the purposes of this section a person uses a sign if, in particular, he –

    (a) affixes it to goods or the packaging thereof;

> (b) offers or exposes goods for sale, puts them on the market or stocks them for those purposes under the sign, or offers or supplies services under the sign;
> (6) Nothing in the preceding provisions of this section shall be construed as preventing the use of a registered trade mark by any person for the purpose of identifying goods or services as those of the proprietor or a licensee.
> But any such use otherwise than in accordance with honest practices in industrial or commercial matters shall be treated as infringing the registered trade mark if the use without due cause takes unfair advantage of, or is detrimental to, the distinctive character or repute of the trade mark.

The purpose of a trade mark is to designate the origin of a product, without any possibility of confusion, as being produced or supplied by a specific undertaking. Its use on a product provides a consumer with a guarantee of its quality, provenance and originality and prevents others from exploiting the reputation of the proprietor by using the trade mark without the proprietor's consent. The Act provides two specific forms of protection to the proprietors of registered trade marks. Section 10(1) prohibits unauthorised copies of the trade mark proprietor's products from being produced and marketed with the protected symbol on them whereas, under s.10(2), attempts to confuse consumers by the use of a symbol similar to that which has been registered or by using the trade mark itself on goods similar to those currently being produced by the proprietor are prohibited.

Where clubs, governing bodies and event organisers have registered as a trade mark a crest, badge, logo or other symbol commonly associated with them, they can prevent anyone from using it to promote the marketing of similar products. Although this form of protection was rarely considered before the late 1980s boom in sports merchandising, it is now commonplace for a range of symbols and words to be registered in an ever increasing range of categories of products and services and for infringements to be vigorously pursued. An additional layer of statutory protection is provided to the Olympic Games, whose symbol, motto and associated words are specifically protected by the Olympic Symbol (Protection) Act 1995 (see further, chapter 14.3).

13.2.3.3 Scarves, badges and retro kits

A number of these issues finally came to a head in respect of a tradesman's sale of Arsenal scarves in the vicinity of their previous home ground, Highbury.

> ▶ *Arsenal Football Club Plc v Reed (No.2)* **[2003] EWCA Civ 96**
>
> Arsenal had registered as trade marks specific symbols related to the club for use with various categories of clothing. Its official merchandise was sold bearing these marks through approved retailers. Reed was a stallholder who had sold both licensed and unlicensed goods from a pitch nearby Arsenal's home ground since 1970. Both classes of goods bore the symbols that Arsenal had registered as trademarks and Reed accepted that he had used the protected marks without Arsenal's consent on the unlicensed products that he was selling. In an attempt to distinguish between the two categories of products, Reed ensured that the licensed products had swing tickets and labels indicating that they were official Arsenal merchandise, whilst the unlicensed products were sold from behind a sign that drew to the attention of potential purchasers that these items had no commercial connection with Arsenal.

Arsenal claimed that by selling unlicensed scarves that bore its registered trade marks alongside officially licensed versions of the same product, Reed was in breach of s.10(1) Trade Marks Act 1994. As its registered trade marks were a designation of the origin of the goods, Arsenal argued that only its officially licensed products were legally entitled to carry the protected symbols so that consumers would be able to distinguish its products from those which were unlicensed. The club also claimed that by using their trade marks in the way that he had, Reed was passing off his unlicensed products as being official Arsenal merchandise.

Reed responded by claiming that there was no breach of s.10(1) because he was not using the registered trade marks in the course of trade. Instead, he was using the symbols as a means of enabling fans to express their support, loyalty and affiliation to Arsenal FC; as he was not in any way trying to assert that the products were official, a claim corroborated by the sign on his stall, he claimed that he could not have infringed Arsenal's registered trade marks. Furthermore, he argued that as he had made it clear to all prospective purchasers which goods were licensed and which were not, he was not misrepresenting the origin of the merchandise but was simply enabling fans to express their support for Arsenal and was not therefore passing off the unlicensed scarves as official club products.

At trial, Laddie J held that Reed's use of the trademarked symbols as a badge of allegiance, rather than as designation of their origin, was not an infringement of Arsenal's rights. Furthermore, as Reed had made no claim that the unlicensed products were anything other than unlicensed, he could not be said to have been passing them off as official Arsenal merchandise.

When the case eventually reached the Court of Appeal, via a reference to the CJEU, the trial court's decision regarding the Trade Marks Act 1994 was reversed; there was no appeal in respect of the finding on passing off. The Court held that the relevant consideration in cases of this nature was to determine whether the use of the trade mark complained of by the proprietor was likely to affect or jeopardise the guarantee of origin, which was the primary function of the protected symbol, not whether it was being used as a trade mark by the infringer. As the unauthorised and unrestricted use of a registered trade mark by another damages this primary function by affecting its ability to act as a guarantee of the origin of the product, an infringement of Arsenal's rights was established.

Each of the courts involved in this litigation appears at various stages to have overcomplicated their analyses of infringement by discussing whether or not there was a need for confusion on the part of potential purchasers of the products. What *Arsenal v Reed* holds is that where the actual trade mark is used on the same products as those on which the proprietor uses the mark, then there is an infringement of s.10(1) Trade Marks Act 1994, even where the infringer is only using the protected symbol as a means of enabling the purchaser to demonstrate their support, loyalty, affiliation or allegiance to the proprietor of the mark; in this case, Arsenal. However, in the course of the reasoning of the CJEU and the Court of Appeal, it was also stated that by using the registered marks in the way that he did, Reed had created a material link between his unlicensed products and Arsenal. This was because anyone who had not seen the sign on his stall would be likely to assume that scarves bearing the Arsenal trade marks would be official Arsenal merchandise. Thus, if he had used the registered trade mark on products similar to those officially licensed by Arsenal or had used a symbol similar in design to the registered trade mark on products actually sold by the club, then he also would have committed an infringement of Arsenal's registered trade marks contrary to s.10(2) Trade Marks Act 1994.

The practical effect of *Arsenal v Reed* was that all major sports clubs, governing bodies and competition and event organisers that had not already done so redesigned the crests, badges and symbols that they used on their merchandise and registered them as trade marks. The degree of change varies dramatically among the many trade mark proprietors in the sports sector, as does the range of products for which protection is sought. However, the growth in the importance of merchandising means that all sports proprietors will now pursue any infringement of their trade marks to ensure that they are able to protect what has become one of their most important income streams.

This leaves traders in the position of Reed able to sell unlicensed products in the club's colours and to use old, unprotected symbols where it is clear that the product on which it is sold is not an official one and where to do so does not create a material link between the merchandise and the club as undertaking. Expressions of loyalty and allegiance, however, are not a justification for infringing the club's trade marks.

The recent growth in the market for old-fashioned/retro replica shirts has given rise to similar legal problems. Whether it is a preference for heavy-duty cotton tops, nostalgia for the kits from the fans' youth or for replicas free from sponsorship logos, the demand for replica kits other than those currently produced officially and under licence continues to expand. As the manufacturers of these shirts seek to produce as authentic a facsimile of the original as is possible, questions have been raised about the legality of the badges and insignia used on these kits.

▶ *Score Draw Ltd v Finch* [2007] EWHC 462 (Ch)

The respondent had registered as a trade mark the official emblem of the former Brazilian Football Federation which had been used as an identifying badge on the football shirts of the Brazilian national football team between 1914 and 1971 (the CBD badge). The respondent had then licensed the use of this mark to TOFFS, a manufacturer and retailer of historical football shirts. The applicant, which was also a manufacturer and retailer of historical football shirts, had used the CBD badge for over ten years prior to the respondent's application to register the CBD badge as a trade mark and wished to continue to do so. The importance of the CBD badge to the parties was that both wanted to use it on replica versions of the football shirts used by the Brazilian World Cup winning teams of 1958, 1962 and 1970, which are amongst the most popular of this kind of merchandise. The applicant appealed against the finding of the hearing officer that the CBD badge was sufficiently distinct to be registered as a trade mark.

In the High Court, Mann J found in favour of the applicant and held that under s.3(1)(b) Trade Marks Act 1994, the symbol under consideration was not sufficiently distinct to be registered as a trade mark. Although it is possible for a trade mark to be both a designation of origin and a badge of affiliation, as with the officially licensed merchandise in *Arsenal v Reed*, that was not the case here. The CBD badge was used by TOFFS and others as a means of maximising the authenticity of the replica shirts that they were producing; the mark was not used by TOFFS in a way that would make consumers automatically assume that on seeing it on an item of historical sportswear, the product could only have been produced by TOFFS and no other undertaking. Thus, the CBD badge was not being used as a designation of origin to denote that the garment had been produced by TOFFS and was not capable of being registered as a trade mark. Further, its use by both parties and others over at least the previous ten years had robbed the mark of its distinctive characteristics as a trade mark and therefore under s.3(1)(b) it was not sufficiently distinct to be used as a trade mark by the proprietor. As the CBD badge was so closely associated with the Brazilian national football team in the minds of the consumers most likely to buy the replica shirts, it could not be used as a designation of origin by any undertaking.

Although technically obiter as the decision of the court turned on the issue under s.3(1)(b), Mann J also held that the CBD badge was, according to s.3(1)(d), descriptive of a characteristic of the clothing which bears it in the sense that it connotes that the clothing has an association with the historic Brazilian national football team. Thus, the judge was reinforcing that the CBD badge was an essential requirement for an authentic replica of the relevant shirts, not a mark that identified a particular manufacturer or producer with the garment.

Only marks or symbols that denote the trade origin of a product can be protected under the Trade Marks Act 1994. If the symbol is used only as a means of producing historical authenticity or accuracy or has been used by so many undertakings that it has become generic, it will be found to be either descriptive or not sufficiently distinctive to be capable of registration.

In the light of *R v Boulter* [2008] EWCA Crim 2375, it is also worth noting that it is no defence for a person accused of infringing a registered trade mark to claim that the reproduction of the mark was of such poor quality that no confusion as to the provenance of the product could have arisen in the minds of potential consumers. The Court of Appeal was not prepared to allow counterfeiters to use this ingenious line of reasoning to undermine the purpose of s.10 Trade Marks Act 1994. A copy of the mark, no matter how poor the quality, is capable of infringing s.10(1) and, if applied to the same category of goods that are produced by the proprietor, will be considered to be capable of confusing a consumer as required by s.10(2).

13.2.4 Ambush marketing

Ambush or parasitic marketing is the unofficial or unauthorised association of a product or service with an event. The undertaking conducts the ambush by strategically attaching itself to the goodwill or high profile of a team, event or competition and in doing so undermines the rights of an official sponsor of a similar product or service, who will usually have paid a substantial sum to be associated exclusively with the primary rights holder. The interpretation and ambit of ambush marketing is far from clear, with many ambushers claiming that their own marketing practices are being unfairly curtailed by anti-ambushing laws. In the UK, the only instance of anti-ambush marketing legislation to date has been the protection provided to the London 2012 Olympic Games (see further, chapter 14.3.4).

The potential impact on fans of anti-ambush marketing strategies is usually only recognised when an event organiser takes particularly unusual action in order to protect the commercial rights of an official sponsor. For example, at the FIFA World Cup 2006 in Germany, male Dutch fans were forced to remove orange lederhosen-style shorts that were emblazoned with the name and logo of the brewer 'Bavaria' before being allowed into the stadium to watch a game. The justification provided by FIFA for requiring the stewards to take this action was that the shorts constituted advertising that conflicted with that of the official beer of the tournament, Budweiser. In protecting the commercial interests of its official partners, FIFA saw nothing wrong with forcing some fans to watch the match in their underwear.

13.3 Regulating access to televised sport

Since BSkyB first acquired the exclusive right to broadcast live Premier League football matches in 1992, the pay TV market for sports events has grown from strength to strength. With sport often being used as a driver for recruiting new subscribers, many events and competitions that were once freely available on terrestrial television are now only available via subscription satellite, cable or Internet services. Although this has often been to the financial benefit of NGBs, event organisers, sports clubs and professional athletes, the impact of collective and exclusive selling practices has been borne predominantly by the fan-consumer.

The creation of this new market in sports broadcasting rights has given rise to a number of specific legal issues. In particular, it has led many people to try and receive subscription services without paying for them, or paying for them at a reduced rate, and it has required the government to update the list of events that cannot be transmitted exclusively by subscription broadcasters. This, in turn, has led to a distortion of the market in favour of terrestrial broadcasters in respect of a limited number of sporting events.

13.3.1 Collective sales and exclusive deals

Two models for the sale of sports broadcasting rights have emerged over the past 20 years. Collective selling is where all teams in a competition join together and sell their rights through one communal body, usually the competition organiser or NGB. In contrast, individual selling is where each participant sells the rights to its home games and is in competition with every other participant when trying to secure broadcasting deals. In the UK, collective selling has become the norm, though this is not the case in other European countries, such as Spain.

Both models require exclusive access to the product in order to maximise profits for the primary rights holder; this is where one broadcaster alone has the right to screen the event to the exclusion of all others. Exclusivity ensures rarity in the supply chain, allowing the primary rights holder to charge a premium to the broadcaster and to maximise its earnings from the rights sale. However, this in turn requires the broadcaster to charge as high a subscription rate as the market will bear in order to recoup its initial outlay and, if possible, make a profit.

The sale of the broadcast rights for English football's Premier League in England was first investigated by the OFT in 1999. The OFT was concerned that the collective and exclusive elements of the agreements entered into by the Premier League, BSkyB and the BBC were distorting competition to the detriment of rival broadcasters and fan-consumers. In *Re Televising Premier League Football Matches* [2000] EMLR 78, the OFT outlined its main concerns with the agreements as being that they stifled competition between broadcasters by making it too difficult for rivals to acquire the rights to show live Premier League matches, that they forced an artificially high sale price of the rights and that too few games were made available live to fan-consumers.

The Restrictive Practices Court disagreed with the OFT and held that the benefits to the consumer of the collective and exclusive selling arrangements outweighed any potentially anti-competitive disadvantages. Four benefits were specifically highlighted by the Court. Firstly, that the combination of collective and exclusive selling of the rights enabled a package of games that was representative of the entire championship to be sold, which was what the public wanted access to. Secondly, that this strategy provided financial benefits to the clubs by enabling them to maximise their income as a group, which in turn improved their solvency and allowed them to develop their stadiums and to purchase better-quality players, thereby producing a better-quality product for fan-consumers. Thirdly, the agreements provided a model for the distribution of the income generated by the rights sale that most effectively provided a financial level playing field among clubs in the same competition and fourthly, they allowed the Premier League to keep a greater degree of control over the timing of fixtures than would a series of individual deals.

Despite these findings, concerns about the legality of collective and exclusive broadcasting agreements persisted, particularly under EU competition law. In an attempt to avoid investigation by the European Commission in respect of the sale of the rights to the Champions League, UEFA applied for an exemption from the application of EU competition law to the broadcasting agreements it had entered into under Art.101(3) TFEU (ex Art.81(3) ECT). By the Commission Decision of 23 July 2003, Comp/C-2/37.398 *Joint Selling of the Commercial Rights to the UEFA Champions League*, the new arrangements devised by UEFA were granted an exemption from Art.101 TFEU (ex Art.81 ECT). UEFA had ensured that there was a variety of rights packages available to both free-to-air and subscription broadcasters and that after the two premium packages per jurisdiction had chosen the two matches each that they wished to show, all remaining matches were available for broadcast on subscription or pay-per-view channels. If any matches were left unsold, the home club would have the non-exclusive right, together with UEFA, to sell the rights to individual games. Additional packages were available for Internet, 3G, audio and delayed broadcast rights. Each of the rights deals was to last for a maximum of three years.

The Commission approved these arrangements on the basis that they improved the production and distribution of a quality branded product through a single point of sale. Further, consumers would benefit by being able to access a variety Champions League packages and that the overall quality of the broadcasting of the product would be likely to improve as a result of these arrangements. Finally, as the restrictions were indispensible for the achievement of these benefits, the exemption was granted.

This Commission Decision had an impact on subsequent sales of the Premier League's broadcast rights, with both the bidding rules and the packages of rights that it offered to broadcasters being amended gradually in an attempt to avoid further investigation by UK and EU competition authorities. As a result of increased cooperation between the Premier League and the Commission, a similar approval was granted to the Premier League's arrangements by Commission Decision of 22 March 2006, Comp/C-2/38.173 *Joint Selling of the Media Rights to the FA Premier League*. The most controversial element of these arrangements was that no single broadcaster was allowed to buy all six of the live TV rights packages, effectively ending the exclusivity that had been enjoyed by BSkyB since 1992. Furthermore, the six available packages had to be more evenly balanced in terms of their content, ensuring that each was genuinely representative of a Premier League season. As with the Champions League Decision, these arrangements were considered to strike an appropriate balance among the needs of the League, the broadcasters and consumers and to be of benefit to each of the affected parties.

Although these collective and exclusive selling practices appear to benefit both the primary rights holders and the broadcasters by enabling them to maximise their incomes, the benefits to the fan-consumer are less easy to indentify, especially in the absence of specific complaints made by the public about either deal. The ability to buy a package that represents an entire championship or tournament from one broadcaster, rather than having to buy individual games or bundles of games from a number of rights holders, is a clear benefit. However, where Premier League games are concerned, the viewer now needs to purchase subscriptions from both Sky and BT, instead of the one subscription from Sky that was previously the case, in order to watch the live games featured in all six packages. This leaves the slightly strange outcome of the Commission's intervention being that where Premier League football is concerned, and as is so often the case this is likely to act as the template for similar deals in other sports, consumers are left paying more for their sport than they were previously.

13.3.2 Live sport in pubs

The increased cost to sports fans of subscription services and the increasing number of events that have migrated to them has led to the watching of live sport in pubs and bars becoming increasingly popular. However, some licensees have found that the higher rate of subscription that they are charged by broadcasters has become prohibitive in recent years. Rather than not showing games at all, some have resorted to showing games via satellite feeds from other countries from both within and outside of the EU. In order to do this, licensees have purchased satellite dishes, decoders and decoder cards from an overseas broadcaster and paid for a subscription that enables them to watch foreign versions of popular British sports events.

The FA Premier League has been particularly vigilant in pursuing what it considers to be the unauthorised screening of football matches in which it owns the copyrights. In *Murphy v Media Protection Services Ltd* [2007] EWHC 3091 (Admin) and [2008] EWHC 1666 (Admin), a pub licensee was prosecuted for breach of copyright under s.297(1) Copyright, Designs and Patents Act 1998 for showing live Premier League football matches on a Greek subscription channel. In *Football Association Premier League Ltd v QC Leisure* [2008] EWHC 1411 (Ch), the League brought civil actions for copyright infringement and the possession of unauthorised decoders against the suppliers of the satellite equipment that enabled the viewing of the foreign feeds of its games and the licensees who had used the equipment to screen live Premier League football matches. The defendants claimed that the legislation prohibiting them from buying or using foreign decoder cards was contrary to Art.56 TFEU as being a restriction on the freedom to provide services throughout the EU and that the Premier League's territorially based broadcasting arrangements were anti-competitive under Art.101(1) TFEU. The CJEU finally delivered its decision in the joined cases of *Football Association Premier League Ltd, NetMed Hellas SA and Multichoice Hellas SA v QC Leisure, David Richardson, AV Station plc, Malcolm Chamberlain, Michael Madden, SR Leisure Ltd, Philip Houghton and Derek Owen* C-403/08 and *Karen Murphy v Media Protections Services Ltd* C-429/08 [2012] 1 CMLR 29 on 4 October 2011.

In order to maximise its income from the sale of its live rights, the Premier League grants media organisations the exclusive right to broadcast its matches on a territorial basis. This framework of territorial exclusivity is supposed to prevent people based in one member state from receiving the broadcasts of broadcasters based in another member state by requiring each official broadcaster to undertake not to sell decoding hardware outside of the territory for which it has bought the live rights. In each of these cases, publicans in the UK had subscribed to receive subscription satellite services from the official broadcaster based in Greece in order to have access to live broadcasts of Premier League football matches at a much lower price than they would have had to pay the official broadcaster in the UK, BSkyB Ltd.

The Court's opinion begins by answering a preliminary technical question, holding that the Greek decoders are not 'illicit devices' that have been used to access the broadcasts without the necessary permissions; in other words, this is not a case of piracy or accessing the broadcasts for free. The decoders are legitimate devices, but they have been used in disregard of the broadcaster's will outside of the geographical area for which they had been issued. The provision of false or misleading information to the Greek broadcaster about the address of the user or that they are a private person as opposed to a commercial entity, does not make a legitimate device an illicit one.

The Court then made its two key findings. First, legislation introduced by one member state that prohibits the importation, sale and use of a decoding device designed for use in another member state is contrary to Art.56 TFEU. This rendered Murphy's conviction unsustainable because the underlying offence, s.297(1) Copyright, Designs and Patents Act 1988, was unlawful for being contrary to Art.56 TFEU, *Murphy v Media Protection Services Ltd* [2012] EWHC 466.

Secondly, a clause of an exclusive licence agreement between the holder of intellectual property rights (the Premier League) and a broadcaster (NetMed Hellas SA and BSkyB Ltd) is a restriction on competition and therefore prohibited by Art.101 TFEU where that clause requires the broadcaster not to supply decoding devices outside of the territory covered by its licence agreement. This would appear to render the entire network of broadcasting arrangements entered into by the Premier League to be anti-competitive. Further, the Court added that these restrictions could not be justified objectively on the grounds that they were necessary to enable the rights holder to maximise its revenue from the sale of its commercial rights or that they encouraged members of the public to attend matches live at the stadium rather than watching them on television. Thus, the absolute territorial protection created by the broadcasting agreements failed to produce any corresponding benefits to the wider public (see further, Hot Topic 13).

13.3.3 Protected events of national importance

The advent of subscription TV channels and their voracious appetite for live sport has forced Parliament to revisit whether some sports events could be said to be of such cultural importance to the British public that they should only be available on free-to-air channels. By protecting some competitions or the finals of some competitions in this manner, it ensures that almost the entire country can watch events that are considered to be of national importance, should they wish to do so. However it also means that the market for selling the rights to these events is significantly restricted as only a limited number of broadcasters are able to screen these events.

The framework for the protection of sports events is provided by ss.97–105 Broadcasting Act 1996 with supplementary provisions including the relevant powers of Ofcom being found in the Television Broadcasting Regulations 2000/54 and the Communications Act 2003. A sports event can be 'listed' where the Secretary of State for Culture, Media and Sport considers that the event or competition has 'national resonance' in that it unites the nation or is a shared date on the national calendar. An event is not protected simply because it is popular; something more than that is needed. Perhaps the best of example of an event of this nature is the Grand National, where many people with no interest in horse racing or gambling will talk about the race, run sweepstakes, bet on the race and eventually watch it for no other reason than it is the Grand National.

Listed events are currently divided into two groups (see box below). If an event or competition does not appear in either group, then any broadcaster is free to purchase the rights to transmit it. Exclusive live coverage of Group A events must be made available in the first instance to 'qualifying broadcasters'; if no qualifying broadcaster purchases the rights to a Group A event, then it can be covered by a non-qualifying broadcaster. Exclusive live coverage of Group B events is allowed by non-qualifying broadcasters, provided that adequate arrangements are made for highlights or delayed coverage to be shown by a qualifying broadcaster.

At present, only BBC 1, BBC 2, ITV 1, Channel 4 and Channel 5 meet the necessary conditions of being freely available and accessible by at least 95 per cent of the population of the UK to be categorised as qualifying broadcasters. Thus, the rights to Group A events must be offered to these channels in the first instance and highlights or delayed coverage packages must be made available to them if they have not secured the exclusive live rights to Group B events. The list of qualifying broadcasters is likely to expand now the switchover to digital terrestrial television is complete.

▶ *Ofcom Code on Sports and Other Listed and Designated Events, Appendix 1 UK Listed Sporting Events*

Group A
  The Olympic Games
  The FIFA World Cup Finals Tournament
  The FA Cup Final
  The Scottish FA Cup Final (in Scotland)
  The Grand National
  The Derby
  The Wimbledon Tennis Finals
  The European Football Championship Finals Tournament
  The Rugby League Challenge Cup Final
  The Rugby World Cup Final
Group B
  Cricket Test Matches played in England
  Non-Finals play in the Wimbledon Tournament
  All Other Matches in the Rugby World Cup Finals Tournament
  Six Nations Rugby Tournament Matches Involving Home Countries
  The Commonwealth Games
  The World Athletics Championship
  The Cricket World Cup – the Final, Semi-finals and Matches Involving Home Nations' Teams
  The Ryder Cup
  The Open Golf Championship

The need for, and impact of, listing sports events in this manner is highly controversial. Some primary rights holders want to have their events delisted so they can charge full market value for their broadcast rights, whilst many fan-consumers want the list to be expanded so they can see more events for free. In *FIFA and UEFA v Commission* T-385/07, T-55/08 and T-68/08, the world and European governing bodies of football challenged the UK's decision to designate the entirety of the World and European football finals tournaments as listed events that can only be available on free-to-air channels. Their argument is that only 'prime' games involving the home nation and other major games, such as the semi-finals and finals, should be restricted in this way; all others should be made available to the highest bidder.

Both the European Commission and the GCEU have held that these finals tournaments are single events that can be protected in their entirety, particularly as many games can have an impact on those identified as 'prime' by the two governing bodies and because these events have large audiences that often comprise viewers who would not watch football on a regular basis. Further, as a member state does not have to provide reasons for designating an event as being of national resonance when informing the Commission of its intention to protect an event in this way, the claims of FIFA and UEFA must fail. These decisions are a major commercial setback to FIFA and UEFA, who continue to claim that it is unfair that they cannot command a market rate for their events; a final appeal to the CJEU has been made and its opinion due to be handed down in 2013.

13.4 Ticket touting and the regulation of secondary ticket sales

Ticket touting involves the unauthorised resale of tickets to a sporting event. It is a practice that has long been associated with UK sport in general and football in particular. Touting refers to any unauthorised resale of a ticket, regardless of how many tickets a tout is selling, whether the sale is made in public or online and whether or not the tout makes or intends to make a profit on those sales. The person who sells a genuinely spare ticket, intending only to recoup their initial outlay, can be considered to be a tout in just the same way as is the person who makes their living from selling tickets on the secondary market.

All unauthorised re-sales are breaches of the original contract between the initial purchaser and the primary rights holder. The initial purchaser of a ticket does not have the right to trade it; all that the ticket represents is a licence granted by the primary rights holder to the purchaser to attend the venue for the purpose of watching the event. However, pursuing each individual breach of contract would usually be too costly and too time-consuming for the primary rights holder, especially as it is difficult to prove that they have suffered a loss when an event is sold out (but see below, 13.4.4); they have still sold a ticket at face value as they wanted to, and it is just that someone else has sold it on, perhaps for a higher sum. Thus, the activities of most touts are ignored by the law unless they are acting in an overtly criminal manner (below, 13.4.2–3).

Not only does touting exist in this grey area between the civil and criminal law, but fans' attitudes towards it are equally confused. Primary rights holders claim to be acting on behalf of fans when they call for all ticket touting to be made criminal, however, there is little call for a generally applicable anti-touting offence from fans who not only see touts as a means of getting hold of tickets to popular events but also expect to be able to sell their own unused tickets on the secondary market, and at a profit, should the need or opportunity arise. It is against this backdrop that the regulation of the secondary market needs to be examined.

13.4.1 The evolution of the secondary market

The conditions necessary for the creation of a secondary market are near perfect where the unauthorised resale of tickets to sports events is concerned. For many popular events, the face value of the ticket is below, and occasionally very far below, its value on the open market. The comparatively low price charged for tickets can be for a variety of reasons: the primary rights holder may be trying to enable the widest possible cross-section of people to attend its event by charging variable ticket prices; it may be trying to guarantee that the event is sold out to ensure the best possible atmosphere is generated; it may be trying to inculcate a culture of attendance and support at the live event; or it may be rewarding fans for their attendance at previous events. In each of these cases, the actual ticket price is less than some people are willing to pay to attend the event in question.

Moreover, the very nature of sports competitions means that the primary rights holder cannot provide an appropriate alternative to attendance live at the event. Fans do not want to go and watch a different team or different sport when tickets to a specific event are sold out and it is not within the power of the event organiser to stage extra performances for those who were unable to buy tickets from official sources. Each game is unique and incapable of substitution for an alternative; matches cannot be played multiple times just because demand outstrips supply.

This situation is exacerbated by the ease with which a ticket holder or potential tout and those seeking to purchase tickets can now engage with the secondary market. Online sales and auction sites have enabled anyone with access to the internet to buy and sell tickets whilst consumer indifference to the ethics and legality of ticket touting ensures that few question the operation of the secondary market, provided that their tickets arrive in time for them to attend the event. Thus, wherever demand outstrips supply, there is the potential for the emergence of a secondary market in tickets to a sports event.

The difficulty for the law in this situation is to determine the basis on which it should regulate this secondary market. The standard terms of most sports event tickets include a prohibition on their resale without the specific authorisation of the primary rights holder, who will also retain property in the ticket itself (*R v Marshall* [1998] 2 Cr App R 282). The only exemption to this general prohibition is where a profit is neither made nor intended to be made by the resale and the original purchaser intends only to sell their tickets to other members of the group with whom they will be attending the event. Despite this specific prohibition, the need to commence multiple actions for breach of contract and the bad publicity generated by excluding those who have bought touted tickets to 'must-see' events make the enforcement of these terms before the courts financially inefficient and practically ineffective as a means of protecting the primary rights holder.

Where touts have provided inadequate, inaccurate or false information about specific qualities of the ticket or fail to provide any ticket at all, they can be prosecuted for fraud or for breaching consumer protection legislation (below, 13.4.2–3). A further justification for legal intervention can be provided where public order may be compromised by causing a breakdown in the segregation of rival fans at designated football matches (below, 13.4.4). However outside of these situations, it is difficult to identify whom has been harmed by ticket touting and who is in need of protection from whom when both parties engage in a process of negotiation and are in possession of all of the facts necessary to enable them to enter into a transaction.

13.4.2 Regulation by generally applicable criminal law provisions

Any person acting as a ticket tout for any sporting event runs the risk of being found guilty of a criminal offence either during the course of negotiating the sale or at the point at which the sale is concluded. Of particular importance in these circumstances are the Fraud Act 2006, the Consumer Protection from Unfair Trading Regulations 2008/1277 and the Consumer Protection (Distance Selling) Regulations 2000/2334.

13.4.2.1 Fraud Act 2006 ss.2 and 3

The offences of fraud defined in ss.2 and 3 Fraud Act 2006 are so widely drafted as to be capable of criminalising almost any ticket-touting transaction where the tout has failed to provide the purchaser with all relevant information about the ticket or where they deliberately fail to provide the ticket that has been paid for.

▶ *Fraud Act 2006 s.2 – fraud by false representation*

(1) A person is in breach of this section if he –
    (a) dishonestly makes a false representation, and
    (b) intends, by making the representation –
        (i) to make a gain for himself or another, or
        (ii) to cause loss to another or to expose another to a risk of loss.
(2) A representation is false if –
    (a) it is untrue or misleading, and
    (b) the person making it knows that it is, or might be, untrue or misleading.
(3) "Representation" means any representation as to fact or law, including a representation as to the state of mind of –
    (a) the person making the representation, or
    (b) any other person.
(4) A representation may be express or implied.
(5) For the purposes of this section a representation may be regarded as made if it (or anything implying it) is submitted in any form to any system or device designed to receive, convey or respond to communications (with or without human intervention).

▶ *Fraud Act 2006 s.3 – fraud by failing to disclose information*

A person is in breach of this section if he –
    (a) dishonestly fails to disclose to another person information which he is under a legal duty to disclose, and
    (b) intends, by failing to disclose the information –
        (i) to make a gain for himself or another, or
        (ii) to cause loss to another or to expose another to a risk of loss.

Under s.2, fraud is committed where the tout makes a false representation about any quality of the ticket, for example, advertising it as being for a front-row seat when it actually has a restricted view or is at the back of the stadium. Alternatively, where the tout fails to disclose that, for example, they are not an authorised seller of the ticket, then the offence under s.3 could be committed. It is important to note that no sale actually has to take place; the offences are complete where the tout intends to make a profit for himself or another, for example, by charging the purchaser a higher amount on the basis of incorrect information about the quality of the ticket or where they intend to cause a loss to the purchaser, for example, by not providing them with any ticket at all or by exposing them to the risk of loss, for example, by failing to inform the purchaser that the ticket is void for having been bought from a tout.

These two sections of the Fraud Act 2006 have the potential to apply to almost all touting transactions and in respect of any sports event. In particular, they can be used to prosecute the more serious forms of ticket touting where the tout is deliberately misleading the purchaser or where the tout has no intention of supplying the purchaser with any tickets. However, this more obviously criminal conduct represents a minority of secondary market transactions and therefore other means of regulation must also be considered.

13.4.2.2 Consumer Protection Regulations

The Consumer Protection from Unfair Trading Regulations 2008/1277 (CPUTR) and the Consumer Protection (Distance Selling) Regulations 2000/2334 (CPDSR) provide further protections to purchasers buying tickets from professional touts who are selling tickets in the course of business or as traders. Although a 'trader' is not defined in the Regulations, it can be assumed that it will require the seller to be engaging with the secondary market with multiple ticket sales on a regular as opposed to an ad hoc basis.

The CPUTR make it a criminal offence for a trader to mislead a consumer in any way and in particular about a specific quality of the ticket being sold such that it materially distorts the purchaser's economic behaviour. Regs.5, 6 and 7 and sch.1 contain comprehensive but non-exhaustive lists of what can amount to unfair commercial practices. Where ticket touting is concerned, this would include providing untruthful or misleading information about the existence or provenance of a ticket, about its material characteristics, for example, its original face value or position in the venue, or about restrictions contained in its terms, such as it becoming invalid when resold by an unauthorised vendor. All of this information must be transmitted to the purchaser before the transaction is completed. Thus, where the average consumer's ability to make an informed decision is impaired by the conduct of the vendor and causes them to purchase a ticket that they would not otherwise have done, an offence is committed.

The CPDSR apply to suppliers who are acting in a commercial or professional capacity when selling tickets otherwise than in a face-to-face transaction, including online and telephone sales. Regulation 7 again requires the supplier to provide the purchaser with the material characteristics of the ticket prior to the conclusion of the contract. Where the purchaser discovers that this has not occurred, Reg.11 provides them with the right to cancel the contract and to have their money refunded. However, as it will often be the case that inaccurate information about the material characteristics of the ticket will only become known upon its receipt, the purchaser is usually left with a choice of either attending the event with the sub-standard ticket that they have purchased or not attending it at all. Further, as only the price of the ticket and not related expenditure, such as travel and accommodation can be recovered, the CPDSR provide only limited protection to consumers.

The protections provided by both sets of Regulations suffer from one significant flaw: they only apply to sales by traders acting in the course of a business or in a professional capacity. As very few touts are able to trade officially in sports event tickets because they are acting in breach of contract by selling the tickets in their possession without the specific authorisation of the primary rights holder, it appears that few secondary market transactions are protected by these Regulations. However, what is left open by both sets of Regulations is whether a seller can be proved to be a 'trader' by reason of the regularity with which they engage with the secondary market or on the basis of the volume of sales that they make. If the concept of a trader is fluid enough to cover sales by such unofficial sellers, then the protection provided to fan-consumers would be greatly enhanced.

13.4.3 Regulation of specific instances of ticket touting

At present, there are only three situations where there is a specific prohibition of the unauthorised resale of tickets to a sporting event. This means that it will always be a criminal offence to sell tickets to a designated football match, whilst the majority of unauthorised sales to events at the London Olympic and Paralympic Games were (and, at the Glasgow Commonwealth Games, will be) crimes.

13.4.3.1 Touting at designated football matches – Criminal Justice and Public Order Act 1994 s.166

Ticket touting at designated football matches was made illegal by s.166 Criminal Justice and Public Order Act 1994. The sole reason for criminalising this specific form of touting was to prevent outbreaks of public disorder caused by a breakdown in the segregation of rival groups of fans at football matches (see further, chapter 10.4.2). Thus, the harm being prevented was harm to society as a whole rather than the protection of the purchaser's financial position or the primary rights holder's commercial interests.

> ▶ *Criminal Justice and Public Order Act 1994 s.166 – sale of tickets by unauthorised persons*
>
> (1) It is an offence for an unauthorised person to –
>   (a) sell a ticket for a designated football match, or
>   (b) otherwise to dispose of such a ticket to another person.
> (2) For this purpose –
>   (a) a person is 'unauthorised' unless he is authorised in writing to sell or otherwise dispose of tickets for the match by the organisers of the match;
>   (aa) a reference to selling a ticket includes a reference to –
>   (i) offering to sell a ticket;
>   (ii) exposing a ticket for sale;
>   (iii) making a ticket available for sale by another;
>   (iv) advertising that a ticket is available for purchase; and
>   (v) giving a ticket to a person who pays or agrees to pay for some other goods or services or offering to do so.

Designated football matches are those where at least one of the teams involved is a member of the Football Association Premier League, the Football League, the Football Conference, the Scottish Football League or the League of Wales or is a team that represents a territory or country or whose home ground is situated for the time being outside of England and Wales; games in the FA Cup, excluding qualifying and preliminary rounds, are also designated, (Football (Offences) (Designation of Football Matches) Order 2004/2410). The Order is updated every year to take account of promotion and relegation to and from the Football Conference and ensures that all major professional and semi-professional games in the UK are covered by the legislation.

Under s.166, all unauthorised sales are prohibited regardless of whether or not the seller is a trader or intends to make a profit. The extended definition given to 'selling' in s.166(2)(aa) was introduced to enable the police to prevent unauthorised sales at the earliest possible opportunity and to counteract the initiative of ticket touts who were, for example, selling vastly overpriced merchandise whilst giving away a free match ticket with every purchase.

In response to the growing number of unauthorised sales taking place online, s.166A clarifies the position of Internet Service Providers (ISP) whose services are being used by touts. An ISP is guilty of a criminal offence where it is aware that information supplied to it by a user of its services contains material that contravenes s.166 and that having become aware that information on its service contravened s.166, it failed to remove it or disable access to it expeditiously. ISPs will usually become aware that they are hosting information that enables sales that breach s.166 to take place when they are informed of the problem by the primary rights holder. In such a case, they must ensure that the information cannot be accessed as soon as is reasonably practicable.

Although the criminalisation of unauthorised ticket sales to some professional football matches is undoubtedly justifiable on public order grounds, the need for an absolute ban on sales to all designated games is not borne out by Home Office arrest statistics. For the 10 seasons between 2002–03 and 2011–12, the police made 981 arrests for ticket touting, averaging fewer than 100 per season, of which 83 per cent were at Premier League, UEFA Champions League or International representative fixtures; during the same period, cumulative attendances increased from 28 million to 37 million spectators at designated football matches in England and Wales. This would seem to suggest that touting is not one of the police's priorities on match days or that the move to online sales has made it more difficult to regulate the activities of touts.

13.4.3.2 Touting at the London Olympics 2012 – London Olympic and Paralympic Games Act 2006 s.31

The unauthorised sale of tickets to any event at the London Olympic and Paralympic Games was an offence under s.31 London Olympic and Paralympic Games Act 2006. The terms and conditions of each ticket included standard prohibitions on their unauthorised resale and on their use in commercial promotions; any breach of these terms and conditions invalidated the ticket and, technically at least, enabled the London Organising Committee of the Olympic Games (LOCOG) to prevent the invalid ticket-holder's entry to the venue. The first of these two prohibitions is the civil or contractual means of preventing ticket touting. The second is an attempt to reduce even further the opportunities available to undertakings to ambush the marketing strategies of the official sponsors and partners by preventing them from offering Olympic tickets as prizes in competitions. In addition, the unauthorised resale of all Olympic tickets was almost always a criminal offence.

▶ *London Olympic and Paralympic Games Act 2006 s.31 – sale of tickets*

(1) A person commits an offence if he sells an Olympic ticket –
    (a) in a public place or in the course of a business, and
    (b) otherwise than in accordance with a written authorisation issued by the London Organising Committee.
(2) For the purposes of subsection (1) –
    (a) "Olympic ticket" means anything which is or purports to be a ticket for one or more London Olympic events,

(b)   a reference to selling a ticket includes a reference to –
    (i)   offering to sell a ticket,
    (ii)   exposing a ticket for sale,
    (iii)   advertising that a ticket is available for purchase, and
    (iv)   giving, or offering to give, a ticket to a person who pays or agrees to pay for some other goods or services, and
(c)   a person shall (without prejudice to the generality of subsection (1)(a)) be treated as acting in the course of a business if he does anything as a result of which he makes a profit or aims to make a profit.

The offence under s.31 is broadly the same as that found in s.166 Criminal Justice and Public Order Act 1994. The one subtle difference is that if a London 2012 ticket was not sold in public and no profit was made or intended to be made on the sale then no offence was committed. It provided the most comprehensive protection for any sporting or cultural event in the UK. The 'traditional' tout selling tickets on the approach to the venue acted unlawfully in respect of all sales, whilst anyone intending to make a profit from the unauthorised resale of an Olympic ticket acted in an equally criminal manner. The only re-sales that were exempted from the operation of s.31 were private sales at face value or below. This enabled a purchaser of multiple tickets to sell them on to friends and family (and others, provided no profit was intended to be made) and allowed a person who finds themselves with a genuinely spare ticket to recoup their initial outlay. Further, s.166 Criminal Justice and Public Order Act 1994 applied to criminalise all unauthorised ticket sales for the Olympic football tournament as the games involved representative sides and are therefore designated football matches (see further, chapter 13.4.3.1).

Little justification was provided by the government for the need for such comprehensive anti-touting provisions. In response to a Freedom of Information Act request, CMS case number 106119, the International Olympic Committee (IOC) assisted the Department for Culture, Media and Sport's explanation of why these provisions were necessary by stating:

> 'Olympic Games events are very popular and must be protected from individuals seeking to profit by selling on tickets above face value. Laws should both forbid: such sales; people from advertising and executing such sales. [Touting] of tickets is detrimental to the image of the Olympic Games particularly at Games-time. Local law enforcement should be able to take appropriate action against [touts] selling Olympic Games tickets.'

In other words, the IOC was concerned solely with the protection of its and LOCOG's commercial rights and required legislation to be implemented that prevented anyone from benefitting unofficially from the goodwill connected to the Olympic Games and the Olympic Movement. Although this aim is one that is pursued by all bodies that have created a commercially successful product, service or event, it is one that is usually protected by commercial means, such as trade marking, or by legal actions, such as passing off or breach of contract, not by a statute imposing criminal liability. Instead, s.31 provided the kind of specific protection to the Olympics and Paralympics that has been consistently denied to other major events that take place in the UK. Without a convincing justification for this individual position, the primary rights holders of other major events are likely to demand similar legislative protection, despite it being used only rarely during the Games, as the pre-emptive enforcement action taken in a few high-profile cases appeared to deter touts to an extent that does not happen at other sporting and cultural events.

13.4.3.3 Touting at the Glasgow Commonwealth Games 2014 – Glasgow Commonwealth Games Act 2008 s.17

The first British event to be granted similar protections is the Glasgow Commonwealth Games.

▶ *Glasgow Commonwealth Games Act 2008 s.17 – ban on ticket touting*

(1) It is an offence to tout a Games ticket ("the touting offence").
(2) A person touts a Games ticket if the person does any act falling within subsection (3) –
   (a) in a public place,
   (b) in relation to the sale, or proposed sale, of a Games ticket for an amount exceeding the ticket's face value, or
   (c) with a view to making a profit.
(3) Acts which fall within this subsection are –
   (a) selling a Games ticket,
   (b) offering to sell a Games ticket,
   (c) exposing a Games ticket for sale,
   (d) advertising that a Games ticket is available for purchase,
   (e) making a Games ticket available for sale by another person, and
   (f) giving away (or offering to give away) a Games ticket on condition that the person given the ticket pays a booking fee or other charge or acquires some other goods or services.

This provision has many similarities with the touting offences at designated football matches and London 2012. As with the Olympic offence, a private sale where the seller either does not charge in excess of the ticket's face value or does not make or intend to make a profit on the transaction appears to be lawful, distinguishing it from the absolute prohibition on sales of tickets to designated football matches. The final form of s.17 is likely to be influenced by developments in ticket-related technological advancements and the demands of other sporting mega-events organisers in the years preceding the opening ceremony of the Glasgow Commonwealth Games in 2014.

13.4.4 Enforcing ticket conditions under the civil law

In all other situations, the only legal option open to a primary rights holder is to pursue a complex series of civil law claims. In *Rugby Football Union v Viagogo Ltd* [2012] UKSC 30, the RFU decided to bring legal actions against everyone who had bought and sold tickets to England Test Matches in contravention of the tickets' terms and conditions. It was claimed that all such sales were a breach of contract in the first instance, that by passing on the ticket without the RFU's permission, the tort of conversion was committed and that any purchaser of a touted ticket gaining entry to the stadium would be a trespasser.

The action was brought against Viagogo in order to obtain the personal details of anyone who had bought or sold one of the RFU's tickets. The Supreme Court held that as this was the only means by which the RFU could get hold of the information necessary to bring actions against the touts and to discourage purchasers from resorting to them, Viagogo must disclose the relevant names and addresses. Although this makes it slightly easier to identify online touts and get hold of sufficient information to sue them, it remains a significantly more difficult, expensive and time-consuming means of regulating the secondary market than if the criminal alternative were more widely available.

Hot topic ... The impact of *Murphy* on the sale of broadcasting rights

In the immediate aftermath of the *Murphy* decision, many commentators were quick to highlight the case's potential importance to the sporting-legal landscape by referring to it as '*Bosman* 2' or the '*Bosman* of TV rights.' Many more seemed particularly pleased by the prospect that this would undermine Sky's position as the dominant provider of live Premier League matches. Although there is no doubt that the case has the potential to be as important to sport as was the *Bosman* decision, that potential has yet to be realised.

The case casts doubt on the legality of the way in which the complex network of interlocking contracts that govern sports broadcasting operate but without declaring that the system as a whole is unlawful. The combination of collective selling of exclusive rights, coupled with clauses that were intended to divide the European market along national lines, was always going to attract the attention of the Commission; what *Murphy* succeeded in doing was bringing these restrictions into the popular consciousness. Whereas the collective and exclusive elements of the various UEFA and Premier League agreements have previously been declared to be compliant with EU law by the Commission, *Murphy* was the CJEU's first opportunity to examine the clauses that had the effect of restricting a broadcaster's ability to sell their services along national/territorial lines. By declaring these clauses to be anti-competitive, and the national laws that prevented the purchase of decoders that enabled UK citizens to subscribe to TV services broadcast from elsewhere in the EU unlawful, it appeared that broadcasting rights would have to be sold in a very different way in the future.

Of the many outcomes that were envisaged, the following were amongst the most plausible and the most often repeated: that subscribers would now be able to choose freely the TV provider from which they received their programming; that primary rights holders (PRHs) would sell their rights based on groups of countries sharing a common language or time-zone; that PRHs would sell one pan-EU package; that PRHs would set up their own TV networks, as many clubs have done; that PRHs would stream packages on the Internet, as the NBA now does on YouTube; or that the charging basis would change to be calculated according to potential audience size. In each case, it assumes that access to sports programming will become easier and cheaper and that the PRHs and broadcasters will receive less revenue. Instead, the total value of the Premier League rights for the 2013–16 seasons increased to record levels and exceeded £5bn for the first time.

What has happened is that the value of UK rights packages has increased as genuinely viable competitors have entered the bidding, with BT replacing ESPN as a prospective future rival to Sky. This has been coupled with a novel approach to the protection of the value of these rights by reducing the availability of live Premier League games to European broadcasters; each broadcaster can now broadcast only one live match per Saturday, making the packages that they have to offer significantly less attractive and comparatively more expensive than they were when Ms Murphy bought her Greek subscription. Finally, any reduction in the value of the European rights has been offset by a significant increase in the value of the rights sold to non-European markets and particularly in the Far East, leaving the status quo largely unaffected.

What appears to be absent from the many analyses of the competition law and free movement provisions is the impact of this contractual framework on the fan-consumer. UK subscribers will pay more for their Premier League football from 2013 and although they can now buy a foreign subscription package lawfully, there is less incentive to do so now that so few games can be broadcast live. The analyses focus on access to the market of other broadcasters and the impact of reduced revenue on PRHs but rarely on the price ultimately paid by the consumer. Where Mrs Murphy had to fight long and hard to clear her name, the impact on the PRHs has been negligible.

Summary

13.1 The rapid commercialisation of sport in recent years has had a significant impact on the ways in which fans now interact with the sports that interest them and the teams that they follow. As sports clubs in particular have sought new income streams to exploit in order to fuel stadium redevelopments and players' wages, the fan has come to be treated as a consumer of the goods and services that it supplies.

13.2 The increase in sales of sports merchandise has led many clubs and event organisers to reassess the importance of officially licensed products as a source of income. Sports clubs and sportswear manufacturers in particular have sought to regulate the use of specific team names, symbols, badges, insignia and crests that were traditionally associated with a club in order to exploit this market with greater efficiency than had been the case. The use of registered trade marks has been particularly effective in preventing the sale of unlicensed merchandise and the growth in anti-ambush marketing laws has ensured that these valuable rights are protected from novel means of infringing them.

13.3 Since 1992, the growth in the value of sports broadcasting rights has been unprecedented. As sport has been used as a driver for new subscriptions to pay TV services, the high price paid by broadcasters for these rights has inevitably been passed on to sports fans. Collectively negotiated exclusive deals have become the norm in the UK are considered capable of being in the public interest despite their anti-competitive appearance and their ability to inflate the value of the rights being sold provided certain safeguards are in place. Innovative attempts to circumvent payment for subscription services remain of dubious legality, however, the *Murphy* decision has highlighted that the framework of broadcasting agreements and underlying criminal sanctions are not the appropriate means of preventing consumers from accessing services provided from elsewhere in the EU. Further restrictions on the ability of some primary rights holders to sell their rights to the highest bidder are found in the listed events procedure under the Broadcasting Act 1996.

13.4 The unauthorised resale of sports tickets has become a controversial sporting, legal, ethical and political issue. Whereas the criminalising of ticket touting in respect of football matches could initially be justified on public order grounds, no similar justification has been proffered for the corresponding offences relating to tickets for events at London 2012 and Glasgow 2014. Although touting at other events is regulated to some extent by the general criminal law and various consumer protection regulations, discussions are ongoing about whether all instances of ticket touting should be criminalised or whether this should remain a civil matter for the primary rights holders to pursue.

Further reading

Intellectual Property

Lewis and Taylor (eds), *Sport: Law and Practice* (2nd edn, 2008, Tottel) ch G1

Dugdale, Jones and Simpson (eds), *Clerk & Lindsell on Torts* (20th edn, 2010, Sweet and Maxwell) chs 25 and 26

Burton and Chadwick, 'Ambush marketing in sport: an assessment of implications and management strategies' (2008) Centre for the International Business of Sport Working Paper Series, No.3

Fields, 'Too poor to be afforded protections as a trade mark?' (2009) 20(4) *Entertainment Law Review* 157

Johnson, 'Look out! It's an ambush!' [2008] 2/3 *International Sports Law Review* 24

Yap, 'Making sense of trade mark use' (2007) 29(10) *European Intellectual Property Review* 420

Further reading cont'd

Broadcasting

Beloff et al., *Sports Law* (2nd edn, 2012, Hart) ch 6

Geey and James, 'The Premier League-European Commission broadcasting negotiations' (2006) 4(1) *Entertainment and Sports Law Review*, online

Hornsby, 'FAPL v QC Leisure and Karen Murphy: what's wrong with the "exclusivity premium" and why can't it be protected?' (2012) 23(6) *Entertainment Law Review* 157

Kaburakis, Lindholm and Rodenberg, 'British pubs, decoder cards and the future of intellectual property licensing after *Murphy*' (2012) 18 *Columbia Journal of European Law* 307

Lefever and Rompuy, 'Ensuring access to sports content: 10 years of EU intervention. Time to celebrate?' [2009] 2 *Journal of Media Law* 243

McAuley, 'Exclusively for all and collectively for none: refereeing broadcasting rights between the Premier League, European Commission and BSkyB' (2004) 25(6) *European Competition Law Review* 370

Parrish and Miettinen, *The sporting exception in European Union Law* (2008, TMC Asser Press) ch 6

Stothers, 'Copyright and the EC Treaty: music, films and football' (2009) 31(5) *European Intellectual Property Review* 272

Wood, 'The CJEU's ruling in the Premier League pub TV cases – the final whistle beckons' (2012) 34(3) *European Intellectual Property Review* 203

Touting

House of Commons Culture, Media and Sport Committee, 'Ticket Touting' (HC 202, 2008)

Secretary of State for Culture, Media and Sport, 'Government Response to the Culture, Media and Sport Select Committee Report on Ticket Touting' (Cm 7346, 2008)

Campbell Keegan Limited, 'The Secondary Market for Tickets (Music and Sport) Qualitative Research Report' (prepared for DCMS, 2007), available at http://www.culture.gov.uk/images/research/secondarymkt_tickets_qrr.pdf

James and Osborn, 'Tickets, policy and social inclusion: can the "European White Paper on Sport" deliver?' [2009] 1/2 *International Sports Law Journal* 61

Links to relevant websites can be found at www.palgrave.com/law/james2e

Chapter 14 follows overleaf.

Chapter 14

Olympic law and sporting mega-events

14.1 Olympic law and its impact on sporting mega-events

The Olympic Games is the largest and most popular sporting and cultural event in the world and the model on which many other major championships base their organisation, regulation and governance. The Olympic Movement has also been a major driving force for the development of sports law and on the laws that are often demanded by organisers of sporting mega-events on an increasingly frequent basis.

Since the Sydney Games in 2000, there has been a systematic formalisation of Olympic Law. Its iterative development from one edition of the Games to the next has seen a range of guarantees be demanded by the International Olympic Committee (IOC) from prospective host governments as an integral part of the bidding process. These guarantees require the host government to pass a variety of specific legal provisions to ensure that the Games run smoothly and that the iconography of the Olympic Movement is protected from unauthorised exploitation and ambush marketing.

Using the Olympic Movement in general and London 2012 in particular, the evolution of Olympic Law will be used as an example of how the commercial rights of sporting mega-events are protected and the demands of primary rights holders are met. The governance structure, bidding process and appointment of local organising committees of many ISFs follow those of the IOC. The importance of Olympic Law as a template for other sporting mega-events will be examined to demonstrate how the specific, individual and supposedly one-off requirements of the IOC are becoming sporting-legal norms that are used in particular to protect the commercial rights of organisations such as FIFA and the Commonwealth Games Committee. This has resulted in some jurisdictions introducing generic legislation to provide the most commonly requested legislative protections to sporting mega-events.

14.2 The modern Olympic Movement

The modern Olympic Movement can trace its roots back to the creation of the original set of Olympic principles at the International Athletic Congress held in Paris in 1894. The IOC, which was created at the same time, has since then become the most powerful sports body in the world and is charged with promoting Olympism and leading the Olympic Movement at a global level. Over time, the original principles have evolved into the Olympic Charter, which now acts as the basic legal document of the Olympic Movement.

By far the most well-known, most visible and most easily identifiable manifestation of Olympism is the Olympic Games. These are held in the first year of each four-year Olympiad, beginning with the Athens Olympics in 1896, and have grown into the largest sporting and cultural event in the world. The Winter Olympics, which were first held in Chamonix, France, in 1924, have been held in the third year of each Olympiad since 1994 rather than the same year as the summer version, to ensure that each edition of the Games has a distinct identity and can exploit the commercial rights associated with the Olympics more efficiently.

The aim of the Olympic Movement is much more than to deliver successful editions of the Olympic Games; it aims to build a better, fairer and more peaceful world through sport. In order to achieve this, it focuses its work in six specific areas: education; development; environmental awareness; the promotion of women's participation in all aspects of sport; the encouragement of grassroots sport and the promotion of peace, particularly during the Games themselves when all participating nations are encouraged to respect the Olympic Truce. Furthermore, one of the IOC's specialist Commissions, Olympic Solidarity, provides funding to emergent and less financially secure National Olympic Committees to enable them to develop their own sport and education programmes so that they can develop their leading athletes to a standard where they will be able to compete in the Olympic Games.

The Olympic Movement has also been actively involved with the creation of two of the most important administrative developments in modern elite-level sport. In 1984, the IOC established the Court of Arbitration for Sport (CAS). Although since 1994 this has been a completely independent institution to ensure that there is a formal separation of powers between the IOC as executive body and CAS in its judicial role, the IOC has helped to establish CAS's credibility by using it as the sole dispute-resolution chamber for Olympic matters (see further, chapter 3). A related development in sporting justice was developed in response to the need for an expedited procedure for use at the Olympic Games leading to CAS creating an Ad Hoc Division that is able to provide a rapid resolution to disputes and is now used at many other major international championships.

The IOC has also been instrumental in ensuring the almost universal acceptance of the authority of the World Anti-Doping Agency (WADA) and the World Anti-Doping Code as the standard by which all doping cases are judged. By requiring all ISFs whose sports are included on the Olympic programme and all those which want to be included to have incorporated the World Anti-Doping Code into their rules, the IOC has ensured its general implementation throughout the sporting world. Moreover, as Arts.13.1.1 and 13.2.1 of the Code require all appeals in doping cases that involve WADA or international level athletes to be heard exclusively by CAS, the IOC has contributed further to the acceptance of CAS as the leading sports law tribunal for international disputes. Thus, the Olympic Movement and its ideals encompass much more than the biennial sporting extravaganza and include the development and promotion of structures through which sport can be made fairer and more accessible and can be governed more effectively and in accordance with universally applicable legal norms.

14.2.1 The structure of the Olympic Movement

Membership of the Olympic Movement requires recognition of a body or individual by the IOC and that it adheres to the Olympic Charter. Rule 1(2) Olympic Charter states that the three main constituents of the Olympic Movement are the IOC, the recognised ISFs and the NOCs. Rule 1(3) acknowledges that the NGBs, clubs and individuals that make up an ISF are automatically considered to be part of the Olympic Movement, as are the Organising Committees of each edition of the Olympic Games for the period of their existence.

The IOC currently recognises 28 sports and their ISFs for inclusion in the summer edition of the Olympics and a further seven for inclusion on the winter programme. Any ISF can apply to be recognised by the IOC even though its sports are not included on the Olympic programmes. An ISF may seek recognition in order to be considered for inclusion at future Games or, in some countries, may need to be recognised in order to qualify for public funding. Recognition of a sport is secured by an ISF where it can demonstrate that it organises a sport or group of related sports at the global level, its membership consists of NGBs, it has incorporated the World Anti-Doping Code into its rules and where it conforms with the requirements of the Olympic Charter. Thirty-three ISFs are currently recognised in this way, including several sports are no longer included on the main Olympic programme or have been demonstration sports.

14.2.2 The Olympic Charter

The Olympic Charter acts as the constitutional instrument for the Olympic Movement as a whole and also serves as the governing statutes of the IOC. It begins with a statement of the Fundamental Principles of Olympism and is then divided into five chapters dealing with the Olympic Movement as a whole, including an explanation of the ownership of all relevant commercial rights associated with it, the establishment and role of the IOC, the recognition process and role of the ISFs, the mission and role of the NOCs and the organisation of, and eligibility, for the Olympic Games.

▶ *Olympic Charter, Fundamental Principles of Olympism*

1   Olympism is a philosophy of life, exalting and combining in a balanced whole the qualities of body, will and mind. Blending sport with culture and education, Olympism seeks to create a way of life based on the joy of effort, the educational value of good example and respect for universal fundamental ethical principles.

2   The goal of Olympism is to place sport at the service of the harmonious development of man, with a view to promoting a peaceful society concerned with the preservation of human dignity.

3   The Olympic Movement is the concerted, organised, universal and permanent action, carried out under the supreme authority of the IOC, of all individuals and entities who are inspired by the values of Olympism. It covers the five continents. It reaches its peak with the bringing together of the world's athletes at the great sports festival, the Olympic Games. Its symbol is five interlaced rings.

> 4   The practice of sport is a human right. Every individual must have the possibility of practising sport, without discrimination of any kind and in the Olympic spirit, which requires mutual understanding with a spirit of friendship, solidarity and fair play. The organisation, administration and management of sport must be controlled by independent sports organisations.
> 5   Any form of discrimination with regard to a country or a person on grounds of race, religion, politics, gender or otherwise is incompatible with belonging to the Olympic Movement.
> 6   Belonging to the Olympic Movement requires compliance with the Olympic Charter and recognition by the IOC.

The most recent version of the Charter was published in 2011 and is updated on a regular basis to reflect sporting, ethical and legal developments. For example, in 2008, the IOC introduced an eligibility rule that prevented any athlete who had been banned from competing for six months or longer as a result of a doping infraction from appearing at the next two editions of the Olympics (one summer and one winter Games) following the completion of their period of suspension. In *United States Olympic Committee v International Olympic Committee* CAS 2011/O/2422, CAS found that this Rule was unlawful on the grounds that the IOC had not followed its own Rules as it was a breach of Art.23 WADA Code to introduce an additional punishment not sanctioned by the Code. Further, CAS noted that by punishing a person twice for the same offence, the Rule offended against the principle of double jeopardy and was therefore unlawful as being a breach of universally applicable legal norms, resulting in the offending Rule being removed from the Charter (see further, Hot Topic 1 and chapter 3.3.5).

14.2.3   The International Olympic Committee

In the context of upholding the fundamental principles of Olympism, by the far the most important member of the Olympic Movement is the IOC. In many ways the IOC has the same basic structure as that which is used by ISFs to govern individual sports; the IOC is the global body to which five continental associations are affiliated and whose membership consists of the 205 NOCs representing the individual nation states that are eligible to send athletes to the Olympic Games. Each of these relationships is governed by the Olympic Charter.

According to Rule 15 Olympic Charter the IOC is an international non-governmental not-for-profit organisation of unlimited duration that is recognised under Swiss Law as an association with a distinct legal personality. The IOC comprises a maximum of 115 members, of which a majority but not more than 70 must be wholly independent of any other function or office that they hold. The remainder, of which there cannot be more than 15 members in any one category, comprise active athletes, senior office holders in ISFs or other IOC-recognised organisations and senior office holders in an NOC. At present, there are 106 active members, of whom three are British: HRH the Princess Royal, Adam Pengilly and Sir Craig Reeide; Sir Craig sits on the Executive Board of the IOC. Each has substantial experience in sports administration and elite-level competition, ensuring that they can provide guidance and leadership on many sports governance issues. Members are expected to be politically and nationally independent; their role is to represent the IOC in their respective countries, not to represent their country at the IOC making their position ambassadorial in nature. Each member is now elected for an eight-year term of office at the end of which they can seek re-election.

The IOC holds an annual general meeting, the Session, at which major issues and policies are debated and developed. The implementation of these policies and the day-to-day administration of the IOC are carried out by its Executive Board, which comprises the President, four Vice-Presidents and ten IOC members. The role of the IOC through the Board is to uphold the Olympic Charter. In order to carry out its functions more effectively, the Session and Executive Board are advised by seven specific Commissions representing the issues that are of the greatest importance to Olympism: the Athletes' Commission, which considers issues relating to competitors at the Olympic Games; the Ethics Commission, which updates the Code of Ethics and informs developments of the World Anti-Doping Code; the Nominations Commission, which oversees the election of IOC members; the Olympic Solidarity Commission, which provides development funding to poorer and emergent NOCs; the Evaluation Commission for Candidate Cities, which determines the application criteria for potential hosts of the Games; the Olympic Games Coordination Commission, which collects information from past host cities and disseminates it to the prospective and eventual hosts to in order to make the bidding procedures fairer and more open; and the Medical Commission, which advises on anti-doping procedures and athlete healthcare issues.

Since its creation in 1894, the IOC has acquired for itself a sporting, cultural and political position unlike any other organisation. It is almost universally and often unquestioningly accepted as the most important sports body in the world. Despite its being self-appointed to this role and to its position as the guardian of the spirit of sport and of sporting good conduct, there have been few serious challenges to its status. The revamped system of governance and the changes made to the procedures for electing its members following the corruption scandals of the 1990s have seen the IOC begin to reclaim its lead on sports ethics, particularly in the development of more robust anti-doping procedures. In 2009, the IOC was granted observer status at the United Nations because of its involvement with peace-keeping missions and its health and education programmes around the world, formalising its leading role in sport in a way that even Baron de Coubertin could not have foreseen.

14.2.4 National representatives

There are three ways in which the Olympic Movement can be represented in a country. Firstly, any nation state recognised as independent by the international community can establish a National Olympic Committee and apply to have it recognised by the IOC. In the UK, this role is fulfilled by the British Olympic Association (BOA). Secondly, it may have one or more nationals who hold membership of the IOC; the UK currently has three active members of the IOC (above, 14.2.3). Thirdly, the city responsible for hosting an Olympic Games must establish an officially recognised organising committee; the London Organising Committee of the Olympic Games (LOCOG) had the task of delivering the Games of the 30th Olympiad in 2012.

14.2.4.1 National Olympic Committees – the British Olympic Association

The BOA was established in 1905 and, like many British sports bodies, is a private company limited by guarantee. Its role is to represent the Olympic Movement in the UK, the Channel Islands, the Isle of Man and any British Overseas Territories that do not have their own NOC and to promote the fundamental principles of Olympism. The BOA is a wholly independent body which, unlike many other NOCs, receives no public money to support its activities. This political and financial independence enabled the

BOA to send a British team to the Moscow Olympics in 1980 against the wishes of the government, who wanted to join a US-led boycott of the Games in protest at the USSR's invasion of Afghanistan. The BOA instead registered its disapproval by competing under the Olympic flag and having the Olympic anthem played at medal ceremonies.

The BOA's activities are entirely self-funded. Its main sources of income are the licensing of its Olympic marks and sponsorship agreements that help to fund Team GB's appearance at each edition of the Olympic Games and the various sporting and educational events that the BOA organises. This funding framework operates in a similar manner to, and is complementary with, those used by the IOC. The BOA is also the owner of the IOC's intellectual property rights in the UK but is only able to exploit them in accordance with instructions from the IOC to ensure that their respective sponsorship and partnership agreements are not in conflict with each other (Bye-laws 1.2 and 1.3 to Rules 7–14 Olympic Charter).

Despite the obvious importance of its commercial activities, the two occasions when the BOA is most visible are when it nominates a UK city hoping to host an edition of the Olympic Games and when it invites athletes to compete on its behalf as members of Team GB. Only an NOC can nominate a city to be a candidate for hosting the Olympic Games; thus, where there are multiple prospective candidates, it may have to run its own domestic competition to determine which city is finally put forward for consideration by the IOC. Once a single candidate is identified, the NOC promotes the bid alongside a team from the prospective host city. If the bid is successful, as was the case with London 2012, the Games is organised by a separate committee such as LOCOG, not the NOC.

The BOA is also responsible for inviting athletes to compete on its behalf at each edition of the Olympic Games. The BOA does not technically pick the members of Team GB; the NGBs in charge of the sports on the Olympic programme nominate those athletes and teams whom they consider to have reached the relevant qualifying standards. The BOA then invites those athletes whom they consider to have fulfilled the eligibility criteria found in Rules 40–44 Olympic Charter to compete at the Games. Rule 44(3) Olympic Charter states that nobody has a right to compete at the Olympics even if they have reached the necessary standard. This enables limits to be placed on the total number of athletes who can be invited to each edition of the Olympic Games and the number of representatives of each NOC who can appear in any particular event. For example, the IOC currently limits the total number of athletes to 10,500 by Bye-law 14 to Rule 44 Olympic Charter and the maximum number of athletes from a single NOC in any event to three according to Bye-law 11 to Rule 44.

The issue of eligibility to compete at the Olympics was the focus of Dwain Chambers' litigation with the BOA in the spring of 2008 (*Chambers v British Olympic Association* [2008] EWHC 2028 (QBD)). BOA Bye-law 25 stated that any athlete who has been banned for a serious doping offence will not be invited to compete in the Olympics even where they have served their suspension and are free to compete in all other competitions authorised by their ISF without further restriction. The BOA made exceptions for minor infringements where it considered that the athlete was not at fault, such as in the case of Christine Ohuruogu, or for minor infringements that are punished by a suspension from competition of six months or less, but effectively banned for life anyone who has been found guilty of doping from representing Team GB at the Olympic Games in any capacity.

Following the decision of CAS in *United States Olympic Committee v IOC* CAS 2011/O/2422 (above, 14.2.2), where the IOC's much more lenient additional doping ban was held to be unlawful, WADA declared that the BOA's Bye-law 25 was incompatible with the WADA Code. In *British Olympic Association v World Anti-Doping Agency* CAS 2011/A/2658, CAS held that the BOA's lifetime ban on participation in the Olympic Games was unlawful on the same grounds as the IOC's eligibility Rule had been; it was an additional punishment that was contrary to the WADA Code and offended the principle of double jeopardy. This enabled Chambers and others to compete in London 2012 after having been prevented from competing at previous editions of the Games.

14.2.4.2 Local organising committees – The London Organising Committee for the Olympic Games

The Olympic Movement's third national-level manifestation is the local organising committee of the next editions of the Games. For London 2012, this role was fulfilled by LOCOG, which was created in 2005 by the BOA, the Mayor of London and the Secretary of State for Culture, Media and Sport. The government's role in the organisation of the Games was overseen by the Minister for the Olympics. All local organising committees cease to exist at the end of the year in which its edition of the Games took place, meaning that LOCOG was formally wound up on 31 December 2012.

LOCOG was a private company limited by guarantee which had the task of organising the Games of the 30th Olympiad and was a member of the Olympic Movement for the period of its existence. It reported through the Olympic Games Coordination Commission to the IOC on all matters relating to the organisation of the London Olympics. At the conclusion of the Games, it passed on its knowledge and experience to the Coordination Commission and on its dissolution the intellectual property and commercial rights in all specifically commissioned works became vested in the IOC. According to Bye-law 4 of Rule 50 Olympic Charter, this includes, for example, the mascots, songs, logos, posters and medals designed for use at a Games. This enables the IOC to exploit the historic rights associated with each edition of the Olympic Games and to continue to generate income for its various sporting and education programmes.

As a private body, LOCOG was self-funding. Its main income-generating streams were ticket sales and the sale of sponsorship and merchandising rights together with a share of the IOC's official partnership and broadcasting deals. Public and lottery funding was distributed through the Olympic Delivery Authority (ODA), which was established by the London Olympic Games and Paralympic Games Act 2006. The ODA was responsible for creating the sporting and transport infrastructure for the Games taking the form of a statutory corporation subject to public law. It was also partially responsible for the enforcement of the offences created by the London Olympic Games and Paralympic Games Act 2006 (below, 14.3.3). After the closing ceremony of the Paralympic Games, the management of the Olympic Park was transferred to the London Legacy Development Corporation.

14.3 Law and the Olympics

Staging the Olympic Games, particularly the main summer edition, has always been seen as one of the most prestigious events that can be hosted by a city. However, it has only been since the Los Angeles Games in 1984 that organisers have broken even or made a profit with any degree of regularity. The Montreal Games in 1976 saddled the city with 30 years of debt, whilst the losses generated by other host cities have often been absorbed by regional and national governments. It is the development of the commercial side of the Olympics and of the Olympic brand, particularly the protections granted to the IOC in respect of its intellectual property and the association rights that it grants to its main sponsors, which have attracted the interest of lawyers and law makers.

The legal protections claimed for the iconography of the Olympic Movement are defined in Rules 7-14 Olympic Charter. By Rule 7 Olympic Charter, all rights in the Olympic Games and the 'Olympic Properties' lie with the IOC, which has the exclusive right to exploit them. Rule 7(2) states that the Olympic Games are the exclusive property of the IOC and that it owns all of the rights and data relating to each individual edition. Rule 7(4) specifically states that the Olympic Properties include the interlocking five-ring Olympic Symbol; the flag; the motto (*citius, altius, fortius*) and any translations of it; the official anthem; depictions of the Olympic flame and the Olympic torches used to transport the flame from Olympia to the host city; any identifications, designations or emblems associated with the Olympic Movement; and the phrases 'Olympic Games' and 'Games of the Olympiad' with more explicit definitions being provided in Rules 8-14 Olympic Charter. The protection of the rights associated with these symbols and words falls to the NOC in each jurisdiction.

The level of protection afforded to the Olympic Properties varies significantly among jurisdictions. At the international level, the Nairobi Treaty on the Protection of the Olympic Symbol provides the IOC with specific protection for the Olympic Symbol (below, 14.3.1). In other jurisdictions, such as the UK, specific legislation has been introduced to protect the Olympic Symbol and specific words and phrases for the benefit of the appropriate NOC (below, 14.3.2 and 14.3.3). In other countries, the relevant protection is enforced by a mixture of copyright and trademark law. The variety of means of protecting the Olympic Properties has led to the IOC requiring legislation to be implemented by the national government of the city where the Olympic Games is to be staged as a condition of the Host City Contract. The focus of legal discussions in the remainder of this chapter is on UK law and in particular the protections that were developed in respect of the London Olympics.

14.3.1 The Nairobi Treaty on the Protection of the Olympic Symbol 1981

As the IOC began to exploit its commercial rights more effectively in order to generate sufficient funding for the host cities of the Olympics, it sought a greater degree of protection for its intellectual property. In 1981, under the auspices of the World Intellectual Property Organization, the Nairobi Treaty on the Protection of the Olympic Symbol came into effect; to date, 68 nations are signatories of the treaty, of which 49 have enacted its provisions into their domestic law. According to Art.1, any party to the treaty is obliged to refuse or to declare as invalid any attempt to register the Olympic symbol consisting of the five interlocking rings unless the use of the symbol is with the consent of the IOC. The only exceptions cover situations where the symbol had already been registered and/or used commercially by an undertaking prior to the date on which the treaty came into force in the signatory nation.

14.3.2 Olympic Symbols etc (Protection) Act 1995

The British government of the time did not ratify the Nairobi Treaty, however similar protection was subsequently provided by the Olympic Symbols etc (Protection) Act 1995 (OPSA 1995) in respect of the generic intellectual property rights of the Olympic

Movement. Two possible explanations can be given for the decision to afford statutory protection to a private body's commercial rights. Firstly, it enables the BOA, rather than the IOC as is the case under the Nairobi Treaty, to exploit the right to be associated with the Olympic symbols more effectively and to raise sufficient funds for it to remain financially independent from the state. Secondly, as British cities began to bid to host the Olympic Games in the 1980s and 1990s, it became apparent that such protection would enhance the prospects of their candidature.

14.3.2.1 The Olympic Association Right

Under s.2 OPSA, specific protection is provided for the Olympic symbol, the Olympic motto and associated protected words by the creation of the Olympics Association Right (OAR). The protected words are defined in s.18(2)(a) as: 'Olympiad'; 'Olympiads'; 'Olympian'; 'Olympians'; 'Olympic'; and 'Olympics.' Further, s.3(1)(b) states that any representations or any words that are so similar to those which have been protected and the use of which is likely to create in the public mind an association with the Olympic Games or the Olympic Movement are also prohibited.

This protection was updated by sch.3 London Olympic Games and Paralympic Games Act 2006 (LOGA 2006) and extended by sch.4 in the light of London's hosting of the 2012 Games. A similar right, the Paralympics Association Right, is created by s.5A OPSA 1995 in respect of the commercial rights associated with the Paralympic Games which are owned by the International Paralympic Committee (IPC). The Paralympics Association Right protects the IPC's symbol and motto 'Spirit in Motion' and the words 'Paralympiad', 'Paralympian', 'Paralympic', and their respective plurals. The OAR grants to the proprietor of the protected symbols the exclusive right to use them. Originally, the BOA was appointed as the sole proprietor of the OAR, however for the period of its existence, LOCOG was a joint proprietor in order to facilitate its funding of the 2012 Games (Olympics and Paralympics Association Rights (Appointment of Proprietors) Order 2006/1119).

Under s.3 OPSA 1995, the OAR is infringed where a person uses the protected symbols and/or words in the course of trade or uses a representation of something so similar to them that it is likely to create in the public mind an association with them or with the Olympic Games or the Olympic Movement. It is drafted widely enough to ensure that any person connected with the manufacture, packaging, supply or sale of an unauthorised or unlicensed product infringes the OAR. Thus, the Act provides the symbols with a statutory version of the protections afforded in other circumstances by trademarks (see further, chapter 13.3.2).

The OAR is not infringed in the limited number of circumstances defined in s.4 OPSA 1995. Two of the exceptions, ss.4(1) and (3), are of particular note. Firstly, there is no infringement where the use of the protected symbols and words is for the purpose of reporting on specific Olympic events or about the Olympic Games in general. This enables the media to report freely on the Games and to advertise the material that they intend to publish or broadcast. Secondly, there is no infringement where the use of the protected symbols and words does not suggest an official contractual, commercial, structural or financial association with either the Olympic Games or the Olympic Movement. The circumstances in which this exception could operate are likely to be extremely limited and when used in conjunction with the anti-ambush marketing provisions (below, 14.4.2) will only very rarely allow any infringement of the OAR.

Infringements of the OAR are actionable by its proprietor the BOA under s.6 OPSA 1995. It enables the BOA to claim damages for any losses caused and an injunction to stop further infringement of the OAR. Under s.7, the proprietors can request erasure of an infringing sign, delivery up or disposal of infringing goods and the forfeiture of counterfeited items. Furthermore, under s.8, anyone involved in the production, packaging, supply or sale of anything that infringes the OAR with a view to making a gain for themselves or another, or with intent to cause loss to another, and doing so without the consent of the proprietor, commits a criminal offence.

In the months preceding London 2012, and in particular during the nationwide Torch Relay, a team of brand enforcement officers was dispatched around the UK to ensure that there were no infringements of either the OAR or the London Olympic Association Right (below, 14.3.2). Prosecutions for infringement were threatened on a number of occasions, though no criminal proceedings were actually commenced. Those threatened included a butcher who had designed and displayed a sign depicting the Olympic rings using sausages, a florist who had made a window display of the rings out of paper flowers and an elderly lady who had knitted a jumper with the rings on the front for a doll that was to be sold at a charity event at a church fair. Although LOCOG obviously needed to ensure that it maximised its commercial income and prevented others from exploiting the goodwill associated with the Olympic Properties, and in particular prevented concerted ambush marketing campaigns (below, 14.3.3), their zero-tolerance approach alienated many individuals and small businesses from engaging fully with the carnival atmosphere that surrounded the Relay and the Games.

A further level of protection has been afforded to the words 'The Olympics' and 'The Games of the Olympiad' and 'Olympic Games' and 'Olympiad' when used in combination with a representation of the Olympic Symbol by their having been registered by the IOC as Community Trade Marks E2827632, E8471369, E876383 and E1118165, respectively. The combination of statutory provisions and trade marking affords an almost unparalleled degree of protection to the Olympic Properties.

14.3.3 London Olympic Games and Paralympic Games Act 2006

LOGA 2006 provided the legislative basis on which London 2012 was organised and gave effect to the commitments made and guarantees provided by the government to the IOC during the bid procedure. The first part of the Act, together with sch.1, established the Olympic Delivery Authority (ODA) and defined its powers to coordinate the planning and transport developments in order to provide the infrastructure necessary to host the London Olympics. Most of the remainder of the Act provided the framework of controls that were applied to prevent ambush marketing and regulate the exploitation of the commercial rights associated with the Games. In particular, it defined the restrictions on advertising and street trading in and around Olympic venues, established a London Olympics Association Right and created an offence of touting tickets to Olympic events (see further, chapter 13.4.3.2).

14.3.3.1 The London Olympics Association Right

In addition to the amendments to the OAR contained in sch.3 LOGA 2006 (above, 14.3.2.1), s.33 and sch.4 created a specific London Olympics Association Right (LOAR) over which LOCOG had sole proprietorship. The framework that was used to protect the specific intellectual property rights associated with London 2012 ran in parallel to the generic protection provided to the Olympic properties by OPSA 1995. Thus, by sch.4 para.1, the LOAR prohibited a person acting in the course of their trade from making any representation of any kind without the consent of LOCOG that suggested to the public that they had an authorised or official association of any kind with the London Olympics. 'Association' was defined in the same way as it is for the OAR as meaning a contractual, commercial, structural or financial link with the London Olympics. When attempting to establish this link, however, there was no limit on the type of representation that could have been used as evidence that an association had been suggested. Use of any of the many trade marks registered by LOCOG would undoubtedly have been considered to be suggesting an association, as would the use of specific words and phrases most commonly connected to London 2012. The wording of the provision was interpreted by LOCOG to be wide enough to include any conduct that might have suggested to the public that an association existed, though such a broad interpretation was never tested before the courts.

▶ *London Olympic Games and Paralympic Games Act 2006 Sch.4 para.3 – infringement: specific expressions*

(1) For the purpose of considering whether a person has infringed the London Olympics association right a court may, in particular, take account of his use of a combination of expressions of a kind specified in sub-paragraph (2).

(2) The combinations referred to in sub-paragraph (1) are combinations of –
    (a) any of the expressions in the first group, with
    (b) any of the expressions in the second group or any of the other expressions in the first group.

(3) The following expressions form the first group for the purposes of sub-paragraph (2) –
    (a) "games",
    (b) "Two Thousand and Twelve",
    (c) "2012", and
    (d) "twenty twelve".

(4) The following expressions form the second group for the purposes of sub-paragraph (2) –
    (a) gold,
    (b) silver,
    (c) bronze,
    (d) London,
    (e) medals,
    (f) sponsor, and
    (g) summer.

(5) It is immaterial for the purposes of this paragraph whether or not a word is written wholly or partly in capital letters.

These restrictions were a non-exhaustive list that could have been amended by statutory instrument, though no such extension of the controlled representations was considered to be necessary. Taken together with the words protected by OPSA 1995 and the wide range of trade marks that were registered by LOCOG to be used as symbols and logos for the promotion of the Games and on related merchandising, it was almost impossible for a person acting in the course of trade or business to use any word, group of words, phrase or symbol that suggested a link with the London Olympics unless they were an official partner of either the IOC, the BOA or LOCOG. Unlike with a claim for passing off or an action under s.10(2) Trade Marks Act 1994, there was no need for confusion to be created in the minds of the public or specific groups of consumers; a much lower standard of suggesting an association with the London Olympics was all that was required. A breach of the LOAR was actionable in the same way as is a breach of the OAR under ss.6 and 7 OPSA 1995 for the period during which the right was in existence.

As was the case with the OAR (above, 14.3.2.1), during the Torch Relay and the Games period a number of individuals and small businesses were threatened with infringement proceedings for making unofficial associations with London 2012. For example, a newsagent in Stratford, East London, was ordered to take down merchandise that he was displaying outside his shop as it was inconsistent with the 'look and feel' of the official display, and the University of Derby was reproached for adding that it 'supported' those running in the Torch Relay to an official banner as it has not paid to be an official 'supporter' of either the Relay or the Games.

LOCOG's interpretation of whether or not the LOAR was infringed was so strict that when easyjet sought clearance for an advert in which Olympic gold medallist Sally Gunnell would re-enact her lap of honour holding a Union Flag above her head as she had on winning the 400m hurdles at the 1992 Barcelona Games, they were refused permission. Despite filming taking place at London Southend airport and Ms Gunnell not wearing athletics kit, LOCOG considered that this would create so strong an association with the Games in the public mind that they might think that easyjet was an official sponsor, which it was not, or the official airline, which was British Airways.

This proactive, and LOCOG's view educational, approach to preventing infringements of the LOAR was set aside on a number of occasions when major companies pushed the limits of the law resulting in LOCOG quickly backing down. The most high-profile instance of LOCOG's interpretation of the law being challenged concerned a campaign run by the Irish bookmakers Paddy Power that began in the week of the Games' Opening Ceremony, in which Paddy Power claimed that it was the 'Official sponsor of the largest athletics event in London this year! (Ahem, London France that is).' Paddy Power was indeed the official sponsor of the largest athletics event in the village of London in southwest France, where they had organised an international egg and spoon race. LOCOG threatened infringement proceedings as the campaign was clearly an attempt to ambush London 2012 but withdrew when Paddy Power threatened to challenge their interpretation of the law in the High Court. Although a strange decision at first sight, particularly in the light of the zero-tolerance stance taken against local traders, LOCOG avoided the risk of a judicial interpretation of the LOAR being handed down that would have been significantly narrower than the one that it was informing the commercial world was applicable.

14.3.4 Preventing ambush marketing at the London 2012 Games

Whereas the creation of the OAR and LOAR can be seen as highly specialised forms of trade mark protection or 'super-IP rights', the framework of regulations that were in place for protecting the commercial rights in the London Olympics from ambush marketing broke entirely new legal ground in the UK. The aim of these provisions was twofold: to provide 'clean' venues for Olympic events and to prevent ambush marketing inside and in the vicinity of Olympic venues. The former is important to the IOC as it does not allow any advertising inside Olympic venues in accordance with Rule 50(2) Olympic Charter; it does not want undertakings providing spectators with items that will provide ambushers with free advertising that is not available to its official partners. The latter is important to both the IOC and LOCOG as they require protection from marketing strategies that undermine the value of the exclusive rights that have been sold to the various categories of official partners. Any diminution in the value of these rights could seriously affect a city's ability to host the Games successfully.

Ambush marketing is the unofficial or unauthorised association of a product or service with an event (13.2.3). In many cases, it is also an attempt to undermine the marketing strategy of one or more of the event's official sponsors by making it seem as though the ambusher is the undertaking with the formal association with the event. In either case, the ambusher is taking advantage of the goodwill associated with an event and is hoping to receive a tangible benefit from creating an apparent association with it for which it has not paid.

14.3.4.1 Regulating advertising in the vicinity of Olympic venues

The difficulties associated with protecting marketing rights through traditional legal means, such as passing off, required additional specific provisions to be introduced to prevent the occurrence of specific types of ambush marketing at the London Olympics. Ambush marketing in the form of unlawful advertising was governed by s.19 LOGA 2006 and the London Olympic Games and Paralympic Games (Advertising and Trading) (England) Regulations 2011/2898 (the Regulations); similar provisions were in place in Wales, SI 2012/60, and Scotland, Scottish SI 2011/458.

It is important to note the breadth of the protections provided to LOCOG in respect of the control of advertising of all kinds. Under s.19 and the Regulations, advertising in the vicinity of all Olympic venues around the country was regulated prior to, during and in the immediate aftermath of London 2012. Specific event zones and event periods were identified for all venues, providing the necessary spatial and temporal definitions within which the Regulations and their restrictions were operative. Advertising was also defined incredibly widely and in ss.19(4) and (5) included advertising of a non-commercial nature, announcements of any kind and the distribution of documents and articles. Further, s.19(7) required all advertising in the vicinity of an Olympic venue to have been authorised by LOCOG.

The width of these provisions ensured that almost any public display that created any kind of link to London 2012 was caught by s.19 LOGA 2006, particularly where LOCOG considered that it impacted negatively on its marketing and intellectual property rights or on those that it had officially licensed to its commercial partners. To ensure compliance with this provision, the police and the ODA, as a designated enforcement agency for offences defined by LOGA 2006, were granted the power under s.22 to enter premises that they reasonably suspected were being used for unlawful advertising or where they suspected advertising that was in breach of s.19 was being created, produced or stored. Any infringing article found on the premises could have been removed, destroyed, concealed or erased. Further, criminal proceedings could have been brought against the infringer, in a similar way to Trading Standards Officers being able to bring actions under consumer protection legislation in circumstances where the breach was particularly flagrant or repeated. Conviction under s.19 or the Regulations could have resulted in an unlimited fine if the case were heard before the Crown Court or a fine of up to £20,000 in the Magistrates' Court (s.21(3) LOGA 2006).

14.3.4.2 Regulating street trading in the vicinity of Olympic venues

In addition to the regulation of advertising, s.25 LOGA 2006 and the Regulations provided a similar framework of regulation over street trading. These further controls were introduced to ensure the quality of goods being sold to the public near Olympic venues, to prevent the sale of unofficial, unlicensed or counterfeited products and to restrict the outlets through which goods that were capable of ambushing official merchandise could be sold. The framework for the regulation of street trading mirrors that for the control of advertising: s.28 created similar powers of enforcement by allowing entry to premises to remove infringing articles, s.29 enabled the ODA to institute criminal proceedings against anyone who committed the offence of unlawful street trading, and s.27 imposed the same levels of punishment on those found guilty as were in s.21.

The provisions of LOGA 2006 only applied to trading that occurred in places to which the public had access, the highway and car parks but not to shops (s.25(4)), and the same event zones and event periods were operative for trading as were for advertising. In order to regulate more specifically the people who could trade in the vicinity of Olympic venues, all existing licences were suspended and anyone wanting to trade in the restricted event zones had to reapply for their right to trade. Although there was no additional cost imposed upon traders, additional conditions were contained in the licences issued for the Olympic period to ensure that traders did not dress their stalls in a manner that conflicted with the official 'look and feel' or branding of London 2012 and to promote health and safety considerations around the entrances to and exists from Olympic venues. Once again, the commercial interests of the IOC and LOCOG were provided with a very high degree of protection from the possibility of ambush marketing of almost any kind. Even though street traders were unlikely to, or unlikely to be able to, mount a sufficiently high-profile marketing campaign that they could interfere with those of the official sponsors or diminish the value of LOCOG's commercial rights, these provisions were rigorously enforced.

14.3.4.3 The impact of the anti-ambush marketing regime

Comparatively few concerns were raised about the framework of protections created for the commercial rights associated with London 2012 even though the legislative provisions introduced to prevent ambush marketing and restrict advertising and street trading went far beyond anything that had been previously seen in the UK. The various provisions in LOGA 2006 were extremely widely drafted and had the potential to be able to catch almost any association made with the Olympics that had not been made by one of the official partners or in the course of legitimate reporting on its constituent events. What became clear during 2012 was that LOGA 2006 provided unprecedented levels of protection for the commercial interests of a major private international undertaking.

The nature of the protections granted went far beyond that which would be available in any other circumstance. For example, there was no need to prove that the public or specific groups of consumers were confused as to the existence of an association between the ambusher and the London Olympics as would be required for an action in passing off; the offence was to advertise a product without the authorisation of LOCOG. Thus, the ability to advertise in the vicinity of an Olympic venue was restricted to the official partners of the IOC and LOCOG or to the suppliers of goods and services that are not in competition with them.

The symbiotic relationship between LOCOG and the ODA meant that these two ostensibly separate and distinct bodies were, in reality, joined to the common purpose of making the London Olympics a success. In respect of the provisions regulating advertising, LOCOG controlled access to prime sites and regulated who could and who could not advertise in the vicinity of Olympic venues whilst the ODA was able to investigate and prosecute breaches of s.19 LOGA 2006. Where street trading was concerned, the ODA was able to authorise, investigate and prosecute breaches of s.25 LOGA 2006 whilst having to work with LOCOG to ensure that the terms of the Host City Contract were complied with. This resulted in the enforcement of the Act being carried out by the two bodies with the most vested interests in its most rigorous application.

In the end, despite these concerns, London 2012 was a resounding success and passed with the provisions contained in LOGA 2006 rarely resorted to. LOCOG appeared to be content to threaten enforcement proceedings rather than pursue them in court and those infringing the OAR and LOAR were quick to comply with little more than a complaint to the local media about how they were only trying to join in the carnival atmosphere surrounding the Games and associated events. Despite this, it is difficult to describe the legislative framework and LOCOG's enforcement of it as an unqualified success. The Olympic laws were used exclusively against individuals, small and local businesses and street traders who could not be described as engaging in ambush marketing according to any accepted definition of the problem and in each reported situation the alleged infringer claimed to be supporting the Games, not attempting to damage them.

In contrast, when presented with the opportunity to enforce the law and test the extent of it powers, particularly against Paddy Power, LOCOG quickly backed down. Once again, where a big business that was capable of defending itself threatened to expose the many problems associated with the legislation, LOCOG, as FIFA has also done in the past (13.2.3), chose not to enforce their rights.

14.3.5 Olympic taxation rules and requirements

The final, and possibly least known, of the legal requirements enforced on host city governments is that special tax-exempt status must be granted to a large contingent of the Olympic family. For London 2012, this was provided by the London Olympic Games and Paralympic Games Tax Regulations 2010/2913 (the Tax Regulations). Regulation 3 exempted all 'accredited individuals' who were either not UK residents or not normally resident in the UK from being liable for income tax on any earnings received in relation to their work at London 2012 during the period 30 March to 8 November 2012. Where competitors were concerned, all income related to competing at London 2012 and supporting or promoting the Games, the Olympic and/or Paralympic Movements was exempted under Reg.4(2), whilst non-competitors were not taxed on the income derived from their accredited status under Reg.4(3). Although competitors do not get paid for competing in the Olympics, the UK tax regime for sports performers would ordinarily require them to pay tax on their annual earnings on a *pro rata* basis. For example, if an athlete were to receive £1m from sponsorship and endorsement agreements and spend one-tenth of the year in the UK, they would be liable for income tax on £100,000; this income would became tax exempt between 30 March and 8 November 2012.

Accredited individuals are defined in Regs.5–7 and include competitors, media workers, representatives of official bodies, service technicians, team officials, technical officials (including match officials, judges and timekeepers), performers in the opening and closing ceremonies and anyone working for one of the commercial delivery partners of London 2012. Official bodies, accredited representatives of which would be covered by the tax exemptions, included: a sovereign, a head of state, a government, a National Olympic and Paralympic Committees, a city that has been selected by the IOC or International Paralympic Committee (IPC) to host a future Olympics and Paralympics or Youth Olympics, a city that has been selected by the IOC or IPC to be a candidate to host a future Olympics and Paralympics or Youth Olympics, a city that the IOC or IPC recognises as an applicant to host a future Olympics and Paralympics or Youth Olympics, the IOC, the IPC, an ISF, CAS or WADA (Reg.5). The Tax Regulations ensured that some of the world's highest-paid professional sports stars and sports administrators were able to live and work in the UK tax-free and are an increasingly common requirement of primary rights holders such as the IOC and FIFA in particular.

14.4 The Court of Arbitration for Sport Ad Hoc Division at London, 2012

In 1996, the Court of Arbitration for Sport (CAS) established an ad hoc division to sit at that summer's Olympic Games in Atlanta. The aim of the ad hoc division was to settle definitively any dispute that arose at the Games within 24 hours to ensure that there was as little disruption to the on-going competitions as possible. The expedited procedure used by the ad hoc division was so successful that it has been used at every edition of both the summer and winter Olympic Games since 1996, at the Commonwealth Games since 1998 and at other major championships around the world; it does not, however, sit at the Paralympic Games. The ad hoc division only hears disputes that are about the Games or championships for which it has been constituted; for London 2012, only disputes that occurred after 17 July 2012 or during events at the Games could be heard before it.

The ad hoc division that sat at London 2012 heard 11 cases, all of which were relatively straightforward. Of the 11, nine raised issues of eligibility to compete at the Games, one challenged the final result of a competition and one an in-game decision; the last two were dismissed for want of jurisdiction as the CAS, whether sitting as the full Court or its ad hoc division, will not interfere with 'field of play decisions' unless there is evidence that the match officials were acting in bad faith, *Swedish Triathlon Federation and Swedish Olympic Committee v International Triathlon Union* CAS OG 12/10 and *Russian Olympic Committee v International Sailing Federation* CAS OG 12/11 (see further, chapter 3.2).

The findings in respect of the eligibility decisions were more varied. Three applications to compete were refused on the basis that the appropriate selection or qualification rules had been correctly applied, *Ward v International Amateur Boxing Association* CAS OG 12/02, *Gezzar v Fédération Française d'Athletisme* CAS OG 12/09 and *Fédération Française de Pentathlon Moderne and Berrou v Union Internationale de Pentathlon Moderne* CAS OG 12/08. One application was refused on the basis that the dispute arose before 17 July 2012 and that the ad hoc division did not have jurisdiction to hear an application that should have been made to the full CAS, *Federación Española de Piragüismo v International Canoe Federation* CAS OG 12/04 and a further one on the basis that there was no right of appeal from the decision-making body in question to CAS, *Lynch v Horse Sport Ireland and the Olympic Council of Ireland* CAS OG 12/03. Only two applications to compete were accepted, both on the basis that the decision-making body had not followed its own selection rules, *Petternell v South African Sports Confederation and Olympic Committee and South African Equestrian Federation* CAS OG 12/01 and *Mullera Rodriguez v Real Federación Española de Atletismo* CAS OG 12/06.

The most unusual of the cases brought before the ad hoc division was in the linked decisions in *Sterba v World Anti-Doping Agency* CAS OG 12/05 and *International Canoe Federation v Sterba* CAS OG 12/07. Shortly before London 2012, Sterba had been found not guilty of a doping offence but was aware that the ICF intended to challenge the decision. In the first case, Sterba sought a declaration that the original finding was correct, but his application was refused on the grounds that he could only appeal against a guilty verdict. As he was not appealing the decision, there was no basis on which the ad hoc division could pass judgment as it only had jurisdiction to hear appeals. In the second case, the ICF appealed against the not-guilty verdict. This time, Sterba was found to have committed a doping offence but not one that was serious enough to warrant his exclusion from the Games.

The most high-profile disciplinary incident of London 2012 did not reach the ad hoc division as it was heard before the disciplinary and appeals committees of the Badminton World Federation. In the women's doubles tournament, the format was such that in the last round of qualifying matches, four teams, two from South Korea and one each from Indonesia and China, deliberately tried to lose their games in order to secure an easier route through the later knockout stages of the competition. All four teams were found to have acted in breach Rules 4.5 and 4.16 of the BWF's Players Code of Conduct by failing to use best efforts and conducting oneself in a manner that is clearly abusive or detrimental to the sport respectively. All were disqualified from competing further in the Olympic tournament. Ultimately, a final appeal could have been made to the ad hoc division, however, none was made as two of the teams accepted the first instance disciplinary committee decision and the remaining two teams accepted the appeals committees' decisions.

14.5 The impact of 'Olympic law' on future sporting mega-events

At each edition of the Olympic Games, new lessons are learned about the most effective means of enforcing the commercial rights owned by the IOC and the local organising committee and how best to regulate the exploitation of those rights. This in turn leads the IOC to require as a condition of the next Host City Contract increasingly sophisticated legal protections to be created by the national government of the country where the host city is based. The success of the Olympic legislation leads organisers of other major events to require similar protections for the commercial rights associated with their championships. In his article 'Look out! It's an ambush!', Johnson referred to these two phenomena as 'horizontal' and 'vertical creep'.

Horizontal creep is where the protection afforded to one edition of an event is used to justify protection of at least the same level at its next edition. Since the introduction of this type of legislative protection in the Sydney 2000 Games (Indicia and Images) Protection Act, a piece of legislation that represented a step change in the degree of protection afforded to an Organising Committee of the Olympic Games, 'Olympic law' has evolved and extended into the protections which are found in LOGA 2006 and its subordinate regulatory frameworks. This horizontal creep can again be witnessed in the development of the laws promulgated to protect the commercial rights of the organisers of the Sochi 2014 Winter Olympics and the next summer Games in Rio 2016.

Under Arts.7 and 8 of the Russian Federal law, 'On the Organisation and Holding of the XXII Olympic Winter Games and XI Paralympic Winter Games 2014 in Sochi, the Development of Sochi as a Mountain Resort and Amendments to Certain Legislative Acts of the Russian Federation' the protections that were available in London 2012 are extended by including Cyrillic versions of the Olympic Properties and criminalising explicitly the use of words or symbols that are similar to those which have been granted legislative protection, which was only LOCOG's enforcement policy, not law at London 2012.

For Rio 2016, the protections are extended further again. Not only has the Nairobi Treaty on the Protection of the Olympic Symbol been enacted into Brazilian law through Legislative Decree 21/1984 but specific protections are granted to Rio 2016 by the 'Lei do alto Olimpico' 12035/2009 that go beyond those enacted for both London 2012 and Sochi 2014. Article 7 of the Act criminalises any improper connection with the Games, including the use of similar terms, words and symbols to those with specific legislative protection, building on the extension of the protections in the Sochi law. Further, it makes provision for the suspension of all advertising agreements around Olympic venues, strategic buildings and transport hubs for up to 180 days around event times, extending the restrictions on advertising that were in place at London 2012 considerably.

Vertical creep is where the protection afforded to the Olympics is then granted to a less prestigious or single sporting event. For example, the Glasgow Commonwealth Games Act 2008 provides an almost identical regulatory framework for advertising, street trading and ticket touting as did LOGA 2006. A Glasgow Commonwealth Games Association Right that mirrors the LOAR is created by Glasgow Commonwealth Games Act 2008 (Games Association Right) Order 2009/1969. Similar legislative protections are also required by FIFA of nations hosting the World Cup Finals.

The result of this process of legislative creep is that all major event organisers, or the ISFs in charge of determining where a championships should be held, are slowly beginning to expect that such protections should be offered to them as a matter of course or demand that their event should be granted those protections as a condition of allowing a city to act as host. What was originally introduced as a specific piece of legislation designed to protect a truly unique, global event is rapidly becoming a sporting-legal norm. This is epitomised by New Zealand's response to such requirements becoming ubiquitous.

In order to improve its chances of hosting major events in the future, New Zealand has passed the Major Events Management Act 2007 to provide Olympic Law-style protections to all significant international sporting events. In order to qualify as a major event under s.7, the organisers must have taken all practicable measures to protect their commercial rights under existing law and further the hosting the event must offer substantial sporting, cultural, social and/or economic or other similar benefits to New Zealand or New Zealanders, thereby extending the range of championships and tournaments which can receive state protection dramatically. With ISFs and their chosen hosts needing to exploit their commercial rights in order to provide the necessary funding to stage an event, specific legislation such as OPSA 1995 and LOGA 2006 and generic legislation such as that now in force in New Zealand are likely to become increasingly commonplace at the world's major sporting events. Where a legislature is unwilling, or unable because of issues relating to personal and corporate free speech, to pass such legislative protections, it is unlikely to be able to host these events in the future.

Hot topic ...   Why are the Olympic Games special?

Since their reintroduction in 1896, the Olympic Games has become the largest and most important sporting event in the world. The summer edition of the Games is unique in terms of its size and scale, the range of events included on its programme, the audience who watches it and the money that it generates. The introduction of the Winter Olympic Games in 1924, and since 1988 the hosting of the Paralympic Games in the same city as the Olympics, has entrenched in the minds of the public the importance of the championships that are encompassed by the Olympic Movement. Only the FIFA World Cup Finals can come close in terms of the popular interest and money generated by the Olympics.

Yet, despite its commercial success and that fully professional athletes are allowed to compete in many of its constituent sports, the Olympic Games continue to be seen by many people as the embodiment of values that are more often associated with amateur sport, including the Fundamental Principles of Olympism, fair play and respect for others. Olympic success is still seen by many athletes in many disciplines as being the pinnacle of achievement in their sport. Even where there are discipline-specific world championships, such as in athletics, or highly lucrative professional tournaments, such as in tennis or basketball, Olympic success of and for itself remains one of the most sought-after sporting distinctions.

However, the tension that has been created between its sporting and commercial aims has seen much criticism directed at the Olympic Movement. Its self-appointed role as the guardian of sporting conduct and ethical play does not always sit well with its need to generate income and protect its commercial rights. Its promotion of the World Anti-Doping Code by requiring all sports included on the Olympic programme to have implemented its provisions has been seen as a major step forward in the regulation of doping and the harmonisation of anti-doping regimes. The promotion and protection of sports ethics and athletes' health is very clearly in accordance with the fundamental principles of Olympism and is the kind of issue that the IOC could be expected to take a lead on.

In contrast, concern has been raised about the rationale for the decision of the IOC Congress in 2009 to include golf in the Olympic programme from 2016 on the grounds that it is too costly to be sufficiently accessible to the majority of people throughout the world to satisfy the requirements of being an Olympic sport. The critics of golf's inclusion claim that this is a commercial decision that will increase the value of broadcasting and sponsorship rights, not a sporting decision based on Olympic values. As the cost of staging the games increases, so does the need to guarantee sufficient income to host them, a commercial necessity not always in accordance with the spirit of Olympism.

There is no doubt that the Olympic Games are special, but are they special enough for the treatment that they receive, particularly in respect of the protections afforded to its commercial rights? In a wider form, this is a question that has been asked of the courts for many years: why is sport so special that it should be treated differently by the law? The CJEU has begun to develop the most effective analytical framework for addressing these questions by directing courts to examine whether the 'specificity of sport' requires that the law should treat certain rules, procedures or conduct differently. Where it can be shown that the conduct of a sporting body is no more than is necessary and proportionate for the proper administration of a sport, to promote sporting competition or protect sports ethics, it will be acting lawfully.

In order to justify its actions, the IOC needs to be able to provide a legally robust explanation for what it is doing. At present, its conduct is often accepted without further question as prospective host cities and their governments accede to the IOC's requests in order to stand the best chance of securing the right to stage the Olympic Games. If it is to continue unchallenged in its current role, the IOC will need to develop a sporting explanation for why its increasingly commercial activities should be treated differently to those of other businesses and other sports organisations. This is particularly the case with the development of super-IP rights to protect its iconography and compulsory tax exemptions for the Olympic family. Simply claiming to be unique may not always be enough; a legally defensible definition of the 'specificity of the Olympic Games' could provide the explanation that the law requires, particularly if this were to focus on how these legislative requirements could promote proactively the Fundamental Principles of Olympism.

Summary

14.1 Since its creation in 1894, the Olympic Movement has grown into being one of the most high-profile and powerful sporting bodies in the world. The members of the Olympic Movement, particularly the IOC, the ISFs and the NOCs, are bound by the principles and rules defined in the Olympic Charter and are responsible for implementing them throughout the world and within their particular sports. The Olympic Games are the most visible celebration of these ideals and as the cost of hosting them has increased, the IOC and the individual organising committees of each edition of the Games have sought ever greater and more sophisticated means of protecting their commercial rights in order to generate sufficient income to enable them to take place, which are often used by other primary rights holders as a template for the protections that they also seek.

14.2 The British Olympic Association represents the IOC on a day-to-day basis in the UK, the Isle of Man, the Channel Islands and Overseas Dependent Territories that do not have their own NOC. It is responsible for promoting host cities' bids to stage the Olympic Games and for inviting athletes to represent Team GB at each edition of them. The UK also provides three members of the IOC, each of whom has substantial competitive and administrative experience, including one who sits on the IOC's Executive Board. The London Organising Committee of the Olympic Games was created to organise the London Olympics in 2012. LOCOG was a member of the Olympic Movement until its dissolution on 31 December 2012.

14.3 The Olympic Symbols etc (Protection) Act 1995 was introduced to provide protection for the generic intellectual property associated with the Olympic Movement. The Olympic Association Right was created for the benefit of the BOA to ensure that it could generate sufficient funds to remain independent of the state. During the period of its existence, LOCOG was also a beneficiary of these quasi-trade mark protections. The London Olympic Games and Paralympic Games Act 2006 created the legislative framework within which the London 2012 Games was organised. It established the Olympic Delivery Authority, a public body responsible for building the infrastructure for the Games and for enforcing the offences created by the Act. The Act also provided specific protections for the commercial rights owned and managed by LOCOG and the BOA. In particular, it created a London Olympics Association Right to protect the words and symbols most closely associated with London 2012. This wide-ranging association right restricted advertising and street trading in the vicinity of Olympic venues and prohibited the unauthorised resale of Olympic tickets in the course of trade or with the intent to make a profit.

14.4 The ad hoc division of the Court of Arbitration for Sport heard 11 cases related to issues concerning London 2012. Nine of the cases were applications by athletes hoping to compete in the Games, only two of which were successful. The remaining two cases were attempts by applicants to overturn the result of an event and an in-game decision of the competition officials; both were refused as neither CAS nor its ad hoc division have jurisdiction to hear 'field of play' decisions.

14.5 The protections afforded to LOCOG were the latest incarnation of 'Olympic law'. The 2006 Act demonstrates how, with each edition of the Olympic Games, the IOC requires the host nation to pass ever more protective legislation in favour of the local NOC and OCOG. This 'horizontal creep' ensures that the previous legislation is used as the basis for extending the law at each subsequent edition of the Games, as can be seen in the developments in the protections afforded to the organising committees of Sochi 2014 and Rio 2016. The impact of the Olympic protections has also begun to produce 'vertical creep' where smaller and single sport championships insist on receiving the same protection that has been afforded previously to the Olympics.

Further reading

Lewis and Taylor (eds), *Sport: Law and Practice* (2nd edn, 2008, Tottel) chs H1 and 2

Maestre, *Law and the Olympics* (2010, Cambridge University Press)

Horsey, Montagon and Smith, 'The London Olympics 2012 – restrictions, restrictions, restrictions' (2012) 7(10) *Journal of Intellectual Property Law and Practice* 715

Greenfield, James and Osborn, 'The Olympics, the law and the contradictions of Olympism' in H. Lenskyj and S. Wagg (Eds), *Handbook of Olympic Studies*, (Palgrave) ch 20.

James and Osborn, 'The Olympic Laws and the tensions and contradictions of promoting and preserving the Olympic Ideal' in V. Girginov (Ed), *Handbook of the London 2012 Olympic and Paralympic Games: Vol. 1 Making the Games*, (Routledge) ch 6.

Johnson, 'Look out! It's an ambush!' [2008] 2/3 *International Sports Law Review* 24

Marcus, 'Ambush marketing: an analysis of its threat to sports rights holders and the efficacy of past, present and proposed anti-infringement programmes' [2011] 3/4 *International Sports Law Journal* 97–101 and 104–115.

Michalos, 'Five golden rings: development of the protection of the Olympic insignia' [2006] 3 *International Sports Law Review* 64

Links to relevant websites can be found at www.palgrave.com/law/james2e

Index

Printed and bound in Great Britain by
TJ International Ltd, Padstow, Cornwall